OLD SILVER AND
OLD SHEFFIELD PLATE

A PAIR OF PLATTER COVERS BY PAUL LAMERIE, LONDON, 1729

These pieces are free from the over-ornamentation that sometimes marked his work and show the exquisite sense of form possessed by the greatest of English silversmiths.

OLD SILVER *and* OLD SHEFFIELD PLATE

A history of the silversmith's art in Great Britain and Ireland, with reproductions in facsimile of about thirteen thousand marks. Tables of date letters and other marks. American silversmiths and their marks. Paris marks and Paris date letters with a description of the methods of marking employed by the Paris Guild of Silversmiths. Hallmarks, and date letters when used, of nearly all the countries of Continental Europe, reproduced in facsimile. A history of Old Sheffield Plate and a description of the method of its production, with the names and marks, in facsimile, of every known maker

WITH TWELVE FULL-PAGE ILLUSTRATIONS

By HOWARD PITCHER OKIE

DOUBLEDAY, DORAN & COMPANY, INC.

GARDEN CITY   1945   NEW YORK

A LADY

whose home is in Kentucky,
but whose duties and responsibilities have
made her name familiar throughout the United
States, years ago perceived that in no other
class of articles of domestic use were combined utility and great beauty to the degree
in which those qualities co-exist in the silver
produced in England during the period that
began with the accession of George I and
ended during the Regency in the early Nineteenth Century. Her unerring taste and judg-
ment, as shown in her own magnificent collection, have made many converts to her belief.
As an inadequate attempt to express the obligation we should all feel, and as a tribute
of personal admiration,
this volume is respectfully dedicated
by its author
to
MRS. ALVIN T. HERT,
of Lexington and Washington.

FOREWORD

THIS book has been written with the single purpose of enabling the reader to establish the origin and authenticity of antique silver and "Old Sheffield plate."

If I have gone rather at length into the history of the silversmith's art in England and the laws under which he worked, it is because I deemed it necessary for the purpose in view. Education in the directions indicated is essential to prevent self-deception; there is no danger of wilful misrepresentation by a reputable dealer.

It has not been thought necessary to go into the methods employed in the production of solid silver. Sheffield plate must, however, be approached from a different angle. One who knows just how "Old Sheffield" rolled plate was made and will apply that knowledge to each piece he examines and will ask and answer the question that should always arise: "Was it possible to produce this article without the aid of electroplating?"—will never, if of average intelligence, mistake electroplate for the older product.

Dealers are deceived every day. This we must believe in view of the fact that a large quantity of electroplate is being marketed as "Old Sheffield." If a wider knowledge is possessed by customers, dealers will be compelled to educate themselves.

Mr. Frederick Bradbury, of Sheffield, has written a book describing in the most minute detail every process used in the older art and illustrating every method and tool employed. Its writing afforded Mr. Bradbury pleasure, no doubt, and certainly he should feel proud of his work, evidencing as it does infinite labour and very great ability.

But, Macaulay said no one but a commentator ever read all of Spenser's "Faërie Queene," and if the seven books of the poem had not been destroyed in Ireland, even a commentator would have baulked.

Hence, I have written just enough to show even a non-industrious reader that the raw material of a maker of Old Sheffield corresponding to the sheet of solid silver in the hands of the silversmith or of copper or nickel silver in the hands of the maker of plated ware presents a uniform colour only on the surface and never at a cross-section. The copper and silver were not amalgamated. They remained distinct but not separate. Every edge of a piece of Sheffield plate must at some time have shown white and red, or white and red and white. That edge had to be masked. How? Never by electroplating: it had not been invented.

I have compiled the tables of marks on solid silver in this book from publications most of which are not readily available to the reading public. The Continental hallmarks (apart from the French) have hitherto only appeared in a German publication—Rosenberg's. The French marks are from Boivin's *Les Ancienns Orfèvres Français*, a costly work practically unknown in America.

It is very important that the collector should be able to identify British provincial silver. "Provincial" as used here includes Ireland and Scotland. This book contains the name and mark of every British and Irish silversmith now known, from the earliest times to the middle of the last century. The value of both English and American silver often depends very largely upon the identity of its maker. For some reason, that is not true of silver of Continental origin unless we hark back to the days of Benvenuto Cellini. It has seemed well, therefore, to give hallmarks only of the European countries other than the British Isles

Our knowledge of early American silversmiths, incomplete as it is, seems almost static. Some few years ago, the Walpole Society published a book containing the names of a number of silversmiths of the Colonies. Copies are infrequently offered at book sales and bring large prices. My friend Colonel Charles Rynesson has given me what we believe to be the only existing copy of the book his late father, Mr. P. A. Rynesson, privately published. It contains data concerning some hundreds of silversmiths not mentioned in the Walpole Society book. Mr. Stephen G. C. Ensko has also published a book containing many names and marks of old and comparatively modern "silversmiths" of this country. No doubt many of his "silversmiths" were only dealers —a fault with which this work also may be charged and for which a reason is given in the proper place. The curious reader will find many very valuable biographical notes in Mr. Ensko's book, and I am indebted to it and to the book of *American Church Silver* (a wonderfully accurate work) for much information I have used in these pages.

That paragon of American collectors, Judge Alphonso T. Clearwater, and Mr. Henry Davis Sleeper, who generously presented his collection of Paul Revere Silver to the Boston Museum of Fine Arts, have given me authoritative decisions as to the distinctions between the marks of the Reveres, father and son.

By following the British and Irish date letters as given by the late Sir Charles Jackson, I have avoided the mistakes made by Chaffers and Cripps and copied by American authors.

HOWARD PITCHER OKIE

Washington, D. C.
   March 1, 1928.

CONTENTS

xii CONTENTS

LIST OF FULL–PAGE ILLUSTRATIONS

OLD SILVER AND
OLD SHEFFIELD PLATE

CHAPTER I
Old English Silver

❖ ❖ ❖ ROM the year 1300, it has been compulsory in England
❖ **F** ❖ to have an official mark impressed upon silverware be-
❖ ❖ ❖ fore offering it for sale. In that year, a statute of
Edward I provided that "no manner of vessel of silver depart out
of the hand of the workers until it be essayed [*sic*] by the wardens
of the craft and further that it be marked with a leopard's head."
To receive that mark it must be of "esterling allay [*sic*]." From
this one would gather that the belief that the word "sterling"
was derived from the name of a North German tribe, the Ester-
lings, who were noted for the uniform fineness of their silver
coins, is based upon fact. Sixty years later, it was provided that
the goldsmith or silversmith should have a "mark by himself." In
neither of these enactments is there any mention of the lion passant which later was to be the sterling mark of every assay office
in England, though the use of the leopard's head was, with certain
exceptions, shown in the tables of marks, restricted to articles
made in London.

We learn, however, from an indictment of the attorney general
that in 1597 "Her Majesty's lion" had a legal status as a mark
of sterling silver. Though that is the earliest mention of the lion
in legal history, it is found on silver with the date letters for
1543, and Sir Charles Jackson says it was never absent "after
1545," a palpable error of Sir Charles, who, no doubt, intended
that his statement apply only to silver produced in London.

In the earlier days, symbols, not letters, were employed by

the English silversmiths to identify their work. In 1515, we find apostle spoons with a "radiant" (fringed) letter S, and in 1545 we find a monogram. Late in the reign of Elizabeth, we find an initial employed with increasing frequency, and toward the end of that reign the silversmith usually used the initials of both his Christian and his surname. This practice continued until 1697, when the statute changing the standard of silver was passed. This act, which raised the standard of silverware above that of the coinage, was designed to prevent the absorption of the silver money in the arts. It provided that the fineness of the silver employed must be 11 ounces, 10 pennyweights to the pound Troy (12 oz.) instead of 11 ounces, 2 pennyweights (.925) the sterling standard. It took more than twenty years for the law-makers to discover that their enactment was futile, as the silversmith could meet the new requirement by simply adding a little pure silver to his melting coins. While the new standard was compulsory, silver was marked in a distinctive way. John Cox no longer marked his silver J. C.: he must use the first two letters of his surname—Co. The lion passant was superseded by the lion erased (the head and neck only of the lion), and the leopard's head was replaced by the figure of Britannia enthroned. In 1720, the old standard and the old system of marking came again into use through the repeal of the statute of 1697, but the maker could, if he wished, continue to use the higher standard, in which case the Britannia hall marks would be affixed, though he could no longer mark his wares with the commencing letters of his surname. He must use his initials, unless it was that, prior to 1697, he used some other mark (a single initial), in which case he was, for a short period, allowed to use his old mark. I revert to this subject in more detail hereafter.

The art of silversmithing doubtless came into England through the development of Christian monastic institutions. There is no evidence of the art having been established in the British Isles during the four centuries of Roman occupation, though the cloth of Britain became famous during that period.

Prior to the Norman Conquest, the work seems to have been confined to the churches. The patron saint of English goldsmiths was the monk Dunstan, who lived in the Tenth Century. He became an archbishop and the chief counsellor of the Saxon king, Edgar.

With the advent of William the Conqueror, it would seem reasonable to suppose that a higher standard of living was brought into England and that the invading nobility would bring with them silver and gold utensils. If they did so, none of them survived the vicissitudes of the intervening centuries. Up to the time of Henry VIII, practically all specimens of the silversmith's craft were in the possession of ecclesiastical bodies.

It is true that, as early as 1238, in the reign of Henry III, an ordinance was passed that shows that goldsmiths were then recognized as a body, but it would seem that only a negligible amount of their output went into the hands of other than the Church and royalty. The reason for that is found in the fact that there was very little raw material in England. Silver has never been found there in the earth in its "free" form, and the small amount that was locked up in refractory ores, such as galena, was unavailable because of the ignorance of any method of separating the precious metal from its base associates.

Henry VII is reported to have died possessed of £1,800,000 in gold and silver, but that monarch's system of appropriating his subjects' money under the name of "benevolences" was so thorough that it is more than likely that his possessions represented the bulk of all the money in England. His successor, Henry VIII, died almost penniless, and probably for that reason we do find a few silver articles of domestic use that were made during the reign of that monarch.

During the reign of Henry VIII the silver currency was so debased that the coinage contained little more than a fourth of its proper content; in other words, it contained about 25 per cent. of silver compared to $92\frac{1}{4}$ per cent., which was the sterling standard. Yet at no time, from the commencement of the legal regulations of the manufacture of silver plate, was it lawful to make silver wares of less than the sterling standard.

When we remember that in the reigns of Henry VIII and Edward VI the silversmiths found their only source of raw material in this debased coinage and the very large purchasing power of that currency, we can understand the scarcity of "Tudor" silver. The reason that, prior to the disestablishment acts of Henry VIII, ecclesiastical institutions (colleges fall within this group) monopolized the ownership of silver is found in the relationship of local monastic institutions to the gentry of their neighbourhoods. If the wealth of a rich English subject were not taken from him by the Sovereign during his life, it would be apt to pass to the Church upon the owner's death. The terrors of hell were very real, and priestly intervention alone stood between the dying and eternal torments.

There was an amusing conflict between the individual and collective belief. The former deemed it the part of wisdom to give all that he had to save his soul. His neighbours deprecated his action, though, as individuals, each would do the same. Various statutes of "mortmain," commencing in the reign of Henry III, were intended to cope with this situation, but none, save the last—that of Henry VIII—was effective.

The idea of the confiscation of church wealth did not originate with Henry VIII; it had often been proposed before, not by kings or their ministers, but by the people. Such a measure nearly succeeded in the reign of Richard II. The King at first favoured the measure, but withdrew his support under threats from Rome.

It is to be noted that the oldest hall-marked piece is an ecclesiastical piece, and it is doubtful if any piece of silver that could be properly termed a domestic article could be found with an earlier date than 1515, although a few apostle spoons have come to light that were made toward the end of the Fifteenth Century. Corpus Christi College, Oxford, has a covered silver cup that was presented to Catherine of Aragon by her loving husband in 1515–1516.

It is doubtful if we can explain the scarcity of even church silver in the pre-Elizabethan period of English history by stating that the monasteries had been depleted of their silver by Henry VIII.

The probabilities are that there was very little silver of any kind in England until the days of Drake and Hawkins, who, with their fellow buccaneers, encouraged the movement of silver from the newly discovered Western world to the British Isles.

The capture of silver-laden Spanish ships, not only while they were en route from Mexico, South America, and the West Indies, but of ships in the English Channel which were taking supplies from Spain to Holland during the reign of Elizabeth, inaugurated an entirely new era. Silver domestic articles were still far from common, yet we are told by the Reverend William Harrison, who wrote *The Description of England* as it fell under his observation from 1577 to 1587, that rather late in the reign of Elizabeth certain noble families sat at table with as much as two thousand pounds' value of plate spread before them.

The coinage was restored to its legal standard early in the reign of Elizabeth. Apart from the fact that this was evidence of an increased supply of silver within the realm, the fact itself would stimulate the industries of the silversmith.

After the apostle spoons, we find with increasing frequency during the Sixteenth Century spoons more clearly intended for domestic use. They have fig-shaped bowls, with four-corner columnar baluster stems, and terminate in a knob which could be used as a seal. The knobs, or finials, are circular or hexagonal.

So-called "rose water" bowls appear at the beginning of the Sixteenth Century, but their original purpose is not clear. At the same time we find tall pedestal salts. They are grand affairs for colleges and the rich "livery" corporations of London. We find a few Elizabethan salts, evidently intended for domestic use. They are oblong, troughlike affairs, something of the shape of the trencher salts made three centuries later, except that they are without pedestals. They are very rare.

During the Sixteenth Century, much church silver was made: patens, communion cups, chalices, and tazzas (small saucers or flat cups with handles and mounted on a stem and base).

The first rat-tail spoon we find bears the mark of 1674. It had a flat stem and a trifid end, i.e., an end divided into three sections like a fragment of a clover leaf.

We find an English three-prong fork—only one—made in 1678. Silver snuffers appear at this time. Tankards, all of silver, had become common in the reign of Charles II, and late in the reign of that monarch toilet sets and toilet boxes were introduced, no doubt a French innovation.

Some two hundred years before, horn beakers had been made with silver bands. That form was preserved in the silver mugs and tankards of a later period, which were ornamented with silver bands, reminders, like the back buttons on a frock coat, of a period when they were of practical use.

In 1683, we find a large oval silver dish, no doubt intended for use upon the table, and about this time silver dinner plates crept into use. There are two in London, dated 1687. In the reign of Queen Anne, and during all the subsequent years, they were common. The author knows of but two or three tea kettles with

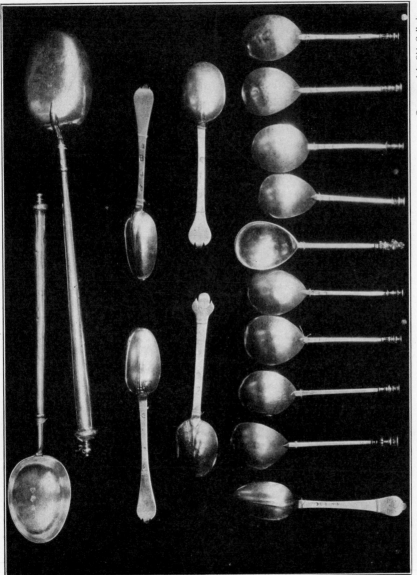

Courtesy of the Okie Galleries

EARLY ENGLISH SPOONS

Commencing at the left, the first nine spoons with fig-shaped bowls are of the reigns of Elizabeth, James I, Charles I, and Charles II. The five spoons with trifid ends and rat-tails are of the reigns of Charles II, James II, William and Mary, and Queen Anne. The smaller of the two pipe-handled spoons was made in 1690; the larger one in 1716.

stands and spirit lamps, made as early as the reign of Queen Anne. One sold in America recently for $5,500. This seems to be a fair price, as the writer saw one in Scotland at about the same time, upon which a trade price of £700 had been set. Tea and coffee pots became common in the reign of Queen Anne. Porringers and caudle cups came on the scene in Elizabethan times, and those of the early Eighteenth Century are very common. The fashion of making complete tea or coffee services seems to have occurred to American silversmiths rather earlier than it did to the English members of that craft. I have never seen a complete three-piece tea set of the same make and date letter and of British origin that was earlier than 1790, and with one exception complete tea and coffee sets seem not to have been made in England before the early years of the Nineteenth Century. The idea of making tea kettles to match the tea sets is a Victorian one. The exception is an authentic three-piece tea set of the time of Queen Anne (1702–1714) sold recently at Christie's in London. No doubt it expressed the idea of a silversmith or customer who failed to create a fashion. No other instance is known to the writer. Replicas of the Queen Anne set are now manufactured and sold.

The source of privately owned silver must have been considerably augmented during the reigns of James I and Charles I. Much of this, however, was destroyed during the Civil War, and it seems that, during the Commonwealth, the production of articles of luxury was discouraged. With the inauguration of Charles II, the trade of the silversmith and goldsmith revived and has flourished ever since. In 1697, there must have been three hundred master silversmiths in London alone, and when one considers that each silversmith employed a number of helpers and apprentices, we can understand that there must have been an enormous output of silverware.

In the reign of Queen Anne, silver domestic utensils were in common use, but, from an artistic standpoint, the silver of the period of that queen leaves much to be desired. We hear much praise of the simplicity of "Queen Anne" silver, but it is an unthinking chorus and rests on no more solid foundation than the admiration expressed for the writings of Laurence Sterne. The candlesticks gave promise of beauty, but they were so small that they lacked dignity and impressiveness.

In 1697, William Hogarth was born. It is known that, in 1720, after having been apprenticed to an English silversmith, he was engaged in engraving silver plate. He became a very famous artist, but it is certain that he never lost touch with the trade with which his youth had been identified. In fact, we know that he designed many pieces for London silversmiths.

In 1745, Hogarth painted that admirable portrait of himself with his dog Trump which is now in the National Gallery in London. In a corner of this he had drawn on a palette a serpentine curve with the words "The Line of Beauty." This was merely a tangible expression of the hitherto undisclosed influence that Hogarth had imposed upon the designers of the preceding twenty years and which was to continue until the Adam Brothers, with their meretricious neoclassicism, captured the public fancy.

During the Hogarthian period—1720–1760—the most exquisite silver the world has ever seen was produced, and in enormous quantities. The geometric figures with straight lines and acute angles of the Queen Anne period gave way to beautiful curved outlines with simple but graceful ornamentation, with none of the stereotyped features that marked the succeeding "Adam" period.

Of course, Hogarth alone could not have brought about this

revolution. It was a happy coincidence that there were many talented and artistic craftsmen in London who were his contemporaries. Some of these were of French Huguenot birth or origin and brought to their trade a refinement that was tempered and strengthened by rugged and less artistic styles than prevailed before this period. An outstanding example is supplied by Paul Lamerie, who worked during the reign of Queen Anne, George I, and George II. He produced pieces of wonderful beauty. He also produced some very ugly pieces. This part of his output may be explained by the fact that he no doubt had mandatory commissions to reproduce silver of the same type as that owned by his patrons' forbears.

Much silver bearing Paul Lamerie's mark is now on the market, and all, beautiful and ugly alike, brings high prices.

Ayme Videau was another great silversmith who was also a great artist. William Fawdery, Robert Abercrombie, and Peter Archambo are names distinguished in the reigns of George I and George II.

The rat-tail spoon, which had originated in the reign of James II and went out of fashion in the reign of Anne, was again made in 1750, and these spoons are commonly found bearing the date letters for the latter half of the Eighteenth Century. Because of a present demand for them, a large number of authentic spoons of the period of George II and early George III are now having tails added to them by clever English artificers. The cost to the antique dealer for each additional caudal appendage is only about three shillings.

Early in the Nineteenth Century, the people of England were obsessed with the desire to encrust every piece of silver they could find with excessive ornamentation. It happened that even during the reign of Queen Anne some beautiful, straight-sided coffee pots were produced. There was also produced at the same time a much greater number of ugly hexagonal and even octagonal coffee pots. The beauty of the former lay in the fact that they presented an unbroken curved surface. Those that survived to the period 1807–1815 were seized upon almost without exception and marred by decoration. This decoration was so indiscriminately applied that in many cases the hall marks, if they were on the side of the vessel, were wholly or partly obliterated. The ugly, angular pieces did not lend themselves to this treatment and have survived, untouched. A straight-sided George I coffee pot standing eleven inches high, if in its original condition, is worth in the neighbourhood of $500. When "re-chased," they sell in the London auction rooms for about one fifth of this sum. The collector must not jump to the conclusion that every piece of silver the hall marks of which have been partially obliterated by chasing is an example of ornamentation put on out of period. It was quite common for silversmiths to send their work to the "hall" to be marked and then chase it afterward.

There is no nicer criterion of a collector's skill than his ability to determine accurately whether or not the ornamentation upon a piece of English silver is contemporary with its birth.

In the year 1300 a statute was enacted which provided that no gold or silver should be sold until it had been assayed by persons duly authorized so to do. Such assay was to be evidenced by impressing upon the article tested a leopard's head. Threescore years later, it was provided by another statute that each goldsmith should have "a mark by himself, which mark shall be known by them assigned by the King to certify their work." This law also provided that the silversmith should not put his mark upon his goods until *after* they had been examined by the proper officials. This feature was found to be attended with inconvenience, and although I have been unable to find a statute that abrogated the one last quoted, we know that in 1583 the

OLD ENGLISH SILVER

The caudle cup shown at the left was made in 1706. The covered dishes are examples of the work of Paul Storr, latest of the great English silversmiths.

workman affixed his mark *before* sending it to the assayer's office, and that custom prevails in Great Britain to-day.

The fashion of denoting the year of manufacture by impressing a date letter, to be determined by the authorities, was probably inaugurated in the reign of Edward IV, and we find that the oldest "hall-marked" English silver pieces are a chalice paten bearing the marks of a leopard's head, the date letter "B," and maker's mark. It has now been determined that that date letter denoted the assay year 1479–1480. As the assay years have from the earliest time commenced in the month of May in each year, it is always necessary to employ figures representing two years in order to designate any particular twelve months represented by a date letter. Up to 1544, the leopard's head served a dual purpose. It certified that the article was silver of a certain standard and that it was made in London. In that year, the lion passant was employed as a stamp for silver of standard (.925) fineness, and thereafter the leopard's head only designated the place of origin.

The use of the lion as a sterling mark was not restricted to London, but for a long period of time, though used in various parts of England, its employment was not universal. Nor was the leopard's head restricted to London, but when employed elsewhere was accompanied by the distinctive mark of the local assay office so that no confusion would ensue.

It is unnecessary now to go into greater particulars, as the reader can get detailed information upon this point by the perusal of the tables of date letters.

CHAPTER II
Frauds and Transformations

❖ ❖ ❖HE collector of Old English silver is confronted with
❖ T ❖ two perils: 1. He may purchase a "dud" with forged hall
❖ ❖ ❖ marks or a "transformation," a term employed to designate an altered genuine piece of silver in which the metamorphosis has been concealed; or (2) he may reject a perfectly good piece from an excess of caution or unhealthy suspicion. The latter is the more common error.

If he adopts the rule never to purchase an unauthenticated piece in which the "antiquity" is the preponderating element of value (i.e., apostle spoons, Elizabethan or Tudor silver), the first danger disappears. The truth of this proposition is apparent upon brief consideration. A forger will starve if he adds a hundred dollars' worth of labour to fifty dollars' worth of silver and sells the finished product for seventy-five dollars. Should he be guilty of this folly, the purchaser will have secured an article worth more than he paid. A corollary to this proposition is that Georgian marks are not forged for the same reason that a bricklayer will not work for five dollars a day when he can get twelve. It is easier to put a credible Charles I mark on a piece of silver than to represent the period of George II, and the Stuart piece would, if genuine, be worth six times as much as the one made a century later. I say "easier" because the later records of Goldsmiths' Hall are more complete than the earlier ones.

Like most rules, this has exceptions arising from peculiar conditions. Paul Lamerie worked in the reigns of the first two

Georges. Authentic pieces by this great silversmith bring such high prices that a forger may be tempted to imitate his mark. Fortunately, the skill required to reproduce the beauty of that master's work as shown in his best pieces is so rare that hitherto the mark alone has been successfully copied and only the inexperienced have been deceived.

A year or so ago, there arose an inexplicable demand for skewers. The price for genuine ones—even those made as late as 1790—rose from $1.25 an ounce to $5.50. Little silver and no skill were required for their production. Thousands of fakes were turned out. I received a consignment of two dozen all bearing the mark of the same maker and the date letter of one year, 1797. My consignor had been tricked. I sent them back. The purchaser who followed the rule I have laid down, "Do not pay more than the intrinsic value for an unpedigreed article," would have been amply safeguarded.

A short time ago, the tremendous demand for silver place plates and their consequent scarcity prompted a forger to make a large number of them bearing the mark of Paul Storr, a prominent London silversmith who commenced his labours in the last decade of the Eighteenth Century and lived into Victorian times —or nearly so. His work is much sought and commands high prices. Some of the forged plates were sold to an American dealer, who became suspicious and took them to Goldsmiths' Hall, where they were pronounced spurious and the forged marks defaced. If a Queen Anne mark had been counterfeited, the selling price could have been doubled and the "Hall" might, probably would, have refused to stamp them as forgeries. The records of the guild are perfect for 1807; for the period a century earlier, their archives are not so complete. The marks of many makers of that period who undoubtedly were duly registered are missing from the records as they survive to-day.

"Transformations" are taken from the rule regarding fakes with forged marks for the reason that fraud is not necessarily connected with their birth. Frequently, the transformation is effected with innocent motives. One may own a silver tureen lining bearing the mark of a famous maker and not have the tureen in which it was intended to rest. A silver base is made and attached, and a beautiful centrepiece is evolved from a piece of metal which, because of its shape, would not retain an upright position upon the table. The hall marks and maker's mark are still plainly visible when the reconstructed piece is viewed from below, and, if the owner parted with it, a purchaser might think that he had acquired an original piece.

The foregoing is an example of a "domestic" "transformation." The commercial transformations are common enough; desk sets from unfashionable cruet stands and salad servers from large spoons are examples most frequently seen.

Many hundreds of pairs of "salad servers" bearing authentic marks of the George III period are sold in this country. Originally, they were serving spoons; their bowls have been elongated and prongs cut in one of the pair. They are sold for utility purposes and not as cabinet specimens. They are imported in such numbers that the price for which they are sold is little if any more than the cost would be for modern articles of corresponding weight and they *are* hand-wrought silver, antique, and admirably adapted to their new purposes. It is very doubtful if salad servers as we identify them were known in Georgian times. Forks of all kinds were scarce. Their purpose seems not to have been understood either in England or her colonies until we had well advanced into the Nineteenth Century. It is true that Queen Elizabeth used them (or exhibited them). They were exotic then; of Italian origin. It is also true that we occasionally come across sets rather late in the Eighteenth Century; one set was found in Norfolk bearing Queen Anne marks, and the author has seen one or two sold in London auction rooms of that early period. Yet the outstanding fact is that whereas now the average household has about as many forks as spoons of modern make, we are offered a thousand Eighteenth Century spoons to one fork of the same period. Political history of the United States teaches us that when John Adams represented this country at Versailles, he and his wife Abigail (the most "advanced" woman of her day) were struck with the cleanliness and utility of the use of forks at the table. When Adams returned to the new republic, he brought forks with him and put them upon his table when guests were entertained as well as when he dined alone. This imprudence nearly cost him the presidency. It was first whispered by his friends and then shouted by his enemies that he had abandoned the ways of democracy.

There is a glut of Georgian spoons; the creation of "salad servers" is helping to reduce the surplus.

Recently writers have exaggerated the dangers in purchasing English silver. Do not believe that "if one is offered by a dealer an antique silver piece much below the current price, it may be an indication that something is wrong." It may be that the dealer is unwise or "hard up." The low price rather tends to negative any presumption of fraud, as it eliminates motive, always a principal factor in wrongdoing. My advice is to buy at once if the price is less than it would cost to produce the article and if the article be one that is desirable if genuine. The matter of provenance can be settled afterward. If you must trust your dealer, you should remember that ability is much more important than honesty. Crime is always a mistake, but dishonest persons are not always fools. A roguish dealer usually realizes that to stay in business he must "ride straight," but there is no protection from a fool. A short time ago, a dealer in London offered me a Queen Anne porringer for £3. I promptly bought and paid for it and then asked why it was so cheap. He said "because it is not marked." It had been made by John Porter, London, 1703. The marks were plain but in an obscure position.

A recent book on this subject warns us: "Articles made since the time of Elizabeth, with only a maker's mark, should be avoided, although the unscrupulous dealer will show you in some book of reference that it is the mark of a celebrated silversmith." So will the scrupulous dealer. Nothing is more certain than that the piece is *not fraudulent* if so marked. My advice is to buy it if the price is low, measured by the intrinsic worth of the article. It may be "Early American"! No forger would bother making a piece that he could not sell except without profit. The penalty for simply copying the dealer's mark and marketing a piece so marked was death, if we hark back to even so late a date as 1820. At the present time, obtaining money by means of "false token" is still a felony and is punishable with a long term of penal servitude. That the forgers of hall marks and makers' marks were prosecuted as violators of the statutes regulating the marking of silver instead of proceeding under the common law of England, is an instance of the tendency of the crown prosecutors to avoid proceedings that would if successful result in the infliction of barbarous penalties. When death was the punishment of crimes now regarded as trivial, judges and prosecutors alike sought to make its infliction as infrequent as possible. Hence the myriad of "technicalities" which a defendant could once invoke, now swept away as the treatment of convicted criminals has become more consonant with an enlightened age.

The absence of the hall marks on an English piece marked only with the maker's punch has two or three reasonable explanations. One is illustrated thus: A tray is shown to me in Washington by a travelling salesman. It bears the mark of Richard Rugg. Rugg was a silversmith of the latter half of the Eighteenth Century, in London. I have had many of his trays; he made little else. This tray bore his mark in three places. It was indubitably a piece of Rugg's handiwork and of the period indicated by his name. Since Elizabethan times, the maker's mark is punched before taking it to Goldsmiths' Hall. In this case, Rugg had made a trifling error in his alloy, in excess of the legally allowable variation, and the "Hall" had refused to mark it. It was still a perfectly good tray for the Rugg family. Perhaps Rugg differed from the conclusions of the authorities and added two more punches to emphasize that fact and put the tray in use. A century and a half later, the tray reached America. The other explanation applies with more force to articles made after 1784 (when the tax upon silver ware was introduced) and intended for export. Hall marks meant so little to our ancestors in this country that Low, Ball & Company (Boston, *circa* 1810), who were the largest importers of English silver of their time, found it necessary to stamp "Coin silver," "Guaranteed by Low, Ball & Company," upon fully hall-marked pieces of silver, made by such well-known makers as the firm of Chawner, Ely & Fearn of London. The author believes that one reason for the large number of pieces attributed to unknown American makers is found here. Pieces made for export were unmarked and, consequently, untaxed.

When one considers that there was a market in America in Colonial and early post-Colonial times for the products of English silversmiths, and that taxes could be evaded without diminishing the sales value of the goods by exporting them without official stamping (a drawback, for tax paid on goods subsequently exported could be successfully claimed, but its collection involved a good deal of trouble), and that such action was lawful, it would seem advisable to look through the lists of British marks wherever American identification cannot be made and the mark consists

of only two initials framed (cartouche, circle, rectangle, oval, etc.).
Writing upon this subject, Sir Charles Jackson says:

From 1597 until 1675 there appears very little of interest to relate concerning the London Goldsmiths' Company. There is not much evidence of any
efforts having been made to enforce the old-time laws and ordinances with
references to the obligation to submit all gold and silver wares to their assayer's
"touch", and it seems probable that a large number of goldsmiths in London
and the provinces . . . sold wrought plate without **being** assayed or marked,
other than with their own stamp.

To pass intelligently pieces purporting or represented to be of
early English origin, it is necessary to have a general knowledge
of all British provincial as well as the London marks.

Many beautiful and very valuable pieces of British silver have
neither the leopard's head nor the lion to identify them. You
may come across a spoon marked on the shaft only with a scallop
shell and the letters IA, AA, or RS, or with the shell alone. It
will have been made in Poole, a town in Dorset, England, *circa*
1540, 1560, 1580, or 1620. It is well not to remember dates, but
one should know the shell mark and that it was not used after
the reign of James I (1625).

Sixteenth Century silver of the finest quality was produced in
Norwich; and York had an assay office and Goldsmiths' Guild in
1563. The earliest known Norwich piece is a communion cup of
1590. It is marked with a castle with a lion beneath, both in the
same shield, and a sea gull also in a shield. The lion designating
sterling was not used there until 1610.

Some time ago, the writer purchased—not as an antique—a
very well-made covered silver tankard of Queen Anne design and
bearing on its base the lion erased, figure of Britannia, and the
date letter for 1697. The maker's mark was Rc. A hopeless combination of letters if intended to represent the beginning of a
surname. The piece was a continental forgery, probably Dutch.

Courtesy of the Okie Galleries

TWO EXAMPLES OF "TRANSFORMATIONS."

The pitcher was originally a tall tankard or "can" made by Edward Vincent in London, 1706. Its lower part has been "belled" out and the spout and decoration added. The only original part of the desk-set is the base or floor, originally a plain platter made by Fred Kandler, London, 1744. Horace Walpole had his silversmith make it into its present form. The rail, bottle-holders, tops, candlestick, snuffers and feet would, if genuine, all be hallmarked; they are not. The hallmark on what was a platter was originally placed upon a flat surface; it now appears partially upon the curve of the groove. It would have been physically impossible to "punch" it in that position.

If the fabricator had used R followed by a vowel or the letter h the fraud might have gone undiscovered.

Though the average intelligence of the successful dealer in antiques is high, many, unfortunately, have not the mental equipment and training necessary for the acquisition of a broad general knowledge so essential to sound deduction from visible facts. The average professional man, even without practical experience, would devote more time and thought to the provenance of a piece of silver and reach a sounder conclusion.

"This is a box for postage stamps; it is over a hundred and fifty years old!" The speaker made his living buying and selling antiques and sold his "expert" testimony. The hall-mark date was 1907, and everyone but an "expert" knows that adhesive stamps were first used in 1840.

A church bazaar sent one of their donations, a transparent green stone, to a pawnbroker for classification and appraisal. He had carried on the business for fifty years and made a specialty of precious stones. He pronounced the green crystal "trash." It was therefore sold for $25. "The purchaser put it before an emerald glass, through which a genuine stone will glow with a dull red light and found that he had a gem. He sold it for $1,500 to a New York jobber, who no doubt doubled his money. The pawnbroker had never heard of the emerald glass. Establish the provenance of your own pieces in order to get the most fun and the most profit from the game.

Though the higher (Britannia) standard of silver ceased to be compulsory in 1720, it has never gone completely into disuse. Once in a while you will come across a piece of silver bearing a maker's mark consisting of a single letter and a later date than 1720; this marking had been comparatively common forty years earlier, but of course had been discontinued during the period of 1697–1720 when the two first letters of the surname had been used as the statute directed. The statute of 1720, repealing the "Britannia" law of 1697, provided that thenceforth the maker must use his initials "unless a different mark had been used by him" prior to 1697. This provision was repealed in the early years of George II's reign, and the use of two initials was made compulsory without exception. During the interim, however, a few dealers had reverted to their ancient custom of using a single initial. This proves a trap for the overcautious collector who may too rashly reject a valuable piece marked with a single initial.

Every year after 1720 some dealer made Britannia standard silver plate; for the most part, they were presentation or "legacy" pieces. Though the date letter and shields showed they were not of the 1697–1720 period, the presence of the lion erased and the figure of Britannia caused purchasers to deceive themselves. Shown a piece thus marked by a non-committal dealer, the customer would hurriedly purchase the article in the belief that the vendor was ignorant. When the modern character of the purchase would be discovered, the dealer would be described as a "crook." The dishonesty was often solely on the side of the buyer. Not always.

Of course, the presence of the King's head on silver made during the period 1784–1890, tended to preclude any such mistake, but after the later date the increase of Britannia marked silver was stimulated by the disappearance of the distinguishing feature and the resultant market with unscrupulous dealers who lay in wait for the "smart-Alecks."

In Devonshire, last summer, an antique dealer handed me a modern silver mustard pot bearing the Britannia marks. "'Ere is a piece I cahn't make 'ed or tail of. Wot do you make of it?"

"You ought to be able to make head or tail of it, for when you showed me a piece exactly like it two years ago, and made the

same remark, I told you that it was made in London by ——
Brothers in 1925."

"Ow! You're the gentleman wot was in 'ere two years ago.
Glad to see you again."

And the piece went back on the shelf. He bought them by
the dozen.

The enormous advance in the price of antique English silver
within the past few months has somewhat altered the conditions
upon which certain statements in the earlier part of this chap-
ter were predicated. Forgeries of the late Eighteenth Century
and even early Nineteenth Century are now much more common
than formerly.

A particular brazen example was seen by the writer while this
volume was in the press. The collar of the lid of a Paul Storr
kettle had been taken from the original piece and attached as a
base rim to a kettle of Continental origin which was unmarked
or from which the marks had been removed. An original Paul
Storr lamp had been found and placed in a silver stand
(unmarked) and the combination was offered to me—as a genuine Paul Storr kettle, lamp, and stand! It was quite usual to omit
the marking from a lid collar so that the robbery of the original
Paul Storr kettle did not impare its value. Naturally enough, the
date letters of the added base-rim and the lamp did not corre-
spond, but that was a small matter compared with the omission
of all hall marks from the lid and body of the kettle itself. Never
before had I seen such confidence in the success of a fraud based
upon such an airy foundation of deceit.

CHAPTER III

Marks on London Plate

EXAMPLES OF THE LEOPARD'S HEAD MARK FOUND ON PLATE OF A DATE ANTERIOR TO 1478.

(THE ASCRIBED DATES ARE APPROXIMATE.)

DATE. (about)	MARK.	ARTICLE AND OWNER.
1390		Spoon with hexagonal stem and acorn knop: in the Author's collection.
1400		„ „ " dyamond poynt " at end of stem : ⎫ Mr. J. H. Walter. „ „ lion sejant „ „ ⎭
1450		„ „ " dyamond poynt " „ „ : Lord Hylton.
„		„ „ „ „ „ „ : Mr. J. H. Walter.

DATE.	MARKS.	ARTICLE AND OWNER.
c. 1470		Spoon topped with seated figure of Our ⎫ Mr. J. H. Walter Lady; leopard's head in bowl, the ⎬ other mark on stem : ⎭
c. 1485 [probably]		Pre-Reformation Paten : Hartshorne, Derbyshire. (The B is probably the maker's mark.)

The marks shown below have been found upon an apostle spoon. The A may designate the first year of the following cycle.

1478-9 ?

CYCLE I.

THREE STAMPS AS BELOW.

	LEOPARD'S HEAD CROWNED.	DATE LETTER.	MAKER'S MARK.
EDW. IV 1478-9			
1479-80		B	
1480-1			
1481-2		D	
1482-3			
RICH. III. 1483-4			
1484-5			
HEN. VII. 1485-6		h	
1486-7			
1487-8			
1488-9		II	
1489-90			
1490-1	,,	n	
1491-2		O	
1492-3			
1493-4	,,	Q	
1494-5	,,	R	W
1495-6			
1496-7		T	
1497-8			

CYCLE II.

THREE STAMPS AS BELOW.

	LEOPARD'S HEAD CROWNED.	DATE LETTER.	MAKER'S MARK.
1498-9		a	
1499 1500		b	
1500-1	,,	c	
1501-2	,,	d	
1502-3			
1503-4	,,	f	
1504-5	,,	g	
1505-6			
1506-7		i	
1507-8	,,	kk	
1508-9		l	
HEN. VIII 1509-10		m	
1510-1	,,	n	
1511-2	,,	o	
1512-3	,,	p	
1513-4	,,	q	
1514-5	,,	r	
1515-6		s	
1516-7	,,	t	
1517-8	,,	u	

* 1492-3   The maker's mark is that of Sir Edmund Shaa, Warden of the Goldsmiths' Company, Master of the Mint, Cup Bearer and Goldsmith to King Richard III., and Lord Mayor in 1482. On Master spoon: Mr. J. H. Walter.

CYCLE III.

THREE STAMPS AS BELOW.

	LEOPARD'S HEAD CROWNED.	DATE LETTER.	MAKER'S MARK.
1518-9		A	
1519-20		B	
1520-1	,,	C	
1521-2		D	
1522-3	,,	E	
1523-4	,,	F	
1524-5	,,	G	
1525-6	,,	h	
1526-7			
1527-8	,,	K	
1528-9	,,	L	
1529-30	,,	M	
1530-1	,,	N	
1531-2		O	
1532-3	,,	P	
1533-4	,,	Q	
1534-5	,,	R	
1535-6	,,	S	
1536-7	,,	T	
1537-8	,,	V	

CYCLE IV.

THREE STAMPS TILL 1544, FOUR STAMPS THENCEFORWARD.

	LEOPARD'S HEAD CROWNED.	DATE LETTER.	LION PASSANT. FROM 1544.	MAKER'S MARK.
1538-9		A		
1539-40		B		
1540-1	,,	C		
1541-2	,,	D		
1542-3				
1543-4	,,	F		
1544-5		G		
1545-6		H		
1546-7	,,	I	,,	
EDW. VI. 1547-8		K		
1548-9	,,	L		
1549-50	,,	M	,,	
1550-1	,,	N		
1551-2		O		
1552-3	,,	P		
MARY. 1553-4	,,	Q	,,	
1554-5	,,	R	,,	
1555-6	,,	S	,,	,,
1556-7	,,	T	,,	
1557-8	,,	V		

1536-7   Marks on seal-top spoon: Mr. E. A. Bennett.

1544-5 G   Marks on seal-top spoon: Mr. E. Brand.

CYCLE V.

FOUR STAMPS AS BELOW.

ELIZ.	LEOPARD'S HEAD CROWNED.	DATE LETTER.	LION PASSANT.	MAKER'S MARK.	
1558-9		a			
1559-60	,,	b	,,		
1560-1	,,	c	,,		
1561-2	,,	d			
1562-3		e			
1563-4	,,	F	,,		
1564-5	,,	g	,,		
1565-6	,,	h	,,		
1566-7	,,	i	,,		
1567-8	,,	k	,,		
1568-9	,,	l	,,	IF	M
1569-70	,,	m	,,		F
1570-1	,,	n	,,		K
1571-2	,,	o	,,		
1572-3	,,	p	,,		EAGLE AS 1562
1573-4	,,	q			IP
1574-5	,,	r	,,		M AS 1568
1575-6	,,	s	,,	HTC	W
1576-7	,,	t	,,		R
1577-8	,,	u	,,		

CYCLE VI.

FOUR STAMPS AS BELOW.

	LEOPARD'S HEAD CROWNED.	DATE LETTER.	LION PASSANT.	MAKER'S MARK	
1578-9		A			
1579-80	,,	B	,,		HTC
1580-1	,,	C	,,	SB	
1581-2	,,	D	,,		
1582-3	,,	E	,,	IF	
1583-4	,,	F	,,	RS	
1584-5	,,	G	,,		
1585-6	,,	H	,,		
1586-7	,,	I	,,		
1587-8	,,	K	,,	N	
1588-9	,,	L	,,	S	W
1589-90	,,	M	,,	D	M
1590-1	,,	N	,,	PW IN	
1591-2	,,	O	,,	TH	
1592-3		P			
1593-4	,,	Q	,,	,,	D AS 1586
1594-5	,,	R		IM	I
1595-6	,,	S	,,	IH	F
1596-7	,,	T	,,		
1597-8	,,	V	,	B	

1593-4 Q Another example of the date letter for this year.

CYCLE VII.
FOUR STAMPS AS BELOW.

	LEOPARD'S HEAD CROWNED	DATE LETTER	LION PASSANT	MAKER'S MARK	
1598-9		T		TF	✠
1599 1600	,,	B		RC	
1600-1	,,	C	,,	HD	
1601-2	,,	D			✠
1602-3	,,	E	,,		VM
JAS. I. 1603-4	,,	F	,,	IG	C
1604-5	,,	G			AB
1605-6	,,	h	,,	HM	,,
1606-7	,,	I		F	RW
1607-8	,,	K	,,		C
1608-9	,,	L	,,		M
1609-10	,,	M	,,		C
1610-1	,,	n		TP	TI
1611-2	,,	O	,,		B
1612-3	,,	P	,,	AB	RB
1613-4	,,	Q	,,	TC	MH
1614-5	,,	R	,,	RB	RC
1615-6	,,	S	,,	CR	IR
1616-7	,,	T	,,	IA	RN
1617-8	,,	V	,,	IV	RS

* Another example of the lion passant for Cycle VIII.

CYCLE VIII.
FOUR STAMPS AS BELOW.

	LEOPARD'S HEAD CROWNED.	DATE LETTER.	LION PASSANT.	MAKER'S MARK.	
*1618-9		a		IP	WR
1619-20	,,	b	,,	E	,,
1620-1	,,	c	,,	IC	II
1621-2	,,	d	,,	EL	a
1622-3	,,	e	,,	RD	ER
1623-4	,,	f	,,		WC
1624-5	,,	g	,,		
CHAS. I. 1625-6	,,	h	,,	LE	IV
1626-7	,,	i	,,	PH	I
1627-8	,,	kk	,,	SW	RI
1628-9	,,	l	,,	RM	
1629-30	,,	m	,,	DTG	RB
1630-1	,,	n	,,	WM	RS
1631-2	,,	o	,,	RS	B
1632-3	,,	p	,,	PB	D
1633-4	,,	q	,,	IBe	WM
1634-5	,,	r	,,	RS	M
1635-6	,,	s	,,	F	LI
1636-7	,,	t	,,	RB	RW
1637-8	,,	v	,,	RM	RC

Examples of forged London marks of the year 1637, found on evnteenth · century apostle spoon : Messrs. Christie.

CYCLE IX.

FOUR STAMPS AS BELOW.

	LEOPARD'S HEAD CROWNED.	DATE LETTER.	LION PASSANT.	MAKER'S MARK.	
1638-9		A B		RA	IH
*1639-40	,,	B	,,	IH	WS
1640-1	,,	C	,,	IM	I·B·
1641-2	,,	D	,,	WM	TH
1642-3	,,	E	,,	IW	F
1643-4	,,	ff	,,		TT
1644-5	,,	G	,,	BB	
1645-6	,,	H	,,	DW	TG
1646-7	,,	I	,,	NW	IL
1647-8		K		IA	RV
1648-9	,,	L	,,	II	H
COMWTH. 1649-50	,,	M	,,		M
1650-1	,,	N	,,	M	IW
1651-2	,,	O	,,		SV
1652-3	,,	P	,,	R·S	IB
1653-4	,,	Q	,,	WH	HC
1654-5	,,	R	,,	,,	,,
1655-6	,,	S	,,	DR	I·L
1656-7	,,	T	,,	C|S	E·L
1657-8	,,	V	,,	TC	KF

CYCLE X.

FOUR STAMPS AS BELOW.

	LEOPARD'S HEAD CROWNED.	DATE LETTER.	LION PASSANT.	MAKER'S MARK.	
1658-9		A		WC	P·B
1659-60	,,	B	,,	TG	G|S
CHAS. II. 1660-1	,,	C	,,	IG	G|S
1661-2	,,	D	,,	SV	T·D
1662-3	,,	E		HN	ET
1663-4	,,	F	,,	I·F	TK
1664-5	,,	G	,,	IW	WH
1665-6	,,	H	,,	AD	TR
1666-7	,,	I	,,	RD	WM
1667-8	,,	K	,,	M	S|S
1668-9		L			I·B
1669-70	,,	M	,,	WG	WW
1670-1	,,	N	,,	TM	TK
1671-2	,,	O	,,	DC	IK
1672-3	,,	P	,,	RP	AH
1673-4	,,	Q	,,	EB	SC
1674-5	,,	R	,,	T·G	GG
1675-6	,,	S	,,	GG	
1676-7	,,	T	,,	M	FS
1677-8	,,	V	,,	KC	WS

Variations of date letters of this cycle :

1639-40   1643-4 ff   1652-3 p   1657-8

*The lion passant is sometimes found thus :

Variations of date-letters of this cycle:

1664-5 G   1667-8 K

1671-2 O   1677-8

CYCLE XI.

	LEOPARD'S HEAD CROWNED.	DATE LETTER.	LION PASSANT.
1678-9		a	
*1679-80	,,	b	
1680-1		c	
1681-2	,,	d	,,
1682-3	,,	e	,,
1683-4	,,	f	,,
1684-5	,,	g	,,
JAS. II. 1685-6	,,	h	,,
1686-7	,,	i	,,
1687-8	,,	k	,,
1688-9	,,	l	,,
WM. & MY. 1689-90		m	
1690-1	,,	n	,,
1691-2	,,	o	,,
1692-3	,,	p	,,
1693-4	,,	q	,,
1694-5	,,	r	,,
WM. III. 1695-6	,,	s	,,
MAY 29, 1696, TO MCH. 27, 1697.	,,	t	,,

*See notes on p. 31

In 1697 a law was passed raising the standard of silver from .925 (sterling) to .958 henceforth to be known as the "Britannia" standard. The same law changed the markings as shown in the column to the right and also provided that the silversmiths should use the first two letters of their surname as a mark and not their initials as theretofore. The law was repealed in 1720. The standard for coin of the realm was not changed from sterling.

Examples of makers' marks of the period 1678–1716 are shown on pp. 58 *et seq.*

CYCLE XII.

	BRITANNIA.	DATE LETTER.	LION'S HEAD ERASED.
*1697 MCH. 27 TO MAY 29.		a	
1697-8	,,	b	,,
1698-9	,,	c	,,
1699 1700		d	
1700-1	,,	e	,,
1701-2	,,	f	,,
ANNE. 1702-3	,,	g	,,
1703-4	,,	h	,,
1704-5	,,	i	,,
1705-6	,,	k	,,
1706-7	,,	l	,,
1707-8	,,	m	,,
1708-9	,,	n	,,
1709-10	,,	o	,,
1710-11	,,	p	,,
1711-2	,,	q	,,
1712-3	,,	r	,,
1713-4	,,	s	,,
GEO. I. 1714-5	,,	t	,,
1715-6	,,	u	,,

CYCLE XIII.

FOUR STAMPS AS BELOW.

	BRIT ANNIA.	DATE LETTER.	LION'S HEAD ERASED.	MAKER'S MARK.	
1716-7		A		HO	KO
1717-8	,,	B	,,	FT	KE
1718 9	,, LEOPARD'S HEAD CROWNED	C	,, LION PASSANT.	HA	FA
1719-20		D		I TE	LA
				WP	BR
1720-1	,,	E	,,	CD	FA
				TS	GB
				FG	IS IS
1721-2		F		EV	IL
1722-3	,,	G	,,	BN	IS
				NG	CO
1723-4	,,	H	,,	I E	TF
1724-5		I		R B	S C
				HU	SH
1725-6	,,	K	,,	WT	IB
1726-7		L L		AV	WD
GEO. II. 1727-8	,,	M M	,,	IR	IS
				RH	WE GW
1728-9	,,	N	,,	WD	IG
1729-30		O		BI	II
1730-1	,,	P	,,	AC	LA
1731-2	,,	Q	,,	IG	EY
1732-3	,,	R	,,	IS	EP
1733-4	,,	S	,,	IE	AC
1734-5	,,	T	,,	R·M	CH
1735-6	,,	V	,,	G·I	T R·C

CYCLE XIV.

FOUR STAMPS AS BELOW.

	LEOPARD'S HEAD CROWNED.	DATE LETTER	LION PASSANT.	MAKER'S MARK.
1736-7		a		HV
1737-8	,,	b	,,	IA MF
*1738-9	,,	c	,,	R·Z
1739-40	,,	d	,,	Wk
				R·B
		d		IW
				Sh
1740-1	,,	e	,,	IR
1741-2	,,	f	,,	Dh
1742-3	,,	g	,,	IG
1743-4	,,	h	,,	WH
1744-5	,,	i	,,	LP
1745-6	,,	k	,,	B·W
1746-7	,,	l	,,	IW
1747-8	,,	m	,,	WG
1748-9	,,	n	,,	EM
1749-50	,,	o	,,	WG
1750-1	,,	p	,,	IP
†1751-2		q		IP
1752-3	,,	r	,,	RC
1753-4	,,	s	,,	GH
‡1754-5	,,	t	,,	P PA M
1755-6	,,	u	,,	IS

*
† } See Notes on p. 31.

CYCLE XV.
FOUR STAMPS AS BELOW.

	Leopard's Head Crowned.	Date Letter.	Lion Passant.	Maker's Mark.
1756-7	(leopard)	A	(lion)	S·W
1757-8	,,	B	,,	D·H
*1758-9	,,	C	,,	I·S
*1759-60	,,	D	,,	I·K
GEO. III. 1760-1	,,	E	,,	R·R
1761-2	,,	F	,,	R·R
1762-3	,,	G	,,	I·I
†1763-4	,,	H	,,	RT
1764-5	,,	I	,,	R D·H
1765-6	,,	K	,,	I·W·L
1766-7	,,	L	,,	L·H
1767-8	,,	M	,,	D·M
†1768-9	,,	N	,,	I·P E·W
1769-70	,,	O	,,	I·A
1770-1	,,	P	,,	B·G
†1771-2	,,	Q	,,	I·C T·H
1772-3	,,	R	,,	I·C WP AS 1761
1773-4	,,	S	,,	R·S
1774-5	,,	T	,,	I·S
1775-6	,,	U	,,	W·T

CYCLE XVI.
FOUR STAMPS TILL 1784, FIVE STAMPS THENCEFORWARD.

	Leopard's Head Crowned.	Date Letter.	Lion Passant.	King's Head.	Maker's Mark.
1776-7	(leopard)	a	(lion)		C·H
1777-8	,,	b	,,		H·G
1778-9	,,	c	,,		I·D
1779-80	,,	d	,,		I·S
1780-1	,,	e	,,		R·D·M
*1781-2	,,	f	,,		C·W
1782-3	,,	g	,,		G·S
1783-4	,,	h	,,		I·L
†1784-5	,,	i	,,	(king's head)	L·I
1785-6	,,	k	,,	,,	W·A
1786-7	,,	l	,,	(head)	S·G E·W
1787-8	,,	m	,,	,,	S·M
1788-9	,,	n	,,	,,	E·I
1789-90	,,	o	,,	,,	H·B 1778
1790-1	,,	p	,,	,,	T·P E·R
1791-2	,,	q	,,	,,	W·P J·P
1792-3	,,	r	,,	,,	H·C
1793-4	,,	s	,,	,,	I·W R·G
1794-5	,,	t	,,	,,	W·F
1795-6	,,	u	,,	,,	T·E

* 1758-60 (shield) On articles bearing the hall-marks of 1758-9-60, the leopard's head crowned is occasionally found in a shield with pointed base.

† Date-letters for 1763-4, 1768-9, and 1771-2, are sometimes found to differ from those in general use thus:

1763-4 (mark)   1768-9 (mark)   1771-2 (mark)

* The author has also noted the date-letters f of 1781-2, and the k of 1785-6 in shields with rounded bases, similar to those of the g, h and i of 1782-3 to 1784-5, as well as in shields with pointed bases as illustrated above. On the other hand, the g and h of 1782-3 and 1783-4, are sometimes found in a shield with a pointed base as in the shield for e of 1780-1.

† On some articles dating from 1784 to 1830, the shield enclosing the date-letter has a rounded base, and the lion passant is sometimes found in an oval stamp.

CYCLE XVII.

FIVE STAMPS AS BELOW.

	LEOPARD'S HEAD CROWNED.	DATE LETTER.	LION PASSANT.	KING'S HEAD.	MAKER'S MARK.
1796-7		A			SP
1797-8	,,	B	,,	,,	RC
*1798-9	,,	C	,,	,,	EM
1799 1800	,,	D	,,	,,	WP
1800-1	,,	E	,,	,,	P·S
1801-2	,,	F	,,	,,	RG
1802-3	,,	G	,,	,,	IH
1803-4	,,	H	,,	,,	B·L
†1804-5	,,	I	,,	,,	GW
1805-6	,,	K	,,	,,	DP
1806-7	,,	L	,,	,,	RH SH
1807-8	,,	M	,,	,,	TG GC IC
†1808-9	,,	N	,,	,,	WE WF WC
1809-10	,,	O	,,	,,	CH
1810-1	,,	P	,,	,,	TP ER
1811-2	,,	Q	,,	,,	JB
1812-3	,,	R	,,	,,	TI
1813-4	,,	S	,,	,,	IC WR
1814-5	,,	T	,,	,,	SH
1815-6	,,	U	,,	,,	IP GP

Notes for p. 28.

*Solid gold articles are marked with the leopard's head and lion passant as 1696 and not with the figure of Britannia and lion's head erased.

 Variation of lion passant occasionally found on plate of 1679 to 1686.

1695-6 ,,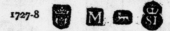

Notes for p. 29:

It is very important to note the variation of the date letter, leopard's head, and lion passant for the year 1726–7 of this cycle. This variation was also found by Sir Chas.

1727-8

Jackson, but the author has found the same variation for the year 1730–1 on authentic specimens and he has no doubt that date letters in square blocks were used alternatively with the conventional shields to the end of the cycle (1735–6). When new dies were made in 1736, no doubt this anomalous fashion of enclosing the date letter was discontinued.

H. P. O.

*1738-9 [mark] C [lion] G·H Variations of leopard's head and lion passant.

† [leopard's head mark] [lion passant mark] Although a punch for the leopard's head mark different in form from that of 1739–40 was used between 1751 and 1756, its use was not entirely general, because articles of the latter period are frequently found stamped with the leopard's head mark as here illustrated.

‡This and other date letters in this cycle are occasionally found with somewhat broader backgrounds.

Notes for p. 31:

*In 1798 the Stat. 38 Geo. III, c.69, authorized a new gold standard of 18 carats fine, and provided that it should be marked with a crown and 18 in place of the lion passant. Up to this time gold and silver of the old standard had been marked alike. Gold of the old standard (22 carats) continued to be marked with the same marks as silver of the old standard until 1844, when a crown and 22 were substituted for the lion passant, for the purpose of distinguishing it from silver-gilt.

1798   An example of the marks on 18 carat gold, as prescribed in the year 1798; on gold snuff box; Mr. Harry Alston.

†For 1804-5, 1808-9; and one or two other years, the duty mark has been found in a trefoil-shaped stamp. It has also been found in the oval stamp in the same years. From 1808 to 1815 the king's head is occasionally found like that shown for 1816-17.

CYCLE XVIII.
FIVE STAMPS AS BELOW.

	LEOPARD'S HEAD	DATE LETTER.	LION PASSANT.	KING'S HEAD.	MAKER'S MARK.
1816-7	(leopard's head)	a	(lion)	(head)	WB
1817-8	,,	b	,,	,,	TR
1818-9	,,	c	,,	,,	GW
1819-20	,,	d	,,	,,	WS
GEO. IV. 1820-1	,,	e	,,	(head)	W·B
1821-2	(leopard's head)	f	(lion)	,,	CdCd
1822-3	,,	g	,,	,,	PS
1823-4	,,	h	,,	,,	IS
1824-5	,,	i	,,	,,	TH GH
1825-6	,,	k	,,	,,	IC
1826-7	,,	l	,,	,,	LL HL CL
1827-8	,,	m	,,	,,	BP
1828-9	,,	n	,,	,,	WS
1829-30	,,	o	,,	,,	RG
WM. IV. 1830-1	,,	p	,,	,,	CP
1831-2	,,	q	,,	(head)	RH
1832-3	,,	r	,,	,,	CP
1833-4	,,	s	,,	,,	PS
1834-5	,,	t	,,	,,	N·M
1835-6	,,	u	,,	,,	CF

CYCLE XIX.
FIVE STAMPS AS BELOW.

	LEOPARD'S HEAD	DATE LETTER.	LION PASSANT.	KING'S HEAD.	MAKER'S MARK.
1836-7	(head)	A	(lion)	(head)	CF JB
VICT. 1837-8	,,	B	,,	(head)	WE AS GW
1838-9	,,	C	,,	,,	WT CR RA GS
1839-40	,,	D	,,	,,	WB FD DB WC
1840-1	,,	E	,,	,,	JA MC JA GA
1841-2	,,	F	,,	,,	JS GA AS CF
1842-3	,,	G	,,	,,	JCE WH RH WS
1843-4	,,	H	,,	,,	WKR JA WB
1844-5	,,	I	,,	,,	RGH BS
1845-6	,,	K	,,	,,	ISU GF
1846-7	,,	L	,,	,,	GPP EB HH &W
1847-8	,,	M	,,	,,	IL RP HL GB
1848-9	,,	N	,,	,,	EJ RH BW JW
1849-50	,,	O	,,	,,	CTE GF FD WRB
1850-1	,,	P	,,	,,	IK GI
1851-2	,,	Q	,,	,,	EB JB
1852-3	,,	R	,,	,,	JE IF
1853-4	,,	S	,,	,,	EB &JB
1854-5	,,	T	,,	,,	WRS
1855-6	,,	U	,,	,,	GA

The shield enclosing the date-letters of Cycle XVIII. and preceding cycles is occasionally found with its base straight, or slightly rounded.

1825-35   (leopard's head)   On plate of the second quarter of the 19th century, the leopard's head is frequently found without whiskers, as here illustrated from an example on a pierced salt cellar: Messrs. Alstons & Hallam.

The date-letter 𝕭 of 1837-8 is accompanied by the head of Wm. IV. from 29 May to 20 June, 1837.

CYCLE XX.

FIVE STAMPS AS BELOW.

	Leopard's Head	Date Letter	Lion Passant	Queen's Head	Maker's Mark
1856-7	[leopard]	a	[lion]	[head]	CTF / GF
1857-8	,,	b	,,	,,	HW
1858-9	,,	c	,,	,,	JA / WM / GR / EB
1859-60	,	d	,	,,	GA / EE / JE
1860-1	,,	e	,,	,,	CR / WS
1861-2	,,	f	,,	,,	RH
1862-3	,,	g	,,	,,	R·H
*1863-4	[Britannia]	h	[lion]	,,	GF
1864-5	*Leopard's head as above*	i	*Lion passant as above*	,,	GA
1865-6	,,	k	,,	,,	IJK / R·H
1866-7	,,	l	,,	,,	GE / GF
1867-8	,,	m	,,	,,	GM / HD
1868-9	,,	n	,,	,,	CS / U
1869-70	,,	o	,,	,,	J·E·B·W·J
1870-1	,	p	,,	,,	WS
1871-2	,	q	,,	,,	HFW
1872-3		r	,,		Rf
1873-4	,,	s	,,		RM / FH
1874-5	,,	t	,,	,,	JEM / GW
1875-6	,,	u	,,	,,	[maker's mark]

CYCLE XXI.

FIVE STAMPS TILL 1890, THENCEFORWARD FOUR ONLY.

	Leopard's Head	Date Letter	Lion Passant	Queen's Head	Maker's Mark
1876-7	[leopard]	A	[lion]	[head]	CFH
1877-8	,,	B	,,	,,	,,
1878-9	,,	C	,,	,,	SS
1879-80	,,	D	,,	,,	DH / CH
1880-1	,,	E	,,	,,	JWD
1881-2	,,	F	,,	,,	FH
1882-3	,,	G	,,	,,	CS / H
1883-4	,,	H	,,	,,	PW
1884-5	,,	I	,,	,,	JRH
1885-6	,,	K	,,	,,	CFH
1886-7	,,	L	,,	,,	
1887-8	,,	M	,,	,,	
1888-9	,,	N	,,	,,	D&C / WD
1889-90	,,	O	,,	,,	CFH
1890-1	,,	P	,,	,,	,,
1891-2	,,	Q	,,		,,
1892-3	,,	R	,,		W.C
1893-4	,,	S	,,		SWS
1894-5	,,	T	,,		JB / ER
1895-6	,,	U	,,		JS

*This is merely an example of the Britannia marks as frequently employed after 1720 to denote the higher standard. It is not typical of 1863–4, or of any particular year. *Vide* p. 20 *infra*.

In 1883 a law was passed decreeing that all silver plate brought into the United Kingdom from abroad should, before being offered for sale, be assayed, and if found of the proper standard, marked with an F in an oval. In 1904, that law changed and it was directed that such silver should have its fineness indicated by a decimal stamp (.925 or .9584) in a long oval and have the symbol of the local assay office (usually a zodiacal sign) also impressed.

CYCLE XXII.

FOUR STAMPS AS BELOW.

	LEOPARD'S HEAD	DATE LETTER	LION PASSANT	MAKER'S MARK
1896-7		a		H&Co
1897-8	,,	b	,,	JRC
1898-9	,,	c	,,	GG
1899 1900	,,	d	,,	GP
1900-1	,,	e	,,	CCd
EDW. VII. 1901-2	,,	f	,,	CK
1902-3	,,	g	,,	WC
1903-4	,,	h	,,	WB JS MRD
1904-5	,,	i		WJ
1905-6	,,	k	,,	TR
1906-7	,,	l	,,	C&Co
1907-8	,,	m	,,	WB JS MS
1908-9	,,	n	,,	JH AS
1909-10	,,	o	,,	IMS
1910-1	,,	p	,,	SJP
1911-2	,,	q	,,	JW
1912-3	,,	r	,,	H&Co LD
1913-4	,,	s	,,	AP FP
1914-5	,,	t	,,	D&J W
1915-6	,,	u	,,	C&R C

CYCLE XXIII.

FOUR STAMPS AS BELOW.

	LION PASSANT	LEOPARD'S HEAD	DATE LETTER	MAKER'S MARK
1916-7			A	G&SCo LD
1917-8	,,	,,	B	,,
1918-9	,,	,,	C	C&R C
1919-20	,,	,,	D	,,

1909-10	SB H	Maker's mark of S. B. Harman: on silver-gilt snuff-box.
1916-17	DF	Mark on Church plate: St. Kerverne, Cornwall.
,,	LAC	Mark of L. A. Crichton.

Date letters of this alphabet will continue in use until 1936–7.

CHAPTER IV

Makers' Marks on London Plate

Arranged
Chronologically

See index, p. 211

DATE.	GOLDSMITHS' MARKS	
1479-80		A jug.*
1481-2		A fetter lock.
1488-9		A key.
1490-1		L.
1491-2		A fish.
1493-4		A horse shoe.
1494-5		A bird's head.
,,		W.
,,		?
1496-7		A leaf slipped.‡
,,		A jug, as in 1479.
,,		?
1498-9		MW in monogram.
1499-1500		SW ,, ,,
,,		Heart as 1516.

DATE.	GOLDSMITHS' MARKS	
1500-1		
1501-2		A hand ?
1503-4		Bow and arrow ?
1504-5		A horse ?
,,		A plant ?
1506-7		A cock's head erased.
,,		A cross pattée.
1507-8		A trellis.
,,		A fleur-de-lys.
,,		A maidenhead.
,,		A fish, as 1491.
1508-9		An incuse cross.
,,		A rising sun.
1509-10		Two links.
1510-1		A flower.
,,		A lamb's head.
1511-2		A foot print.
1512-3		A barrel or tun.
1513-4		Head of pastoral staff
1514-5		Orb and cross.
,,		Gemini.
,,		A leaf.
,,		A gate ?
,,		,,
1515-6		
,,		A fringed S.

DATE.	GOLDSMITHS' MARKS.		DATE.	GOLDSMITHS' MARKS.	
1516-7		A heart.	1527-8		Double-headed arrow.
1517-8		A sheep.	,,		T, incuse, charged with 3 pellets.
1518-9		Two links.	1528-9		Crescent enclosing mullet.
,,		HK in monogram ?	,,		Orb and cross between I C.—John Carswell.
,,		D ?	,,		A fringed S, as 1527.
1519-20			1529-30		Orb and cross between I C, as 1528.
,,		A fringed S.	1530-1		A fringed S, as 1519.
,,		A bunch of grapes.	1531-2		A coronet.
1520-1		A crescent enclosing a mullet.	,,		Orb and cross between I C, as 1528.
1521-2		An escallop.	1532-3		A hanap.
,,			,,		A hand erect.
,,		Two links.	,,		?
,,		A sun.	1533-4		An arbalist ?
1522-3		A short sword.	,,		Rose and crown.
,,		A serpent.	,,		Thomas Wastell.
1523-4		A sceptre ?	1534-5		Double-headed arrow.
,,		A sun, as 1521.	,,		A basket.
1524-5		An orb and cross.	,,		A fringed S, as 1519.
,,		A heart, as 1516.	,,		A pair of compasses.
1525-6		Implements crossed.	1535-6		A negro's head.
,,		A sceptre ? see 1523.	,,		?
,,		Sc ?	,,		?
,,		{ A heart, see 1516. ,, ,,	,,		An eagle displayed.
1527-8		A maid's head.	,,		A hand grasping a hammer between H C. (Henry Colville ?)
,,		A fringed S, as 1519.			
,,		An eagle displayed.			

DATE.		GOLDSMITHS' MARKS.	DATE.		GOLDSMITHS' MARKS.
1536-7		A sheaf of arrows.	1551-2		Crescent enclosing mullet.
1537-8		A fringed S, as 1519.	,,		A K conjoined.
1538-9		A pheon ?	,,		Stag's head caboshed.
1539-40		A fringed S, as 1519.	,,		Swan's head erased.
1540-1		A spray of leaves.	1552-3		T L in monogram.
,,			1553-4		Robert Danbe, as 1549.
1541-2		A fringed S, as 1519.	,,		As 1551.
1543-4		Orb and cross incuse.	1554-5		As 1552.
,,		A fringed S, as 1519.	,,		Queen's head as 1545.
,,		Marigold and letter E.	1555-6		I F (John Freeman).
1514-5		A crab.	,,		T L., as 1554.
,,		A fringed S, as 1541.	1556-7		Stag's head, as 1551.
1545-6		A queen's head.	,,		W.
,,		N B in monogram (Nicholas Bartlemew).	1557-8		H crowned.
,,		A head	,,		W over a crescent.
1546-7		A fleur-de-lys.	1558-9		A rose (Henry Gillard).
1547-8		N B in monogram as 1545.	,,		C A in monogram.
1548-9		A covered cup.	1559-60		H W.
,,			,,		A lamp.
,,		M, or W inverted.	,,		A bird's claw, see 1565.
1549-50		F B.	,,		A mullet.
,,		R D in monogram (Robert Danbe).	,,		A fleur-de-lys.
,,		C A in monogram.	,,		C C linked.
,,		Crowned cross moline.	,,		S K.
1550-1		A high boot.	1560 1		
,,		A hand under a coronet.	,,		A bird.

DATE.	GOLDSMITHS' MARKS.	
1561-2		A spur.
,,		P. C.
,,		A star radiant.
,,		Crossed compasses within a radiant circle.
,,		A fleur-de-lys (Wm. Dyxson).
,,		R B.
,,		{ Three mullets over a crescent (R. Durrant) }
1562-3		S R.
,,		Sun in splendour.
,,		R M.
,,		W C over a pig (Wm. Cater).
,,		A wallet hook palewise on a cross bendwise.
,,		N S in monogram (Nicholas Sutton).
,,		H K conjoined.
,,		R D in monogram, see 1549 (Robert Danbe).
,,		An eagle displayed (Fras. Jackson).
,,		Crescent enclosing mullet.
,,		Eagle's (?) head between I C.
,,		A fleur-de-lys incuse.
,,		A hand grasping a cross, see 1564.
,,		A holly leaf incuse.
1563-4		3 mullets over a crescent, as 1561.
,,		I P (John Pikenynge).
,,		H W, as 1559.
,,		A bird.
,,		W in radiant circle.

DATE.	GOLDSMITHS' MARKS.	
1563-4		A spur.
,,		R D (Robt. Danbe), as 1549.
1564-5		A mullet.
,,		
,,		A fleur-de-lys, as 1561.
,,		I C { John Cross or John Clark }
,,		A horse's head couped (Robert Medley ?)
,,		I S in monogram.
,,		A campanula, as 1566.
,,		A.
1565-6		A bird's claw, see 1559.
,,		I P (John Pikenynge), see 1563.
,,		As 1562.
,,		
,,		H W, as 1559.
,,		R K.
1566-7		Stars and crescent.
,,		A.
,,		A star radiant, as 1561.
,,		
,,		A campanula, as 1564.
,,		Acorns.
,,		
,,		W H, pellet below.

DATE.	GOLDSMITHS' MARKS.		DATE.	GOLDSMITHS' MARKS.	
1567-8		A bull's head erased (Affabel Partridge?)	1569-70		A hooded falcon (Thomas Bampton).
,,		A wallet hook.	,,		R V, a heart beneath.
,,		A bird.	,,		A bunch of grapes, see 1568.
,,		F G in monogram.	1570-1		A millrind.
,,		A horse's head couped, as 1564.	,,		An orb and cross.
,,		R D (Robert Danbe), as 1549.	,,		A beaked bassinet.
,,		A hand grasping a hammer, see 1535.	,,		A K conjoined, see 1551.
,,		E R in monogram (Edward Ranklyn).	,,		T E o, in monogram (Thomas Heard).
,,		T B in monogram (Thos. Brown or Benson).	,,		T H in monogram (Thos. Harrison or Hampton).
,,		A talbot? sejant (Thos. Conell).	,,		A pair of bellows.
,,		A cock's comb?	,,		H B conjoined (Hy. Boswell).
1568-9		I F, see 1555 (Jasper Fysher?).	,,		M in plain shield.
,,		M.	,,		Covered cup (John Mabbe).
,,		A wallet hook.	,,		I H (John Harryson)..
,,		A bunch of grapes.	,,		A campanula, see 1564.
,,		F R in monogram.	,,		R H conjoined.
,,		I H, see 1570.	1571-2		F?
,,		?	,,		A heart.
,,		A globe.	,,		Porcupine over T A.
,,		Two birds.	,,		L reversed.
,,		R A.	,,		A bird (John Bird?)
1569-70		A bunch of grapes, see 1568.	,,		A hand grasping a crosslet, see 1562.
,,		F, enclosing T, in monogram.	,,		I piercing G.
,,		A hand grasping hammer, see 1567.	,,		A beaked bassinet, see 1570.
,,		Animal's head couped.	,,		T G in monogram.

DATE.	GOLDSMITHS' MARKS.		DATE.	GOLDSMITHS' MARKS.	
1571-2		T L.	1575-6		R E in indented border.
,,		Lombardic A.	,,		A K conjoined, see 1570.
,,		A B conjoined.	,,		W T.
,,		N R conjoined.	,,		T B.
1572-3		A trefoil.	,,		M.
,,		A trefoil slipped.	,,		?
,,		H B conjoined, see 1570.	,,		A millrind, as 1570.
,,		H R.	,,		A pair of bellows, as 1570.
,,		A cross couped.	1576-7		t b.
,,		Grotesque object and bunch of grapes.	,,		Three trefoils in a trefoil.
1573-4		B.	,,		I H, bear below.
,,		I F.	,,		An arrow piercing H.
,,		N O in monogram.	,,		A fox sejant (John Foxe).
,,		I P in shaped shield.	,,		R H in monogram.
,,		A beaked helmet, see 1571.	,,		A caltrap.
,,		A millrind, as 1570.	,,		A bouget.
,,		A pelican displayed.	,,		An arrow piercing H, see above.
,,		H S in monogram (Henry Sutton).	,,		W C over a grasshopper (Wm. Cocknidge ?)
,,		H R conjoined.	,,		A snail.
,,		A bird, see 1571.	,,		t b, see above.
,,		Escallop.	,,		A mullet between a pair of compasses.
1574-5		Sun in splendour, see 1562.	1577-8		L R.
,,		C P, an axe between.	,,		Do.
,,		V S, fleur-de-lys below.	,,		M.
1575-6		Hand grasping hammer between H C, see 1535.			

DATE.		GOLDSMITHS' MARKS.
1577-8		A branch.
"		S E in monogram.
"		A H.
"		W H (Wm. Holborne).
"		A bird in shaped shield, see 1571.(John Bird?)
"		R P, crescent below (Robert Planckney).
"		t b, see 1576.
1578-9		S on a cross (Isaac Sutton?)
"		A windmill (Robert Wright).
"		P G in monogram.
"		C B in monogram.
"		A rose slipped.
1579-80		An escallop, see 1573.
"		Hand grasping hammer between H C, as 1535 (Hugh Crook?)
"		Three trefoils slipped within a trefoil.
c. 1580		I H in monogram.
1580-1		S B (Simon Brooke).
"		Sun in splendour.
"		A four petalled rose seeded.
1581 2		Tudor rose.
"		Fleur-de-lys incuse.
"		t b, as 1576.
"		H W, rose below.
"		R W.
"		R B in monogram (Richard Brooke).

DATE.		GOLDSMITHS' MARKS.
1581-2		H W over a star.
1582-3		An escallop.
"		A fleur-de-lys.
"		A bull's head.
"		I F, see 1555, 1568 and 1583.
".		Small letter b ?
1583-4		R S, fleur-de-lys below (Robert Signell).
"		A banner bendwise.
"		I F, see 1555, 1568 and 1582.
"		I H.
1584-5		I C.
"		W C conjoined.
"		A crown.
"		Mullet and pellet.
"		Mullet and annulet.
"		R W, as 1581.
1585-6		A caltrap, as 1576.
"		An escallop.
"		Three trefoils voided.
"		M (line across).
1586-7		A newt on a tun (for Newton).
"		A crescent enclosing W. (Christopher Waiste?)
"		T, over a crescent.
"		T, within a bordure.
"		A mullet and annulet.
"		Orb and cross.

DATE.	GOLDSMITHS' MARKS.		DATE.	GOLDSMITHS' MARKS.	
1587-8		D or I D in monogram. Or E D.	1593-4		I G, as 1592-3.
,,		A chanticleer.	,,		D, as 1587.
,,		An escallop.	1594-5		I M over a billet (John Morley ?).
,,		I N in monogram.	,,		An anchor.
,,		T S over a double-headed eagle.	,,		T H, a rose above and below.
1588-9		C B in monogram, see 1578.	,,		W H, a rose in base (Wm. Holborne ?).
,,		I S in monogram, see 1578 (John Speilman).	,,		A crescent enclosing a mullet, see 1590.
·,		W over a rose.	1595-6		I H.
,,		R F (Robert Frye).	,,		T N in monogram.
,,		W S over a rosette.	,,		G S, mullet below (Giles Sympson ?),
1589-90		D, as in 1587 (Edward Delves ?).	,,		I B, rose in base (John Brode ?).
,,		I M (John Morris).	,,		T N, rose in base (T. Newton ?).
,,		H L conjoined.	,,		C B in monogram.
1590-1		P W over I N.	,,		G A, pheon in base.
,,		A crescent enclosing a mullet.	1596-7		D.
,,		A heart over two clubs in saltire.	,,		Crescent enclosing W.
,,		R M (Richard Matthew?).	,,		Sun in splendour.
1591-2		T F (Thos. Francknall ?).	,,		Mullet over annulet, see 1584.
,,		T S over a double-headed eagle, as 1587.	,,		T, see 1599.
·,		N R conjoined.	1597-8		H B conjoined.
,,		T F (Thos. Francknall ?).	,,		I H over a bear passant, see 1576.
1592-3		I G in monogram.	,,		I D over a doe lodged (I. Doe).
,,		A crescent inclosing W.	,,		I B, badge above.
,,		R W.	,,		R B, mullet below (Richard Brooke ?).
,,		P W.			

DATE.		GOLDSMITHS' MARKS.
1597-8		I B, bow in chief.
1598-9		T F, see 1591 (Thos. Francknall ?).
,,		Crescent enclosing W, see 1592.
,,		Branch between R.P.
,,		E R.
1599-1600		B W.
,,		I A.
,,		R C.
,,		A squirrel.
,,		I B, rosette below.
,,		T, see 1596.
,,		An anchor, see 1594.
,,		A branch.
1600-1		S O, a roundlet below.
,,		Dove, holding olive branch.
,,		H D, rosette below.
,,		A cock, see 1587.
,,		C B in monogram, see 1595.
,,		M in plain shield.
,,		Three trefoils slipped, see 1585.
1601-2		Tau with bar across.
,,		b, see 1582.
,,		Cross couped.
,,		Two crescents.
,,		A merchant's mark.

DATE.		GOLDSMITHS' MARKS.
1601-2		A wine skin tied at the neck.
,,		T S in monogram.
1602-3		An animal's head erased between W I.
,,		A harp, between L M.
,,		D enclosing C.
,,		M W in monogram.
,,		T S, over an Imperial eagle, see 1587.
,,		T W in monogram.
,,		Anchor.
,,		A B conjoined, see 1571.
,,		b, see 1582.
1603-4		I G, annulet below.
,,		C I in monogram.
,,		A T, tun below.
,,		Three gouttées.
,,		I B, fleur-de-lys below.
,,		A bird over H I.
,,		A triangle intersected.
1604-5		W I, as 1602.
,,		A B conjoined, as 1602.
,,		W I.
,,		I A.
,,		I E.
,,		M B conjoined, a billet below.
1605-6		H M conjoined.

DATE.		GOLDSMITHS' MARKS.
1605-6		{ A B, as 1602. { I A, as 1604.
"		Crescent circling W, see 1598.
"		G.
"		R W, rosette below.
1606-7		F T in monogram (F. Terry).
"		R W.
"		T R in monogram over W.
"		Orb and cross.
"		L B, rosette above and below.
"		R S.
"		F S, star below.
"		H B.
"		T H, bugle below.
"		W T, animal's head, erased between, see 1602.
"		G. C.
1607-8		A collar and jewel ?
"		C enclosing W.
"		C enclosing M.
"		Crescent enclosing I.
"		C enclosing W.
"		T W in monogram.
"		R S.
"		I S, crescent under line in base.
"		Crescent enclosing saltire.
1608-9		T C.

DATE.		GOLDSMITHS' MARKS.
1608-9		A fruit slipped.
"		F W in monogram.
"		A B, as 1602.
"		T A, mullet below.
"		W R.
"		S O.
"		I K.
"		A helm, see 1573.
"		N R over a head couped.
"		A ship.
"		?
1609-10		A bird over R P.
"		A cross within a bordure.
"		C enclosing I, see 1607.
"		E W.
"		Crescent enclosing saltire, see 1607.
"		Staves in saltire, between B T.
"		A growing plant.
"		F S in monogram.
"		W.
1610-11		I W in monogram (John Wardlaw?).
"		T P.
"		T I, star below.
"		T, over crescent.
"		E M in monogram.
"		H B.

DATE.		GOLDSMITHS' MARKS.	DATE.		GOLDSMITHS' MARKS.
1610-11		T C.	1613-14		T C between pellets.
,,		T A, star above.	,,		M H conjoined.
,,		H S, gerbe in base.	,,		W L conjoined.
,,		L M in monogram.	,,		N.
,,		A pair of compasses.	,,		H B conjoined, star below (H. Babington).
,,		Trefoil slipped.	,,		R S.
1611-12		T Y Z.	,,		I M, a bow between.
,,		Key between W C.	1614-15		R B.
,,		T B in monogram.	,,		R C.
,,		F W in monogram.	,,		B F, a trefoil in base (Benjamin Francis).
,,		Two clubs in saltire.	,,		I M and F B.
,,		I T.	,,		S O, mullet below.
,,		Crescent enclosing **W**, see 1598 and 1605.	,,		I D, rose below.
1612-13		St. Catherine's wheel.	,,		R M, bird over.
,,		A crested helmet.	,,		H M conjoined.
,,		Unicorn's head.	1615-16		C R, key between.
,,		A B conjoined, as 1602.	,,		I R, bow beneath.
,,		R B.	,,		M H conjoined, as 1613.
,,		N R.	,,		H S, star below.
,,		Key between W C, see 1611.	,,		I S in monogram.
,,		F S in monogram, see 1609.	,,		Anchor in shaped shield, see 1594.
,,		W R.	,,		T F, a dragon between.
,,		T H in monogram.	,,		An escallop.
,,		A pair of compasses, see 1610.	,,		R D.
			,,		A bear.

DATE.		GOLDSMITHS' MARKS.
1615-16		A double-headed eagle.
,,		W. F.
1616-17		I A.
,,		R N.
,,		I P over a bell.
,,		I A, pellet below.
,,		A phœnix incuse.
,,		R over W.
,,		R C, pheon below.
,,		E enclosing C.
,,		A trefoil within a bordure.
,,		F G in monogram.
,,		I C.
1617-18		R W.
,,		H B conjoined.
,,		I V, star below.
,,		R S, heart below.
,,		I C, rose below.
,,		R P, mullet below.
,,		An arrow between W C.
,,		I F.
,,		T H in monogram.
,,		A tree between C C.
1618-19		I P, as 1616.
,,		W R, as 1608.

DATE.		GOLDSMITHS' MARKS.
1618-19		A V.
,,		I C.
,,		Crescent enclosing mullet, see 1594.
,,		C enclosing I, see 1609.
,,		R C, mullet below.
,,		R W, rose below.
,,		An arrow between W C, as 1617.
,,		R C.
,,		I S.
1619-20		T E in monogram.
,,		F M.
,,		A B, roundlet below.
,,		R K, rose below.
,,		R G.
1620-1		I C, mullet below.
,,		I I, mullet below.
,,		I S, rose below.
,,		A I over W T.
1621-2		E L, fleur-de-lys below.
,,		Small italic *a*.
,,		H T in monogram.
,,		T B in monogram within a bordure.
,,		R over W.
,,		C.
1622-3		R D, over crescent.

DATE.	GOLDSMITHS' MARKS.	
1622-3		E R.
,,		Crescent and mullet.
,,		A H over W W, as 1626.
,,		H T in monogram, as 1621.
,,		I F crowned.
1623-4		A trefoil slipped.
,,		W C, mullet below.
,,		I M, mullet below.
,,		R C, pheon below, as 1616.
,,		E H, pellet above and below.
,,		R S, a heart below.
,,		T B, head below.
,,		R S and anchor.
,,		I F.
1624-5		T H.
,,		A mullet over an escallop.
,,		A flower slipped.
,,		A in a lozenge.
,,		J in a wreath.
,,		B Y, a gate below (Benj. Yate).
1625-6		I E, a billet below.
,,		I V, a star below.
,,		H S, mullet below.
,,		S over W.
,,		H S, star below.
,,		W S.
,,		T B.

DATE.	GOLDSMITHS' MARKS.	
1625-6		C B.
1626-7		P H in monogram, annulet below.
,,		A tree.
,,		H S, star below.
,,		H B conjoined, as 1613.
,,		R B, mullet below.
,,		A H over W W.
,,		B Y, see 1624 (Benj. Yate).
,,		W S.
,,		W S.
1627-8		S over W, see 1625.
,,		R I, mullet below.
,,		W S linked (Walter Shute).
,,		T B.
,,		T E, fleur-de-lys in base.
,,		J in wreath, as 1624.
,,		T V, star below.
1628-9		R M, heart below.
,,		An escallop, see 1615.
,,		D crossed by a bow sinister wise ?
,,		A pegasus ?
,,		B Y, gate in base, as 1626, for B. Yate.
,,		Bow & arrow between W S (Walter Shute ?)
,,		D enclosing C.
1629-30		Anchor between D G.
,,		R B, mullet below.

DATE.	GOLDSMITHS' MARKS.	
1629-30		B P, mullet below.
,,		R C, pheon below, in dotted border.
,,		{ C C, as 1617. { W S, as 1628-9.
,,		I T.
,,		G G, rose above, roundlet below.
,,		P G.
1630-1		T D in monogram (T. Dove).
,,		W over M (W. Maunday).
,,		R S, heart below.
,,		A bolt.
,,		I M, a bear below.
,,		I A, mullet below.
,,		W C, mullet below.
,,		R S, star below.
1631-2		R S, heart below.
,,		T B in monogram.
,,		H M, rose below.
,,		W C, heart below.
,,		D W.
,,		W R, arch above, pellet below (W. Rainbow).
,,		An orb and star.
,,		C B.
,,		V S over fleur-de-lis.
1632-3		E H.
,,		P B between crescents, see 1658.
,,		T E, mullet below.

DATE.	GOLDSMITHS' MARKS.	
1632-3		D enclosing C, see 1602.
,,		I M, bird below.
•		Owl holding mouse.
,,		C B in monogram.
,,		I G over a covered cup.
,,		I H between pellets.
1633-4		I B, a buckle below (J. Buckle ?)
,,		W over M (W. Maundy).
,,		Walter Shute, as 1628.
,,		An escallop, as 1628.
,,		E S in dotted circle.
,,		H B conjoined, a sun above, see 1626.
,,		R C.
1634-5		R S, mullet above and below.
,,		W over M, see 1633.
,,		P G, rose below.
,,		R W between mullet and pellets.
,,		D W, a mullet below.
,,		R C, a rosette below.
,,		P B between two crescents.
1635-6		F.
,,		L I, flower below.
,,		R S under sun in splendour.
,,		An escallop, as 1633.
,,		R H.
,,		R O.
,,		R S between a mullet and a heart.

DATE.		GOLDSMITHS' MARKS.
1635-6		E C in dotted circle.
"		I B, buckle below, as 1633
"		E R in rayed shield.
"		H M conjoined.
"		B B crowned, six pellets below.
"		Owl holding mouse, see 1632.
1636-7		R W, mullet below.
"		G M, bird below, in dotted border.
"		R W between mullets in lozenge.
"		I over W between three mullets.
"		R over W.
"		R H between pellets.
"		B F (Benj. Francis ?)
"		C R in monogram.
"		E S, pellet above.
1637-8		R G, heart below.
"		R S, heart below.
"		I intersecting C.
"		A star over an orb with annulets.
"		A star over an orb, see 1631.
"		R B over an escallop.
"		R M, rose below.
"		R C, as 1634.
"		A pillar between G S.
"		G D, mullet and pellets below (Geo. Day ?)
"		W C, heart below.

DATE.		GOLDSMITHS' MARKS.
1637-8		W M, pellets above and below.
"		R G, heart below.
1638-9		R A, quatrefoil below.
"		I H in circle.
"		W T.
"		T I over star and pellets.
"		T H conjoined.
"		H L conjoined.
"		S V (Stephen Venables), see 1645, 1651-3.
"		R C.
"		F C in monogram.
"		W M, mullet and two pellets below.
"		I G, mullet below.
"		F C between mullets.
"		F, as 1635.
"		R R.
"		B E crowned.
"		I H.
"		W S linked, as 1627.
1639-40		C P, rose below.
"		T P in shaped shield.
"		H B conjoined, see 1613.
"		T b in monogram, bird below.
"		B F, pellet below.
"		A crowned escallop.
1640-1		D I.

DATE.		GOLDSMITHS' MARKS.	DATE.		GOLDSMITHS' MARKS.
1640-1		T I.	1643-4		TT (indistinct marks).
,,		I M, bear below, as 1630.	,,		T M, see 1641.
,,		I B.	1644-5		B B.
,,		R P, mullet below.	1645-6		D W, mullet below.
,,		R W, mullet above.	,,		T G.
,,		H B conjoined, see 1639.	,,		S V (Stephen Venables).
,,		W W in monogram.	1646-7		W T.
,,		W C.	,,		N W, cinquefoil below (Nicholas Wollaston?)
1641-2		W M.	,,		I L, pellet below.
,,		T H conjoined.	,,		C O (Cardinal Orme?)
,,		R W.	,,		A F (an ancestor of Ant. Ficketts?).
,,		I F.	1647-8		I A.
,,		E I.	,,		R V. (Richard Vaughan?)
,,		O M, pheon below.	,,		W M, see 1641.
,,		T H, fleur-de-lys above and below.	,,		S A in monogram.
,,		I I, mullet below.	,,		A bird with branch in beak.
,,		W C, heart below.	1648-9		A hound sejant.
,,		I T, pellet below.	,,		I I, pellet below.
,,		T over M (Thomas Maundy).	,,		I H in monogram.
1642-3		I W, tun below.	,,		I G, escallop below.
,,		F.	,,		B E, see 1638.
,,		R S between mullets.	1649-50		Hound sejant.
,,		R C, 3 pellets above, star below.	,,		M, star below.
,,		W S, mullet below.	,,		C T, two pellets above.
,,		R K, mullet below.	,,		A bird.
1643-4		I W, as 1642-3.			

DATE.		GOLDSMITHS' MARKS.
1649-50		S A in monogram.
1650-1		I C crowned.
,,		A M in monogram (probably A. Moore).
,,		I W.
,,		H G, between mullets and pellets.
,,		I G, crescent below.
1651-2		Cock on reversed C.
,,		S V, see 1638 (Stephen Venables ?)
,,		I T between 3 pellets.
,,		I R, cinquefoil below.
,,		I I.
1652-3		I B.
,,		A F.
,,		S V (Stephen Venables).
,,		R S between mullets.
,,		I B, buckle below, as 1635.
,,		S A in monogram, see 1647.
,,		R F, mullet below.
,,		A F, see 1646.
1653-4		W H, star above, pellet in annulet below.
,,		H G between mullets and pellets (Henry Greenway ?)
,,		C T in monogram.
,,		I V, pellet below.
,,		S V, as 1651.
,,		E D, roundlet below.

DATE.		GOLDSMITHS' MARKS.
1653-4		R R.
1654-5		W H, as 1653-4
,,		H G, as 1653-4.
,,		H N, bird between.
,,		W C, pellets above, rose and pellets below.
,,		I R, crescent above.
1655-6		D R, pellet above and below (Daniel Rutty ?)
,,		I L in plain shield.
,,		R N between mullets (Richard Neale ?)
,,		T B in monogram, see 1631.
,,		R F between pellets.
,,		R over W.
,,		F W in a circle (Field Whorwood ?)
,,		I W, tun below.
,,		W G between pellets.
,,		M G.
,,		W G.
,,		W G.
1656-7		A D conjoined.
,,		C S, a sword in pale (Christopher Shaw ?)
,,		E L, escallop below.
,,		G D, mullet and two pellets below.
,,		W M, as 1647.
,,		B or J B in monogram.
,,		E T, crescent below.
1657-8		N W, as 1646-7.
,,		T G in dotted oval.

DATE.	GOLDSMITHS' MARKS.	
1657-8		K F, mullet below.
,,		I G, pellet between.
,,		I H in monogram between three mullets.
,,		A F, see 1652.
,,		R W.
,,		H W, mullet below.
1658-9		H B conjoined, mullet below, see 1640.
,,		W C, rose below.
,,		P B, see 1632-3.
,,		I or T.
,,		?
,,		G B, flower below.
,,		S A in monogram, mullet below, see 1652.
,,		F L, bird below.
,,		Crozier between G S.
,,		F L over a bird.
1659-60		S.
,,		T G in dotted circle.
,,		G S, a bolt in pale, see 1658.
,,		A F, a rose below (Ant. Ficketts ?), see 1657.
,,		T A, mullet and pellets below.
,,		I G, crescent below.
,,		M, star below.
,,		I C, mullet below.
,,		S V, see 1651.
,,		R D, fleur-de-lys below.

DATE.	GOLDSMITHS' MARKS.	
1660-1		I G, mullet below.
,,		G S, as 1658.
,,		T over M for Thomas Maundy, see 1641.
,,		An orb and cross.
,,		R F between pellets.
,,		R F and pellets.
,,		G D, mullet below.
,,		E T, crescent below.
,,		R A, mullet and two pellets below.
,,		S V, see 1659.
,,		T B in monogram, as 1631.
,,		W M, mullet below.
1661-2		S V, see 1659.
,,		T D between pellets and a rose.
,,		R D over I B.
,,		I I, mullet below.
,,		R N between 2 mullets.
,,		T G, 3 pellets above and below.
,,		T D between mullets and pellets.
,,		T A C in monogram.
,,		T T, mullet below
,,		R N, mullet and two pellets below.
,,		R L over fleur-de-lys.
,,		S R.
1662-3		D R, stars and pellets above and below.

DATE.		GOLDSMITHS' MARKS.
1662-3		D R.
,,		C A in monogram.
,,		H N, bird with olive branch below.
,,		E T, crescent below. Do. without crescent.
,,		R F.
,,		F P, quatrefoil below.
,,		W C.
,,		G V.
,,		D R, as 1655.
,,		I N, mullet below.
,,		K S between 2 mullets.
,,		T P between 2 pellets.
,,		M, as 1659.
,,		W M, pellet above, mullet below.
1663-4		I F, fleur-de-lys below.
,,		T K, fleur-de-lys below.
,,		I N, bird below.
,,		E T between mullets and pellets.
,,		A F, mullet and 2 pellets below.
,,		W N, 4 pellets below.
,,		I G, mullet below.
,,		T K, cinquefoil below, see 1663.
,,		I S in heart.
,,		C H, billet below.
,,		H N, as 1662.
,,		N B, mullet and 2 pellets below.
1664-5		I W, woolsack below.

DATE.		GOLDSMITHS' MARKS.
1664-5		W H, cherub's head below.
,,		I G, pellet below.
,,		H G between pellets and a mullet.
,,		F W, a mullet and 2 pellets above and below.
,,		An escallop, a mullet above, see 1624.
,,		B, 2 mullets over and 1 below.
,,		H I, mullet below, see 1657.
,,		R M, between mullets and pellets.
,,		H in engrailed shield.
,,		T P, pellets and rosette below.
,,		D R between mullets.
,,		T P, a rosette above and below.
,,		H B conjoined, a mullet below.
,,		I K, two pellets above, a mullet below.
,,		T L, a pellet above and below.
1665-6		A D conjoined.
,,		T R, crescent above.
,,		P D, 3 pellets above, cinquefoil below.
,,		I I, as 1661.
,,		H R, 3 pellets above and 3 below.
,,		P P, star below.
,,		I G, crescent below.
,,		A M in monogram, see 1650.
,,		C Y in monogram.
,,		T A, mullet between.

DATE.		GOLDSMITHS' MARKS.
1665-6		P M in monogram, a coronet over.
,,		F L, bird below.
,,		W G crowned, in a dotted circle.
1666-7		E M in a dotted circle, see 1673 (Edmund Michell).
,,		R D crowned.
,,		W M crowned.
,,		M, mullet below.
,,		A , key between two pellets.
1667-8		T M in monogram.
,,		S S crowned.
,,		S V, pellet below.
,,		R S, a fleur-de-lys below.
,,		T S, a bird below.
,,		J W in monogram.
,,		B P, escallop below.
1668-9		T I, two escallops between.
,,		T L in plain stamp.
,,		B E C G in monogram, star above.
,,		I B, crescent below.
,,		A M in monogram, crowned, see 1665.
,,		R S, mullet above, six pellets below.
,,		P P, six pellets below, see 1665.
,,		I C, mullet below.
,,		G V in engrailed shield.
,,		I C, pellet below.

DATE.		GOLDSMITHS' MARKS.
1668-9		R D, mullet below.
,,		R D, mullet above, crescent below.
,,		I A in dotted circle.
,,		A L between three mullets.
1669-70		W G, trefoil below.
,,		W W, fleur-de-lys below.
,,		T A, star below.
,,		S N, star below.
,		I W, three pellets above, billet below.
,,		R S.
,,		F W between mullets and pellets.
,,		T C in monogram, pellet below.
,,		R P, pellet below.
,,		I L, flower below.
,,		T H crowned.
,,		T E H (T E conjoined).
,,		F C.
,,		T B E in monogram.
,,		C over W.
,,		O G, fleur-de-lys below.
,,		I S, rosette below.
,,		T P, 3 mullets below.
,,		E G.
,,		D R, coronet over.
,,		L C crowned. (Lawrence Coles).
,,		I I, anchor between.

DATE.		GOLDSMITHS' MARKS
1670-1		T M over a crown.
,,		T K, rosette below.
,,		I R between rosettes. (John Ruslen ?)
,,		R H, a cinquefoil and 2 pellets below.
,,		T H, anchor between.
,,		R N, mullet below.
,,		R P between pellets.
,,		R D, cinquefoil below.
,,		G crowned, 3 mullets below.
,,		W H conjoined, mullet below.
,,		E R, mullet below.
,,		I D between pellets and a gerbe.
,,		E G in oblong punch.
,,		I L over a crescent and pellet.
1671-2		G W over a crescent and pellets.
,,		I L, a mullet below.
,,		W G conjoined.
,,		I H over a fleur-de-lys and pellets.
,,		M G over a trefoil and pellets.
,,		D C, rossette below.
,,		I K, rose and 2 pellets below.
,,		I D, pellet below.
,,		W W linked.
,,		R S between mullets.
,,		O S, a trefoil slipped below.

DATE.		GOLDSMITHS' MARKS.
1671-2		A flower slipped.
,,		P D, five pellets below.
,,		C M, three pellets below.
,,		C M, mullet and two pellets below.
,,		E G, crescent below.
,,		I S, two mullets and fleur-de-lys above.
,,		I P, rosette below.
,,		R P, star below.
1672-3		D L, a trefoil over and mullet below.
,,		R K, a star and pellets below.
,,		I P, a pellet above and below.
,,		A H, star above, crescent below.
,,		W G, pellet below.
,,		S V, mullet below.
,,		I C, a pellet below.
,,		H L, a pellet below.
,,		S R, cinquefoil below.
,,		H.
,,		H E, a pellet below.
,,		R G, star above.
,,		I F, crescent above.
,,		T R in monogram.
,,		D L.
1673-4		E B crowned.
,,		S C, fleur-de-lys above and below.

DATE.		GOLDSMITHS' MARKS.
1673-4		I K, rosette below.
"		E H crowned, crescent below.
"		S S, fleur-de-lys below.
"		L C, crown and crescent (Lawrence Coles).
"		H E conjoined.
"		R L, rosette and pellets below.
"		Another mark of Lawrence Coles.
"		E M, see 1666 (Edmund Michell ?)
"		Ed. Jones ?
"		M W (Mathew West ?)
"		G W, crescent below.
1674-5		E M crowned.
"		T G, 3 pellets above and 3 below.
"		G G, George Garthorne (probably).
"		I S, John Sutton (probably), see 1683.
"		T L, pellet below.
"		R D, comet below.
"		G T over a mullet voided.
"		H K, pellet above and below.
"		W W between mullets and pellets.
"		E H, pellet above, crescent below.
"		W R conjoined, coronet above.
"		J M in monogram.
"		W S.
"		D W crowned (David Willaume or Williams ?)

DATE.		GOLDSMITHS' MARKS.
1674-5		A M in monogram, see 1665.
"		G S, a crown and fleur-de-lys above.
1675-6		G C, mullet below.
"		F C, a rosette below.
"		R A, winged figure between.
"		N.
"		B.
"		T D, star below.
"		M, fleur-de-lys below.
"		T I between 2 mullets.
"		I S crowned (Sir Jeremiah Snow).
"		A R.
"		I B, see 1684 (J. Buck ?)
"		I H.
"		I F, mullet below.
"		T L, a pellet below.
"		I E, a pellet between and below.
"		S crowned.
"		C W, a fleur-de-lys above and below.
1676-7		R M in monogram (Richard Morrell ?)
"		F S.
"		Y I between escallops.
"		F A, fleur-de-lys below
"		K S between mullets.
"		T F, mullet below (Sir Thomas Fowles or ffowles).

DATE.		GOLDSMITHS' MARKS.
1676-7		I O or O I.
,,		W A in monogram.
,,		T C, a cat above.
,,		A S H in monogram (Thomas Ash ?)
,,		W W, see 1674.
,,		C E, a pellet above and below.
,,		S H in dotted circle.
,,		S R, a cinquefoil and pellets below.
,,		O S, a pellet above.
,,		I R, a trefoil above, a pellet below.
,,		B R in monogram.
1677-8		A castle between I C.
,,		W S, a mullet and two pellets above & below.
,,		S G crowned.
,,		W G, a trefoil below.
,,		W S, a rosette below.
,,		H H conjoined, a fleur-de-lys and pellets below.
,,		M P conjoined under a crown.
,,		I S crowned.
,,		W C, fleur-de-lys below.
,,		F G, mullet below, for Fras. Garthorne ?
,,		A K, pellets above and below.
,,		F S, a pellet above and below.
,,		D R, a coronet above.
,,		W S linked.

DATE.		GOLDSMITHS' MARKS.
1677-8		J G in monogram.
,,		I B between pellets.
,,		E M in monogram.
1678-9		I B, pellet below.
,,		S R, cinquefoil voided below.
,,		R N crowned.
,,		N C, four pellets below.
,,		W N.
,,		T R crowned.
,,		I A, crescent below.
,,		A R, mullet and two pellets below.
,,		W over S (Wm. Sanberry or W. Scarlett ?)
,,		I B, fleur-de-lys below.
,,		C K, pellet below.
,,		I P crowned.
,,		T B in monogram.
,,		Double-seed rose.
,,		R S.
,,		A H, pellet above, mullet below.
,,		S crowned.
,,		N W.
,,		I R, crescent below.
,,		T A, three pellets above, a device below.
,,		K S between mullets.
,,		T E in monogram, a coronet above.
,,		E C crowned.

DATE.		GOLDSMITHS' MARKS.
1678-9		I L, a coronet above.
1679-80		T H in monogram.
,,		I T.
,,		I M conjoined.
,,		R H crowned.
,,		C K, mullet below.
,,		T C, a fish above.
,,		T A between pellets (Thos. Allen ?)
,,		B P, escallop below (Benj. Pyne ?)
,,		T M in monogram.
,,		H C crowned.
,,		T S in monogram, crowned.
,,		R H, mullet below.
,,		I S, as 1674.
,,		O S, between trefoils.
,,		I S, billet below.
,,		I N, as 1662.
,,		D C, a pellet above and below.
,,		B, see 1675 and 1687.
c. 1680		Mark indistinct.
,,		F S.
1680-1		A goose in dotted circle.
,,		I H, fleur-de-lys below.
,,		L C crowned (Lawrence Coles).
,,		R S, fleur-de-lys below.
,,		D G and 2 fleur-de-lys in lozenge.
,,		F G, star below, see 1677 (Fras. Garthorne).
,,		I B, see 1677.

DATE.		GOLDSMITHS' MARKS.
1680-1		W I, star below.
,,		R K, mullet below.
,,		I S, cinquefoil below.
,,		I H, pellets above and one below.
,,		T A in lozenge, mullet below.
,,		T I, two escallops between, see 1668 & 1684.
,,		T L, an escallop and pellets below.
,,		F N, a crescent above and pellets below.
,,		R L, a trefoil below.
,,		B over W, with trefoils.
,,		R H crowned, crescent below.
,,		W F conjoined.
,,		S E.
1681-2		P B in monogram.
,,		I C, mullet below.
,,		R C in dotted circle.
,,		P L in monogram.
,,		S H linked.
,,		F B, pellets between.
,,		I M in dotted circle.
,,		P H.
,,		M K in lozenge.
,,		T E, a coronet above.
,,		L S crowned.
,,		I I between pellets.

DATE.		GOLDSMITHS' MARKS.
1681-2		T S, an escallop above and below.
"		N W, a star below.
"		E N conjoined, under a crown.
"		T A, three pellets above, one below.
"		B crowned.
"		I H.
1682-3		I S, cinquefoil below, see 1680.
"		A D.
"		T A in monogram.
"		H E conjoined, crowned, see 1673.
"		A R.
"		F W, cinquefoil below.
"		E G crowned.
"		P M, star above, fleur-de-lys below.
c. 1682		I A in monogram.
1682-3		T E B in monogram.
1683-4		I H crowned.
"		W F, knot above, rosette below.
"		R L (Richd. Lassels or Ralph Leeke).
"		M H, rosette below.
"		P R in cypher, pellet below.
"		L C crowned (Lawrence Coles).
"		S H.
"		I P, star above, crescent below.
"		C enclosing K.

DATE.		GOLDSMITHS' MARKS.
1683-4		G C, duplicated in reverse.
"		T Z, a crown above, a crescent below.
"		I intersecting S, see 1674 and 1684.
"		T H conjoined.
"		T M (T. Mammal?)
"		W F, knot above.
"		I H, 3 pellets above.
"		R P, pellet below.
"		S H, fleur-de-lys below.
"		M P conjoined.
"		I S crowned.
"		F H E in monogram.
"		R I.
"		I W crowned.
"		W S, a bird below.
"		E B, a rosette below.
"		C K, fleur-de-lys below.
"		T E, fleur-de-lys above, pellet below.
"		M K, between cinquefoils.
1684-5		I Y, a horse between.
"		I S crowned.
"		I I, fleur-de-lys below (John Jackson).
"		C T.
"		I B, see 1675 (J. Buck?)

DATE.		GOLDSMITHS' MARKS.
1684-5		W B, a mullet below.
"		T W conjoined.
"		D B, a star above, an annulet below.
"		N G, a pellet between.
"		R A, pellets above and below.
"		I intersecting S, see 1674 and 1683 (John Sutton, probably).
"		I I, a pellet between, a fleur-de-lys below.
"		T I, escallop above and below in quatrefoil.
"		C D.
"		T C in monogram.
"		A H between pellets.
"		J S in monogram within a wreath.
"		P crowned. (Benjn. Pyne).
"		T A between pellets.
"		O S, trefoil below.
"		E H, crescent below.
"		I G crowned.
"		R K, annulet below.
"		E O, pellet below.
"		I S, cinquefoil below, see 1680.
"		G G, pellet below, see 1674.
1685-6		D.
"		W H, fleur-de-lys below.
"		P R, coronet over.
"		Y Z crowned, crescent below.

DATE.		GOLDSMITHS' MARKS.
1685-6		P K, rosette below.
"		W K conjoined.
"		B B, crescent below.
"		B M, between pellets.
"		I S, coronet over (John Shepherd ?)
"		T B between pellets.
"		T D in monogram.
"		G M, 2 crescents above, 1 below (Geo. Middleton ?)
"		A F conjoined, a trefoil below.
"		I S under a coronet.
"		R B.
"		Benj. Bathurst (ent. 1677).
"		H R between pellets.
"		S E between a crescent and annulet.
"		L C.
"		W R, mullet below.
"		T M in monogram.
"		W L, annulet below.
"		M W between pellets.
"		I L, escallop above and below.
"		W F conjoined.
"		P M between two stars.
1686-7		R S, mullet below.
"		W M, plume and pellets above, and pellet below.
"		C K, mullet below.

DATE.		GOLDSMITHS' MARKS.
1686-7		T R B in monogram.
,,		T P, a trefoil above, a pellet between.
,,		I C crowned.
,,		C K under a mitre ?
,,		I C, rosette and 2 pellets below.
,,		W. C, cherub's head above.
,,		Y T, 2 pellets above, fleur-de-lys below.
,,		D B, mullet above, crescent inverted below.
,,		R I in dotted circle.
,,		F O in monogram.
,,		C R, mullet below (Christopher Riley ?)
1687-8		R H.
,,		C O, mullet below.
,,		E G between mullets.
,,		R L, fleur-de-lys below (Ralph Leeke).
,,		I B.
,,		N G (Nathaniel Greene ?)
,,		M H.
,,		T G in dotted circle.
,,		F F, escallop below.
,,		I C in monogram.
,,		H T crowned.
,,		B, see 1679.
,,		E C.
,,		G S crowned.

DATE.		GOLDSMITHS' MARKS.
1688-9		I I S and three pellets.
,,		E L, fleur-de-lys below.
,,		A dagger between I D.
,,		W M crowned.
,,		W N crowned.
,,		S D, pellet below (Samuel Dell ?)
,,		O S, trefoil below.
,,		I I, a crown and cinquefoil between.
,,		M S.
,,		A pillar between I S.
,,		T V between plumes.
,,		I F, crescent below.
,,		I R, annulet below.
,,		G S, mullet below.
,,		T A.
1689-90		H G between mullets.
,,		F D in monogram.
,,		E B.
,,		T C and fish, as 1679.
,,		W B.
,,		I I, see 1684.
,,		M E conjoined, bird above.
,,		H H between rosettes.
,,		N B under a coronet.
,,		D A.
,,		I E.

DATE.		GOLDSMITHS' MARKS.
1689-90		R L (Richard Lassels ?)
,,		C S in dotted oval (Clement Stonor).
,,		T S in monogram in dotted octagon.
,,		A N in monogram (Anthony Nelme).
,,		R E.
,,		W P, mullet below.
,,		S over W.
c. 1690		N G (Nathaniel Green).
1690-1		T S H E in monogram.
,,		W B under a coronet.
,,		S H linked as 1681.
,,		K crowned. (Jonah Kirke ?)
,,		I D crowned.
,,		E K.
,,		R L in dotted circle.
,,		R C in monogram (Robt. Cooper ?)
,,		T S O I.
,,		R Timbrell.
,,		J S.
,,		T L (Timothy Ley).
,,		T A, fleur-de-lys above.
,,		T S between scroll and star.
,,		W M.
,,		G M.
,,		G N.
,,		T T crowned.
,,		G S under a crown and fleur-de-lys.

DATE.		GOLDSMITHS' MARKS.
1690-1		W B (William Bainbridge ?)
,,		I I in dotted oval, see 1684 and 1689.
,,		I D, a sexfoil above and crescent below.
,,		T H, a crescent below.
,,		D G under crown and fleur-de-lys (Daniel Garnier).
,,		A H, a crown above and cinquefoil below.
1691-2		M H crowned.
,,		I C crowned (Jas. Chadwick ?)
,,		D.
,,		W S.
,,		S D crowned, fleur-de-lys below.
,,		H P in monogram (Henry Penstone ?)
,,		B S.
,,		S I.
,,		I E crowned.
,,		I G.
,,		G M between mullets.
,,		R G.
,,		Bird over monogram, and 3 annulets.
,,		N G (Natl. Greene ?), see 1687.
,,		M H.
,,		A N in monogram (Anthony Nelme).
,,		I C over star.
1692-3		Three storks.

DATE.		GOLDSMITHS' MARKS.
1692-3		I W.
,,		S C, crown and star (Stephen Coleman).
,,		R T (Robert Timbrell ?)
,,		G G, as 1684 (Geo. Garthorne ?)
,,		N L.
,,		W E, mullet above and below.
,,		I C in monogram, crowned.
,,		G F, fleur-de-lys below.
,,		I H crowned.
,,		L B do.
,,		B.
,,		W G crowned (Wm. Gamble ?)
,,		W H crowned.
,,		T A, 3 pellets, and a trefoil.
,,		D G crowned.
,,		C A between cinquefoils.
,,		I G crowned.
,,		I S (John Spackman ?)
1693-4		I N, star below.
,,		D A crowned.
,,		I L, mullet above, fleur-de-lys below.
,,		B B, addorsed, in monogram (Benj. Bathurst ?)
,,		H C, 3 pellets, mullet and 2 annulets.
,,		C C in monogram (Christopher Canner ?)
,,		D W (Dd. Willaume ?)
,,		M E, mullet below.

DATE.		GOLDSMITHS MARKS.
1693-4		H P between 2 mullets.
,,		O, enclosing R.
,,		T K, fish above, trefoil below.
,,		E T between 2 pellets.
,,		W S (William Scarlett).
,,		R M.
,,		I G crowned.
1694-5		E M.
,,		S L in monogram, see 1695.
,,		S T.
,,		A N in monogram (Anthony Nelme).
,,		R D linked, with 4 annulets.
,,		P crowned (Benj. Pyne).
,,		R F conjoined.
,,		H B between 2 mullets.
,,		H V.
,,		S H in monogram (Sam Hood).
,,		I in dotted ellipse.
,,		I R crowned (John Ruslen ?)
,,		T A, see 1690 (Thomas Allen ?)
,,		M G, bird above, crescent below.
,,		W H bird below.
,,		I F.
1695-6		R G, two sexfoils above and one below.
,,		T H conjoined.

DATE.	GOLDSMITHS' MARKS.	
1695-6		I intersecting S, see 1684.
,,		Peter Harache.
,,		John Hodson.
,,		M B conjoined (Moses Brown ?)
,,		William Keatt.
,,		S.
,,		A G, crescent below.
,,		M M (Mat. Madden ?)
,,		Jonah Kirk.
,,		Isaac Davenport.
,,		Anchor between E S crowned.
,,		S L in monogram.
,,		S over W.
,,		M E conjoined.
,,		I S, see 1692.
1696-7		W V in monogram.
,,		G M.
,,		T Z, crown above, mullet below, see 1683.
,,		John Penfold (probably).
,,		T B, crescent below.
,,		H C in monogram.
,,		T Z crowned, with mullet below.
,,		T B, mullet above, crescent below.
,,		Lawrence Jones

DATE.	GOLDSMITHS' MARKS.	
1696-7		Thomas Brydon.
,,		Jonathan Bradley.
,,		R W.
,,		Fras. Garthorne.
,,		F.
,,		Christopher Canner.
,,		R G.
,,		I S in monogram.
,,		T B, crescent below.
c. 1696-8		G a (possibly Fras, Garthorne).

DATE.		MAKERS' MARK AND NAME.	DATE.		MAKERS' MARK AND NAME.
1697	Co	Lawrence Coles ent. 1697	1697	CH	Jas. Chadwick ent. 1697
,,	TH	——— Thriscross ,, ,,	,,	Gi	Wm. Gibson ,, ,,
,,	RO	Alexr. Roode ,, ,,	,,	Ba	Name not traced.
,,	WE	Mathew West ,, ,,	,,	Al	Thos. Allen ,, ,,
,,	ED	Jas. Edgar ,, ,,	,,	BR	Moses Brown ,, ,,
,,	M	Andrew Moore ,, ,,	,,	GA	Danl. Garnier ,, ,,
,,	TO	Edmd. Townsend ,, ,,	,,	Ash	Thos. Ash ,, ,,
,,	WI	C. Williams ,, ,,	,,	AS	,, ,, ,, ,,
,,	MA	Mathew Madden ,, ,,	,,	AS	,, ,, ,, ,,
,,	Jo	Lawrence Jones ,, ,,	,,	AR	Fras. Archbold ,, ,,
,,	FR	Wm. Francis ,, ,,	,,	BR	Benj. Bradford ,, ,,
,,	H	John Hodson ,, ,,	,,	BA	Wm. Bainbridge ,, ,,
,,	IR	Edward Ironside ,, ,,	,,	SM	Jno. Smithsend ,, ,,,
,,	AS	? Thos. Ash ,, ,,	,,	WI	——— Wimans ,, ,,
,,	GA	Geo. Garthorne ,, ,, (probably)	,,	Py	Benj. Pyne ,, ,,
,,	GA	Daniel Garnier ,, ,, (see p. 153)	,,	SH	Jno. Shepherd ,, ,,
,,	DI	Isaac Dighton ,, ,, (see p. 155)	,,	HO	Frances Hoyte ,, ,,
,,	Gi	Wm. Gimber ,, ,,	,,	RO	Hugh Roberts ,, ,,
,,	Co	Edwd. Courthope ,, ,,	,,	Jo	Ed. Jones ,, ,,
,,	HO	Sam. Hood ,, ,,	,,	Br	Wm. Brett ,, ,,
,,	CA	Christr. Canner ,, ,,	,,	GR	Dorothy Grant ,, ,,
,,	GA	Fras. Garthorne ,, ,,	,,	Co	Stephen Coleman ,, ,,
,,	PA	Thos. Parr ,, ,,	,,	BR	Jno. Brassey ,, ,,
,,	DB	Wm. Denny & ⎫ ,, ,, John Backe ⎭	,,	NI	Rich. Nightingale ,, ,,
			,,	Ti	Geo. Titterton ,, ,,
			,,	LA	Jn'th'n Lambe ,, ,,

The date in the left-hand column means that the piece of silver found was dated in that year. It is often much later than the year when the mark was entered.

DATE.	MAKERS' MARK AND NAME.		
1697-8		Jos. Bird	ent. 1697.
,,		Chas. Overing	,, ,,
,,		Thos. Brydon	,, ,,
,,		Thos. Issod	,, ,,
,,		Robt. Peake	,, ,,
,,		Wm. Scarlett	,, ,,
,,		Jos. Stokes	,, ,,
,,		Philip Rolles	,, ,,
,,		John Fawdery	,, ,,
,,		Thos. Ash	,, ,,
,,		James Edgar	,, ,,
,,		Richard Syngin	,, ,,
,,		Joseph Bird	,, ,,
,,		Andrew Moore	,, ,,
,,		Joyce Issod	,, ,,
,,		Isaac Dighton	,, ,,
,,		———— Wimans	,, ,,
,,		Anthy. Nelme	,, ,,
,,		Geo. Cox	,, 1698.
,,		John Cove	,, ,,
,,		Wm. Bull	,, ,,
1698-9		Geo. Garthorne	,, 1697.
,,		Wm. Mathew	,, ,,
,,		Jonath'n Bradley	,, ,,
,,		Edwd. Yorke	,, 1705.

DATE.	MAKERS' MARK AND NAME.		
1698-9		Henry Collins ?	ent. 1698.
,,		Richard Nightingale ?	,, 1697.
,,		Isaac Dighton (see pp. 152 and 154)	,, ,,
,,		Name not traced.	
,,		,, ,, ,,	
,,		Jos. Sheene.	
,,		Benj. Bentley	,, 1698.
,,		Wm. Matthew	,, 1697.
,,		Wm. Fawdery	,, 1698.
,,		John Ruslen	,, 1697.
,,		Wm. Scarlett	,, ,,
,,		Jno. Ladyman	,, ,,
,,		Robt. Cooper	,, ,,
,,		Lawrence Coles	,, ,,
,,		John Sutton	,, ,,
,,		John Hely	,, 1699,
,,		Job Hanks	,, ,,
,,		Jno. Porter	,, 1698.
,,		White Walsh	,, ,,
,,		Benj. Bentley	,, ,,
1699 1700		Wm. Lukin	,, 1699.
,,		Benj. Traherne	,, 1687.
,,		John Cory	,, 1697.
,,		John Diggle	,, ,,

DATE.	MAKERS' MARK AND NAME.				DATE.	MAKERS' MARK AND NAME.			
1699 / 1700		Fras.	Singleton	ent. 1697.	1700-1		Phillip	Roker	ent. 1697.
,,		Sam.	Thorne	,, ,,	,,		Mat.	Madden	,, ,,
,,		Isaac	Davenport	,, ,,	,,		George	Lewis	,, 1699.
,,		Jno.	Chartier	,, 1698.	,,		Henry	Aubin	,, 1700.
,,		Sam	Dell	,, 1697.	,,		Rich.	Biggs	,, ,,
,,		Pierre	Platel	,, 1699.	,,		Steph.	Edmonds	,, ,,
,,		John	Downes?	,, 1697.	,,		Wm.	Gossen	,, ,,
,,		Isaac	Davenport	,, ,,	,,		Edm.	Proctor	,, ,,
,,			Gould.		,,		John	Tiffin	,, 1701.
,,		John	Leach	ent. 1697.	,,		Alex.	Roode?	,, 1697.
,,		Joseph	Ward	,, ,,	1701-2		Frans.	Singleton (see p. 156).	
,,		John	Cory	,, ,,	,,		Ed.	Gibson	ent. 1697.
,,		Richd.	Syngin	,, ,,	,,		Pierre	Harache	,, ,,
,,		Andrew	Raven	,, ,,	,,		Benj.	Watts	,, 1698.
,,		John	Laughton	,, ,,	,,		Sam	Hood	,, 1697.
,,		Alex.	Roode	,, ,,	,,		Sam	Jefferys	,, ,,
,,		Philip	Oyle	,, 1699.	,,		Henry	Green	,, 1700.
,,		John	Broake	,, ,,	,,		Wm.	Andrews	,, 1697.
1700-1		Wm.	Fawdery	,, 1700.	,,		Thos.	Brydon	,, ,,
,,		Jos.	Stokes	as 1697.	,,		Wm.	Keatt	,, ,,
,,		Sam.	Wastell	ent. 1701.	,,		Willo'by	Masham	,, 1701.
,,		Jno.	Jackson	,, 1697.	,,			Name not traced.	
,,			Name not traced		,,		Wm.	Keatt	,, 1697.
,,		Thos.	Jenkins	,, ,,	,,		Sam	Hawkes	,, ,,
,,		David	Willaume	,, ,,	,,		Fras.	Archbold	,, ,,
,,		Ralph	Leeke	,, ,,	,,		Josh.	Field	,, 1701.

DATE.	MAKERS' MARK AND NAME.			DATE.	MAKERS' MARK AND NAME.		
1701-2	John	Goode	ent. 1700.	1702-3	Jonathan Madden		ent. 1702.
,,	Ralph	Leeke	,, 1697.	,,	Robt.	Lovell	,, ,,
,,	John Danl.	Read & Sleamaker }	,, 1701.	,,	Matt.	Cooper	,, ,,
,,	Alexr.	Hudson	,, ,,	1703-4	Jno.	Rand	,, 1704.
,,	Stepn.	Coleman	,, 1697.	,,	Thos.	Jenkins	,, 1697.
1702-3	Henry	Greene	,, 1700.	,,	Ed.	Gibson	,, ,,
,,	Richd.	Syngin	,, 1697.	,,	Wm.	Andrews	,, ,,
,,	John	Eckfourd	,, 1698.	,,	Name not traced.		
,,	Wm.	Gamble	,, 1697.	,,	J.	Broake.	
,,	Jonath'n Crutchfield		,, ,,	,,	Soane or Soame.		
,,	Humph.	Payne	,, 1701.	,,	Jonah	Kirke	,, ,,
,,	Name not traced.			,,	Gabl.	Player	,, 1700.
,,	Thos.	Sadler	,, ,,	,,	Saml.	Smith	,, ,,
,,	Jos.	Ward	,, 1697.	,,	Chas.	Williams	,, 1697.
,,	Jno.	Downes	,, ,,	,,	Jno.	Snelling	,, ,,
,,	Jno.	Cope	,, 1701.	,,	Nat.	Greene	,, 1698.
,,	Thos.	Waterhouse	,, 1702.	,,	Name not traced.		
,,	Wm.	Barnes	,, ,,	,,	Wm.	Warham	,, 1703.
,,	Abm.	Russell	,, ,,	,,	Wm.	Charnelhouse	,, ,,
,,	Jas.	Chadwick	as 1697.	,,	Andr.	Archer	,, ,,
,,	Matt.	Cooper	ent. 1702.	,,	Thos.	Peele	,, 1704.
,,	Hy.	Greene	,, 1700.	,,	Wm.	Petley	,, 1699.
,,	Name not traced.			1704-5	Robert	Stokes ?	
,,	Henry Aubin, see 1700. (earliest ment. 1700).			,,	Wm.	Denny	,, 1697.
,,	?	Fraillon.		,,	Geo.	Lewis	,, 1699.
,,	Name not traced.						

DATE.		MAKERS' MARK AND NAME.
1704-5		Thos. Saddler ent. 1701.
,,		Henry Penstone ,, 1697.
,,		Jno. Cole ,, ,,
,,		Jno. East ,, ,,
,,		Jno. Gibbon ,, 1700.
,,		Chas. Adam ,, 1702.
,,		Geo. Havers ,, 1697.
,,		Wm. Middleton ,, ,,
,,		Alex. Hudson ,, 1704.
,,		Wm. Spring ,, 1701.
,,		Jno. Cooke ,, 1699.
,,		Ishml. Bone ,, ,,
,,		Jno. Fletcher ,, 1700.
1705-6		Robt. Timbrell ,, 1697.
,,		Wm. Fawdery ,, ,,
,,		Samuel Pantin ,, 1701.
,,		Jon. Madden ,, 1702. (see 1702)
,,		Isaac Liger ,, 1704. (see below)
,,		Matthew Pickering ,, 1703.
,,		Wm. Fleming ,, ,,
,,		Thos. Spackman ,, 1700.
,,		Mathw. Lofthouse ,, 1705.
,,		Saml. Wastell ,, 1701.
,,		Josh. Readshaw ,, 1697.
,,		Isaac Liger ,, 1704.

DATE.		MAKERS' MARK AND NAME.
1705-6		Jonah Clifton ent. 1703.
,,		Jno. Corosey ,, 1701.
,,		Wm. Warham ,, 1705.
,,		Thos. Corbet ,, 1699.
,,		Natl. Lock ,, 1698.
,,		John Barnard ,, 1702.
1706-7		Jos. Barbitt ,, 1703.
,,		Wm. Matthew ,, 1700.
,,		Wm. Juson ,, 1704.
,,		Timothy Ley ,, 1697.
,,		John Backe ,, 1700.
,,		Launcelot Keatt ,, 1701.
,,		Benj. Pyne ,, 1697.
,,		Jacob Margas ,, 1706.
,,		Jno. Ladyman ,, 1697.
,,		Louys Cuny ,, 1703.
,,		Jno. Abbot ,, 1706.
,,		Wm. Spring ,, 1701.
,,		Jno. Crutcher ,, 1706.
,,		Wm. Fordham ,, ,,
,,		Name not traced.
1707-8		Danl. Sleath ,, 1704.
,,		Wm. Fleming ,, 1697.
,,		Thos. Burridge ,, 1706.
,,		John Leach ,, 1697.
,,		Anthy. Nelme ,, ,,

DATE.	MAKERS' MARK AND NAME.				DATE.	MAKERS' MARK AND NAME.			
1707-8		Pierre	Le Cheaube	ent. 1707.	1708-9		Thos.	Wall	ent. 1708.
,,		Richard	Hutchinson	,, 1699.	,,		Jno.	Clifton	,, ,,
,,		Philip	Roker	,, 1697.	,,		Richard	Clarke	,, ,,
,,		Benj.	Harris	,, ,,	,,		John	Chartier	,, 1698.
,,		Chr.	Atkinson	,, 1707.	1709-10		Jno. W. Edw.	Stocker & Peacock }	,, 1705.
,,		Phil.	Rainaud	,, ,,	,,		Jno.	Clifton (?)	
,,		Thos.	Fawler	,, ,,	,,		Thos.	Allen	,, 1697.
,,		Jos.	Smith	,, ,,	,,		Fras.	Turner	,, 1709.
,,		Samuel	Lee	,, 1701.	,,		Isr'l.	Pincking	,, 1697.
,,		Benj.	Pyne	,, 1697.	,,		Hy.	Greene	,, 1700.
,,		Saml.	Wastell	,, 1701.	,,		Laun.	Keatt	,, 1701.
,,		John	Backe	,, 1700.	,,		Jno.	Rand	,, 1704.
1708-9		Mary	Matthew	,, ,,	,,		Simon	Pantin	,, 1701.
,,		Jos.	Bird	,, 1697.	,,		Phil.	Rolles	,, 1705.
,,		Thos.	Farren	,, 1707.	,,		See 1702.		
,,		Philip	Rolles, Jr.	,, 1705.	,,		Wm.	Francis	,, 1697.
,,		Wm.	Warham	,, 1703	,,		Andrw.	Dalton	,, 1708.
,,		Lawrence	Jones	,, 1697.	,,		Ebenezr.	Roe	,, 1709.
,,		Chris.	Riley	,, ,,	,,		Thos.	Prichard	,, ,,
,,		Alice	Sheene	,, 1700.	,,		Hen.	Clarke	,, ,,
,,		Jno.	Read	,, 1704.	,,		Jas.	Wethered	,, ,,
,,		Jno.	Bodington	,, 1697.	,,		Richd.	Watts	,, 1710.
,,		Wm.	Fawdery	,, 1698.	1710-1		Thos.	Folkingham	,, 1706.
,,		Henry	Greene	,, 1700.	,,		Jno.	Smith	,, 1710.
,,		Anty.	Blackford	,, 1702.	,,		Wm.	Hinton	,, 1704.
					,,		Geo.	Gillingham	,, 1703.

DATE.	MAKERS' MARK AND NAME.			DATE.	MAKERS' MARK AND NAME.		
1710-1	ME	Lewis	Mettayer ent. 1700.	1711-2	PO	John	Porter ent. 1698.
,,	CO	Ed.	Cornock ,, 1707.	,,	WI	Richard Williams ,, 1712.
,,	WI	Jno.	Wisdom ,, 1704.	,,	PE	Wm.	Penstone ,, ,,
,,	PE	Wm.	Pearson ,, 1710.	,,	Ie	Ed.	Jennings ,, 1709.
,,	TW	Wm.	Twell ,, 1709.	,,	Re	Jno.	Read ,, 1704.
,,	BE	Jas.	Beschefer ,, 1704.	,,	Me	Lewis	Mettayer (probably).
,,	MA	Jacob	Margas ,, 1706.	,,	CL	Nich.	Clausen ent. 1709.
,,	RO	Jas.	Rood ,, 1710.	,,	HO	Ed.	Holaday ,, ,,
,,	KE	Jno.	Keigwin ,, ,,	,,	CO	Aug.	Courtauld , 1708.
,,	SL	Gabriel Sleath ,, 1706.		,,	GR	Hen.	Greene ,, 1700.
,,	HY	Name not traced.		,,	CH	Jno.	Chamberlen ,, 1704.
,,	MA	Jacob	Margas ,, ,,	,,	DA	Isaac	Dalton ,, 1711.
,,	GO	Jas.	Goodwin ,, ,,	,,	MA	Wm.	Matthew ,, ,,
,,	RV	Abm.	Russell (?) ,, 1702.	,,	Ne	Jonthn. Newton ,, ,,
,,	Ke	Robt.	Keble ,, ,,	1712-3	SU	Thos.	Sutton ,, ,,
,,	SH	Jos.	Sheene ,, ,,	,,	Ra	Jno.	Rand ,, 1704.
,,	St	Jno.	Stockar ,, ,,	,,	LO	Seth	Lofthouse ,, 1697.
,,	TR	Wm.	Truss ,, ,,	,,	DA	Isaac	Dalton ,, 1711.
,,	MO	Hezk.	Mountfort ,, 1711.	,,	GI	Ed.	Gibson ,, 1697.
,,	MA	Isaac	Malyn ,, 1710.	,,	Lu	Wm.	Lukin , 1699.
,,	FL	Jno.	Flight ,, ,,	,,	BA	Richd.	Bayley ,, 1708.
1711-2	PE	Edmd.	Pearce ,, 1704.	,,	RA	Richd.	Raine ,, 1712.
,,	GR	Dorothy Grant ,, 1697.		,,	H	John	Hobson ,, 1697.
,	EA	John	East ,, ,,	,,	IO	Glover Johnson ,, 1712.
,,	BA	Joseph	Barbitt ,, 1703.	,,	Tv	Wm.	Turbitt ,, 1710.
				,,	WI	Richd.	Williams ,, 1712.

DATE.	MAKERS' MARK AND NAME.			
1712-3		Thos.	Bevault	ent. 1712.
,,		Jno. M.	Stockar	,, 1710.
1713-4		Samuel	Margas	,, 1706.
,,		Ambrose	Stevenson	,, ,,
,,		Natl.	Locke	1698.
,,		Hugh	Roberts	,, 1697.
,,		Gabriel	Sleath	,, 1706.
,,		Mark	Paillet	,, 1698.
,,		Henry	Collins	, ,,
,,		Edw.	Vincent	(?)
,,		Jno.	Ludlow	,, 1713.
,,		Gundry	Roode	,, 1709.
,,		Thos.	Mann	,, 1713.
,,		Thos.	Ewesdin	,, ,,
,,		Wm.	Looker	,, ,,
,,		John	Bathe	,, 1700.
,,		Wm.	Juson	,, 1704.
,,		Seth	Lofthouse	,, 1697.
1714-5		Robt. Timbrell & Benj. Bentley }		,, ,,
,,		David	Tanqueray	,, 1713.
,,		Joseph	Fainell	,, 1710.
,,		Thomas	Bevault	,, 1712.
,,		Glover	Johnson	,, ,,
,,		Mich'l	Bou't	,, ,,
,,		Name not traced.		

DATE.	MAKERS' MARK AND NAME.			
1714-5		Wm. John	England & Vane }	ent. 1714.
,,		Sam	Welder	,, ,,
,,		Rich'd	Green	,, 1703.
,,		Jno.	Holland	,, 1711.
,,		Saml.	Hitchcock	,, 1712.
,,		Saml.	Welder	,, 1714.
,,		Philip	Brush	,, 1707.
,,		Josiah	Daniel	,, 1714.
,,		Nathl.	Bland	,, ,,
,,		Richd.	Gines	,, ,,
,,		Henry	Beesley	,, ,,
,,		Henry	Miller	,, ,,
1715-6		Thos.	Allen	,, 1697.
,,		David	Killmaine	,, 1715.
,,		Fras.	Plymley	,, ,,
,,		John	Corporon	,, 1716.
,,		Danl.	Sleamaker	,, 1704.
,,		Humph.	Payne	,, 1701.
,,		Petley	Ley	,, 1715.
,,		Thos.	Port	,, 1713.
,,		Richard	Greene	,, 1703.
,,		Edward	Jones	,, 1697.
,,		Josiah Daniel (see 1714)		,, 1714.
,,		Jas.	Goodwin	,, 1710.
,,		Danl.	Yerbury	,, 1715.
,,		Geo.	Lambe	,, 1713.

DATE.	MAKERS' MARK AND NAME.			DATE.	MAKERS' MARK AND NAME.		
1715-6		Robt. Hill	ent. 1716.	1717-8		Joseph Ward	ent. 1717.
,,		Thos. Holland	,, 1707.	,,		Edward Barnet	,, 1715.
1716-7		John Holland	,, 1711.	,,		Chas. Jackson (see 1718 below)	,, 1714.
,,		Nat. Roe	,, 1710.	,,		William Pearson (see 1716)	,, 1710.
,,		Jos. Clare	,, 1713.	,,		Isaac Riboulau	,, 1714.
,,		Thos. Mason	,, 1716.	,,		Edw. Barnet	,, 1715.
,,		Paul Lamerie	,, 1712.	,,		Phil. Robinson	,, 1713.
,,		Thos. Ewesdin	,, 1713.	,,		Thos. Holland	,, 1707.
,,		Jas. Seabrook	,, 1714.	,,		Jno. Harris	,, 1716.
,,		Petley Ley	,, 1715.	,,		Wm. Street	,, 1717.
,,		Phillip Robinson	,, 1713.	,,		Jas. Smith	,, 1718.
,,		Joseph Clare (see above and 1719)	,, ,,	,,		Thos. Shermer	,, 1717.
,,		Anty. Nelme	,, 1697.	,,		Starling Wilford	,, ,,
,,		Geo. Lambe	,, 1713.	,,		Paul Hanet	,, ,,
,,		Wm. Bellassyse	,, 1716.	,,		Thos. Burridge	,, ,,
,,		David Green	,, 1701.	,,		Wm. Bellamy	,, ,,
,,		Jno. Guerrie	,, 1717.	,,		Sam. Welder	,, ,,
,,		Danl. Cunningham	,, 1716.	1718-9		Ambrose Stevenson	,, 1706.
,,		Jos. Bell	,, ,,	,,		Wm. Petley	,, 1717.
,,		Richd. Edwards	,, ,,	,,		Paul Hanet	,, 1715.
,,		Jas. Morson	,, ,,	,,		John Farnell	,, 1714.
,,		Wm. Pearson	,, 1717.	,,		Chas. Jackson	,, ,,
1717-8		Jas. (?) Fraillon	,, 1710.	,,		Thos. Parr	,, 1697.
,,		Robt. Kempton	,, ,,	,,		Geo. Beale	,, 1713.
,,		Wm. Penstone	,, 1717.	,,		Ed. Holaday	,, 1709.

DATE.	MAKERS' MARK AND NAME.
1718-9	David Tanqueray ent. 1713. (see 1714)
"	Henry Clarke „ 1709. (see 1709)
"	Thomas Mason „ 1716.
"	Thomas Tearle „ 1719. (see 1719 below)
"	John Keigwin „ 1710.
"	John Sanders „ 1717.
"	Wm. Fawdery „ 1697. (as 1705)
"	Wm. Darkeratt „ 1718.
"	Hugh Saunders „ „
"	John Bignell „ „
"	Geo. Gillingham „ „
"	Jno. Millington „ „
"	Jno. Lingard „ „
"	Do. do. (for O.S.) „ 1719.
1719-20	Thos. Tearle „ „ (see 1718-9)
"	Thos. Langford „ 1715.
"	Réné Hudell „ 1718.
"	Wm. Spackman „ 1714.
"	Geo. Boothby „ 1720.
"	John White „ 1719.
"	John le Sage „ 1718.
"	Benj. Blakeley „ 1715.
"	Wm. Paradise „ 1718.
"	Lawrence (?) Jones „ 1697.

DATE.	MAKERS' MARK AND NAME.
1719-20	John Gibbons ent. 1700.
"	Thomas Shermer „ 1717.
"	Wm. Darkeratt „ 1718. (see 1718)
"	Edw. Barrett „ 1715.
"	James Smith „ 1718.
"	Gabriel Sleath „ 1706.
"	Thos. Allen „ 1697. (2nd Mark)
"	Thos. Morse „ 1718.
"	Edw. Gibbon „ 1719.
"	Saml. Smith „ „
"	Jos. Steward „ „
"	Jos. Clare, as 1716-7.
"	Chris. Gerrard ent. 1719.
"	Edmd. Hickman „ „
"	Wm. Pearson „ „
"	Geo. Brydon „ 1720.
"	Thos. Gladwin „ 1719.
"	Starling Wilford „ 1720.
"	John Lingard „ 1719.
"	John Jones „ „
"	Paul Hanet „ 1717.
"	Edwd. Hall „ 1720.
"	Bowles Nash „ „
"	—— Hodgkis „ 1719.
"	Phyllis Phillip „ 1720.

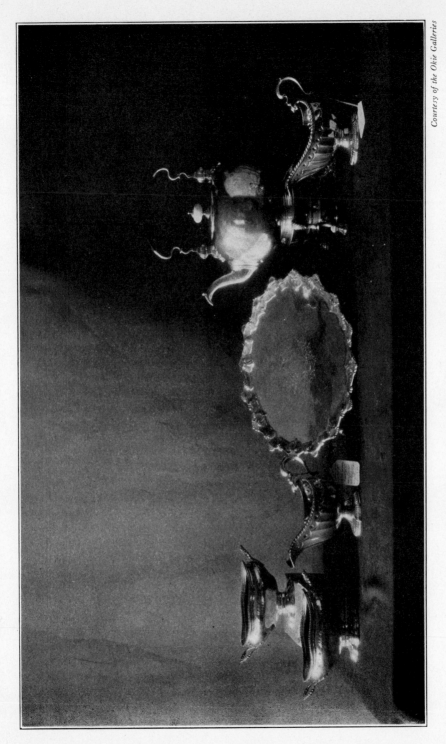

LONDON SILVER OF THE REIGN OF GEORGE II

DATE.	MAKERS' MARK AND NAME.		DATE.	MAKERS' MARK AND NAME.	
1719-20	Joseph Fainell	ent. 1710.	1720-1	Jno. Bromley	ent. 1720.
,,	Phyllis Phillip	,, 1720.	,,	Benj. Watts	,, ,,
,,	Richard Gines	,, ,,	,,	John Bignell	,, ,,
,,	Wm. Scarlett (O.S. as before 1697)	,, ,,	,,	John Betts	,, ,,
,,	Mary Rood	,, ,,	,,	Michl. Boult.	,, ,,
,,	Christr. Gerrard	,, ,,	,,	Saml. Hitchcock	,, ,,
1720-1	John Edwards	,, 1697.	,,	Thos. Sadler	,, ,,
,,	Thos. Evesdon (see 1721-2)	,, 1713.	,,	Geo. Boothby	,, ,,
,,	William Looker	,, ,,	,,	Phil. Rolles	,, ,,
,,	Paul Lamerie	,, 1712.	,,	Jno. Hopkins	,, ,,
,,	Paul Crespin	,, 1720.	,,	Do. do.	,, ,,
,,	Geo. Lambe (widow of)	,, 1713.	,,	Saml. Welder	,, ,,
,,	William Fawdery	,, 1720.	,,	John Penfold (probably)	,, ,,
,,	Henry Millar	,, ,,	,,	Fras. Turner	,, ,,
,,	Thomas Folkingham	,, ,,	,,	Jas. Morson	,, ,,
,,	Petley Ley (see 1716)	,, 1715.	,,	Jno. Millington	,, ,,
,,	John Fawdery	,, 1697.	,,	Thos. Folkingham	,, ,,
,,	Matt. Cooper	,, ,,	,,	John Ludlow	,, ,,
,,	Ann Tanqueray	,, 1720.	,,	Thos. Mann	,, ,,
,,	Chas. Jackson	,, 1714.	,,	Ed. Jennings	,, ,,
,,	Sarah Holaday	,, 1719.	,,	Do. do. (O.S.)	,, ,,
,,	Hugh Arnett & Ed. Pocock	,, ,,	,,	Richd. Watts	,, ,,
,,	Name not traced.		,,	Name not traced.	
,,	Thos. Bamford	,, ,,	,,	J. Burridge	,, ,,
			,,	Jno. Barnard	,, ,,
			,,	A'brose Stevenson	,, ,,

DATE.	MAKERS' MARK AND NAME.			DATE.	MAKERS' MARK AND NAME.		
1720-1		Edw.	Feline	ent. 1720.	1721-2		Simon	Pantin	ent. 1717.
"		Jas.	Seabrook	" "	"		John	Wisdome (probably)	" 1720.
"		Jos.	Steward	" "	"		Jane	Lambe	" 1719.
"		Henry	Miller	" "	"		Ed.	Turner	" 1720.
"		Geo.	Squire	" "	"		Abm.	Buteux	" 1721.
"		Gabl.	Sleath	" "	"		Saml.	Lee	" "
"		Phil.	Roker (N.S.)	" "	"		Geo.	Wickes	" "
"		Do.	do. (O.S.)	" "	"		Hugh	Spring	" "
"		Geo.	Brydon	" "	"		Mary	Rood	" "
"		Hen.	Greene	" "	"		Gundry	Roode	" "
"		Edwd.	Pearce	" "	"		Wm.	Truss	" "
"		Jno.	Brumhall	" 1721.	"		Do.	do.	" "
"		Jno.	Newton	" 1720.	"		Name not traced.		
"		Wm.	Matthew	" "	"		Sarah	Holaday (see 1720-1)	" 1719.
"		Saml.	Lee	" "					
"		Henry	Clarke	" "	"		Joseph	Bell ?	" 1716.
"		Jno.	Corosey	" "	"		Thos.	Evesdon (see 1720-1)	" 1713.
"		Jno.	Farnell	" "	"		Edmund Pearce		" 1720.
"		Glover	Johnson	" "	"		Simon	Pantin (see above)	" 1717.
"		Wm.	Looker	" "					
"		Phil.	Rainaud	" "	1722-3		Bowles	Nash	" 1721.
1721-2		Ed.	Vincent (probably)	" "	"		Edward	Feline (see 1720)	" 1720.
"		Isaac	Líger	" "	"		Jno. le	Sage	" 1718.
"		Henry	Jay	" "	"		Ed.	Wood	" "
"		Jos.	Clare	" "	"		Benj.	Pyne	as 1706.
"		M.	Arnett &	" "	"		Name not traced.		
		Ed.	Pocock		"		Anth.	Nelme	as 1716.
					"		Edw.	Jennings	ent. 1720.

DATE.	MAKERS' MARK AND NAME.				DATE.	MAKERS' MARK AND NAME.			
1722-3	IB	Jno.	Bignell	ent. 1720.	1722-3	RW	Richard	Watts	ent. 1720.
,,	GU	Natl.	Gulliver	,, 1722.	,,	ED	Ed.	Dymond	,, 1722.
,,	DW	David	Willaume	,, 1720.	,,	KI	Jeremiah King		,, 1723.
,,	IE	Jno.	Eckford	,, ,,	,,	IK	Do.	do.	,, ,,
,,	IR	Isaac	Riboulau	,, ,,	,,	SO	Wm.	Soame	,, ,,
,,	PI	Pere	Pilleau	,, ,,	,,	WS	Do.	do.	,, ,,
,,	W	Edw.	Wood	,, ,,	,,	IO	John	Jones	,, ,,
,,	GO	Jas.	Gould	,, 1722.	,,	II	Do.	do.	,, ,,
,,	NC	Nich.	Clausen	,, 1720.	,,	HD	Henry	Dell	,, 1722.
,,	PR	Phil.	Robinson	,, 1723.	,,	WO	Wm.	Owen	,, 1723.
,,	GO	Phil.	Goddard	,, ,,	,,	IG	John	Gibbons	,, ,,
,,	PG	Do.	do.	,, ,,	,,	GO	Meshach Godwin		,, 1722.
,,	NG	Natl.	Gulliver	,, ,,	1723-4	IE	John	East	,, 1721.
,,	CO	Isaac	Cornasseau	,, 1722.	,,	TF	Thos.	Farrer	,, 1720.
,,	IC	Do.	do.	,, ,,	,,	TM	Thos.	Morse	,, ,,
,,	NI	Michl.	Nicholl	,, 1723.	,,	CO	Aug.	Courtauld	,, 1708.
,,	CL	John	Clarke	,, 1722.	,,	MA	Jnthn.	Madden	,, 1702.
,,	GY	Geo.	Young	,, ,,	,,	Pe	Edw.	Peacock	,, 1710.
,,	IC	Jno.	Clarke	,, ,,	,,	RS	Richd.	Scarlett	,, 1723.
,,	IF	Jas.	Fraillon	,, 1723.	,,	IC	John	Chartier	,, ,,
,,	DY	Ed.	Dymond	,, 1722.	,,	DI	Arte	Dicken	,, 1720.
,,	A	Joseph	Adams ?	,, ,,	,,	LA	Paul	Lamerie	,, 1712.
,,	SA	John le Sage		,, 1718.	,,	IO	John	Jones	,, 1719.
,,	PB	Philip	Brush ?	,, 1707.	,,	EG	Edw.	Gibbons	,, 1723.
,,	IC	Isaac	Cornasseau	,, 1722.	,,	WS	Wm.	Spackman	,, 1720.
					,,	RO	Jnthn.	Robinson	,, 1723.

DATE.	MAKERS' MARK AND NAME.			DATE.	MAKERS' MARK AND NAME.		
1723-4		John	Bignell ent. 1718. (see 1720 and 1722)	1724-5		Jas.	Burne ent. 1724.
"		Geo.	Squire „ 1720.	"		Do.	do, „ „
"		Thos.	Wall (?) „ 1708.	"		Saml.	Hutton „ „
"		Arte John	Dicken ? or „ 1720. Diggle „ 1697.	"		Do.	do „ „
"		John	Motherby (?) „ 1718.	"		Ed.	Peacock „ „
"		Sam	Hitchcock „ 1712.	"		John	Owing „ „
"		Wm.	Fawdery ? „ 1720.	"		Peter	Simon „ 1725.
"		Jnthn.	Robinson „ 1723.	"		John	Gibbons „ 1723.
"		Richd.	Edwards „ „	"		Aug,	Courtauld „ 1708.
"		John	Owing „ 1724.	"		Josiah	Daniel „ 1714.
"		John Geo.	Edwards & Pitches „ 1723.	"		Peter	Simon „ 1725.
1724-5		Richd.	Bigge „ 1700. (probably)	"		John	Motherby „ 1718.
"		Richd.	Scarlett „ 1719.	"		John	Pero „ 1717.
"		David	Tanqueray „ 1720.	"		Jnthn.	Newton „ 1718.
"		Abm.	Buteux „ 1721.	1725-6		Abm. de Oliveyra „ 1725.	
"		Meshach	Godwin „ 1722.	"		John	Eckfourd „ „
"		Humphy.	Payne „ 1720.	"		Josh.	Healy „ „
"		Paul	Crespin „ „	"		Do.	do. „ „
"		Jacob	Margas „ „	"		Robt.	Lucas „ 1726.
"		Fleurant	David „ 1724.	"		Harvey Price	„ „
"		Do.	do. „ „	"		John	Gorsuch „ „
"		Mathw.	Lofthouse „ 1721.	"		Wm.	Toone „ 1725.
"		John	Edwards „ 1724.	"		Jos.	Bird „ 1724.
"		Edw.	Conen „ „	"		Hugh	Saunders „ 1718.
"		John	Jones „ 1723.	"		Paul	Hanet „ 1721.
"		W'sc'mbe Drake „ 1724.		"		Fras.	Garthorne „ „
"		John	White „ „				

DATE.		MAKERS' MARK AND NAME.
1725-6		Jacob Margas ent. 1720. (see 1724)
"		Starling Wilford (?) " " (see 1728 and 1737).
"		Edward Feline " " (see also 1722-1729)
"		John Gibbons " 1723.
"		Edw. Vincent " " (see 1729)
"		Thos. Mason " 1720.
"		Jas. Gould " 1722.
"		John Edwards " 1724.
"		Geo. Wickes " 1721.
"		Thos. Clark " 1725.
"		Thos. England " "
"		Wm. Scarlett " "
"		Peter Tabart " "
"		Do. do. " "
"		Mathew Cooper " "
"		Do. do. " "
"		Louis Laroche " "
"		John Flavill " 1726.
1726-7		Name not traced.
"		Wm. Darkeratt " 1724.
"		Richd. Green " 1726.
"		Benj. Pyne (as before 1697).
"		Peter Archambo ent. 1722.
"		Wm. Fawdery " 1720.
"		Wm. Atkinson " 1725.

DATE.		MAKERS MARK AND NAME.
1726-7		Robt. Lucas ent. 1726. (variant of mark of)
"		Thos. Evesdon " 1713. (see 1720 and 1721)
"		Fras. Nelme " 1722.
"		Bern'd. Fletcher " 1725.
"		Thos. Bamford " 1720.
"		Robt. Williams " 1726.
"		Do. do. " "
"		Gawen Nash " "
"		Chas. Perier " 1727.
"		Do. do. " "
"		Geo. Brome. " 1726.
"		Peter le Chaube " "
1727-8		Isaac Riboulead " 1720.
"		Jas. Smith " "
"		Edw. Wood " 1722.
"		Ed. Cornock " 1707.
"		Saml. Bates " 1727.
"		Thomas England " 1725.
"		Richard Pargeter " 1730.
"		Matt. Cooper " 1725. (see 1725)
"		?Andrew Raven " 1706.
"		Jno. le Sage " 1722.
"		Name not traced.
"		Sarah Holaday " 1725.
"		John East " 1721.
"		Jonah Clifton " 1720.

DATE.	MAKERS' MARK AND NAME.			DATE.	MAKERS' MARK AND NAME.		
1727-8		Saml. Laundry	ent. 1727.	1727-8		Saml. Green	ent. 1721.
,,		Edmd. Bodington	,, ,,	,,		Wm. Shaw	,, 1728.
,,		Chas. Kandler & } Jas. Murray }	,, ,,	1728-9		Wm. Darkeratt	,, 1720.
,,		Do. do.	,, ,,	,,		James Goodwin	,, 1721.
,,		Edw. Bennett	,, ,,	,,		Tim. Ley (as before 1697)	
,,		Hester Fawdery	,, ,,	,,		Blanche Fraillon	ent. 1727.
,,		Thos. Cooke	,, ,,	,,		Isaac Callard	,, 1726.
,,		Richd. Hutchinson	,, ,,	,,		Name not traced.	
,,		Chas. Kandler	,, ,,	,,		James Wilkes	,, 1722.
,,		Geo. Weir	,, ,,	,,		Peter Archambo	,, 1720.
,,		Do. do.	,, ,,	,,		Josh. Holland	,, ,,
,,		Name not traced.		,,		Simon Pantin (see 1729)	,, ,,
,,		Abel Brokesby	,, ,,	,,		John Millington	,, 1728.
,,		Dike Impey (probably)	,, ,,	,,		Edward Bennett	,, 1727.
,,		Benj. Bentley	,, 1728.	,,		Ralph Frith	,, 1728.
,,		Mary Johnson	,, 1727.	,,		Do. do.	,, ,,
,,		L. Wichalles	,, 1728.	,,		Geo. Hodges	,, ,,
,,		Chas. Hatfield	,, 1727.	,,		Do. do.	,, ,,
,,		Sam. Laundry	,, ,,	,,		John Fawdery	,, ,,
,,		Matw. Cooper	,, 1725.	,,		John Montgomery	,, ,,
,,		David Willaume	,, 1728.	,,		? John Richardson	,, 1723.
,,		Danl. Cunningham	,, 1720.	,,		? Wm. Fordham	,, 1706.
,,		Richd. Gines	,, ,,	,,		Starling Wilford (see 1725 and 1737)	,, 1729.
,,		Geo. Gillingham	,, 1721.	1729-30		John Tuke	,, 1721.
,,		Chas. Hatfield	,, 1727.	,,		Thos. Tearle	,, 1720.
,,		Jacob Foster	,, 1726.	,,		Ed. Vincent (see 1725)	,, ,,

DATE.	MAKERS' MARK AND NAME.	DATE.	MAKERS' MARK AND NAME.
1729-30	Anthony Nelme ent. 1722.	1730-1	Richd. Bayley ent. 1720.
„	Chas. Martin „ 1729.	„	Wm. Belassyse „ 1723.
„	Edwd. Feline „ 1720. (see 1722 and 1725)	„	Isaac Callard „ 1726.
„	Abel Brokesby „ 1727. (see 1727)	„	Wm. Petley „ 1720.
„	Simon Pantin „ 1717. (see 1728)	„	Perè Pilleau „ „
„	George Jones „ 1724. (see 1735-6)	„	Chas. Kandler „ 1727.
„	Name not traced.	„	John White „ 1719.
„	Paul Lamerie „ „	„	Anne Tanqueray „ 1720.
„	Ralph Maidman „ 1730.	„	? Saml. Laundry „ 1727. (see also 1727)
„	Richd. Scarlett „ 1720. (see 1723)	„	John Chapman „ 1730. (see 1737)
„	Name not traced.	„	Samuel Hitchcock „ „
„	John Jones „ 1729.	„	Jas. Jenkins „ 1731.
„	Saml. Margas „ 1720.	„	Wm. Justis „ „
„	Chas. Alchorne „ 1729.	„	Wm. Reeve „ „
„	Sam. Welder „ „	„	Aaron Bates „ 1730.
„	Benj. Goodwin „ „	„	Aug. Courtauld „ 1708.
„	Name not traced.	1731-2	John Gamon „ 1728.
„	Edith Fletcher „ „	„	Edwd. Yorke „ 1730.
„	Eliz. Goodwin „ „	„	Geo. Hindmarsh „ 1731.
„	Jas. Maitland „ 1728. of the "Grasshopper," Suffolk Street.	„	David Willaume „ 1728.
1730-1	Aug. Courtauld ent. 1729.	„	Wm. Darker „ 1731.
„	Paul Lamerie „ 1712.	„	Thos. England „ 1725.
„	Saml. Jefferys „ 1697.	„	Jane Lambe „ 1729.
„	Gabl. Sleath „ 1720.	„	Mary Lofthouse „ 1731.
		„	Thos. Merry „ „
		„	Jeffrey Griffith „ „

DATE.		MAKERS' MARK AND NAME.
1731-2	SP	Sarah Parr ent. 1720.
,,	GRAH	Robt. Abercromby & } ,, 1731. Geo. Hindmarsh
,,	WW	Wm. Woodward ,, ,,
,,	TC	Thos. Causton ,, 1730.
,,	ER	Etienne Rongent ,, 1731.
,,	WD	Wm. Darker ,, ,, (see 1731)
1732-3	R·B	Richd. Beale ,, ,,
,,	L I G	Sam Laundry & } ,, ,, Jeffy Griffith
,,	I·S	Joseph Smith ,, 1728.
,,	EP	Edw. Pocock ,, ,,
,,	I·S	John Sanders ,, 1720.
,,	I·F	John Fawdery ,, 1728. (see 1728)
,,	F·P	Fras. Pages ,, 1729.
,,	LO	? Matt. Lofthouse ,, 1705.
,,	DL	Name not traced.
,,	WL	Wm. Lukin ,, 1725.
,,	FS	Fras. Spilsbury ,, 1729. (same mark found in square stamp).
,,	TP	Thos. Parr ent. 1732.
,,	WM	Wm. Matthews ,, 1728.
,,	IS	Jas. Savage ,, ,,
,,	IP	John Pero ,, 1732.
,,	IG	Jas. Gould ,, ,,
,,	GS	Geo. Smith ,, ,,
,,		R. W. (as 1696).
,,	WS	Wm. Soame ,, ,,
,,	C·G	Chas. Gibbons ,, ,,
,,	SH	Wm. Shaw ,, 1728.
1733-4	IE	John Eckfourd, jr. ,, 1725.

DATE.		MAKERS' MARK AND NAME.
1733 4	AC	Aug. Courtauld ent. 1729.
,,	IS	Jas. Slater ,, 1732.
,,	RB	Richd. Bayley ,, 1720.
,,	HH	Henry Herbert ,, 1734. (of the " Three Crowns ")
,,	WS	Wm. Soame ,, 1732.
,,	EB	Eliz. Buteux ,, 1731.
,,	DC	Danl. Chapman ,, 1729.
,,	LP	Lewis Pantin ,, 1733.
,,	CS	Chas. Sprage ,, 1734.
,,	R·A	Robt. Abercromby ,, 1731. (see 1734)
,,	GB	Geo. Braithwaite ? earliest ment. 1728.
1734-5	R·M	Ralph Maidman ent. 1731.
,,	CH	Caleb Hill ,, 1728.
,,	LM	Lewis Mettayer ,, 1720.
,,	WG	Wm. Gould ,, 1732.
,,	R·A	Robt. Abercromby ,, 1731. (see 1733)
,,	IN	John Newton ,, 1726.
,,	MP	Mary Pantin ,, 1733.
,,	RP	Richd. Pargeter ,, 1730.
,,	HA	Hugh Arnell ,, 1734.
,,	AC EF	Alex. Coates & } ,, ,, Edw. French
,,	IT	John Taylor ,, ,,
,,	CO	Wm. Gould ,, ,,
,,	II	John Jacob ,, ,,
,,	IP	John Pollock ,, ,,
,,	IM	Jas. Manners ,, ,,

DATE.	MAKERS' MARK AND NAME.	DATE.	MAKERS' MARK AND NAME.
1734-5	Edw. French ent. 1734.	1736-7	Benj. West ent. 1737.
,,	Jas. Brooker ,, ,,	,,	Robt. Brown ,, 1736.
,,	Sam. Hutton ,, ,,	,,	Ann Hill ,, 1734
,,	Wm. Kidney ,, ,,	,,	Thos. Mason ,, 1733.
1735-6	Geo. Jones ,, 1724.	,,	John Jones ,, ,,
,,	Richd. Gurney & Thos. Cook } ,, 1734.	,,	John Fossey ,, ,,
,,	Edw. Bennett ,, 1731.	,,	Bennet R. Bradshaw & Tyrill } ,, 1737.
,,	Fred Kandler ,, 1735.	,,	Jerem. King ,, 1736.
,,	Benj. Godfrey ,, 1732. (see 1739)	,,	Thos. Mann ,, ,,
,,	Grif. Edwards ,, ,,	,,	David Hennell ,, ,,
,,	Wm. Shaw ,, 1727.	,,	Benj. West ,, 1737.
,,	Peter Bennett ,, 1731.	,,	Henry Herbert ,, 1734.
,,	John White ,, 1724.	,,	? Harvey Price ,, 1726.
,,	Wm. Atkinson ,, 1725.	1737-8	Joseph Allen & Co. ,, 1729.
,,	Wm. Young ,, 1735.	,,	Geo. Weekes ,, 1735.
,,	Name not traced, (see 1729-30)	,,	Jos. Sanders ,, 1730.
,,	Francis Nelme ,, ,,	,,	Saml. Blackborrow ,, 1720.
,,	John Barbe ,, ,,	,,	Thos. Whipham ,, 1737.
,,	Geo. Hindmarsh ,, ,,	,,	Geo. Hindmarsh ,, 1735. (see 1735-6)
,,	Christn. Hilland ,, 1736.	,,	Starling Wilford ,, 1729.
,,	Name not traced.	,,	John Chapman ,, 1730. (see 1730)
,,	Henry Herbert ,, 1734. (of the "Three Crowns")	,,	Robt. Williams ,, 1726.
,,	Lewis Hamon ,, 1735.	,,	Richd. Beale ,, 1731.
1736-7	Name not traced.	,,	Simon Jouet ,, 1723.
,,	Wm. Garrard ,, 1735.	,,	Thos. Jackson ,, 1736.
,,	Sam. Wood ,, 1733-7.	,,	Thos. Gladwin ,, 1737.

DATE.	MARKERS' MARK AND NAME.			DATE.	MARKERS' MARK AND NAME.		
1737-8	IB	John Barrett	ent. 1737.	1739-40	HP	Humphrey Payne	ent. 1739.
"	GB	Geo. Baskerville	" 1738.	"	SH	Sarah Holaday	" 1719.
"	PP	Philip Platel	" 1737.	"	BG	Benj. Godfrey (see 1735)	" 1732.
"	I·I	Jas. Jenkins	" 1738.	"	TW	Thos. Whipham	" 1737.
"	GR	Gundry Roode	" 1737.	"	CH	Chas. Hillan	" 1741.
"	IR	John Robinson	" 1738.	"	WK	Wm. Kidney	" 1739.
"	IS	Jas. Schruder	" 1737.	"	PL	Paul Lamerie	" "
"	WE	Wm. Soame	" 1738.	"	BB	Ben. Blakeley	" "
"	SW	Sam. Wood	" 1737.	"	IC	Isaac Callerd	" "
"	DW	Denis Wilks	" "	"	I·G	Jeff. Griffith	" "
1738-9	RZ	Richd. Zouch	" 1735.	"	TT	Thos. Tearle	" "
"	TW	Thos. Whipham	" 1739	"	IF	Jnthn. Fossy	" "
"	FK	Fred Kandler	" 1735.	"	PC	Paul Crespin	" "
"	IR	Jno. Robinson	" 1738.	"	IH	John Harwood	" "
"	LD	Louis Dupont	" 1736.	"	RB	Richd. Bayley	" "
"	TR	Thos. Rush	" 1724.	"	Ab	Robt. Abercromby	" "
"	BB	Benj. Blakeley	" 1738.	"	LD	Lewis Dupont	" "
"	HB	Henry Bates	" "	"	WH	Wm. Hunter	" "
"	PB	Philip Brugier	" "	"	WG	Wm. Gwillim	" "
"	WW	Wm. West	" "	"	GB	Geo. Boothby	" "
"	FP	Fras. Pages	" 1739.	"	EA	Edw. Aldridge	" "
"	RH	Robt. Hill	" "	"	WS	Wm. Soame	" "
"	IL	James Langlois	" 1738.	"	PB	Peter Bennett	" "
1739-40	FK	Fred Kandler	" 1735.	"	HB	Henry Bates	" "
"	RB	? Richd. Bayler	" 1739.	"	IT	John Tuite	" "
"	IP	John Pero (see 1732)	" "				

DATE.		MAKERS' MARK AND NAME.		
1739-40		Thos.	England	ent. 1739.
"		Robt.	Lucas	" "
"		Ben.	Godfrey	" "
"		Do.	do.	" "
"		Gawen	Nash	" "
"		John	Bryan	" "
"		Richard	Beale	" "
"		John	Cam	" 1740.
"		J.	Barbitt	" 1739.
"		Richd.	Pargeter	" "
"		Marmdk.	Daintry	" "
"		Ed.	Bennett	" "
"		Do.	do.	" "
"		Bennett	Bradshaw & Co.	" "
"		Thos.	Bamford	" "
"		John	Eckfourd	" "
"		Wm.	Shaw	" "
"		John	Jacobs (see 1750)	" "
"		John	Pero (see p. 190)	" "
"		John	White	" "
"		Henry	Herbert	" "
"		Richd.	Zouch	" "
"		Susan'h	Hatfield	" "
"		J.	McFarlane	" "
"		Henry	Morris	" "
"		John	Luff	" "

DATE.		MAKERS' MARK AND NAME.		
1739-40		Benj.	Sanders	ent. 1739.
"		Abm. de	Oliveyra	" "
"		Thos.	Mason	" "
"		Chas.	Martin	" 1740.
"		Jos.	Steward	" 1739.
"		Geo.	Smith	" "
"		Louis	Laroche	" "
1740-1		John	Robinson	" "
"		Griff.	Edwards	" "
"		John	Pollock	" "
"		Jos.	Sanders	" "
"		Benj.	Sanders	" 1737.
"		Wm.	Garrard	" 1735.
"		Gabl.	Sleath	" "
"		Richd.	Gurney & Co.	" 1739.
"		Ed.	Wood	" 1740.
"		Chas.	Bellassyse	" "
"		Sarah	Hutton	" "
"		Ed.	Lambe	" "
"		Thos.	Mercer	" "
"		John	Barbe	" 1739.
"		Paul	Crespin	" 1740.
"		Isabel	Pero	" "
"		Lewis	Ouvry	" "
"		Jas.	Gould	" 1741.
"		Edwd.	Aldridge (see 1744)	" 1739.

DATE.	MAKERS' MARK AND NAME.			DATE.	MAKERS' MARK AND NAME.		
1740-1		? John Owing	ent. 1724.	1742-3		Paul Crespin	ent. 1739.
,,		Name not traced.		,,		Jos. Allen & } M'decai Fox	,, ,,
,,		Do. do.		,,		Robt. Brown	,, ,,
,,		John Roker	,, 1740.	,,		Fras. Spilsbury	,, ,,
,,		Abm. le Francis	,, ,,	,,		Eliz. Tuite	,, 1741.
,,		Benj. Gurdon	,, ,,	,,		Anne Craig & } John Neville (see 1745)	,, 1740.
1741-2		David Hennell	,, 1739.	,,		Saml. Wells	,, ,,
,,		James Shruder	,, ,,	,,		Robt. Abercromby	,, 1739.
,,		Eliza Godfrey	,, 1741.	,,		Jas. Montgomery	,, 1742.
,,		Saml. Roby	,, 1740.	,,		Jos. Timberlake	,, 1743.
,,		Geo. Wickes	,, 1739.	,,		Phillips Garden	,, 1739.
,,		Thos. Farren	,, ,,	,,		Paul Crespin	,, ,,
,,		Dinah Gamon	,, 1740.	,,		John Cam	,, 1740.
,,		John Newton	,, 1739.	1743-4		Dd. Williams	,, 1739.
,,		Thos. Gilpin	,, ,,	,,		Benj. Sanders	,, ,,
,,		Chas. Hillan	,, 1741.	,,		? Robt. Abercromby	,, ,,
,,		John Stewart (?)		,,		Wm. Hunter	,, ,,
,,		Peter Archambo	,, 1739.	,,		Wm. Gould	,, ,,
,,		Jas. Willmott	,, 1741.	,,		Jas. Wilks	,, ,,
,,		John Spackman	,, ,,	,,		Ed. Feline	,, ,,
,,		Chas. Laughton	,, 1739.	,,		Aug. Courtauld	,, ,,
,,		Thos. Lawrence	,, 1742.	,,		Geo. Jones	,, ,,
,,		Jer'mi'h King	,, 1739.	,,		Jer'mi'h Ashley	,, 1740.
,,		Benj. Gurdon	,, 1740.	,,		Henry Brind	,, 1742.
,,		Robt. Tyrrill	,, 1742.	,,		Robt. Abercromby	,, 1739.
1742-3		Jno. Gould	,, 1739.	,,		Pere Pilleau	,, ,,

DATE.	MAKERS' MARK AND NAME.				DATE.	MAKERS' MARK AND NAME.			
1743-4		Thos.	Whipham	ent. 1737.	1744-5		Jas.	Morrison	ent. 1740.
,,		Name not traced.			1745-6		Benj.	West	,, 1739.
,,		Isaac	Duke	,, 1743.	,,		Thos. Wm.	Whipham & Williams }	,, 1740.
,,		Ed.	Malluson	,, ,,	,,		Ann John	Craig & Neville } (see 1742)	,, ,,
,,		Geo.	Methuen	,, ,,	,,		John	Holland	,, 1739.
,,		Chas.	Johnson	,, ,,	,,		Ben.	Cartwright	,, ,,
,,		Ann	Farren	,, ,,	,,		Fred.	Kandler	,, ,,
,,		Geo.	Ridout	,, ,,	,,		Wm.	Cripps	,, 1743.
,,		Robt.	Swanson	,, ,,	,,		Fras.	Crump	,, 1741.
1744-5		Wm. Wm.	Soame or Shaw	,, 1723. } ,, 1727. }	,,		John	Higginbotham	,, 1745.
,,		Edwd.	Aldridge (see 1740)	,, 1739.	,,		Geo.	Baskerville	,, ,,
,,		Ed.	Feline	,, ,,	,,		Jas.	Manners, Jr.	,, ,,
,,		Lewis	Pantin	,, ,,	,,		? Jer'mi'h King		,, ,,
,,		Robt.	Pilkington	,, ,,	,,		John	Swift (probably, see 1754-5)	,, 1739.
,,		Chas.	Hatfield	,, ,,	,,		Sam	Key	,, 1745.
,,		Peter	Archambo	,, ,,	,,		Robt.	Andrews	,, ,,
,,		John	Quantock	,, ,,	,,		John	Harvey	,, ,,
,,		Aymé	Videau	,, ,,	1746-7		Sam	Wood	,, 1739.
,,		John	Barbe	,, ,,	,,		Jas.	Gould	,, 1743.
,,		John	Edwards	,, ,,	,,		Wm.	Hunter	,, 1739.
,,		Wm.	Bagnall	,, 1744.	,,		Wm.	Peaston	,, 1746.
,,		Wm. Peter	Gwillim & Castle }	,, ,,	,,		Jas.	Morrison	,, 1744.
,,		Jas.	Smith	,, ,,	,,		Henry	Morris	,, 1739.
,,		John	Neville	, 1745.	,,		Jos.	Barker	,, 1746.
,,		Thos.	Jackson	,, 1739.	,,		Ed.	Vincent	,, 1739.
,,		Nich's	Sprimont	,, 1742.	,,		Ann	Kersill	,, 1747.

DATE.	MAKERS' MARK AND NAME.		
1746-7	ES	Ernest Sieber	ent. 1746.
"	GY	Geo. Young	" "
"	SM	Saml. Meriton	" "
"	HH	Henry Herbert	" 1747.
"	HH	Do. do.	" "
"	SJ	Simon Jouet	" "
"	BC	Benj. Cartwright	" 1739.
1747-8	IS	Jno. Sanders	" "
"	WG	Wm. Gould	" "
"	RK	Richd. Kersill	" 1744.
"	WW	Wm. Williams	" 1742.
"	SC	Saml. Courtauld (see 1750).	" 1746.
"	IM	Jacob Marsh	" 1744.
"	TC	Thos. Carlton	" "
"	JE	? John Eckfourd	" 1739.
"	BG	? Benj. Griffin or Benj. Gignac	" 1742. " 1744.
"	JR	John Richardson	" 1743.
"	JP	Thos. Parr	" 1739.
"	MD	M'duke Daintry	" "
"	WS	Wm. Solomon	" 1747.
"	SH	Saml. Herbert	" "
"	I·F	John Fray	" 1748.
"	BC	Ben. Cooper	" "
1748-9	EM	Edwd. Medlycott	" "
"	JW	John Wirgman	" 1745.
"	HP	Hmphy. Payne (see 1739)	" 1739.
"	EC	Elias Cachart	" 1742.

DATE.	MAKERS' MARK AND NAME.		
1748-9	MF	M'decai Fox	ent. 1746.
"	WG	Wm. Grundy	" 1748.
"	JC	John Carman	" "
"	GY	Geo. Young	" 1746.
"	JB	John Barbe	" 1739.
"	GH	Geo. Hunter	" 1748.
"	PG	Phillips Garden	" "
"	WS	Wm. Shaw	" 1749.
"	EH	Eliz. Hartley	" 1748.
"	EJ	Eliz. Jackson	" "
"	EO	Eliz. Oldfield	" "
"	ED	Ed. Dowdall	" "
"	DS	Danl. Shaw	" "
"	W·B	Walter Brind	" 1749.
1749-50	WG	Wm. Grundy	" 1743.
"	DP	Dan. Piers	" 1746.
"	BC	Benj. Cartwright	" 1739.
"	PC	Paul Crespin	" "
"	EbA	Name not traced.	
"	JKing	Jerem'h King	" "
"	AP	Abm. Portal	" 1749.
"	AL	Abm. le Francis	" 1746.
"	JD	Jabez Daniel	" 1749.
"	WM	Wm. MacKenzie	" 1748.
"	WK	Wm. Kersill	" 1749.
"	A·K	Andrew Killick	" "
"	HH	Henry Haynes	" "

DATE.	MAKERS' MARK AND NAME.			
1749-50	GB	Geo.	Bindon	ent. 1749.
,,	TM	Thos.	Mann	,, 1739.
,,	I·A	John	Alderhead	,, 1750.
,,	IT	Jas.	Tookey	,, ,,
,,	WW	Wm.	Wooler	,, ,,
,,	GM	Geo.	Morris	,, ,,
,,	TJ	Thos.	Jeannes	,, ,,
1750-1	IP	John	Priest	,, 1748.
,,	C·C	Chas.	Chesterman	,, 1741.
,,	EC	Eben.	Coker	,, 1739.
,,	I·R	John	Rowe	,, 1749.
,,	RG	Richd.	Gurney & Co.	,, 1750.
,,	S·H	S.	Herbert & Co.	,, ,,
,,	LG	Louis	Guichard	,, 1748.
,,	GC	Geo.	Campar	,, 1749.
,,	FW JF	Fuller	White & John Fray	,, 1750.
,,	HB	Henry	Bayley	,, ,,
,,	JJ	John	Jacobs (see 1739)	,, 1739.
,,	S·C	Saml.	Courtauld (see 1747 and 1755)	,, 1746.
,,	PL	Paul	Lamerie (see 1729 and 1730)	,, 1732.
,,	AM	A.	Montgomery	,, 1750.
,,	MW	Michl.	Ward	,, ,,
,,	GB	Geo.	Bindon	,, 1749.
,,	JH	John	Harvey	,, 1750.
,,	TS	Thos.	Smith	,, ,,
1750-1	IB	John	Berthelot	ent. 1750.
,,	L·I	L'r'nce	Johnson	,, 1751.
,,	PG	Phillips	Garden	,, ,,
,,	MB	Math.	Brodier	,, ,,
,,	F·C	Fras.	Crump	,, 1750.
,,	FC	Do.	do.	,, ,,
c. 1750-60	W·F	Name not traced.		
1751-2	IW	? John	Wetherell	,, 1743.
,,	JP	John	Payne	,, 1750.
,,	DW	Denis	Wilks	,, 1747.
,,	FK	Fred	Knopfell	,, 1752.
,,	ST	Saml.	Taylor	,, 1744.
,,	PW	P.	Werritzer	,, 1750.
,,	TM	Thos.	Moore	,, ,,
,,	WW	Wm.	Woodward	,, 1743.
,,	GS S	G. & S. Smith		,, 1751.
,,	GM	Geo.	Morris	,, ,,
,,	NW	Nicks	Winkins	,, ,,
,,	P·P	Paul	Pinard	,, ,,
,,	ED	Ed.	Doweal	,, ,,
,,	TB	Thos.	Beere	,, ,,
,,	PB	Phil.	Bruguier	,, 1752.
1752-3	RC	Robt.	Cox	,, ,,
,,	LH	Lewis	Haman	,, 1739.
,,	RC	Robt.	Cox (see above)	,, 1752.
,,	WA	Wm.	Alexander	,, 1742.
,,	JP	John	Payne	,, 1751.

DATE.	MAKERS' MARK AND NAME.		
1752-3	WH	Wm. Homer	ent. 1750.
"	W S P	Wm. Shaw & Wm. Priest	" 1749.
"	JB	John Berthelot	" 1741.
"	JR	John Richardson	" 1752.
"	DP	Danl. Piers	" 1746.
"	CC	Chas. Chesterman	" 1752.
"	I·C	John Carman	" "
"	RG	Richd. Goldwire	" 1753.
"	PG	Phillips Garden	" 1751.
1753-4	GH	Geo. Hunter	" 1748.
"	DP	Danl. Piers	" "
"	T&W	Turner & Williams	" 1753.
"	RG	Richd. Gosling	" 1739.
"	RH	Robt. Hennell	" 1753.
"	J·C	John Cafe	" 1742.
"	AJ	Alex. Johnston	" 1747.
"	FW	Fuller White	" 1744.
"	DW IF	Denis John Wilks & Fray	" 1753.
"	WB	Wm. Bond	" "
"	TT	Thos. Towman	" "
"	I·E	John Edwards	" "
"	GFSC	Gabl. Sleath & Fras. Crump	" "
"	DCF	D. C. Fueter	" "
"	DS	Dorothy Sarbit	" "
"	GA	Edward Aldridge (see 1740 and 1744)	" 1743.
"	EIA JS	Edwd. Aldridge & John Stamper	" 1753.

DATE.	MAKERS' MARK AND NAME.		
1753-4	TR	Thos. Rowe	ent. 1753.
"	SS	Saml. Smith	" 1754.
"	LL	Simon Le Sage	" "
"	HC	Henry Corry	" "
"	BC	Benj. Cartwright	" "
"	SB	Sarah Buttall	" "
1754-5	P A M	Peter Archambo & Peter Meure	" 1749.
"	RP	? Robt. Perth.	
"	WC	Wm. Cripps	" 1743.
"	I·Q	John Quantock	" 1754.
"	E A J S	Ed. Aldridge & John Stamper	" 1753.
"	PG	Phillips Garden	" "
"	IM	John Munns	" "
"	DM	Do'thy Mills	" 1752.
"	JH	John Holland	" 1739.
"	IS	John Steward	" 1755.
"	TC	Thos. Collier	" 1754.
"	HD	Henry Dutton	" "
"	W·B	Walter Brind	" 1749.
"	GB WS	Geo. Baskerville & Wm. Sampel	" 1755.
"	DPW	Dobson Prior & Williams	" "
"	D	John Delmester	" "
"	W·I	? Wm. Justus	" 1739.
"	JS	John Swift (see 1745 and below)	" "
"	HM	Henry Miller	ent. 1740.
1755-6	JS	John Swift	" 1739.

DATE.		MAKERS' MARK AND NAME.
1755-6	W·S	Wm. Sanden ent. 1755.
,,		Simon Le Sage ,, 1754.
,,		Magd'n Feline ,, 1753.
,,	J·W	? Thos. Wright ,, 1754.
,,	S·C	Saml. Courtauld ,, 1746. (see 1750)
,,	P·C	Paul Crespin ,, 1739. (see 1749)
,,	W·B J·P	Wm. Bond & } ,, 1754. John Phipps }
,,	W·T	Wm. Turner ,, ,,
,,	W·B	Wm. Bond ,, 1753.
,,	J·J	Jas. Jones ,, 1755.
,,	P·T	Peter Taylor ,, 1740.
,,	F·V	Fred Vonham ,, 1752.
,,	S·S	Saml. Siervent ,, 1755.
,,	J·W	John Wirgman ,, 1745.
,,	R·M	Richd. Mills ,, 1755.
,,	B·B	Benj. Brewood ,, ,,
,,	E·D	Ed. Doweal ,, 1751.
,,	R·Cox	Robt. Cox ,, 1755.
,,	R·C	Do. do. ,, ,,
,,	T·B	Thos. Beezley ,, ,,
,,	A·S	Albert Schurman ,, 1756.
,,	J·R	John Robinson ,, 1739.
1756-7	S·W	Saml. Wheat ,, 1756.
,,	P·G	Pierre Gillois ,, 1754.
,,	W·R	Wm. Robertson ,, 1753.
,,	W·C	Wm. Caldecott ,, 1756.

DATE.		MAKERS' MARK AND NAME.
1756-7	T·G	? Thos. Gilpin ent. 1739.
,,	T·H	Thos. Heming ,, 1745.
,,	R·P W·P	Name not traced.
,,	M·R	Mathew Roker ,, 1755.
,,	P·C	Paul Callard ,, 1751.
,,	I·E	John Edwards ,, 1753.
,,	W·G	Wm. Gould ,, ,,
,,	T·D W·W	T. Devonshire } ,, 1756. & W. Watkins }
,,	B·C	Ben. Cartwright ,, ,,
,,	E·J	Edw. Jay ,, 1757.
1757-8	D·H	David Hennell ,, 1736.
,,	CL ARE	Joseph Clare ,, 1713. (see 1716)
,,	E·G	Eliza Godfrey ,, 1741.
,,	J·J	John Jacobs ,, 1739.
,,	R·P W·P	W. & R. Peaston ,, 1756.
,,	E·D	Ed. Darvill ,, 1757.
,,	R·I	Robert Innes ,, 1742.
,,	S·A	Stephen Ardesoif ,, 1756.
,,	E·B	Ed. Bennett ,, 1739.
,,	I·K T·G	John Kentenber & } 1757. Thos. Groves }
,,	J·F	John Frost ,, ,,
,,	J·F	Do. do. ,, ,,
,,	J·H C·S	John Hyatt & } ,, ,, Chas. Semore }
,,	A·A	Arthur Annesley ,, 1758. (see 1761)
,,	R·B	Robt. Burton ,, ,,

DATE.	MAKERS' MARK AND NAME.			DATE.	MAKERS' MARK AND NAME.		
1757-8	JS	John	Schuppe ent. 1753.	1759-60	SW	? Saml.	Wheat ent. 1756.
"		Wm.	Cafe " 1757.	"	SWIA	Stephen Wm.	Abdy & Jury } " 1759.
1758-9		Fras.	Nelme " 1722.	"	AB	Alex.	Barnett " "
"		Saml.	Taylor " 1744.	"	TC	Thos.	Congreve " 1756.
"	WC	Wm.	Cripps " 1743.	"	TD	Thos.	Doxsey " "
"	S·C	Name not traced.		"	WM	Wm.	Moody " "
"	WSP	Wm. Wm.	Shaw & Priest } " 1749.	"	WD	Wm.	Day " 1759.
"	C·B	Name not traced.		"	S·E	Saml.	Eaton " "
"	I·H	John	Hague " 1758.	"	JK	? Jno.	Kentenber
"	WB	Wm.	Bell " 1759.	1760-1	R·R	Robt.	Rew " 1754.
"	LFHB	Lewis Francis	Herne & Butty } " 1757.	"	EW	Edwd.	Wakelin " 1747.
"	I·BELL	Jos.	Bell " 1756.	"	C·D	Name not traced.	
"	ISA	Name not traced.		"	FW	Fuller	White " 1758.
1759-60	SHB	S.	Herbert & Co. " 1750.	"	AS	Alex.	Saunders " 1757.
"	FK	Fred.	Kandler " 1739.	"	JM	John	Moore " 1758.
"	LD	John	Delmester " 1755.	"	CT	C'nst'ne	Teulings " 1755.
"	IP	John	Perry " 1757.	"	WH	Wm.	Howard " 1760.
"	SW	Saml.	Wood, 2nd mk. " 1739.	"	GM	Geo.	Methuen " 1743.
"	IBBOT	Geo.	Ibbott " 1753.	"	IE	John	Eaton " 1760.
"	I·P	John	Perry " 1757.	c. 1760-1	W·L	Name not traced.	
"	SL	Simon	Le Sage " 1754.	"	Lee	Jeremy	Lee " 1739.
"	WB	? Walter	Brind " 1749.	1761-2	R·R	Richd.	Rugg " 1754.
"	WC	Wm.	Cripps " 1743.	"	WP	Wm.	Plummer " 1755.
"	IH	John	Hyatt " 1748.	"	LFHB	Louis Fras.	Herne & Butty } " 1757.
"	HB	Henry	Bayley (probably).	"	FBND	Fras. Nicks.	Butty & Dumee } " "
				"	WS	Wm.	Shaw " 1749.

DATE.	MAKERS' MARK AND NAME.			
1761-2	I·H	John	Horsley.	
"	JG	John	Gorham	ent. 1757.
"	A·A	Arthur	Annesley	" 1758.
		(see 1757)		
"	GH	Geo.	Hunter	" 1748.
"	MF	Magdalen Feline		" 1753.
"	T·H	Thomas	Heming	" 1745.
		(see 1756)		
"	MP	Mary	Piers	" 1758.
"	T·P	Thos.	Powell	" "
1762-3	JJ	Jas.	Jones	" 1755.
"	WT	Wm.	Tant	" 1773.
			(probably)	
"	WS	Wm.	Sampel	" 1755.
"	L·B	Louis	Black	" 1761.
"	C·TW	Thos.	Whipham & }	" 1757.
		Chas.	Wright	
"	GI	Geo.	Ibbott	" 1753.
"	SD	Saml.	Delamy	" 1762.
"	D W·I	W. & J.	Deane	" "
"	I·B	Jos.	Bell	" 1756.
"	E E A A	Edwd.	Aldridge & Co.	
"	WD	Wm.	Day	" 1759.
"	W Wa	Wm.	Watkins	" 1756.
"	E✱A	Edward	Aldridge	" 1739.
"	R✝P	R.	Peaston	" 1756.
1763-4	RT	Richd.	Thomas	" 1755.
"	JD	Tmpsn.	Davis	" 1757.
"	EA	Edward	Aldridge	" 1739.
"	C·TW	Thos.	Whipham & }	" 1758.
		Chas.	Wright	

DATE.	MAKERS' MARK AND NAME.			
1763-4	DS RS	Danl.	Smith & }	
		Robt.	Sharp	
"	T·WC	T. & W. Chawner (probably).		
"	EC	Ebenezer Coker		"
"	PV	Phil	Vincent	ent. 1757.
"	WK	Wm.	King	" 1761.
"	JB	John	Buckett.	
"	IA	John	Aspinshaw	" 1763.
"	J·L	John	Lamfert	" 1748.
c. 1763-4	NH	Name not traced.		
"	TE GS	Do.	do.	
1764-5	R D·H	D. & R.	Hennell	" 1768.
"	TH RM	? Thos.	Hannam }	
		Rich.	Mills	
"	CM	Name not traced.		
"	W·P R·P	W. & R. Peaston (probably).		
"	I V V L	Names not traced.		
"	H·I I·S·C	John	Hyatt & }	ent. 1757.
		C.	Semore	
"	A·L	Aug.	Le Sage	" 1767.
"	TF IM	Thos.	Freeman & }	" 1764.
		J.	Marshall	
"	AC	Anthy.	Calame	" "
"	IAC	J. A.	Calame	" "
"	I·I	John	Innocent (probably).	
"	W·P R·P	W. & R.	Peaston	"
		(see above)		
"	WC	Wm.	Cafe	ent. 1757.
"	ER	Name not traced.		
"	BM	Do.	do.	
"	C TW	Thos.	Whipham & }	" 1758.
		Chas.	Wright	

DATE.	MAKERS' MARK AND NAME.	DATE.	MAKERS' MARK AND NAME.
1765-6	I W V L — Names not traced.	1767-8	O T B I — Thos. Bumfries & Orlando Jackson } ent. 1766.
,,	GS — Do. do.	,,	S.H H B — S. Herbert & Co. ,, 1750.
,,	WC — Wm. Caldecott ent. 1756.	,,	C·B — Name not traced.
,,	EC — Eben. Coker (probably).	,,	WA — Wm. Abdy ,, 1767.
,,	W F — Name not traced.	,,	G·F — Geo. Fayle ,, ,,
,,	ER — Emick Romer	,,	W·T — Wm. Tuite (probably).
,,	BM — Name not traced.	,,	J E — Name not traced.
,,	R✶P — ? R. Peaston.	1768-9	I·P E·W — John Parker & Edwd. Wakelin }
,,	I·A — John Allen ent. 1761.	,,	I·H — James Hunt ent. 1760.
,,	SH — Sam. Howland ,, 1760.	,,	W·C T·C — T. & W. Chawner (probably).
,,	GH — Geo. Hunter ,, 1765.	,,	R D·S — Dan. Smith & Robt. Sharp }
,,	T·C W·C — T. & W. Chawner (probably).	,,	W A L — Name not traced.
1766-7	LH — Name not traced.	,,	F·S — Fras. Spilsbury, Jr.
,,	L·C — Louisa Courtauld.	,,	E·T — ? Eliz. Tuite ent. 1741. (see 1742)
,,	J·L — John Lampfert ent. 1748.	,,	W J — Name not traced.
,,	I·L S — John Langford & John Sebille }	,,	E·C — Edward Capper (probably).
,,	MF — Matthew Ferris ,, 1759.	,,	F·C — Fras. Crump ent. 1756.
,,	T·H I·C — Thos. Hannam & John Crouch }	,,	W·P J·P — W. & J. Priest.
,,	FC — Fras. Crump ,, 1756.	,,	J·L — John Lamfert ,, 1748.
,,	GA — Geo. Andrews ,, 1763.	,,	B·B — Benj. Blakeley ,, 1739.
,,	J·D — Thos. Dealtry ,, 1765.	,,	I·D — John Darwall ,, 1768.
,,	C·M — Chas. Miegg ,, 1767.	1769	I·N — John Neville (probably).
,,	DM — Dorothy Mills (probably).	,,	H·G C·A — Chas. Aldridge & Henry Green }
,,	T·W — Thos Wynne ent. 1754.	,,	F·C — Fras. Crump ent. 1756.
1767-8	I R — Jno. Richardson ,, 1752.	,,	GS — Geo. Seatoun.
,,	I W·F K — Names not traced.	,,	CW — Chas. Woodward.

A COFFEE URN MADE IN LONDON IN 1765 BY PARKER & WAKELIN

DATE	MAKERS' MARK AND NAME.
1769-70	I·K — John Kentenber ent. 1757.
"	AL — Aug. Le Sage " 1767.
"	E·L — Edwd. Lowe " 1777.
"	W·B — Walter Brind " 1757.
"	W·G — Wm. Grundy " 1748.
"	SC I·C — Septimus & James Crespell }
"	T·I — Thos. Jackson " 1769.
"	LC GC — Louisa & Geo. Courtauld Cowles. }
"	RR — Robt. Rogers " 1773.
"	JB — John Baker " 1770.
1770-1	B·G — Benj. Gignac " 1744.
"	T·H — Thos. Heming " "
"	JA — Jas. Allen " 1766.
"	SC I·C — Septimus & James Crespell } see 1769.
"	T·P — ? Thos. Powell ent. 1756.
"	T·A — Thos. Arnold " 1770.
"	IB — John Baxter " 1773.
"	C·W — Chas. Wright.
"	I·B — ? John Buckett " 1770.
"	I·I·S — John Langford & John Sebille }
"	G·S — Name not traced.
"	ER — E. Romer (probably).
"	OJ — Orlando Jackson ent. 1759.
"	SW — Sam. Wheat " 1756.
"	W·G·V — John Wm. Gimblett & Vale } " 1770.
"	I·B — J. Bassingwhite " "
1771-2	I·C T·H — John Thos. Crouch & Hannam }

DATE	MAKERS' MARK AND NAME.
1771-2	T·F — Thos. Foster ent. 1769.
"	D·B — David Bell " 1756.
"	R I·S — ? Robt. & Jno. Schofield } " 1776.
"	T I·D — Thos. & Jabez Daniel }
"	S·B — ? Sarah Buttall " 1754.
"	J·A — Jonathan Alleine.
"	W·P — Wm. Penstone.
"	W·S — Wm. Sheen " 1755.
"	T·C — Thos. Chawner.
"	S·H — Saml. Howland " 1760.
"	A·U — A. Underwood.
"	C·C — Chas. Chesterman " 1771.
"	E·I — Edwd. Jay " 1757.
"	T·T — Thos. Towman (probably).
"	W·T — Wm. Tuite ent. 1756.
"	I·R — John Romer ent. before 1773.
1772-3	I·C — John Carter " "
"	T·C — Thos. Chawner " "
"	E·T — Eliz. Tookey " "
"	W·F — Wm. Fearn " "
"	B·D — Burrage Davenport " "
"	I·A — John Arnell " "
"	J·S — John Swift " "
"	P·N — Philip Norman " "
"	C·W — Chas. Wright " "
"	P·D — Peter Peter Desergnes or Deveste. }
"	W·a — ? Wm. Watkins " 1756.

DATE.	MAKERS' MARK AND NAME.	DATE.	MAKERS' MARK AND NAME.
1772-3	Henry Hallsworth.	1774-5	P. Freeman ent. 1774.
,,	Name not traced.	,,	Wm. Fennell.
,,	John Fayle ent. 1772.	,,	Jas. Young ,, 1775.
,,	Wm. Eley (probably).	,,	Jas. Stamp ,, 1774.
1773-4	Dan. Smith & ent. before Robt. Sharp 1773.	1775-6	Walter Tweedie ent. before 1773.
,,	Orlando Jackson ,, 1759.	,,	? Ed. Capper (see 1776).
,,	John Harvey ,, 1739.	,,	? Wm. Cox.
,,	Thos. Smith ,, 1750.	,,	? John Kentish Jas. King or ent. 1773. Jas. Kingman
,,	Name not traced.	,,	Wm. Sumner & Richd. Crossley ,, 1775.
,,	Abr'm Barrier & Lewis Ducornieu	,,	Jas. Young ,, ,,
,,	Wm. Sheen ,, 1775.	,,	Thos. Langford (probably).
,,	Jabez & Daniel see 1771. Thos.	,,	? John Easton & Wm. Fearn or Wm. Fennell, etc.
,,	Burrage Davenport.	,,	Robt. Ross ent. 1774.
,,	Saml. Wood (probably).	,,	Mark Cripps ,, 1767.
,,	P. Freeman ent. 1773.	,,	Chris. Woods ,, 1775.
,,	Mary Makemeid ,, ,,	,,	Richd. Rugg ,, ,,
,,	Thos. Tookey ,, ,,	,,	Robt. Jones ,, 1776.
,,	Louis de Lisle ,, ,,	,,	Geo. Baskerville & T. Morley ,, 1775.
,,	Wm. Le Bas ,, ,,	,,	Robt. Piercy ,, ,,
1774-5	Jas. Stamp ,, 1774.	,,	Louis Ducomieu ,, ,,
,,	Wm. Penstone ,, ,,	,,	Ben Stephenson ,, ,,
,,	Eliz. Tookey ,, 1773.	1776-7	Name not traced.
,,	Thos. Evans ,, 1774.	,,	Henry Sardet.
,,	Jas. Young & Orlando Jackson ,, ,,	,,	Robt. Piercy ,, ,,
,,	John Deacon ,, 1773.	,,	Alexr. Barnet ,, 1759.
,,	Thomas Daniel (probably).	,,	Nich. Dumee ,, 1776.
		,,	Geo. Heming & Wm. Chawner ,, 1774.

DATE.	MAKERS' MARK AND NAME.	DATE.	MAKERS' MARK AND NAME.
1776-7	I·L	John Lautier ent. 1773.	1778-9	NH	Nichs. Hearnden ent. 1773.
,,	I·W T	John Wakelin & Wm. Taylor } ,, 1776.	,,	ED	Ed. Dobson ,, 1778.
,,	H G C A	Chas. Aldridge & Henry Green } ,, 1775.	,,	RC DS RS	Rich. Carter, Danl. Smith & Robt. Sharp } ,, ,,
,,	A·C	A. Calame ,, 1764.	,,	WE GP	Wm. Eley & Geo. Pierpoint } ,, 1778.
,,	EC	Edwd. Capper or Edwd. Cooke } ,, 1773.	,,	ID	John Deacon ,, 1776.
,,	A·L	Aug. Le Sage ,, 1767.	,,	CK	Chas. Kandler ,, 1778.
,,	PR	Phil. Roker ,, 1776.	,,	EL	Ed. Lowe ,, 1777.
,,	ER	Eliz. Roker ,, ,,	,,	GR	Geo. Rodenbostel ,, 1778.
1777-8	HG	Henry Greenway ,, 1775.	,,	TW	Thos. Wallis ,, 1773.
,,	JA	Jon'th'n Alleine.	1779-80	IS	John Schofield ,, 1778.
,,	RM RC	Robt. Makepeace & Richd. Carter } ,, 1777.	,,	EF d	Edith Fennell ,, 1780.
,,	I·H	Joseph Heriot ,, 1750.	,,	W G H C	Geo. Heming & Wm. Chawner } ,, 1774. (see also 1781)
,,	WH	Wm. Holmes ,, 1776.	,,	HB	Hester Bateman ,, 1774.
,,	WP	Wm. Potter ,, 1777.	,,	T·S	Thos. Satchwell ,, 1773.
,,	W WH C	Wm. Howe & Wm. Clark } ,, ,,	,,	TP RP	Thos. & Richd. Payne } ,, 1777.
,,	WG	Wm. Grundy ,, ,,	,,	WF	W. L. Foster ,, 1775.
,,	GN	Geo. Natter ,, 1773.	,,	E WG F	Wm. Grundy & Ed. Fernell } ,, 1779.
,,	RI IS	Robt. Jones & John Schofield } ,, 1776.	,,	LC SC	Louisa & Samuel Courtauld } ,, 1777.
,,	GN	Name not traced.	1780-1	FS	Fras. Stamp ,, 1780.
,,	TD	T. Daniel ,, 1774.	,,	WG	Wm. Garrard (probably).
1778-9	H C A G	Name not traced.	,,	R D M	Jane Dorrell & Rich. May } ent. 1771.
,,	AF	Andrew Fogelberg.	,,	I·S	Jas. Sutton ,, 1780.
,,	JD	J. Denzilow.	,,	WV	Wm. Vincent ,, 1773.
,,	WE	Wm. Eley.	,,	IM WH	Jas. Mince & Wm. Hodgkins } ,, 1780.
,,	HB	Hester Bateman. ,, 1774.	,,	TB AH	T. P. Boulton & Arthur Humphreys } ,, ,,
,,	WH ND	Wm. Holmes & Nichs. Dumee } ,, 1773.	,,	IL IR	John Langlands & John Robertson } ,, ,, of Newcastle

DATE.	MAKERS' MARK AND NAME.		
1780-1	H·P	Name not traced.	
"	IP	Joseph Preedy.	
,"	I·K	John Kidder	ent. 1780.
1781-2	TP AH	T. B. Pratt & Arthur Humphreys }	" 1773.
"	C·W	Chas. Wright	" 1775.
"	RC	Robt. Cruickshank	" 1773.
"	IC TH	John Crouch & Thos. Hannam }	" "
"	I·L	Josh. Lejeune	" "
"	LK	Luke Kendall	" 1772.
"	GH WC	Geo. Heming & Wm. Chawner }	" 1781.
"	WP WW	Wm. Playfair & Wm. Wilson }	" 1782.
"	TD IW	Thos. Daniel & John Wall }	" 1781.
1782-3	GS	Geo. Smith	" 1782.
"	JW	John Wren	" 1777.
"	GG	George Giles (probably).	
"	AF SG	Andr. Fogelberg & Steph. Gilbert } ent. 1780.	
"	RH	Robt. Hennell	" 1773.
"	WB	Wm. Bayley.	
"	N A·A	This mark is A N S A. Name not traced.	
"	AP PP	Abm. Peterson & Peter Podie }	" 1783.
1783-4	I·L	John Lamb	" "
"	IS IB	Jas. Sutton & Jos. Bult }	" 1782.
"	WT	Wm. Tant	" 1773.
"	W·B	Wm. Brown (probably).	
"	S·B	?·Saml. Bradley.	
"	A·F S·G	Name not traced.	

Note. The interpretation given by Sir Charles Jackson, in the column, of the mark $\smash{^{N}_{A}}$A is incorrect; the mark complete is N A A S, and though found on a piece in the Draper collection, is probably bogus. The author has found the mark upon two fraudulent pieces of silver. The fact that no marks for "N A" or "A S" as individual silversmiths working during this period have appeared is a suspicious circumstance, as members of a partnership usually engage in business "on their own" either before or after the partnership. H. P. O.

DATE.	MAKERS' MARK AND NAME.				DATE.	MAKERS' MARK AND NAME.			
1783-4	E·F	Ed.	Fennell	ent. 1780.	1786-7	SG EW	Saml. & Edwd.	Godbehere Wigan }	ent. 1785.
,,	SW	Saml.	Wintle	,, 1783.	,,	T·P·AH	T. Arth.	Pratt & Humphreys }	,, 1780.
,,	W·S	Wm.	Sumner	,, 1782.	,,	W·S	Wm.	Sutton	,, 1784.
,,	JH	Name not traced.			,,	WR	Wm.	Reynolds	,, 1773.
,,	IT	John	Townshend	,, 1783.	,,		Robt.	Hennell	as 1782.
,,	TC	Thos.	Chawner	,, 1773.	,,	HC	Henry	Chawner	ent. 1786.
,,	IT	John	Tayleur	,, 1775.	,,	GG	Name not traced.		
,,	I·S	John	Schofield	,, 1778.	,,	CA	Chas.	Aldridge	,, 1786.
1784-5	LI	Name not traced.			,,	TD	Thos.	Daniel	,, 1774.
,,	BM	Do.	do.		,,	DD	Danl.	Denny	,, 1782.
,,	CH	Chas.	Hougham	,, 1785.	,,	WP	Wm.	Pitts	,, 1786.
,,	HG	Hen.	Greenway	,, 1775.	1787-8	SM	Saml.	Massey (probably).	
,,	SA	Stephen	Adams	,, 1760.	,,	JH	Name not traced.		
,,	SG	Saml.	Godbehere	,, 1784.	,,	WE	Wm.	Eley.	
,,	WS	Wm.	Simmons	,, 1776.	,,	T·M	Thos.	Mallison	ent. 1773.
,,	PG	Peter	Gillois	,, 1782.	,,	DS RS	Danl. Robt.	Smith & } Sharp }	,, 1780.
,,	RI	Robt.	Jones	,, 1778.	1788-9	EI	Edwd.	Jay	,, 1773.
1785-6	WA	Wm.	Abdy	,, 1784.	,,	IC	John	Carter	before ,,
,,	I·MF	Name not traced.			,,	TP	Thos.	Powell, probably 1770.	
,,	HV	Do.	do.		,,	GB	Geo.	Baskerville (probably).	
,,	B·L	Ben.	Laver	,, 1781.	,,	HC	Henry	Cowper	ent 1782.
,,	W·T	Walter	Tweedie	,, 1775.	,,	CB	Cornls.	Bland	,, 1788.
,,	TW	Thos.	Wallis	,, 1778.	,,	TO	Thos.	Ollivant	,, 1789.
,,	TD	Thos.	Daniel	,, 1774.	1789-90	HB	Hester	Bateman	,, 1774.
,,	I·K	John	Kidder	,, 1780.	,,	HG	Henry	Greenway	,, 1775.
,,	TS	Thos.	Shepherd	,, 1785.	,,	IT	John	Thompson	,, 1785.
,,	A·B	Abm.	Barrier	,, 1775.	,,	I·E	John	Edwards	,, 1788.

DATE.	MAKERS' MARK AND NAME.				DATE.	MAKERS' MARK AND NAME.			
1789-90	TW	Thos.	Willmore	ent. 1790.	1792-3	WF PS	Wm. Paul.	Frisbee & Storr }	ent. 1792.
,,	PC	Name not traced.			,,	IF	John	Fountain	,, ,,
1790-1	P·P	Peter	Podie	,, 1783.	,,	TG	Thos.	Graham	,, ,,
,,	TP ER	T. E.	Phipps & Robinson }		,,	EI	Edwd.	Jay	,, ,,
,,	GS WF	Geo. Wm.	Smith & Fearn }	,, 1786.	1793-4	I·W R·G	J. Robt.	Wakelin & Garrard }	,, ,,
,,	RH	Robt.	Hennell	,, 1773.	,,	IM	John	Moore	,, 1778.
,,	PB IB	Peter & Jonath'n	Bateman }	,, 1790.	,,	I·S	John	Schofield	,, ,,
,,	SD	Saml.	Davenport	,, 1786.	,,	PB AB	Peter & Ann	Bateman	,, 1791.
,,	WA	Wm.	Abdy	,, 1784.	,,	RM TM	Robt. & Thos.	Makepeace	,, 1794.
,,	AP	Abm.	Peterson	,, 1790.	,,	DU NH	Duncan Naphtäli	Urquhart & Hart }	,, 1791.
1791-2	WP JP	Wm. Jos.	Pitts & Preedy }	,, 1791.	,,	I·F I·B	John John	Fountain & Beadnall }	,, 1793.
,,	GB	Geo.	Baskerville (probably).		,,	W·F I·F	Wm. & John	Fisher	,, ,,
,,	GS	Geo.	Smith	ent. 1773.	1794-5	WF	Wm.	Frisbee	,, 1792.
,,	RS	Robt.	Salmon	,, ,,	,,	I·K	John	King	,, 1785.
,,	WF DP	Wm. Danl.	Fountain & Pontifex }	,, 1791.	,,	MB	? Mark	Bock (see 1798).	
,,	IB EB	Jas. & Eliz.	Bland }	,, ,,	,,	F·T	? Francis Thurkle.		
,,	JL	John	Lamb	,, 1783.	,,	JR	John	Robins	ent. 1774.
,,	TS	Thos.	Streetin	,, 1791.	,,	JW	John	Wren	,, 1777.
,,	EB	Name not traced.			,,	MP	Michl.	Plummer	,, 1791.
,,	SG RW	Do.	do.		,,	WJ	W.	Fountain	,, 1794.
1792-3	W·L	Do.	do.		,,	TN GB	Thos. Geo.	Northcote & Bourne }	,, ,,
,,	W·P I·P	Wm. Jos.	Pitts & Preedy { see above }		1795-6	RG	Richd. Robt.	Gardner or Gaze	,, 1773. ,, 1795.
,,	HC	Henry	Chawner	ent. 1786.	,,	TE	Thos.	Ellis	,, 1780.
,,	TH	Thos.	Howell	,, 1791.	,,	RM	Robt.	Makepeace	,, 1795.
,,	TN	Thos.	Northcote.		,,	PB AB	Peter & Ann	Bateman	,, 1791.
,,	GS TH	Geo. Thos.	Smith & Hayter }	ent. 1792.	,,	TP AH	T. B. Arthur	Pratt & Humphreys }	,, 1780.
					,,	WE	Wm.	Eley.	

DATE.	MAKERS' MARK AND NAME.			
1795-6	SH	Name not traced.		
"	IP IP	J. & J.	Perkins	ent. 1795.
"	HN	Henry	Nutting	,, 1796.
1796-7	SP	Name not traced.		
"	RH DH	Robt. & David	Hennell }	,, 1795.
"	IM	John	Mewburn	,, 1793.
"	IBO	Jos. B.	Orme	,, 1796.
"	WEH	Wm.	Hall	,, 1795.
"	HC IE	Hy. Jno.	Chawner & Eames }	,, 1796.
1797-8	RC	Richd.	Crossley	,, 1782.
"	HC IE	Henry John	Chawner & Emes }	,, 1796.
"	GC	Geo.	Cowles	,, 1797.
1798-9	EM	E.	Morley.	
"	IP	Jos.	Preedy	,, 1777.
"	IB	John	Beldon	,, 1784.
"	WE WF	Wm. Wm.	Eley & Fearn }	,, 1797.
"	GS	Geo.	Smith.	
"	IH TL	Jos. Thos.	Hardy & Lowndes }	,, 1798.
"	M·B	? Mark Bock.		
"	JE	John	Emes.	
"	T·D	Thos.	Dealtry	,, 1765.
1799 1800	WP	Wm.	Pitts	,, 1781.
"	WB	Wm.	Bennett	,, 1796.
"	WP	Wm.	Pitts	,, 1799.
"	RC	Richd.	Cooke	,, ,,
"	AF	Andrew	Fogelberg	,, 1776.
"	IH	John	Hutson	,, 1784.
"	WS	Name not traced.		

DATE.	MAKERS' MARK AND NAME.			
1799 1800	IP	Jos.	Preedy	ent. 1800.
1800-1	P·S	Paul	Storr	,, 1793.
"	I·W R·G	J. Robt.	Wakelin & Garrard }	,, 1792.
"	WH	Wm.	Hall	,, 1795.
"	SG EW IB	Saml. Ed. J.	Godbehere Wigan & Bult }	,, 1800.
"	TH IC	Thos. John	Hannam & Crouch }	,, 1799.
1801-2	RG	Robt.	Garrard	,, 1801.
"	I·P	John	Parker.	
"	JE	John	Emes	,, 1796.
"	PB AB WB	Peter, Ann & Wm.	Bateman }	,, 1800.
"	GS TH	Geo. Thos.	Smith & Hayter }	,, 1792.
"	RH DH SH	Robert, David & Saml.	Hennell }	
1802-3	IH	John	Harris	,, 1786.
"	DS BS	Digby Benj.	Scott & Smith }	,, 1802.
"	HB	Wm.	Burwash	,, ,,
"	PB AB WB	Peter, Ann & Wm.	Bateman }	,, 1800.
"	AB GB	Alice & George	Burrows	,, 1802.
"	CB TB	Christr. & T. W.	Barker	,, 1800.
1803-4	BL	Benj.	Laver	,, 1781.
"	TH	Thos.	Holland	,, 1798.
"	GB TB	G. & T.	Burrows.	
"	SG W	Saml. & George	Whitford	,, 1802.
"	AJ	Name not traced.		
"	IR	John	Robins (probably).	
"	TR	? Timothy Renou.		
"	JA	John	Austin.	
1804-5	W·P	Wm	Purse.	

DATE.	MAKERS' MARK AND NAME.
1804-5	S·B Name not traced.
„	RB&R Rundell, Bridge & Rundell.
„	GW Geo. Wintle ent. 1804.
„	RG Robt. Garrard „ 1802.
„	I·H Jos. Hardy „ 1799.
„	HN Hannah Northcote „ 1798.
1805-6	DP Danl. Pontifex „ 1794.
„	J·E John Emes.
„	TA ? T. Ash.
„	W·B R·S Wm. Burwash & Richd. Sibley } „ 1805.
„	TS Name not traced.
1806-7	RH SH R. & S. Hennell „ 1802.
„	PB WB Peter & Wm. Bateman „ 1805.
„	JS John Sanders (probably).
„	CF Crespin Fuller „
„	IS John Salkeld „
„	T·R Thos. Robins „
„	WF Wm. Fountain ent. 1794.
1807-8	TG IC T. & J. Guest & Josh. Cradock } „ 1806.
„	PB WB P. & W. Bateman „ 1805.
„	SW Saml. Whitford „ 1807.
„	T·H Thos. Halford „ „
„	BS Name not traced.
„	IR T. Robins „ „
„	IWS ? J. W. Storey.
1808-9	I·C John Crouch „ 1808.
„	RSW Name not traced.

DATE.	MAKERS' MARK AND NAME.
1808-9	TM ? T. W. Matthews.
„	I·C John· Crouch ent. 1808.
„	E·M E. Morley.
„	WE WF WC Wm. Eley, Wm. Fearn & Wm. Chawner } „ „
„	HN RH Henry. Nutting & Robt. Hennell } „ „
„	RC GS Richard Crossley & Geo.. Smith } „ 1807.
„	W·S Wm. Sumner „ 1802.
„	JC John Crouch „ 1808.
1809-10	CH Chas. Hougham „ 1785.
„	TW Thos. Wallis „ 1792.
„	DW David Windsor (probably).
„	TJ Thomas Jenkinson „
„	SJ Name not traced.
1810-1	TH SH Do. do.
„	RC ? Richd. Cooke ent. 1799.
„	BS IS Benj. Smith & Jas. Smith. }
„	TP ER T. Phipps & E. Robinson }
„	SB IB Name not traced.
„	TW JH Thos. Wallis & Jonath'n Hayne } „ 1810.
„	IC TH John Cotton & Thos. Head. } „ 1809.
1811-2	JB James Beebe „ 1811.
„	BS Benj. & Jas. Smith.
„	WK Wm. Kingdon (probably).
„	RR Robt. Rutland ent. 1811.
„	SH Saml. Hennell „ „
„	DS BS IS Digby Scott, Benj. Smith, Jas. Smith } (probably).

AN EARLY GEORGE III ÉPERGNE. MADE BY THOMAS POWELL, LONDON, 1765

DATE.	MAKERS' MARK AND NAME.
1812-3	**T·B** ? T. Barker.
"	**JS** ? John Sanders.
"	**TI** Thos. Jenkinson (probably).
"	**RE EB** Rebecca Emes & Edwd. Barnard } ent. 1808.
"	**GS** Geo. Smith " 1812.
"	**MS ES** Mary & Eliz. Sumner " 1809.
1813-4	**IC WR** Jos. Craddock & Wm. Reid } " 1812.
"	**P·S** BRITANNIA Paul Storr " 1793.
"	**IWS WE** J. W. Story & W. Elliott } " 1809.
1814-5	**SH** Saml. Hennell " 1811.
"	**RE EB** Emes & Barnard " 1808.
"	**SA** Stephen Adams, junr.
"	**W·B** Wm. Bell (probably).
"	**W·E** Wm. Elliott ent. 1810.
"	**IL WA** Name not traced.
"	**SH IT** S. Hennell & J. Taylor } (probably).
1815-6	**TP ER JP** Name not traced.
"	**JE EF** Do. do.
"	**I·P G·P** Do. do.
"	Emes & Barnard as above.
"	**RG** Robt. Garrard ent. 1801.
"	**CR DR** Christ'n Reid & ano'r of Newcastle " 1815.
1816-7	**W·B** Wm. Burwash " 1813.
"	**IL** Jas. Lloyd.
1817-8	**S SR IED** Name not traced.

DATE.	MAKERS' MARK AND NAME.
1817-8	**WB** Wm. Bateman ent. 1815.
"	**M·S** Name not traced.
"	**WC** Wm. Chawner " "
"	**TR** T. Robins (probably).
"	**WC** Wm. Chawner ent. 1815.
"	**GP** Geo. Purse.
1818-9	**GW** Geo. Wintle " 1813.
"	**IW** Joseph Wilson.
"	**RG** Robt. Garrard " 1801.
1819-20	**SR ID** Name not traced.
"	**AH** Do. do.
"	**HN** Henry Nutting " 1809.
"	**WS** Wm. Stevenson (probably).
"	**TI** See 1812-3 above.
"	**PR** Philip Rundell ent. 1819.
1820-1	**W·B** Wm. Bateman " 1815.
"	**I·L H·L** John & Henry Lias " 1819.
1821-2	**TB** Thos. Baker " 1815. or Thos. Balliston " 1819.
"	**IET** ? J. E. Terry & Co. " 1818.
"	**ICF** ? John Foligno.
"	**COCO** An Exeter maker (probably).
"	**JA IA** J. & J. Aldous "
1822-3	**PS** Paul Storr "
"	**WA** William Abdy "
"	**WT** Wm. Trayes ent. 1822.
1823-4	**IS** Name not traced.
"	**JA** John Angell (probably).

DATE.		MAKERS' MARK AND NAME.
1823-4	I·B	John Bridge ent. 1823.
,,	BS	Benj. Smith.
1824-5	TH GH	Thos. & Geo. Hayter ,, 1816.
,,	SC	Name not traced.
,,	R·H	Robt. Hennell.
,,	F·F	Name not traced.
,,	WE CF IE	Do. do.
,,	GK	Geo. Knight (probably).
,,	WE	Wm. Edwards· (,,).
1825-6	IC	James Collins (,,).
,,	IB	John Bridge ent. 1823.
,,	RP	R. Peppin (probably).
,,	CE	C. Eley (,,).
,,	FH	Fras. Higgins (,,).
1826-7	IL HL CL	John, Henry } Lias ent. 1823. & Chas.
,,	A·B·S	A. B. Savory ,, 1826.
,,	RC	Randall ·Chatterton ,, 1825.
1827-8	BP	Name not traced.
,,	T·C·S	T. Cox Savory ,, 1827.
,,	JW	Jacob Wintle ,, 1826.
,,	ME	Moses Emmanuel (probably).
1828-9	WS	Wm. Schofield (,,).
,,	ES	E. S. Sampson (,,).
1829-30	IH	Jas. Hobbs (,,).
,,	EE	Edward Edwards.
,,	RG	Robt. Garrard ent. 1801.
1830·1.	C·P	Chas. Plumley (probably).

DATE.		MAKERS' MARK AND NAME.
1830-1	T·D	Thos. Dexter (probably).
,,	RA WS	Name not traced.
1831-2	W·H	,, ,,
,,	R·H	R. Hennell.
1833-4	PS	Paul Storr ent. 1793.
,,	AS S AS	Adey, Joseph } Savory ,, 1833. & Albert
1834-5	N·M	N. Morrison (probably).
,,	IF	Jas. Franklin ,,
,,	WB	W. Bellchambers ,,
,,	RP CP	Name not traced
,,	T·E	T. Eley.
1835-6	CF	Chas. Fox ent. 1822.
,,	J.C.E	J. Chas. Edington ,, 1828.
,,	CR GS	Reily & Storer (probably).
1836-7	CF	See 1835-6.
,,	EB EB JB W	Edwd. Barnard, Edwd. Barnard, jr., } ent. 1829. John Barnard, & Wm. Barnard
1837-8	WE	Wm. Eaton.
,,	RS	Richard Sibley (probably).
,,	GW	George Webb ,,
,,	RG	Robert Garrard ent. 1821.
,,	MC	Mary Chawner.
1838-9	WT RA	Wm. Theobalds } ,, 1838. & Robt. Atkinson
,,	CR GS	Rawlins & Sumner.
1839-40	WB DB	Wm. Bateman & } ,, 1839. Danl. Ball
,,	FD	Francis Dexter ,, ,,
,,	WC	Wm. Cooper (probably).
,,	I·T	Jos. Taylor ,,

DATE.	MAKERS' MARK AND NAME.			DATE.	MAKERS' MARK AND NAME.		
1839-40	EE	Ed.	Edwards (probably).	1847-8	EE	Eliz.	Eaton.
1840-1	GL	Name not traced.		1848-9	EJ BW	E. J. & W.	Barnard. }
,,	TC	Thos.	Cording ,,	,,	RH	R.	Hennell.
,,	GA	Geo. W. Adams	ent. 1840.	,,	JW	Jacob	Wintle (probably).
,,	JA JA	J. & J. Aldous."		1849-50	CTF GF	Chas. T. Geo.	Fox & Fox }
,,	MC GA	Mary Chawner & Geo. W. Adams } ,, ,,		,,	FD	Frans.	Douglas.
1841-2	JS AS	Jos. & Albert Savory ,, ,,		,,	WRS	W. R.	Smily.
,,	J·L	John Lacy or John Law } (probably).		1850-1	IK	John	Keith.
1842-3	JCE	J. Chas. Edington ent. 1828.		,,	GI	George	Ivory.
,,	R·H	R.	Hennell.	1851-2	EB JB	E. & J.	Barnard.
,,	WB WS	Brown & Somersall (probably).		1852-3	JE	James	Edwards (probably).
1843-4	WKR	Wm. K. Reid.		,,	IF	I.	Foligno.
,,	WB	Wm.	Brown (possibly).	1853-4	EB &JB	E. & J.	Barnard.
,,	J·A J·A	Joseph & John Angel see 1844.		1854-5	WR S	W. R.	Smily.
,,	R·S	Richd. Sibley ent. 1837.		1855-6	GA	George	Angell.
1844-5	R·G	R.	Garrard ,, 1801.	1856-7	CTF GF	Chas. T. Geo.	Fox & Fox }
,,	J·A & J·A	Joseph & John Angel.		1857-8	HW	Henry	Wilkinson of Sheffield.
,,	RGH	R. G.	Hennell.	1858-9	J·A	Joseph	Angell.
,,	BS	Benj.	Smith (probably).	,,	W·M	W.	Mann.
1845-6	ISH	John S. Hunt ent. 1844.		,,	GR EB	Roberts & Briggs.	
,,	CTF GF	Chas. T. Fox & Geo. Fox. }		1859-60	GA	George	Angell.
1846-7	GFP	G. F.	Pinnell.	1860-1	EE JE	Messrs.	Eady.
,,	H·H	Hyam	Hyams.	,,	CR WS	Rawlins & Sumner.	
,,	EB J &W	E. J. & W.	Barnard.	1861-2	RH	Robt.	Harper.
1847-8	IL HL	John & Henry Lias.		1862-3	R·H	Richard	Hennell.
,,	RP GB	R. Pearce & G. Burrows. }		1863-4	GF	Geo.	Fox.
				1864-5	GA	Geo.	Angell.

CHAPTER V

Marks on York Plate

From 1411 to 1560 all silver plate made in York should have been marked with the leopard's head and fleur-de-lys, both dimidiated (cut vertically in half) and joined in a single stamp. The use of date letters probably commenced in 1560 though no earlier example than the D given in Table I has been found. The assay office in York was abolished in 1858.

TABLE I.

	TOWN MARK.	DATE LETTER.	MAKER'S MARK.	MAKER'S NAME.
ELIZ. 1559-60		A		... ...
1560-1		B		... .
1561-2		C		...
1562-3	[mark]	D	RG	Robert Gylmyn.
1563-4		E		... ...
1564-5	[mark]	F	M	... ...
1565-6		G		... ...
1566-7	[mark]	H	[mark]	Christopher Hunton.
1567-8		I		... ...
1568-9	[mark]	K	RB / TS / WX	Robert Beckwith. / Thomas Symson. / ...
1569-70	[mark]	L	RG	Robert Gylmyn.
1570-1		M	[heart]	Name not traced.
1571-2		N		
1572-3	[mark]	O	{mark / WF}	John Lund. / William Foster.
1573-4		P		... ...
1574-5	"	Q	GK	George Kitchen.
1575-6	[mark]	R	"	" "
1576-7		S	TW	Thomas Waddie.
1577-8	"	T		Indistinguishable.
1578-9		V		... ...
1579-80		W		... ...
1580-1		X		... ...
1581-2		Y		... ...
1582-3	"	Z	WR	William Rawnson.

TABLE II.

	TOWN MARK.	DATE LETTER.	MAKER'S MARK.	MAKER'S NAME.
1583-4	[mark]	a	WR	Wm. Rawnson.
1584-5	[mark]	b	"	" "
1585-6		c		... ...
1586-7		d		... ...
1587-8	"	e	GK	Geo. Kitchen.
1588-9		f		... ...
1589-90		g		... ...
1590-1	"	h	GK	Geo. Kitchen.
1591-2		i		... ...
1592-3	[mark]	k	{WR / RG}	Wm. Rawnson. / Robt. Gylmyn.
1593-4	"	l	WH	? Wm. Hutchinson.
1594-5	"	m	GK	Geo. Kitchen.
1595-6	'	n		... ...
1596-7	'	o		... ...
1597-8	"	p	CH	Chris. Harrington.
1598-9		q		... ...
1599 1600	"	r	FT	Fras. Tempest.
1600-1		s		... ...
1601-2	"	t	"	" "
1602-3		u		... ...
JAS. I. 1603-4		w		... ...
1604-5	"	x	CH	Chris. Harrington.
1605-6		y		... ...
1606-7		z		... ...

TABLE III.

	TOWN MARK.	DATE LETTER.	MAKER'S MARK.	MAKER'S NAME.	
1607-8				John	Moody ?
1608-9				Robt.	Casson.
				Peter	Pearson.
1609-10	,,			Fras.	Tempest.
1610-1	,,			Peter	Pearson.
			,,	,,	,,
1611-2	,,			Chris.	Harrington
1612-3	,.			Fras.	Tempest.
1613-4				Peter	Pearson.
1614-5	,,			,,	,,
1615-6				Chris.	Mangy.
				Fras.	Tempest.
1616-7	,,		,,	,,	,,
1617-8				...	... ...
1618-9	,,			Sem.	Casson.
1619-20	,,			Peter	Pearson.
1620-1	,,			Sem.	Casson.
1621-2	,,			Peter	Pearson.
1622-3			,,	,,	,,
1623-4				Robt.	Williamson.
				...	... ...
1624-5				Thos.	Harrington.
CHAS. I 1625-6				Robt.	Harrington.
1626-7	,,			?	
1627-8	,,			James	Plummer.
1628-9				...	... ..
1629-30	,,			Chris.	Mangy.
1630-1	,,			Thomas	Waite.

TABLE IV.

	TOWN MARK.	DATE LETTER.	MAKER'S MARK.	MAKER'S NAME.	
1631-2				Sem.	Casson.
1632-3			,,	,,	,,
1633-4	,,			Robt.	Harrington.
1634-5	,,			Thos.	Harrington.
1635-6	,,			John	{ Thomason or Thompson.
1636-7				Robt.	Harrington.
1637-8				Thos.	Harrington.
1638-9	,,			Robt. or Richd.	Williamson, Senr. Waite.
1639-40	,,			Francis	Bryce.
1640-1				...	... ...
1641-2	,,			John	Thomason.
1642-3	,,			Thos.	Harrington.
1643-4	,,			John	Thomason.
1644-5				...	... ...
1645-6	,,			Chris.	Mangy.
1646-7				...	... ...
1647-8				...	... ...
1648-9				...	... ..
COMWTH. 1649-50				James	Plummer.
1650-1				,,	,,
1651-2	,,			,,	,,
1652-3	,.			,,	,,
1653-4				...	... ...
1654-5	,,			Thomas	Waite.
1655-6	,,			,,	,,
1656-7	,,			Philemon Marsh.	

TABLE V.

	TOWN MARK.	DATE LETTER	MAKER'S MARK	MAKER'S NAME.	
1657-8		A	IP	John	Plummer.
1658-9		B	"	"	"
1659-60		C	{W, IT	Wm. John	Waite. Thomason.
1660-1	"	D	IP	John	Plummer.
1661-2	"	E	"	"	"
1662-3		F	{GM	" George	" Mangy.
1663-4		G	MB	Marmaduke Best.	
1664-5	"	H	RW	Robt.	Williamson.
1665-6	"	J	IP	John	Plummer.
1666-7		K	TM	Thos.	Mangy.
1667-8	"	L	MB	Marmaduke Best.	
1668-9	"	M	PM	Philemon	Marsh.
1669-70	"	N	TM	Thomas	Mangy,
1670-1		O	MB	Marmaduke Best.	
1671-2	"	P	{RK	Roland "	" Kirby.
1672-3		Q	IT	John	Thompson.
1673-4	"	R	MB	Marmaduke Best.	
1674-5	"	S	{RW, TM	Robt Thos.	Williamson. Mangy.
1675-6	"	T	WM	Wm.	Mascall.
1676-7	"	U	HL	Henry	Lee.
1677-8	"	V	WB	Wm.	Busfield.
1678-9	"	W	IP	John	Plummer.
1679-80		X	IT	John	Thompson.
1680-1	"	Y	WB	Wm.	Busfield.
1681-2	"	Z	TM	Thos.	Mangy.

TABLE VI.

	TOWN MARK.	DATE LETTER	MAKER'S MARK	MAKER'S NAME.	
1682-3		A	GG	George	Gibson.
*1683-4	"	B	WB	Wm.	Busfield.
1684-5 JAS. II.		C	{JC, IP	John John	Camidge. Plummer.
1685-6		D	RC	Richd.	Chew.
1686-7	"	E	IS	John	Smith.
1687-8	"	F	IO	John	Oliver.
1688-9	"	G	CW	Chris.	Whitehill.
WM. & MY. 1689-90	"	H	WB	Wm.	Busfield.
1690-1		J	W	Robt.	Williamson.
1691-2		K	CR	Charles	Rhoades.
1692-3	"	L	CW	Chris.	Whitehill.
1693-4	"	M	MG	Mark	Gill.
1694-5		N	WB	Wm.	Busfield.
1695-6 WM. III.		O	CR	Clement	Reed.
1696-7	"	P	WB	Wm.	Busfield.
1697-8	"	Q	IS	John	Smith.
1698-9	"	R		Wm.	Busfield as above.
1699 / 1700		S		...	... ...

* 1683-4   B   TM   Thomas   Mangy.

The missing date letter for 1676–7 was found by the author while this book was in the press. It is and is on the spoon shown on plate facing page 6.

TABLE VII.

	TOWN MARK.	BRIT. ANNIA.	LION'S HEAD ERASED.	DATE LETTER.	MAKER'S MARK.	MAKER'S NAME.
1700-1				A	CG	Chas. Goldsborough (probably)
1701-2				B	Tu BE	Danl. Turner. John Best.
ANNE. 1702-3	,,	,,	,,	C	Bu	Wm. Busfield.
1703-4	,,	,,	,,	D	LA	John Langwith.
1704-5						
1705-6	,,	,,	,,	F	,,	,, ,,
1706-7	,,	,,	,,	G	RH	Chas. Rhoades.
1707-8					LA	John Langwith.
1708-9	,,	,,	,,	J	WI	Wm. Williamson.
1709-10					WA	?
1710-11						
1711-2	,,	,,	,,	M	LA	John Langwith.
1712-3						
1713-4	,,	,,	,,	O	,,	,, ,,
GEO. I. 1714-5						

Possibly a variation of the date letter for 1701-2.

The York Assay Office was closed in 1716 and re-opened in 1776.

In Table VIII letters not in shields are hypothetical. A new alphabet was employed from 1787-8.

TABLE VIII.

FIVE STAMPS UNTIL 1784–5, THENCEFORWARD SIX STAMPS AS BELOW.

	Town Mark.	Lion Passant.	Leopard's Head Crowned.	Date Letter.	King's Head.	Maker's Mark.	MAKER'S NAME.	ARTICLES AND OWNERS.
1776-7				A			,, ,,, ,,,	Date-letter conjectured.
1777-8				B			,, ,,, ,,,	Do. do.
1778-9				C			,, ,,, ,,,	Do. do.
1779-80				D		HP	J. Hampston & J. Prince }	Communion cup: Warthill. Bowls (1783): Messrs. Crichton.
1780-1				E			,, ,, ,,	Date-letter conjectured.
1781-2				F			,, ,, ,,	Communion flagons: All Saints', North Street, York.
1782-3	,,	.		G			,, ,, ,,	Paten on foot; All Saints', North Street, York.
1783-4	,,	.	,,	H		HP	,, ,, ,,	Com. cup: Huntington, nr. York. (no town mark.)
1784-5	,,	.	.	J		HP	Hampston & Prince.	Plate . Messrs. Crichton. Com. cup: Holme, nr. York.
1785-6				K		.	- - -	Date-letter conjectured.
1786-7				L		.	,, - .	Do. do.

TABLE IX.

SIX STAMPS AS BELOW.

	TOWN MARK.	LION PASSANT.	LEOPARD'S HEAD CROWNED	KING'S HEAD.	DATE LETTER.	MAKER'S MARK.	MAKER'S NAME.	ARTICLES AND OWNERS.
1787-8	⊕	🦁	🐆	👑	A	HP&P	J. Hampston & J. Prince.. }	Noted by the Author.
1788-9					b		... ...	Date-letter conjectured.
1789-90	,,	,,	,,	,,	c	,,	,, ,,	Table-spoons : Mr. Greenwood.
1790-1	,,	,,	,,	,,	d	,,	,, ,,	Com. flagon, dated 1791 : St. John's, Micklegate, York.
1791-2	,,	,,	,,	,,	e	,,	,, ,,	Com. flagon, dated 1792 : Kirk Deighton, York.
1792-3					f		... ...	Date-letter conjectured.
1793-4	,,	,,	,,	,,	g	,,	,, ,,	Table-forks : Mr. Greenwood.
1794-5					h		... ...	Date-letter conjectured.
1795-6	,,	,,	,,	,,	i	HP&P	,, ,,	Com. cup : Askham Bryan, Yorks.
1796-7	,,	,,	,,	🐆	K	,,	,, ,,	Goblet : Mr. J. H. Walter, Drayton, Norwich.
1797-8					l or L		... ...	Date-letter conjectured.
1798-9	,,	,,	,,	,,	M	HP &Co	H. Prince & Co.	Com. flagon, dated 1798 : Warter, Yorks.
1799 1800	,,	,,	,,	,,	N	,,	,, ,,	Table-forks : Mr. Greenwood.
1800-1	,,	,,	,,	,,	O	HP&C	,, ,,	Plain cup : Mr. Bradford.
1801-2	,,	,,	,,	,,	P	HP&C	,, ,,	Tea-spoons : Mr. Lowe.
1802-3	,,	,,	,,	,,	Q	,,	,, ,,	Gravy-spoon : Do.
1803-4	,,	,,	,,	,,	R	,,	,, ,,	Beakers and waiter : Messrs. Crichton.
1804-5	,,	,,	,,	,,	S	,,	,, ,,	Trowel : Mr. Colburne.
1805-6	,,	,,	,,	,,	T	,,	,, ,,	Noted by the Author.
1806-7					U		... ...	Date-letter conjectured.
1807-8	,,	,,	,,	,,	V	RC JB	Robt. Cattle & J. Barber. }	Communion cups : St. John's, Micklegate, York.
1808-9	,,	,,	,,	,,	W	,,	,, ,,	Skewer : Messrs. Crichton.
1809-10	,,	,,	,,	,,	X	,,	,, ,,	Salt-cellars and spoon : Mr. Williams.
1810-1	,,	,,	,,	,,	Y	,,	,, ,,	Table-spoon : Messrs. Robinson & Fisher.
1811-2					Z		... ...	Date-letter conjectured.

1805-6 [T]   1807-8 [V]   1809-10 [X]   Possibly variants of date-letters in above cycle. Stamped on small brass plate from the Assay Office.

[leopard's head] Also example of leopard's head, probably used from 1790 to 1836. Stamped on small brass plate from the Assay Office.

1787 to 1796 [head]   1796 to 1815-6 [head]   1816 to 1820 [head]   1820 to 1830 [head]   [head] Variants of Sovereigns' heads. Stamped on small brass plate from the Assay Office.

TABLE X.

SIX STAMPS AS BELOW.

	TOWN MARK.	LION PASSANT.	LEOPARD'S HEAD CROWNED.	KING'S HEAD.	DATE LETTER.	MAKER'S MARK.	MAKER'S NAME.	ARTICLES AND OWNERS.
** 1812-3	✠	🦁	👑	👤	𝖆	JB WW	James Barber & Wm. Whitwell }	Dessert-forks: Messrs. Crichton.
1813-4					𝖇		... ...	Date-letter recorded.
1814-5					𝖈		... ...	Do. do.
1815-6	,,	,,	,,	,,	𝖉	,,	,, ,,	Dessert-spoons: Messrs. Crichton.
1816-7					𝖊		... ...	Date-letter recorded.
1817-8	,,	,,	,,	,,	𝖋	,,	,, ,,	Salt-cellars and milk-jug: Messrs. Crichton.
1818-9	,,	,,	,,	,,	𝖌	,,	,, ,,	Com. flagon: St. Cuthbert's, York.
1819-20					𝖍		.. ..	Date-letter recorded.
GEO. IV. 1820-1		,,	,,	,,	𝖎	,,	,, ,,	Table-forks: Messrs. Crichton.
1821-2		,,	,,	,,	𝖐	,,	,, ,,	Table-forks and snuffers tray: Messrs. Crichton.
1822-3					𝖑			Date-letter recorded.
1823-4					𝖒		... ...	Do. do.
1824-5	,,	,,	,,	,,	𝖓	JB &Co	Jas. Barber & Co.	Com. cup: St. John's, Micklegate, York.
1825-6	,,	,,	,,	,,	𝖔	BC &N	Jas. Barber, Geo. Cattle & Wm. North }	Mustard-pot: Messrs. Crichton.
1826-7		,,	,,	,,	𝖕	,,	,, ,,	Noted by the Author.
1827-8					𝖖		... ...	Date-letter recorded.
1828-9	,,	,,	,,	,,	𝖗	,,	,, ,,	Table-forks: Mr. Maurice Freeman.
1829-30	,,	,,	,,	,,	𝖘	JB GC WN	,, ,,	Fish-slice: Messrs. Crichton.
WM. IV. 1830-1	🅓	,,	,,	🅒	𝖙	JB GC WN	,, ,,	Table-forks: Mr. Arthur J. Brown.
1831-2		,,	,,	,,	𝖚	,,	,, ,,	Communion paten: Slingsby Yorks.
1832-3					𝖛		... ...	Date-letter recorded.
1833-4					𝖜		... ...	Do. do.
1834-5					𝖝		... ...	Do. do.
1835-6					𝖞		... ...	Do. do.
1836-7					𝖟		... ...	Do. do.

* In examples of marks from 1812 onward, the leopard's head is sometimes found with whiskers and sometimes without.

1812-3 🅐   1813-4 🅑   1815-6 🅓   1819-20 🅗

1820-1 🅘   1821-2 🅚   1823-4 🅜   1831-2 🅤   1833-4 🅦

Possibly variants of date-letters in above cycle. Stamped on small brass plate from the Assay Office.

TABLE XI.

SIX STAMPS TILL 1848, FIVE AFTERWARD AS BELOW.

	TOWN MARK.	LION PASSANT.	LEOPARD'S HEAD CROWNED, TILL 1848.	QUEEN'S HEAD.	DATE LETTER.	MAKER'S MARK.	MAKER'S NAME.	ARTICLES AND OWNERS.
VICT. 1837-8					A	JB WN	Jas. Barber & Wm. North }	Waiter: Messrs. Crichton.
1838-9	,,	,,	,,	,,	B	,,	,, ,,	Noted by the Author.
1839-40	,,	,,	,,	,,	C	,,	,, ,,	Communion cup: Otley.
1840-1	,,	,,	,,		D	,,	,, ,,	Communion plate: Bishopthorpe.
1841-2	,,	,,	,,	,,	E	,,	,, ,,	Noted by the Author.
1842-3	,,	,,	,,	,,	F	,,	,, ,,	Com. cup: St. Maurice, York.
1843-4	,,	,,	,,	,,	G	,,	,, ,,	Noted by the Author.
1844-5	,,	,,	,,	,,	H	,,	,, ,,	Paten: Dishforth.
1845-6	,,	,,	,,	,,	I	,,	,, ,,	Alms plate: Bishopthorpe.
1846-7					K	...	... ...	Date-letter conjectured.
1847-8	,,	,,	,,	,,	L	,,	,, ,,	Com. cup: St. Cuthbert's, York.
1848-9	,,	,,		,,	M	JB	James Barber	Paten: Scrayingham.
1849-50	,,	,,		,,	N	,,	,, ,,	Do. do.
1850-1	,,	,,		,,	O	,,	,, ,,	{ Noted by the Author: also (with maker's mark IG) communion paten: Snainton, Yorks.
1851-2					P	...	... ...	Date-letter conjectured.
1852-3					Q	...	... ...	Do. do.
1853-4					R	...	... ...	Do. do.
1854-5					S	...	... ...	Do. do.
1855-6					T	...	... ...	Do. do.
1856-7	,,	,,		,,	V	JB	James Barber	Communion cup: St. Helen's, York.*

*There is at St. Michael-le-Belfry, York, a communion paten stamped with the same marks as those on the communion cup at St. Helens, except that the town-mark is not visible. These examples are understood to have been amongst the last of the plate marked at York, as the office was closed almost immediately afterwards.

1851-2 P   1852-3 Q   Possibly date-letters used in the above Cycle. Stamped on small brass plate from the Assay Office.

CHAPTER VI

Marks on Norwich Plate

The marking of silver plate at an assay office was made compulsory in Norwich in 1565. The office was closed not later than 1697 or 1698.

TABLE I.

THREE STAMPS AS BELOW.

	CASTLE OVER LION.	DATE LETTER.	MAKER'S MARK.	DESCRIPTION OF MAKER'S MARK.	ARTICLES AND OWNERS.
1565-6		A		Orb and cross in lozenge.	Communion cup: Diss, Norfolk. Do. do. : Saxlingham, (1566-7).
1566-7	,,	B		Sun in splendour. Mark of Peter Peterson.	Standing cup: South Kensington Museum.
				IV over a heart.	Communion cup : Bintry, Norfolk.
1567-8		C		Maidenhead in shield.	Communion cup: dated 1568: Northwold, Norfolk.
				Flat fish in oval.	Communion cup, dated 1568 : St. Martin-at-Oak, Norwich.
				Estoile of six curved rays.	Communion cup, undated : Beighton, Norfolk.
1568-9		D		Trefoil slipped.	Communion cup, dated 1570: St. Stephen, Norwich.
1569-70		E		Orb and cross in plain shield.	Communion cup, inscribed " Made by John Stone and Robert Stone " : Haddiscoe, Norfolk.
1570-1		F		Mark of Christ'r. Tannor.	Com. cup : Little Witchingham. Patens at Arminghall and Burgh, Norfolk.
1571-2	,,	G		Orb and cross in shaped shield.	Mounts of stone-ware jug : Mr. W. Boore.
1572-3		H		... ...	Date-letter conjectured.
1573-4	,,	I		Trefoil slipped.	Wine-taster : Messrs. Crichton.
1574-5	,,	K		A flower with foliated stem and orb and cross as 1571-2	Seal-top spoon : Messrs. Christie.
1575-6		L		... ...	Date-letter conjectured.
1576-7		M		... ...	Do. do.
1577-8		N		... ...	Do. do.
1578-9		O		... ...	Do. do.
1579-80		P		... ...	Do. do.
1580-1		Q		... ...	Do. do.
1581-2	ROSE CROWNED.	R		Flower of five petals.	Mounts of coco-nut cup: South Kensington Museum.
1582-3		S		... ...	Date-letter conjectured.
1583-4		T		... ...	Do. do.
1584-5		V		... ...	Do. do.

c. 1570 — Norwich mark, and mark of Christopher Tannor (free 1562) on seal-top spoon : Mr. J. H. Walter.

113

TABLE II.

STAMPS VARIOUS AS BELOW.

DATE (ABOUT).	MARKS.	DESCRIPTION OF MAKER'S MARK.	ARTICLES AND OWNERS.
1590		A bird.	Communion cup and paten, Guestwick.
1595		Orb and cross, and wyvern's head erased	Four beakers from the Old Dutch Church, Norwich, now in the possession of Mr. Wm. Minet, F.S.A., Miss Colman, and the Nederlandsch Museum, Amsterdam.
1600-10		Orb and cross.	Goblet on baluster stem: Messrs. Crichton.
1610		* Indistinguishable.	Seal-top spoon: Mr. J. H. Walter.
1620		Lion rampant.	Do. do.
''		Mark of Wm. Hayden.	Beakers: Mr. R. Levine.
''		W. is probably an Assayer's mark.	Spoon: Mr. J. H. Walter.
1620-40		T.S.	Castle struck twice at right angles, one over the other, and castle (in bowl), maker's mark and castle on back of stem; massive seal-top spoon, pricked 1640: Messrs. Crichton.
1624		Arthur Heaslewood (free 1625).	The first mark in bowl, the other three marks on stem; seal-top spoon: Mr. J. H. Walter.

During the intervals when no date letters were used at Norwich the Assay Office was not functioning and the local productions were sporadic and uncontrolled.

TABLE III.

FOUR STAMPS AS BELOW.

	CASTLE OVER LION.	ROSE CROWNED.	DATE LETTER.	MAKER'S MARK.	DESCRIPTION OF MAKER'S MARK.	ARTICLES AND OWNERS.
1624-5			A		A pelican, as 1628.	Seal-top spoon: Mr. J. H. Walter.
1625-6	,,	,,	B		A pegasus, as 1632.	Do. do.: Messrs. Crichton. { Mounts of wood bowl: Mr. Theodore Rossi.
1626-7		,,	C		Timothy Skottowe.	Seal-top spoon: Mr. J. H. Walter.
1627-8	,,	,,	D	{	Orb and cross.	Chalice: Attleburgh.
					A ship.	{ Seal-top spoon: Messrs. Lambert. { Do. do.: Mr. R. Levine.
1628-9		,,	E		A pelican in her piety.	Seal-top spoon, dated 1629: Mr. A. D. George.
1629-30			F		... ...	Date-letter conjectured.
1630-1	,,		G		W. D. conjoined.	{ Tall flagon: Norwich Corporation. { Seal-top spoon: Mr. J. H. Walter.
1631-2			H		... ...	Date-letter conjectured.
1632-3	,,	,,	I	{	A pegasus.	Com. cup: Great Melton, Norfolk
					A lion rampant.	Seal-top spoon: Mr. J. H. Walter.
1633-4	,,	,,	K		Arthur Heaslewood.	Com. cup: Aspall, Suffolk.
1634-5	,,	,,	L		A lion rampant,	Com. cup: S.S. Simon & Jude, Norwich.
*1635-6			M		Do. do.	Spoon with virgin and child finial: Mr. R. Levine.
1636-7			N		A crowing cock † (Herald of the Morn.)	Seal-top spoon: Burlington Fine Arts Club Exhibition.
1637-8			O	{	Timothy Skottowe.	Beaker, dated 1638, from a Congregational Ch., Great Yarmouth: Pierpont Morgan Collection.
					A pelican in her piety.	Seal-top spoon, pricked 1637: Mr. J. H. Walter.
1638-9	,,	,,	P		A crowing cock,† see above.	Com. paten: Skeyton, Swanton-Abbot, Norfolk.
1639-40			Q		A pelican in her piety.	Communion cup at St. Margaret's, Swanington, Norfolk.
1640-1	,,	,,	R		Timothy Skottowe.	Com. paten: Riddlesworth, Norfolk.
1641-2	,,	,	S	{	A tower incuse.	Mounts of coco-nut cup: The Marquess of Breadalbane, K.G.
					D.	Com. paten: St. Etheldreda, Norwich.
1642-3	,,	,,	T		Timothy Skottowe. †	Seal-top spoon: Messrs. Christie.
1643-4			V		.. ..	Date-letter conjectured.

* 1635-6 M Accompanying this date-letter, are the mark of Arthur Heaslewood (maker) as 1633-4 and Norwich town-marks as 1637-8; communion paten: Coston, Leicestershire.

† Crowing cock rising from pot or skillet (old legend).

TABLE IV.

FROM ABOUT 1645 TO ABOUT 1685. MARKS VARIOUS AS BELOW.

DATE (ABOUT).	MARKS.	ARTICLES AND OWNERS.
1645		Seal-top spoon: Mr. W. Boore.
,,		* Seal-top spoon (pricked 1650): Mr. J. H. Walter.
1653		* Seal-top spoon; (pricked 1653 EM SA : Mr. J. H. Walter.
1661		* Trifid-spoon: Messrs. Crichton.
,,		Communion cup, inscribed 1661: Southwold, Suffolk.
1670		* Spoon, flat stem, trifid end: Mr. J. H. Walter.
,,	,, ,,	* Do. do. do. : Do. do.
,,		* Seal-top spoon, pricked WF PC : Do. do.
,,		* Table-spoon: Mr. Thurlow Chamness,
1675		† Communion paten: St. Peter Hungate, Norwich.
1676	,, ,,	† Flat-top tankard, dated 1676: Messrs. Christie.
1679	,, ,,	† Communion paten, dated 1679; St. Peter's, Mountergate, Norwich.
,,	,, ,, ,,	Seal top spoon: Mr. A. D. George.
1680		Communion cup, dated 1680: East Dereham, Norfolk.
1685		† Crown, rose, and maker's mark of Thos. Havers; cream jug: Lord Hastings.

c. 1660   Small jug; Mr. J. H. Walter.

* This maker's mark is probably that of Arthur Heaslewood.
† Maker's name: Thomas Havers.

TABLE V.

FROM 1688 TO 1697. FOUR STAMPS AS BELOW.

	ROSE CROWNED.	CASTLE OVER LION.	DATE LETTER.	MAKER'S MARK.	MAKER'S NAME.	ARTICLES AND OWNERS.
1688			a	EH	... ...	Beaker : Messrs. Christie.
1689			b	TH	Thomas Havers.	{ Tankard : Major H. S. Marsham. { Bleeding bowl : Mr. J. H. Walter.
1690			C		... ...	Date-letter conjectured.
1691	„	„	D	„	Thomas Havers.	Communion flagon, dated 1694 : St. Michael's-at-Plea, Norwich.
	„	„	„	ID	James Daniel.	{ Alms-dish and basin : St. Stephen's, Norwich. { Dome-top tankard : Mr. R. J. Colman.
	„	„	„	EH	... ...	{ Small mug : Messrs. Christie. { Salver on foot : Mr. R. J. Colman.
	„	„	„	LG	... ...	Communion cup, dated 1694 : Stockton, Norfolk.
1692			E		... ...	Date-letter conjectured.
1693			F		... ...	Do. do.
1694			G		... ...	Do. do.
1695			H		... ...	Do. do.
1696	„	„	I	ID	James Daniel.	Spoon, flat stem, trifid end : Messrs. Spink.
1697	„	„	K	PR	... ...	Beaker, pricked 1697 : Messrs. Spink.
	„	„	„	EH	... ...	Beaker and spoon : Mr. J. H. Walter.

c. 1697   „ Castle as 1688, no date-letter.   ... ...   Trifid spoon : Mr. Arthur Irwin Dasent.

1701-2    HA   Robt. Hartsonge ? Communion paten on foot : Kirkstead, Norfolk.

CHAPTER VII

Marks on Exeter Plate

The Exeter Assay Office was established in 1701 and discontinued in 1883. A guild of goldsmiths flourished in Exeter from a time long anterior to the reign of Elizabeth. No Exeter town mark has been found of earlier date than c. 1571; before that date only makers' marks appear to have been used.

TABLE I.

FROM 1544 TO 1592 OR THEREABOUT.

DATE.	MARKS.	MAKER'S NAME.	ARTICLES AND OWNERS.
c. 1544-98		Richard Hilliard.	Communion cups: St. Edmund's and St. Sidwell's, Exeter.
c. 1562 / 1607		Richard Osborne.	Communion cups: Catteleigh.
c. 1568-74		John North.	Do. cup: Curry Mallett.
c. 1570		Henry Hardwicke.	Chalices: Parkham and Holsworthy.
1570-3		John Ions (Jones).	Communion cup: St. Petrock's, Exeter.
"		Do. do. do.	Cover paten: Whitstone.
c. 1570 / 1600		Steven More.	Communion cup: Halwell.
1571		John North.	Do. do., dated 1571: St. Davids, Exeter.
"		Do. do.	Communion cup: Messrs. Crichton.
"		John Jons.	Do. do., dated 1571: Trevalga.
1572		John Withycombe.	Trencher used as paten: Berrynarbor.
1575		John Jons.	Mounts of cylindrical salt (ivory drum): Lord Swaythling.
"		Do. do.	Standing salt: Mr. J. Dixon.
"		Do. do.	Com. cup, dated 1575: Lympstone, nr. Exeter.
"		Do. do.	Com. cup: Duloe, Cornwall.
1576		Do. do.	Do. do., dated 1576: Tamerton, Devon.
"		... ...	Do. co.: Eggesford and Broadwoodwiger, dated.
1580		Wm. Horwood.	Mounts of stone-ware jug: Messrs. Christie.
c. 1580		John Eydes.	Mounts of stone-ware jug: Victoria and Albert Museum. / Chalice and paten: Harpford.
1582		C. Eston.	Com. cup, dated 1582: Cadbury, Devon. / Do. do. do. 1585: Talaton, do. / Lion-sejant spoon: Mr. A. S. Marsden Smedley.
"		C. Easton.	Com. cup, dated 1582: formerly at Fen Ottery, Devon.
1585		— Bently.	Mounts of stone-ware jug: Ashmolean Museum.
"		R. Herman.	Seal-top spoon: Messrs. Christie.
1590		C. Eston.	Com. cup, dated 1590: St. Andrew's, Plymouth.
1592		Do. do.	Lion-sejant spoon: Victoria and Albert Museum.

TABLE II.

FROM 1600 TO 1640 OR THEREABOUT.

(The dates are approximate except where the articles are described as dated.)

DATE.	MARKS.	MAKER'S NAME.	ARTICLES AND OWNERS.
1600		Richd. Osborn.	Maidenhead spoon : Mr. J. H. Walter.
,,		R. Herman.	Seal-top spoon : Do. do.
,,		No maker's mark.	Lion-sejant spoon : Do. do.
c. 1600		Richd. Osborn.	Apostle spoon : Mr. Crichton.
1606		,, ,,	Lion-sejant spoon, pricked 1606 : Noted by the Author.
. 1610-20		William Bartlett. (1597-1646).	{ Com. cup : Crewkerne. { Seal-top spoons : Mr. W. Boore.
1620	,, ,, ,,	,, ,,	Lion-sejant spoon : Messrs. Christie.
,,	,,	Edward Anthony (1612-67).	Seal-top spoon : The Author's Collection.
,,		,, ,,	Do. do. : Dunn-Gardner Collection.
,,		?	Six maidenhead spoons . Mr. R. E. Brand.
c. 1630	WB	Wm. Bartlett (probably).	Communion cup and paten, dated 1630 : Helston.
,,	T	Anthony mark, &c.*	Exeter mark in bowl, other marks on stem of seal-top spoon : Mr. H. D. Ellis.
c. 1635	IL	John Lavers.	{ (Crowned X repeated after second IL). { Chalice : Ashwater.
,,	IP	I. P.	Apostle spoon : noted by the Author.
c. 1635-8	IL	John Lavers.	{ Seal-top spoon, pricked 1638 : do. do. { Do. do. : Sir Edward Marshall Hall, K.C.
c. 1640		... ...	Apostle spoon : Messrs. Crichton.
,,	HP HP	H. P.	Do. do : Messrs. Bruford.
,,	RADCLIFF	Jasper Radcliffe.	Do. do. : Messrs. Christie.
,,	,,	L. M.	Snuff-box : Mr. G. Henderson.
,,	,, ,,	Jasper Radcliffe.	Com. cup, dated 1640 : St. Petrock's, Exeter.
,,	OSBORN ,,	Richd. Osborn.	Apostle spoon : Messrs. Christie.
,,	IL IL IL	John Lavers.	{ Do. do. : Holburne Museum. { Seal-top spoon, with dot at each side of X : Sir E. Marshall Hall, K.C.
,,		No maker's mark.	Apostle spoon : Holburne Museum.

TABLE III.

Date	Marks	Maker's Name
c. 1640-50		{ John Elston / Anthony Tripe
"		P. R.
"		Thomas Bridgeman.
"		Edward Anthony.
"		Do. do.
c. 1646-98		I. F.
c. 1670		Jasper Radcliffe.
1676		M. W.
"		— S.
c. 1680		... ...
"		No maker's mark.
"		I. S.
1690		John Mortimer.
c. 1690		Daniel Slade.
"		Wm. Ekins.
"		Do. do.
"		John Mortimer.
"		... ...
"		I. P. (See Barnstaple, p. 459 infra).
"		I. P.
1694		Nichs. Browne.
1698		

TABLE IV.

Date	Castle.	Brit. Annia.	Lion's Head Erased.	Date Letter.	Maker's Mark.	Maker's Name.
1701-2				A		J. Elston.
ANNE. 1702-3		"	"	B		Thos. Foote.
1703-4		"	"	C		Hy. Muston. / John Audry.
1704-5	"	"	"	D		Wm. Briant.
1705-6		"	"	E		Richd. Freeman.
1706-7	"	"	"	F		Thos. Reynolds.
1707-8		"	"	G		Richd. Wilcocks. / Thos. Salter.
1708-9		"	"	H		Richd. Plint.
1709-10		"	"	I		Name not traced.
1710-1	"	"	"	K		Ed. Richards.
1711-2	"	"	"	L		Geo. Trowbridge. / Ed. Sweet.
1712-3	"	"	"	M		Ed. Richards.
1713-4		"	"	N		Danl. Slade.
GEO. I. 1714-5	"	"	"	O		— Tolcher. / John Mortimer.
1715-6	"	"	"	P		Geo. Trowbridge. / Pent. Symonds.
1716-7	"	"	"	Q		Ab'm. Lovell.
1717-8	"	"	"	R		Pent. Symonds.
1718-9	"	"	"	S		Peter Arno.
1719-20	"	"	"	T		Andr. Worth.
1720-1	"	"	"	V		Saml. Blachford. / J. Elston.
1721-2				W		Thos. Sampson.
1722-3	"	"	"	X		Saml. Blachford.
1723-4	"	"	"	Y		J. Elston.
1724-5	"	"	"	Z		Jas. Williams.

TABLE V.

	CASTLE.	LEOPARD'S HEAD CROWNED.	LION PASSANT.	DATE LETTER.	MAKER'S MARK.	MAKER'S NAME.	
1725-6				a	SB	Saml.	Blachford.
1726-7	,,	,,	,,	b	TS	Thos.	Sampson.
GEO. II. 1727-8	,,	,,	,,	c	JC / PE	Joseph / Philip	Collier. / Elliott.
1728-9	,,	,,	,,	d	JE	John	Elston, jr.
1729-30	,,	,,	,,	e	Do. / JS	Do. / James	do. / Strang.
1730-1	,,	,,	,,	f	IB	John	Burdon.
1731-2	,,	,,	,,	g	PE	Peter	Elliott.
1732-3	,,	,,	,,	h	JC	Joseph	Collier.
1733-4	,,	,,	,,	i	JE	John	Elston, jr.
1734-5	,,	,,	,,	k	SB	Sampson	Bennett.
1735-6	,,	,,	,,	l	PE	Philip	Elston.
1736-7	,,	,,	,,	m	JS	James	Strang.
1737-8	,,	,,	,,	n	PE	Philip	Elston.
1738-9	,,	,,	,,	o	PS	Pent.	Symonds.
1739-40	,,	,,	,,	p	JB	John	Burdon.
1740-1	,,	,,	,,	q	JB	Do.	do.
1741-2	,,	,,	,,	r	Sy	Pent.	Symonds.
1742-3	,,	,,	,,	s	IF	Name not traced. J.	Freeman ?
1743-4	,,	,,	,,	t	JB	John	Babbage ?
1744-5	,,	,,	,,	u	,,	Do.	do.
1745-6	,,	,,	,,	w			
1746-7	,,	,,	,,	x	PS	Pent.	Symonds.
1747-8	,,	,,	,,	y	TB	Thos.	Blake.
1748-9	,,	,,	,,	z	JS	Jas.	Strang.

Variant of date-letter for 1748-9

TABLE VI.

	CASTLE	LEOPARD'S HEAD CROWNED	LION PASSANT.	DATE LETTER	MAKER'S MARK	MAKER'S NAME.	
1749-50				A	TB	Thomas	Blake.
1750-1	,,	,,	,,	B	,,	,,	,,
1751-2	,,	,,	,,	C	,,	,,	,,
1752-3	,,	,,	,,	D	WP	W.	Parry.
1753-4	,,	,,	,,	E	DC	Danl.	Coleman.
1754-5	,,	,,	,,	F	WP	W.	Parry.
1755-6	,,	,,	,,	G	,,	,,	,,
1756-7	,,	,,	,,	H	TB	Thomas	Blake.
1757-8	,,	,,	,,	I	,,	,,	,,
1758-9	,,	,,	,,	K			
1759-60	,,	,,	,,	L	SF	Name not traced.	
GEO. III. 1760-1	,,	,,	,,	M			
1761-2	,,	,,	,,	N			
1762-3	,,	,,	,,	O	MS	Mat'w	Skinner.
1763-4	,,	,,	,,	P			
1764-5	,,	,,	,,	Q			
1765-6	,,	,,	,,	R			
1766-7	,,	,,	,,	S	RS	Richard	Sams.
1767-8	,,	,,	,,	T	,,	,,	,,
1768-9	,,	,,	,,	U	JH	James	Holt.
1769-70	,,	,,	,,	W	TC	Thomas	Coffin.
1770-1	,,	,,	,,	X	IF	J.	Freeman.
1771-2	,,	,,	,,	Y	RS	Richard	Sams.
1772-3	,,	,,	,,	Z		... ...	

TABLE VII.

	CASTLE.	LEOPARD'S HEAD CROWNED	LION PASSANT.	DATE LETTER.	MAKER'S MARK.	MAKER'S NAME.
1773-4	[castle]	[leopard]	[lion]	A	RS	Richd. Sams.
1774-5	"	"	"	B		
1775-6	"	"	"	C	{ RS / WW }	Thos. Eustace. William West of Plymouth.
1776-7	"	"	"	D		
1777-8	"	"	"	E		
1778-9	"	"	[lion]	F	"	Thos. Eustace.
1779-80	"	"	"	G	"	" "
1780-1	"	"	"	H		
1781-2-3	"	"	"	I	"	" "
1783-4	"	KING'S HEAD	"	K	WP	W. Pearse.
1784-5	"	[head]	"	L		Thos. Eustace (as 1775-6).
1785-6	"	"	"	M	TE	Thos. Eustace.
1786-7	"	[head]	"	N	JH	Joseph Hicks.
1787-8	"	"	"	O	"	" "
1788-9	"	"	"	P	"	" "
1789-90	"	"	"	q	JP	J. Pearse.
1790-1	"	"	"	r		
1791-2	"	"	"	s	JH	Joseph Hicks.
1792-3	"	"	"	t		
1793-4	"	"	"	u		
1794-5	"	"	"	w		
1795-6	"	"	"	X	RF	Richd. Ferris.
1796-7	"	"	"	y		

TABLE VIII.

	CASTLE.	LION PASSANT.	DATE LETTER.	KING'S HEAD.	MAKER'S MARK.	MAKER'S NAME.
1797-8	[castle]	[lion]	A	[king's head]	RF	Richd. Ferris.
1798-9	"	"	B	"	"	" "
1799 / 1800	"	"	C	[king's head]	JH / WW	Joseph Hicks. W. Welch.
1800-1	"	"	D	"	JH	Joseph Hicks.
1801-2	"	"	E	"	"	" "
1802-3	"	"	F	"	"	" "
1803-4	"	"	G	"	TE	Thos. Eustace.
1804-5	"	"	H	"	RF	Richd. Ferris.
1805-6	[castle]	[lion]	I	"	"	" "
1806-7	"	"	K	"	"	" "
1807-8	"	"	L	"	"	" "
1808-9	"	"	M			
1809-10	"	"	N	"	JL	J. Langdon
1810-1	"	"	O	"	WW	W. Welch.
1811-2	"	"	P	"	JH	Joseph Hicks.
1812-3	"	"	Q	"	"	" "
1813-4	"	"	R	"	GT	G. Turner.
1814-5	"	"	S	"	"	" "
1815-6	"	"	T	"	"	" "
1816-7	"	"	U	"	GF	Geo. Ferris.

TABLE IX.

	CASTLE.	LION PASSANT.	DATE LETTER.	KING'S HEAD.	MAKER'S MARK.	MAKER'S NAME.
1817-8			a		GF	Geo. Ferris.
1818-9	,,	,,	b	,,	,,	,, ,,
1819-20	,,	,,	c	,,	JH	Joseph Hicks.
GEO. IV. 1820-1	,,	,,	d	,,	,,	,, ,,
1821-2	,,	,,	e	,,	,,	,, ,,
1822-3	,,	,,	f		GF	Geo. Ferris.
1823-4	,,	,,	g	,,	,,	,, ,,
1824-5	,,	,,	h	,,	,,	,, ,,
1825-6	,,	,,	i	,,	IE	John Eustace.
1826-7	,,	,,	k	,,	GM	Name not traced.
1827-8	,,	,,	l	,,	JO	J. Osmont.
1828-9	,,	,,	m	,,	,,	,, ,,
1829-30	,,	,,	n	,,	JH	Joseph Hicks.
WM. IV. 1830-1	,,	,,	o	,,	,,	,, ,,
1831-2			p		WS	W. Sobey.
1832-3	,,	,,	q	,,	J·S	John Stone.
1833-4			r	,,	W·P	Wm. Pope.
1834-5	,,	,,	s		J·O	J. Osmont.
1835-6	,,	,,	t	,,	WRS	W. R. Sobey.
1836-7	,,	,,	u	,,	WW	William Welch.

TABLE X.

	CASTLE.	*LION PASSANT.	DATE LETTER.	QUEEN'S HEAD.	MAKER'S MARK.	MAKER'S NAME.
VICT. 1837-8			A		SOBEY	W. R. Sobey.
1838-9	,,	,,	B		J·O	J. Osmont.
1839-40	,,	,,	C		TB	Thos. Byne.
1840-1			D	,,	J·S	J. Stone.
1841-2		,,	E	,,	RAMSEY	— Ramsey.
1842-3	,,	,,	F	,,	SOBEY	W. R. Sobey.
1843-4		,,	G	,,	,,	,, ,,
1844-5	,,	,,	H	,,	WRS	,, ,,
1845-6	,,	,,	J	,,	SOBEY	,, ,,
1846-7	,,	,,	K	,,	,,	,, ,,
1847-8	,,	,,	L	,,	WWW	? Williams.
1848-9	,,	,,	M	,,	J·S	J. Stone.
1849-50	,,	,,	N	,,	WRS	W. R. Sobey.
1850-1	,,	,,	O	,,	,,	,, ,,
1851-2	,,	,,	P	,,	J·O	J. Osmont.
1852-3	,,	,,	Q	,,	,,	,, ,,
1853-4	,,	,,	R	,,	IP	Isaac Parkin.
1854-5	,,	,,	S	,,	,,	,, ,,
1855-6	,,	,,	T	,,	,,	,, ,,
1856-7	,,	,,	U	,,	J·S	J. Stone.

TABLE XI.

	CASTLE.	LION PASSANT.	DATE LETTER.	QUEEN'S HEAD.	MAKER'S MARK.	MAKER'S NAME.		
1857-8	🏰	🦁	A	👑	J·S	J.	Stone.	
1858-9	,,	,,	B	,,	,,	,,	,,	
1859-60	,,	,,	C	,,		...	...	...
1860-1	,,	,,	D	,,	PO	Name not traced.		
1861-2	,,	,,	E	,,	JW	Jas.	Williams.	
1862-3	,,	,,	F	,,		...	...	...
1863-4	,,	,,	G	,,		...	...	...
1864-5	,,	,,	H	,,		...	...	...
1865-6	,,	,,	I	,,		...	...	...
1866-7	,,	,,	K	,,		...	...	...
1867-8	,,	,,	L	,,		...	...	...
1868-9	,,	,,	M	,,	HL	Henry	Lake.	
1869-70	,,	,,	N	,,		...	...	...
1870-1	,,	,,	O	,,		...	...	...
1871-2	,,	,,	P	,,		...	...	...
1872-3	,,	,,	Q	,,		...	...	...
1873-4	,,	,,	R	,,		...	...	...
1874-5	,,	,,	S	,,		...	...	...
1875-6	,,	,,	T	,,		...	...	...
1876-7	,,	,,	U	,,		...	...	...

TABLE XII.
FIVE STAMPS AS BELOW.

	CASTLE.	LION PASSANT.	DATE LETTER.	QUEEN'S HEAD.	MAKER'S MARK	MAKER'S NAME.	ARTICLES AND OWNERS.
1877-8			A		J.W. &Co.	J. Whipple & Co.	Engraved goblet: Mr. Bruford.
1878-9	,,	,,	B	,,		... ...	From the Assay Office plate.
1879-80	,,	,,	C	,,		... ...	Do. do. do.
1880-1	,,	,,	D	,,		... ...	Do. do. do.
1881-2	,,	,,	E	,,		... ...	Do. do. do.
1882-3	,,	,,	F	,,	WE FD JT	Ellis, Depree & Tucker }	Com. plate· St. Matthew's, Exeter.

The communion plate at St. Matthew's above-mentioned appears to have been some of the last work assayed at Exeter, as the office was finally closed in 1883.

SUPPLEMENTARY LIST OF MARKS OF GOLDSMITHS
Impressed at Exeter, but not illustrated in the preceding tables.

DATE.	MARK.	NAME.	DATE.	MARK.	NAME.
1701	SI	Daniel Slade.	1722	PS	Pentecost Symonds.
c 1706	JO	Peter Jouett.	1728	TC	Thomas Coffin.
1707	Sa	Thos. Sampson.	1730	IR	John Reed
1708	Wi	Richard Wilcocks. ?	1732	TC	Thomas Clarke.
1709	SY	Pentecost Symonds.	,,	IS	John Suger
1710	PI	John Pike.	1741	MM	Micon Melun.
,,	Bc	Joseph Bennick.	1771	RB	Richd. Birdlake (Plymouth).
1713	Su	John Suger.	1825	SL	Simon Lery.
1714	Tr	Anthony Tripe.	1830	IP	Isaac Parkin.
1717	Wi	Zacariah Williams.	1835	GT TTT	G. Turner & partner (? Son).
1719	BE	Joseph Bennick.	1845	JG	J. Golding (Plymouth).
1721	ER	Edward Richard.	1847	HE	Henry Ellis.
,,	IM	John March.	1850	IP GS	Isaac Parkin & Geo. Sobey.

CHAPTER VIII

Marks on Newcastle Plate

Money was minted at Newcastle in 1248 and in the reign of Henry VI (1423) it was ordained that Newcastle-upon-Tyne should have a "touch" (assay office). A proper assay office for marking silver plate was established in 1702.

TABLE I.

Date	Marks	Maker's Name
1658		John Wilkinson.
1664		" "
1668		" "
1670		John Dowthwaite.
1672		" "
"		Wm. Ramsay.
1675		" "
"		" "
1680		" "
1684		" "
"		" "
"		" "
1685		Wm. Robinson.*
"		" "
1686-7		Eli Bilton.
1686-8		Wm. Robinson.
1690		" "
1692		" "
1694		Robt. Shrive.
"		Eli Bilton.
"		" "
1695		Wm. Robinson.
1697		Thos. Hewitson.
1698		" "
1698-9		Eli Bilton.
1700		" "
"		John Ramsay.
1701		Eli Bilton.

TABLE II.

Date	Three Castles.	Brit. Annia.	Lion's Head Erased.	Date Letter.	Maker's Mark.	Maker's Name.
ANNE. 1702-3				A	Ra	John Ramsay.
1703-4	"	"	"	B	Ba	Fras. Batty.
1704-5	"	"	"	C	Sh	Robt. Shrive.
1705-6	"	"	"	D	Bi	Eli. Bilton.
1706-7	"			E	Yo	" " / John Younghusband.
1707-8	"	"	"	F	Yo / Fr	" " / J'nath'n French.
1708-9	"	"	"	G	Bv	John Buckle of York.
1709-10	"	"	"	"	Ki	James Kirkup.
1710-11						
1711-2					Bi	Eli. Bilton.
1712-3				H	Ho	Richd. Hobbs.
1713-4					LA	John Langwith.
GEO. I 1714-5		"	"	D	Fr / Ba	J'nath'n French. / Fr. Batty, jr.
1715-6					Sh	Nathl. Shaw.
1716-7						
1717-8	"	"	"	P	BV	Joseph Buckle.
1718-9	"	"	"	M	Ba / Ki	Fras. Batty, as above. / James Kirkup.
1719-20	"	"	"	D	Ma Ba	R. Makepeace & F. Batty.
					Ca	John Carnaby.
1720-1	"	"	"	E	Wh	Wm. Whitfield.

The dates assigned in table I must be regarded as approximate.

TABLE III.

	THREE CASTLES.	LION PASSANT.	LEOPARD'S HEAD CROWNED.	DATE LETTER.	MAKER'S MARK.	MAKER'S NAME.
1721-2	⛉	🦁	👑	A	FB / IR	Fras. Batty, jr. / John Ramsay, jr.
1722-3	⛉	🦁	,,	B	RM / I·K	Robt. Makepeace. / Jas. Kirkup.
1723-4	,,	🦁	,,	C	IF	Jthn. French.
1724-5	,,	,,	,,	D	IC / TP	John Carnaby. / Thos. Partis.
1725-6	⛉	🦁	👑	E	IR	Fras. Batty, jr.
1726-7	,,	,,	,,	F	WW / IB	Wm. Whitfield. / John Busfield of York. ?
GEO. II. 1727-8	⛉	,,	👑	G	IC	Isaac Cookson.
1728-9	,,	🦁	,,	H	GB / WW / WD	Geo. Bulman. / Wm. Whitfield. / Wm. Dalton.
1729-30	,,	,,	,,	I	GB	Geo. Bulman.
1730-1	,,	,,	,,	K	WD	Wm. Dalton.
1731-2	,,	,,	,,	L	TG / IF	Thos. Gamul ? / Jon. French.
1732-3	,,	,,	,,	M	TM / IB	Thos. Makepeace. / John Busfield of York. ?
1733-4	,,	,,	,,	N	IC	Isaac Cookson.
1734-5	,,	,,	,,	O	TP	Thos. Partis.
1735-6	,,	,,	,,	P	GB	Geo. Bulman.
1736-7	,,	,,	,,	Q	WP	Wm. Partis.*
1737-8	,,	,,	,,	R	IC	Isaac Cookson.
1738-9	,,	,,	,,	S	WB / IB	Wm. Beilby&Co.?
1739-40	,,	,,	,,	T	IC / R·M	Isaac Cookson. / Robt. Makepeace.

*Possibly Wm. Prior.

TABLE IV.

	THREE CASTLES.	LION PASSANT.	LEOPARD'S HEAD CROWNED.	DATE LETTER.	MAKER'S MARK.	MAKER'S NAME.
1740-1	⛉	🦁	👑	A	SB / I·K	Stephen Buckle. / James Kirkup.
1741-2	,,	,,	,,	B	WB / IB	W. Beilby & Anor. / Perhaps Jno. Busfield (of York.)
1742-3	,,	,,	,,	C	IC	Isaac Cookson.
1743-4	,,	,,	,,	D	TS / WP	Thomas Stoddart. / William Partis.
1744-5	,,	,,	,,	E	FM	F. Martin (probably).
1745-6	,,	,,	👑	F	IB	Thomas Blackett (probably).
1746-7	⛉	🦁	👑	G	IC	Isaac Cookson.
1747-8	,,	,,	,,	H	IW	John Wilkinson of Sheffield (probably).
1748-9	,,	,,	,,	I	TR	? Thos. Reid of York.
1749-50	,,	,,	,,	K	RG / R·M / TP	R. Gillson (of Sunderland). / Robert Makepeace. / Thos. Partis II. (of Sunderland).
1750-1	,,	🦁	👑	L	WB	William Beilby.
1751-2	,,	,,	,,	M	WP	William Partis.
1752-3	,,	,,	,,	N	WD / IB	William Dalton. / Perhaps John Barrett (of Sunderland).
1753-4	,,	,,	,,	O	IC	Isaac Cookson.
1754-5	,,	,,	,,	P	IL / IG	Langlands & Goodriche.
1755-6	,,	,,	,,	Q	IK	John Kirkup.
1756-7	,,	,,	,,	R	IL	John Langlands.
1757-8	⛉	,,	👑	S	IL / IL	" " / " "
1758-9				T	RB	Ralph Beilby.

Note. The letter T is presumed. No doubt the shield was identical with that of the other date letters.

TABLE V.

	THREE CASTLES.	LION PASSANT.	LEOPARD'S HEAD CROWNED.	DATE LETTER.	KING'S HEAD.	MAKER'S MARK.	MAKER'S NAME.
1759-60	⬡	⬡	⬡	A		SI	Samuel James.
						SJ	Saml. Thompson.
GEO. III. 1760-8	,,	,,	,,	B		IB	John Barrett of Sunderland.
						SI	Saml. James.
1769-70	,,	,,	,,	C		RP	Robt. Peat.
1770-1	⬡	,,	⬡	D		{ IK	John Kirkup.
						{ IF	John Fearny of Sunderland.
						{ I-L	John Langlands.
1771-2	,,	,,	,,	E			
1772-3	⬡	,,	,,	F		IC	James Crawford.
1773-4	,,	,,	,,	G		JH	John Jobson.
						I-H	Jas. Hetherington.
1774-5	,,	,,	,,	H		WS IM	Stalker & Mitchison.
1775-6	,,	,,	,,	I		{ HH HE	Hetherington & Edwards.
						{ FS	Francis Solomon of Whitehaven.
1776-7	,,	,,	,,	K		H&E	Hetherington & Edwards.
1777-8	,,	,,	,,	L		JH	James Hetherington.
						DC	David Crawford.
1778-9	,,	,,	,,	M		{ I.L L.R	Langlands & Robertson. }
1779-80	,,	⬡	⬡	N		DC	David Crawford.
1780-1	,,	,,	,,	O		RP RS	Pinkney & Scott.
1781-2	,,	,,	,,	P		I-L I-R	Langlands & Robertson (as below). }
1782-3	,,	,,	,,	Q		IS	John Stoddart.
						BD	Ben. Dryden.
1783-4	,,	,,	,,	R		JS	John Stoddart.
1784-5	,,	,,	,,	S	◉	RP RS	Pinkney & Scott.
1785-6	,,	,,	,,	T	,,	IM	John Mitchison.
1786-7	,,	,,	,,	U	◔	,,	,, ,,
1787-8	,,	⬡	⬡	W	,,	TG	Name not traced.
						L&R	Langlands & Robertson. }
1788-9	,,	⬡	,,	X	,,	C-R	Chrstn. Reid.
1789-90	,,	,,	,,	Y	,,	P&S	Pinkney & Scott.
1790-1	,,	,,	,,	Z	,,	IM	John Mitchison.

TABLE VI.

	LION PASSANT.	THREE CASTLES.	LEOPARD'S HEAD CROWNED.	KING'S HEAD.	DATE LETTER.	MAKER'S MARK.	MAKER'S NAME.
1791-2	⬡	⬡	⬡	◔	A	IL IR	Langlands & Robertson. }
1792-3	,,	,,	,,	,,	B	RS	Robert Scott.
*1793-4	,,	,,	,,	,,	C	AH	Anth. Hedley.
1794-5	,,	,,	,,	,,	D	MA GW	Mary Ashworth of Dur. G. Weddell.
1795-6	,,	,,	,,	,,	E	I-R D-D	Robertson & Darling. }
1796-7	,,	,,	,,	,,	F	TW R&D	Thos. Watson. Robertson & Darling.
1797-8	,,	,,	,,	◔	G	GL JW	Geo. Laws & John Walker. }
1798-9	,,	,,	,,	,,	H	CR IR	Chrstn. Reid. John Robertson.
1799 1800	,,	,,	,,	,,	I	JR SC	,, ,, Sarah Crawford.
1800-1	⬡	⬡	⬡	◔	K	IL TW	John Langlands, jr. Thos. Watson.
1801-2	,,	,,	,,	,,	L	A-R	Ann. Robertson.
1802-3	,,	,,	,,	,,	M	D-D CR DR	David Darling. Chrstn. K. Reid & David Reid.
1803-4	⬡	,,	,,	◔	N	A-K	Alexr. Kelty.
1804-5	,,	,,	,,	,,	O	IL	John Langlands, jr.
1805-6	,,	,,	,,	,,	P	GM	George Murray.
1806-7	,,	,,	,,	,,	Q	TW	Thos. Watson.
1807-8	,,	,,	,,	,,	R	,,	,, ,,
1808-9	,,	,,	,,	,,	S	DD TB	Darling & Bell.
1809-10	⬡	⬡	⬡	◔	T	I-L	John Langlands.†
1810-1	,,	,,	,,	,,	U	T-W	Thos. Watson.
1811-2	,,	,,	,,	,,	W	D-L IR IW	Drthy. Langlands. Robertson & Walton. }
1812-3	,,	,,	,,	,,	X	RP M-R	Robert Pinkney. Name not traced.
1813-4	,,	,,	,,	,,	Y	CR DR CR	Chrstn. Ker Reid, David Reid, & Chrstn. Bruce Reid.
1814-5	⊙	,,	,,	,,	Z	IW	John Walton.

* 1793-4   C ⬡ ⬡ M.MILLER   Maker, M. Miller.

1805-6   AC ⬡ ⬡ ⬡ P   Maker, Alexander Cameron, of Dundee.

†Probably used by the son of John Langlands after his father's death.

TABLE VII.

SIX STAMPS AS BELOW.

	DATE LETTER	KING'S HEAD	LION PASSANT	THREE CASTLES	LEOPARD'S HEAD CROWNED	MAKER'S MARK	MAKER'S NAME.	ARTICLES AND OWNERS.
1815-6	A					T·W	Thos. Watson.	Punch-ladle: General Meyrick.
1816-7	B	,,	,,	,,	,,	T·W	,, ,,	Tea-spoons: Messrs. Crichton.
1817-8	C	,,	,,	,,	,,	C·D	Christ'r. Dinsdale, of Sunderland.	Milk jug: S. & A. Mus., Dublin.
1818-9	D	,,	,,	,,	,,	I·R T·W	Robertson & Walton.	From Assay Office plate.
1819-20	E	,,	,,	,,	,,			
GEO. IV. 1820-1	F	,,	,,	,,	,,	T·W	Thos. Watson.	Do. do. do.
1821-2	G		,,	,,	,,	,,	,, ,,	Marrow scoop: Submitted to the Author.
1822-3	H	,,	,,	,,	,,	,,	,, ,,	Tea-spoon: Mr. E. Heron-Allen.
1823-4	I	,,	,,	,,	,,	,,	,, ,,	Small mug: Messrs. Debenham.
1824-5	K	,,	,,	,,	,,	T·W	,, ,,	Large two-handled cup: The Earl of Yarborough.
1825-6	L	,,	,,	,,	,,			
1826-7	M	,,	,,		,,			
1827-8	N	,,	,,	,,	,,			
1828-9	O	,,	,,	,,	,,			
1829-30	P	,,	,,	,,	,,			
WM. IV. 1830-1	Q	,,	,,	,,	,,			
1831-2	R	,,	,,	,,	,,			
1832-3	S		,,	,,	,,	,,	Thos. Watson.	Sauce-ladle: Mr. J. B. Stansby.
1833-4	T	,,	,,	,,	,,			
1834-5	U	,,	,,	,,	,,	W·L	Wm. Lister.	From Assay Office plate.
1835-6	W	,,	,,	,,	,,			
1836-7	X	,,	,,	,,	,,			
VICT. 1837-8	Y		,,	,,	,,	T·W	Thos. Watson.	Salt-spoons: Messrs. Crichton.
1838-9	Z	,,	,,	,,	,,	W·L C·L W·L	Lister & Sons.	From Assay Office plate.

See supplementary List of Makers' Marks on p. 131.

TABLES VIII. AND IX.

SIX STAMPS AS BELOW. LEOPARD'S HEAD UNCROWNED FROM 1846.

	KING'S HEAD.	LION PASSANT.	THREE CASTLES.	LEOPARD'S HEAD CROWNED.	DATE LETTER.	MAKER'S MARK.	MAKER'S NAME.	ARTICLES & OWNERS.		DATE LETTER.
1839-40	(stamp)	(stamp)	(stamp)	(stamp)	A	JW	John Walton.	Com. cup & paten : Aspatria.	†1864-5	a
1840-1	„	„	„	„	B	„	„ „	Do. do. do.	1865-6	b
1841-2	(stamp)	„	„	„	C	TW	Thos. Watson.	Small mug : Col. Fitzgerald.	1866-7	c
1842-3	„	„	„	„	D	„	„ „	Goblet : Mr. W. Boore.	1867-8	d
1843-4	„	„	„	„	E				1868-9	e
1844-5	„	„	„	„	F		Lister & Sons (as 1838-9).	Sugar ladle : Messrs. Crichton.	1869-70	f
1845-6	„	„	„	„	G				1870-1	g
*1846-7	„	(stamp)	(stamp)	(stamp)	H	GG	Name not traced.	Egg-spoon : Mr. Lowe.	1871-2	h
1847-8	„	„	„	„	I				1872-3	i
1848-9	„	„	„	„	J				1873-4	k
1849-50	„	„	„	„	K				1874-5	l
1850-1	„	„	„	„	L				1875-6	m
1851-2	„	„	„	„	M				1876-7	n
1852-3	„	„	„	„	N				1877-8	o
1853-4	„	„	„	„	O				1878-9	p
1854-5	„	„	„	„	P				1879-80	q
1855-6	„	„	„	„	Q				1880-1	r
1856-7	„	„	„	„	R				1881-2	s
1857-8	„	„	„	„	S				1882-3	t
1858-9	„	„	„	„	T				1883-4	u
1859-60	„	„	„	„	U					
1860-1	„	„	„	„	W					
1861-2	„	„	„	„	X					
1862-3	„	„	„	„	Y					
1863-4	„	„	„	„	Z					

The office was closed in 1884.

†Mustard spoon of this year with leopard's head *un*crowned : Messrs. Reid & Sons.

	KING'S HEAD.	LION PASSANT.	THREE CASTLES.	LEOPARD'S HEAD CROWNED.	DATE LETTER.	MAKER'S MARK.	MAKER'S NAME.	ARTICLES & OWNERS.
1850-1	(stamp)	„	„	(stamp)	M	DR	David Reid.	Marrow scoop : Mr. A. J. Grimes.
1869-70	(stamp)	(stamp)	(stamp)	(stamp)	f	CJR	C. J. Reid.	Pair of salt-spoons : Messrs. Reid & Sons.

* In some cases the leopard's head has been found with a crown.

SUPPLEMENTARY LIST OF MARKS OF GOLDSMITHS.

Impressed at Newcastle from c. 1750 to c. 1880, but not illustrated in the preceding tables.

MARK.	NAME.	MARK.	NAME.	MARK.	NAME.
GL	Name not traced.	L&SONS	Lister & Sons.	I·M	John Miller.
W.F.	„ „	L&S	„ „	CD	Cuthbert Dinsdale.
WB	Mr. Bartlett ?	I·B	John Brown.	GL	Geo. Sam. Lewis.
SI	Samuel Jones.	J·B	„ „	MY&SONS	M. Young & Sons.
PI	Peter James.	JB	„ „	SJ	Simeon Joel.
HII	Name not traced.	WS	Wm. Sherwin.	J.C	John Cook.
F·S	F. Somerville or Summerville, Sen., and F. S. Junr.	J·D	James Dinsdale.	RD	R. Duncan of Carlisle.
P·B	Peter Beatch.	JS	Name not traced.	J&IJ	Joseph and Israel Jacobs.
I·T	Name not traced.	CJR	Chrstn. J. Reid.	JF	James Foster.
R·D	„ „	RR	Robert Rippon.	W&JW	Wm. and Jno. Wilson.
R·W	Robt. Wilson.	JS	John Sutler.	TR	Thos. Ross of Carlisle ?
D&B	Darling & Bell.	J.W	John White.	TALBOT	A. Y. Talbot of Crook, Darlington.
T·H	Thos. Huntingdon.	DR	David Reid.	TS	Thos. Sewill.
H·B	Hugh Brechinridge.	BUXTON	Wm. Buxton of Bishop Auckland.	IR	Name not traced.
PL	Peter Lambert of Berwick.	I·D	John Deas ?	EJC	„ „
CR DR	Chrstn. K. Reid & David Reid.	OSWALD	Robt. Oswald of Durham.	WR	„ „
CAMERON	Alexr. Cameron of Dundee.	OY	Oliver Young.	E·O	„ „
J·R	John Robertson.	IC	John Cook.	RO	„ „
		WW&SONS	W. Wilson & Sons.	I·H HB	„ „
		LP	L. Pedrine of Carlisle.		
		A&S	Alder & Sons of Blyth.		

CHAPTER IX
Marks on Chester Plate

The Chester Assay Office was established in 1687, though a guild of silver-smiths existed as early as 1573. The assay office was suspended in 1696 but re-established in 1701. It still functions.

TABLE I.

DATE.	MAKER'S MARK, TOWN MARK AND DATE-LETTER.				MAKER'S NAME.
1668					George Oulton.
c. 1683					Ralph Walley.
"					Nathanl. Bullen.
c. 1685					" "
"					" "
1686-90					Alexand'r Pulford.
"					Peter Edwards.
"					" "
"					Ralph Walley.
1690-2					" "
"					Peter Pemberton.
"					" "
"					" "
c. 1692					" "
1692-4					" "
1695-1700					Name not traced.
1695					... ...
1696					... ...
1697					... ...

TABLE II.

FIVE STAMPS AS BELOW.

	BRIT-ANNIA.	LION'S HEAD ERASED.	DATE LETTER.	TOWN MARK.	MAKER'S MARK.	MAKER'S NAME.	ARTICLES AND OWNERS.
1701-2			A		Ri	Richd. Richardson.	Rat-tail spoon : Mr. G. Lambert.
ANNE. 1702-3	,,	,,	B	,,	Bi	John Bingley.	Do. do. : Messrs. Christie.
1703-4	,,	,,	C	,,	Bu Bi	Nath. Bullen. Chas. Bird.	Table-spoon: Mr. Lowe, Chester. Assay Office Plate, Chester.
1704-5	,,	,,	D	,,	Ri	Richd. Richardson.	Oval tobacco box, dated 1704 : Chester Corporation.
1705-6	,,	,,	E	,,	Pe Ho	Peter Pemberton. Name not traced.	Large rat-tail table-spoon: Mr. Lowe. Assay Office Plate, Chester.
1706-7	,,	,,	F	,,	Ho	,, ,,	Do. do. do.
1707-8	,,	,,	G	,,	Ro	Thos. Robinson.	Tumbler cup: Judge Wynne-Ffoulkes.
1708-9	,,	,,	H	,,	Gi	Name not traced.	Assay Office Plate, Chester.
1709-10	,,	,,	I	,,	Co	,, ,,	Do. do. do.
1710-11	,,	,,	K	,,	Ie	,, ,,	Do. do. do.
1711-2	,,	,,	L	,,	Sa	,, ,,	Do. do. do.
1712-3	,,	,,	M	,,	Ta	— Tarleton.	Do. do. do.
1713-4	,,	,,	N	,,	Ri	Richd. Richardson.	Com. cup and flagon, "given 1716.": St. Peter's, Chester.
GEO. I. 1714-5	,,	,,	O	,,	Ri	,, ,,	Com. paten : Church of St. John Baptist, Northgate, Chester.
1715-6	,,	,,	P	,,	Du	Barth. Duke.	Gravy spoon : Mr. Hignett.
1716-7	,,	,,	Q	,,	Ma Ma	Thos. Maddock. ,, ,,	Rat-tail spoon : Mr. Crichton. Assay Office Plate, Chester.
1717-8	,,	,,	R	,,	Ri	Richd. Richardson.	Alms-plate, inscribed 1719 : St. John's, Chester.
1718-9	,, LION PASSANT.	,, LEOP'S HEAD C.?	S	,,	,,	,, ,,	Com. cup : St. Bridget's (now at St. Mary's), Chester.
1719-20			T	•	Ri	,, ,,	Small oar : Chester Corporation.
1720-1	,,	,,	U	,,	Ma	Thos. Maddock.	Rat-tail spoon : The Day Collection.
1721-2	,,	,,	V	,,	Ri	Richd. Richardson.	Small cup with one handle: Cordwainers' Guild, Carlisle.
1722-3	,,	,,	W	,,	Ri	,, ,,	Rat-tail spoon : Chester Corpn.
1723-4	,,	,,	X	,,	Ri	,, ,,	{ Paten, on foot, dated 1723 : St. Michael's, Chester. { Gravy spoon : late Miss Farmer.
1724-5	,,	,,	Y	,,	Ri	,, ,,	Plate paten : St. Michael's, Ches. Com. cup : St. John's, Chester.*
1725-6	,,	,,	Z	,,	JM	John Melling.	Table-spoon : Judge Wynne-Ffoulkes.

1716-7   Ri   Mark on small cup at Llanerchymedd ; possibly the mark of a Richardson widow.

* Also water-bailiff's oar, dated 1726, badge of jurisdiction over the river : Beaumaris.

TABLE III.

FIVE STAMPS AS BELOW.

	LION PASSANT.	LEOPARD'S HEAD CROWNED.	TOWN MARK.	DATE LETTER.	MAKER'S MARK.	MAKER'S NAME.	ARTICLES AND OWNERS.
1726-7	🦁	👑	🛡	*A*	BP	Benj'n Pemberton.	Small salver : Messrs. Christie.
GEO. II. 1727-8	,,	,,	,,	*B*	BP	,, ,,	Large skewer : Messrs. G.
1728-9	,,	,,	,,	*C*	RR	Richd. Richardson.	Com. cup, dated 1728 : Kendal.
1729-30	,,	,,	,,	*D*	RP	Richd. Pike.	Rat-tail spoon : Mr. W. Boore.
1730-1	,,	,,	,,	*E*	WR	Wm. Richardson.	Do. do. : Do.
1731-2	,,	,,	,,	*F*		R.R. conjoined as at 1728 above.	Pipkin : Mr. Lowe, Chester.
1732-3	,,	,,	,,	*G*	RR	Richd. Richardson.	Com. cup and cover, dated 1732 : Whitehaven.
1733-4	,,	,,	,,	*H*	RR	,, ,,	Assay Office Plate.
1734-5	,,	,,	,,	*I*	,,	,, ,,	Com. cup and cover : Workington.
1735-6	,,	,,	,,	*K*	{ ,, RR	,, ,,	Do. do. : Kirkby Lonsdale. Do. do., dated 1735 : Poulton-le-Fylde, Lancashire.
1736-7	,,	,,	,,	*L*	,,	,, ,,	Half-pint mug : Messrs. Comyns.
1737-8	,,	,,	,,	*M*	RR	,, ,,	Pair of alms-basins, dated 1737 : Chester Cathedral.
1738-9	,,	,,	,,	*N*	,,	,, ,,	Large gravy spoon : Mr. W. Boore.
1739-40	,,	,,	,,	*O*	WR	Wm. Richardson.	Assay Office Plate.
1740-1	,,	,,	,,	*P*	BP	Benj'n Pemberton.	Table-spoon : Mr. G. Lambert.
1741-2	,,	,,	,,	*Q*	RR	Richd. Richardson.	Sauce-boat : Judge Wynne-Ffoulkes.
1742-3	,,	,,	,,	*R*	TM	Thos. Maddock.	Pap bowl : Messrs. Spink.
1743-4	,,	,,	,,	*S*	RR	Richd. Richardson.	Do. do. : Mr. Lowe, Chester.
1744-5	,,	,,	,,	*T*	,,	,, ,,	Sauce pan : Messrs. Crichton.
1745-6	,,	,,	,,	*U*		... ...	Date-letter conjectured.
1746-7	,,	,,	,,	*V*		... ...	Do. do. do.
1747-8	,,	,,	,,	*W*		Thos. Maddock as above.	Table-spoon : Mr. Payne.
1748-9	,,	👑	,,	*X*	RR	Richd. Richardson.	Pair of beakers : Judge Wynne-Ffoulkes.
1749-50	,,	,,	,,	*Y*	,,	,, ,,	Plate : Messrs. Comyns.
1750-1	🦁	,,	,,	*Z*	RR	,, ,,	Tumbler : Mr. W. Keir, Corwen.

Y Variant of date-letter for 1749-50 : Assay Office Plate ; and tumbler : Mr. Lowe.

TABLE IV.

	LION PASSANT.	LEOPARD'S HEAD CROWNED.	TOWN MARK.	DATE LETTER.	MAKER'S MARK.	MAKER'S NAME.
1751-2				a	RR	Richd. Richardson.
1752-3	"	"	"	Borb		
1753-4	"	"	"	C	"	" "
1754-5	"	"	"	Dord		
1755-6	"	"	"	e	"	" "
1756-7	"	"	"	Forf		
1757-8	"	"	"	G	RR	" "
1758-9	"	"	"	h	RR	" "
1759-60	"	"	"	Iori		
GEO. III, 1760-1	"	"	"	Kork		
1761-2	"	"	"	Lorl		
1762-3	"	"	"	m	RR RR	" "
1763-4	"	"	"	n	RR	" "
1764-5	"	"	"	O P	RR	" "
1765-6	"	"	"	P	"	" "
1766-7	"	"	"	Qorq		
1767-8	"	"	"	R	RR	" "
1768-9		"	"	S	"	" "
1769-70	"	"	"	T	BWF	Bolton & Fothergill, Birm.
1771-2	"	"	"	U	IW	Joseph Walley.
1773	"	"	"	V	GW I·D	Geo. Walker. James Dixon or Jos. Duke.
1774	"	"	"	W	ID	" "
1775	"	"	"	X	GW	Geo. Walker.
1775-6	"	"	"	Y	RR	Richd. Richardson, jr.

1755-6   E   Another example of date-letter for this year: Assay Office Plate. Also on a sugar basin (with mark of Joseph Walley): The Goldsmiths' Co.

TABLE V.

	LION PASSANT.	LEOPARD'S HEAD CROWNED.	TOWN MARK.	DATE LETTER.	MAKER'S MARK.	MAKER'S NAME.
1776-7				a	RR	Richd. Richardson.
1777-8	"	"	"	b	GW	George Walker.
1778-9	"	"	"	c	RR	Richd. Richardson.
1779-80				d	IW	Joseph Walley.
1780-1	"	"	"	e	"	" "
1781-2	"	"	"	f	GW	George Walker.
1782-3	"	"	"	g	"	" "
1783-4	"	"	"	h i	JA	John Adamson.
	"	"	"	i	KING'S HEAD. BF	Richd. Richardson.
1784-5				k	RR	" "
1785-6	"	"	"	l	JC	J. Clifton or James Conway.
1786-7	"	"	"	l	TP	T. Pierpoint.
1787-8	"	"	"	m	RB	Robt. Boulger.
1788-9	"	"	"	n	IG RJ	John Gilbert. Robert Jones.
1789-90	"	"	"	o	WH	Wm. Hull.
1790-1	"	"	"	p	WT WT	Wm. Tarlton.* " "
1791-2	"	"	"	q	IB	James Barton.
1792-3	"	"	"	r	EM	E. Maddock.
1793-4	"	"	"	s	TA	Thos. Appleby.
1794-5	"	"	"	t	TH	Thos. Hilsby.
1795-6	"	"	"	u	TM	Thos. Morrow.
1796-7		"	"	v	IA&S	John Adamson & Son.

IH   John   Hewitt.

TABLE VI.

SIX STAMPS AS BELOW.

	LION PASSANT.	LEOPARD'S HEAD CROWNED.	TOWN MARK.	DATE LETTER.	KING'S HEAD	MAKER'S MARK.	MAKER'S NAME.	ARTICLES AND OWNERS.
1797-8	[lion]	[leopard]	[town]	A	[head]	GL	George Lowe.	Large skewer : Judge Wynne-Ffoulkes.
1798-9	,,	,,	,,	B	,,	R·I	Robt. Jones.	Extinguisher : Messrs. Crichton.
1799 1800	,,	,,	,,	C	,,	RG	Robert Green.	Watch-case, noted in Manchester.
1800-1	,,	[leopard]	,,	D	,,	NC	Nicholas Cunliffe.	Do. do. do.
1801-2	,,	,,	,,	E	,,		Maker's mark indistinct.	Goblet : Messrs. Welby.
1802-3	,,	,,	,,	F	,,	GW	George Walker.	Gravy-spoon : Messrs. Debenham.
1803-4	,,	,,	,,	G	,,		,, ,,	Table-spoon : Mr. W. Boore.
1804-5	,,	,,	,,	H	,,	I·E	Name not traced.	Marks noted by the Author.
1805-6	,,	,,	,,	I	,,	NL	Nicholas Lee.	Watch-case, noted in Manchester.
1806-7	,,	,,	,,	K	,,		,, ,,	Do. do. do.
1807-8	,,	,,	,,	L	,,	GL	George Lowe.	Skewer : Mr. Lowe, Chester.
1808-9	,,	,,	,,	M	,,		Mark indistinct.	Table-spoon : Mr. Wills.
1809-10	,,	,,	,,	N	,,	WJ	Name not traced.	Marks noted by Author.
1810-1	,,	,,	,,	O	,,	IW	John Walker.	Watch-case : Mr. Spiridion.
1811-2	,,	,,	,,	P	,,	WP	William Pugh (of Birmingham).	Sugar-tongs : Mr. Harris.
1812-3	,,	,,	,,	Q	,,	A&I	Abbott & Jones.	Watch-case noted by the Author.
1813-4	,,	,,	,,	R	,,		,, ,,	Do. do. do.
1814-5	,,	,,	,,	S	,,	JM	Jas. Morton.	Sauce-boat : Mr. Crichton.
1815-6	,,	,,	,,	T	,,		,, ,,	Fish-slice : Mr. Phillips.
1816-7	,,	,,	,,	U	,,	H·A	Hugh Adamson.	Watch-case noted by the Author.
1817-8	,,	,,	,,	V	,,	JA	John Abbott.	Do. do. do.

TABLE VII.

SIX STAMPS AS BELOW.

	LION PASSANT	LEOPARD'S HEAD.	TOWN MARK.	DATE LETTER.	KING'S HEAD.	MAKER'S MARK.	MAKER'S NAME.	SOURCE OF MARKS.
1818-9	🦁	⛊	⛊	A	👤	J.W	J. Walker.	From wax impression : Mr. J. F. Lowe, B.A.
1819-20 GEO. IV.	,,	,,	,,	B	,,	V&R	Vale & Co.	Assay Office Plate and Records.
1820-1	,,	,,	,,	C	,,	I&R	Jones & Reeves.	Do. do. do.
1821-2-3	,,	,,	,,	D	,,	HVA	Hy. Adamson.	Do. do. do.
1823-4	,,	⛊	,,	E	👤	MH	Mary Huntingdon.	Do. do. do.
1824-5	,,	,,	,,	F	,,	JT	John Twemlow.	Do. do. do.
1825-6	,,	,,	,,	G	,,	JM	J. Morton.	Small cream-jug : Mr. Crichton.
1826-7	,,	,,	,,	H	,,	G.L	Geo. Lowe.	Plate : Mr. Lowe, Chester.
1827-8	,,	,,	,,	I	,,	RB	Robt. Bowers.	Assay Office Plate, Chester.
1828-9	,,	,,	,,	K	,,	TN	Thos. Newton.	Do. do. do.
1829-30 WM. IV.	,,	,,	,,	L	,,	JH JH	John Hilsby, L'pool. ,, ,, ,, }	Do. do. do.
1830-1	,,	,,	,,	M	,,	JC	John Coakley.	Gravy spoon : Mr. Lowe, Chester.
1831-2	,,	,,	,,	N	,,	JP	John Parsonage.	Assay Office Plate, Chester.
1832-3	,,	,,	,,	O	,,	TW	Thos. Walker or Thos. Woodfield }	Do. do. do.
1833-4	,,	,,	,,	P	,,	R.L	Robt. Lowe.	Do. do. do.
1834-5	,,	,,	,,	Q	,,	R.L	Richd. Lucas.	Do. do. do.
1835-6	,,	,,	,,	R	👤	IW	John Walker.	Do. do. do.
1836-7 VICT.	,,	,,	,,	S	,,	ILS	Jos. L. Samuel.	Do. do. do.
1837-8	,,	,,	,,	T	,,	JS	John Sutters.	Large quantity of table plate, Liverpool.
1838-9	,,	,,	,,	U	,,	HC	Henry Close.	Pocket compass case : Captain Williams.

TABLE VIII.

FIVE STAMPS AS BELOW.

	LION PASSANT.	TOWN MARK.	DATE LETTER.	QUEEN'S HEAD.	MAKER'S MARK.	MAKER'S NAME.		SOURCE OF MARKS.		
1839-40	🦁	🛡	A	👑	IL TL	J. & Thos.	Lowe.	Sauce-boat; Mr. P. Lannon.		
1840-1	,,	,,	B	,,	I&TL	,, ,, ,,		Assay Office Plate and Records.		
1841-2	,,	,,	C	,,	HA	Henry	Adamson.	Do.	do.	do.
1842-3	,,	,,	D	,,	PL	P.	Leonard.	Do.	do.	do.
1843-4	,,	,,	E	,,	WS	Wm.	Smith.	Do.	do.	do.
1844-5	,,	,,	F	,,	RS	Ralph	Samuel.	Do.	do.	do.
1845-6	,,	,,	G	,,	AB / WC	Adam / Wm.	Burgess. / Crofton.	Do. / Do.	do. / do.	do. / do.
1846-7	,,	,,	H	,,	JB	J.	Burbidge.	Do.	do.	do.
1847-8	,,	,,	I	,,	IFW	John F.	Wathew.	Do.	do.	do.
1848-9	,,	,,	K	,,	CJ	Christr.	Jones.	Do.	do.	do.
1849-50	,,	,,	L	,,	TW	T.	Wilson.	Do.	do.	do.
1850-1	,,	,,	M	,,	EK	E.	Kirkman.	Do.	do.	do.
1851-2	,,	,,	N	,,	GW	Geo.	Ward.	Do.	do.	do.
1852-3	,,	,,	O	,,	TC	T.	Cubbin.	Do.	do.	do.
1853-4	,,	,	P	,,	RA / GCL	Richard / G. C.	Adamson. / Lowe. (Manchester).	Do. / Do.	do. / do.	do. / do.
1854-5	,,	,,	Q	,,	TW	Thos.	Wooley.	Do.	do.	do.
1855-6	,,	,,	R	,,	AGR	A. G.	Rogers.	Do.	do.	do.
1856-7	,,	,,	S	,,	JL	John	Lowe.	Do.	do.	do.
1857-8	,,	,,	T	,,	JM	Joseph	Mayer.	Do.	do.	do.
1858-9	,,	,,	U	,,	EJ	Edwd.	Jones.	Do.	do.	do.
1859-60	,,	,,	V	,,	EN	Elias	Nathan.	Do.	do.	do.
1860-1	,,	,,	W	,,	GR	Geo.	Roberts.	Do.	do.	do.
1861-2	,,	,,	Y	,,	HF	H.	Fishwick.	Do.	do.	do.
1862-3	,,	,,	Y	,,	HS	H. J.	Stuart.	Do.	do.	do.
1863-4	,,	,,	Z	,,	FB	Francis	Butt.	Do.	do.	do.

TABLE IX.

FIVE STAMPS AS BELOW.

	LION PASSANT.	TOWN MARK.	DATE LETTER.	QUEEN'S HEAD.	MAKER'S MARK.	MAKER'S NAME.
1864-5	🦁	🛡	a	👑	WD	Wm. Dodge.
1865-6	,,	,,	b	,,	IR	John Richards.
1866-7	,,	,,	c	,,	SW	Saml. Ward, Manchester.
1867-8	,,	,,	d	,,	GL	Geo. Lowe, junr.
1868-9	,,	,,	e	,,	HT HT	Henry Tarlton, Liverpool.
1869-70	,,	,,	f	,,	WR	W. Roskell, Liverpool.
1870-1	,,	,,	g	,,	S.Q	S. Quilliam.
1871-2	,,	,,	h	,,	GR	Geo. Roberts.
1872-3	,,	,,	i	,,	RO	Robt. Over.
1873-4	,,	,,	k	,,	TR	Thos. Russell.
1874-5	,,	,,	l	,,	HG	Hugh Green.
1875-6	,,	,,	m	,,	S&R	Samuel & Rogers.
1876-7	,,	,,	n	,,	AC	A. Cruickshank.
1877-8	,,	,,	o	,,	SQ	S. Quilliam.
1878-9	,,	,,	p	,,	GFW	Geo. F. Wright, Liverpool.
1879-80	,,	,,	q	,,	JK	Joseph Knight, Birmingham.
1880-1	,,	,,	r	,,	TP &S	T. Power & Son, Liverpool.
1881-2	,,	,,	s	,,	BN	Benge Nathan.
1882-3	,,	,,	t	,,	WS	Wm. Smith, Liverpool.
1883-4	,,	,,	u	,,	AR	A. Rogers, Liverpool.

TABLE X.

FIVE STAMPS TILL 1890, FOUR AFTERWARD.

	LION PASSANT.	TOWN MARK.	DATE LETTER.	QUEEN'S HEAD.	MAKER'S MARK.
1884-5	🦁	🛡	A	👑	NBS
1885-6	,,	,,	B	,,	A.B
1886-7	,,	,,	C	,,	JT&S
1887-8	,,	,,	D	,,	A&M
1888-9	,,	,,	E	,,	W.T
1889-90	,,	,,	F	,,	EW
1890-1	,,	,,	G		J.W
1891-2	,,	,,	H		T.C
1892-3	,,	,,	I		J H A H
1893-4	,,	,,	K		H.W
1894-5	,,	,,	L		J D W D
1895-6	,,	,,	M		A.M
1896-7	,,	,,	N		W.N
1897-8	,,	,,	O		HK
1898-9	,,	,,	P		W.A
1899 1900	,,	,,	Q		T.P.B
1900-1	,,	,,	R		G N R H
EDW. VII. 1901-2	,,	,,	A		J.F
1902-3	,,	,,	B		B.B

TABLE XI.

FOUR STAMPS, WITH MAKER'S MARK.

DATE.	LION PASSANT.	TOWN MARK.	DATE-LETTER.	SOURCE OF MARKS.		
1903-4			C	From Assay Office Records.		
1904-5	,,	,,	D	Do.	do.	do.
1905-6	,,	,,	E	Do.	do.	do.
1906-7	,,	,,	F	Do.	do.	do.
1907-8	,,	,,	G	Do.	do.	do.
1908-9	,,	,,	H	Do.	do.	do.
1909-10	,,	,,	J	Do.	do.	do.
1910-1	,,	,,	K	Do.	do.	do.
1911-2	,,	,,	L	Do.	do.	do.
1912-3	,,	,,	M	Do.	do.	do.
1913-4	,,	,,	N	Do.	do.	do.
1914-5	,,	,,	O	Do.	do.	do.
1915-6	,,	,,	P	Do.	do.	do.
1916-7	,,	,,	Q	Do.	do.	do.
1917-8	,,	,,	R	Do.	do.	do.
1918-9	,,	,,	S	Do.	do.	do.
1919-20	,,	,,	T	Do.	do.	do.
1920-1	,,	,,	U	Do.	do.	do.
1921-2	,,	,,	V	Do.	do.	do.

CHAPTER X
Marks on Birmingham Plate
The Birmingham Assay Office was established in 1773.
TABLE I.
FOUR STAMPS UNTIL 1784, THENCEFORWARD FIVE, AS BELOW.

	LION PASSANT.	ANCHOR.	DATE LETTER.		MAKER'S MARK.	MAKER'S NAME.	ARTICLES AND OWNERS.
1773-4	🦁	⚓	A		MB IF	Matthew Boulton & John Fothergill.	Pair of salts: Birmingham Assay Office.
1774-5	,,	,,	B		,, ,,	{ ,, ,, ,, ,,	Candlesticks: Mr. M. B. Huish. Do. : B'm'ham Assay Office.
1775-6	,,	,,	C		CF	Charles Freeth.	Mounts of horse-pistols . Mr. F. Weekes.
1776-7	,,	,,	D		,,	,, ,,	Light striker : Mr. F. Weekes.
1777-8	,,	,,	E		RB CF MB IF	Richard Bickley, Charles Freeth. Boulton & Fothergill.	Mounts of pistol: Mr. Dudley Westropp. Cake-basket : Mr. H. D. Ellis.
1778-9	,,	,,	F		,, ,,	,, ,,	Candlesticks: Mr. W. Boore.
1779-80	,,	,,	G		TW	T. Willmore & Alston.	Pair of shoe buckles: B'm'ham Assay Office.
1780-1	,,	,,	H			... ...	Marks from B'm'ham Assay Office Records.
1781-2	,,	,,	I			... ...	Do. do. do.
1782-3	,,	,,	K		TW	T. Willmore & Alston.	Pair of shoe buckles: B'm'ham Assay Office.
1783-4	,,	,,	L	KING'S HEAD	,,	,, ,,	Pair of shoe buckles: Mr. Dicker.
1784-5	,,	,,	M	👤	SP	Samuel Pemberton.	Snuff-box : Mr. Falk.
1785-6	,,	,,	N	,,	HH	Henry Holland.	Watch-case : B'm'ham Assay Office.
1786-7	,,	,,	O	👤	SP	Samuel Pemberton.	Snuff-box : Messrs. Robinson and Fisher.
1787-8	,,	,,	P	,,	IT	Joseph Taylor.	Caddy spoon : Do. do.
1788-9	,,	,,	Q	,,	,,	,, ,,	Marrow spoon : Mr. Simmonds.
1789-90	,,	,,	R	,,	T.W	Thos. Willmore.	Pair of shoe buckles: The Author's Collection.
1790-1	,,	,,	S	,,	MB	Mathw. Boulton.	Tripod fruit stand : B'm'ham Assay Office.
1791-2	,,	,,	T	,,	SP	Samuel Pemberton.	Patch-box : B'm'ham Assay Office.
1792-3	,,	,,	U	,,	,,	,, ,,	Snuff-box : Mr. Lowe, Chester.
1793-4	,,	,,	V	,,	MB	Mathw. Boulton.	Candelabrum : Birmingham Assay Office.
1794-5	,,	,,	W	,,	IT	Joseph Taylor.	Caddy spoon : Birmingham Assay Office.
1795-6	,,	,,	X	,,	IS	John Shaw.	Vinaigrette : The Author's Collection.
1796-7	,,	,,	Y	,,	T.W	Thos. Willmore.	Scent bottle case : B'm'ham Assay Office.
* 1797-8	,,	,,	Z	👤	,,	,, ,,	Vinaigrette : B'm'ham Assay Office.

* The King's head is found in stamps both of oval and indented outline for the year 1797-8, and in some instances the King's head mark is stamped twice.

TABLE II.

FIVE STAMPS AS BELOW.

	LION PASSANT.	ANCHOR.	DATE LETTER.	KING'S HEAD	MAKER'S MARK.	MAKER'S NAME.	ARTICLES AND OWNERS.
1798-9	🦁	⚓	**a**	👑	TW	Willmore & Alston.	Nutmeg box : Mr. Fitzhenry.
1799 1800	,,	,,	**b**	,,	SP	Samuel Pemberton.	Snuff-box : Messrs. Spink.
1800-1	,,	,,	**c**	,,	F&W	Forrest & Wasdell.	Nutmeg grater : Messrs. Spink.
1801-2	,,	,,	**d**	,,	IT TW	John Turner ? Thos. Willmore ?	Vinaigrette : B'ham Assay Off. Patch-box : The Author's Collection.
1802-3	,,	,,	**e**	,,	MB	Matthew Boulton.	Toast rack : B'ham Assay Off.
1803-4	,,	,,	**f**	,,	IS	John Shaw.	Vinaigrette : The Author's Collection.
1804-5	,,	,,	**g**	,,	IT	Joseph Taylor.	Mustard spoon : Mr. Fitzhenry.
1805-6	,,	,,	**h**	,,	ML WP	Matthew Linwood. William Pugh.	Snuff-box : The Author's Coll. Caddy spoon : B'm Assay Off.
1806-7	,,	,,	**i**	,,	JW C&B	Joseph Willmore. Cocks & Bettridge.	Snuff-box : Do. do. Nutmeg grater : Mr. Ballard.
1807-8	,,	,,	**j**	,,	WP	William Pugh.	Snuff-box : The Author's Coll.
1808-9	,,	,,	**k**	,,	MB	Matthew Boulton.	Cheese scoop : Messrs. Christie.
1809-10	,,	,,	**l**	👑	IS	John Shaw.	Snuff-box : Mr. Bruford.
1810-1	,,	,,	**m**	,,	T&T	Thropp & Taylor.	Do. : B'ham Assay Office.
1811-2	,,	,,	**n**	,,	S&S	T. Simpson & Son.	Snuff-box : Messrs. Spink.
1812-3	,,	,,	**o**	👑	IT	Joseph '' Taylor.	Do. : B'ham Assay Office. Salt-spoons : Messrs. M. & S. Lyon.
1813-4	,,	,,	**p**	,,	C&B	Cocks & Bettridge.	Mustard-spoon : The Author.
1814-5	,,	,,	**q**	,,	L&C	W. Lea & Co.	Vinaigrette : Do.
1815-6	,,	,,	**r**	,,	,,	,, ,,	Snuff-box : Messrs. Spink.
1816-7	,,	,,	**s**	,,	SP W&K	Samuel Pemberton. Wardell & Kempson.	Vinaigrette : Mr. G. Lowe. Child's coral : Miss Jackson.
1817-8	,,	,,	**t**	,,	E·T	Edward Thomason.	Tea-spoon : B'ham Assay Off.
1818-9	,,	,,	**u**	,,	J.W	Joseph Willmore.	Snuff-box : Do. do.
1819-20 GEO. IV. 1820-1	,,	,,	**v** **w**	,, ,,	,, ML	,, ,, Matthew Linwood & Son.	Vinaigrette : The Author's Collection. Sandwich box : Messrs. Robinson & Fisher.
1821-2	,,	,,	**x**	,,	L&C	Lea & Clark.	Seal : Birmingham Assay Office.
1822-3	,,	,,	**y**	,,	L&Cº	John Lawrence & Co.	Snuff-box : Do. do.
1823-4	,,	,,	**z**	,,	J.W	Joseph Willmore.	Vinaigrette : Do. do.

On plate of 1801 to 1811 the King's head mark is frequently found in a stamp of oval shape, and on plate of 1812 to 1825 it is sometimes found in a foliated stamp as shown at 1797-8 and 1809-10.

TABLE III.

	LION PASSANT.	ANCHOR.	DATE LETTER.	KING'S HEAD.	MAKER'S MARK.	MAKER'S NAME.	ARTICLES AND OWNERS.
1824-5			A		T·P C·J	T. Pemberton & Son. Charles Jones.	Salt-spoons: B'm. Assay Office. Sugar-tongs: Do. do.
1825-6	,,	,,	B	,,	LV&W T·S	Ledsam, Vale & Wheeler. Thomas Shaw.	Snuff-box: Messrs. Spink. Do. : Mr. John Fullerton.
1826-7	,,	,,	C		L&Cº N·M	John Lawrence & Co. Nathaniel Mills.	Do. : The Author's Coll'n. Do. : B'm'ham Assay Office.
1827-8	,,	,,	D	,,	U&H M·B J·W	Unite and Hilliard. M. Boulton & Plate Co. Joseph Willmore.	Caddy spoon: Do. do. Taper-stand : Do. do. Snuff-box: The Author's Coll'n.
1828-9	,,	,,	E	,,	E·T W·F	Edward Thomason. William Fowke.	Cake-basket : M's'rs. Smith & Rait. Table-spoon: B'm'ham Assay Off.
1829-30	,,	,,	F		I·B LV&W	John Bettridge. Ledsam, Vale & Wheeler.	Snuff-box : Do. do. Wine-labels : Do. do.
WM. IV. 1830-1	,,	,,	G	,,	TR&S M·B	Thos. Ryland & Sons. M. Boulton & Plate Co.	Pair of spurs : Do. do. Cake-basket : Do. do.
1831-2	,,	,,	H		J·W	Joseph Willmore.	Handles of knife and fork : Birmingham Assay Office.
1832-3	,,	,,	I	,,	,, ,,	,, ,,	Silver-gilt knife, fork, and spoon: Birmingham Assay Office.
1833-4	,,	,,	K	,,	E·S V·R	Edward Smith. Vale & Ratheram.	Snuff-box : Messrs. Spink. Watch-case : B'm'ham Assay Off.
1834-5	,,	,,	L		T&P W·P	Taylor & Perry. William Phillips.	Caddy-spoon : Do. do. Snuff-box : Mr. Bruford.
1835-6	,,	,,	M	,,	G·W	Gervase Wheeler.	Vinaigrette : Mr. G. Lowe.
1836-7	,,	,,	N	,,	F·C J&Cº	Francis Clark. Joseph Jennens & Co.	Snuff-box : The Author's Coll'n. Baron's coronet : Messrs. Crichton.
VICT. 1837-8	,,	,,	O	,,	T·S R.E.A	Thomas Spicer. Robinson, Edkins & Aston.	Watch-case : B'm'ham Assay Off. Standish : Do. do.
*1838-9	,,	,,	P		G·U N·M	George Unite. Nathaniel Mills.	Wine labels: Do. do. Snuff-box : Do. do.
1839-40	,,	,,	Q	,,	N&R	Neville & Ryland ?	Do. : Do. do.
1840-1	,,	,,	R		,, ,,	,, ,,	Do. : B'm'ham Assay Office.
1841-2	,,	,,	S	,,	... ...	... ...	From Birmingham Assay Office Records.
1842-3	,,	,,	T	,,	R.E.A	Robinson, Edkins & Aston.	Hand candlestick: Messrs. M. & S. Lyon.
1843-4	,,	,,	U	,,	E·S	Edward Smith.	Snuff-box: Messrs. Spink.
1844-5	,,	,,	V	,,	N·M	Nathaniel Mills.	Do. : B'm'ham Assay Office.
1845-6	,,	,,	W	,,	W&E·T	Wm. & Ed. Turnpenny.	Oval strainer : Mr. Peters.
1846-7	,,	,,	X	,,	Y&W N·M	Yapp & Woodward. Nathaniel Mills.	Apple scoop : B'm'ham Assay Off. Snuff-box : Do. do.
1847-8	,,	,,	Y	,,	,,	,, ,,	Vinaigrette : Messrs. Spink.
1848-9	,,	,,	Z	,,	... ...	... ...	From Birmingham Assay Office Records.

* On plate of the early part of 1838-9 the head of King William is sometimes found stamped, although Queen Victoria succeeded to the throne in 1837.

TABLE IV.

FIVE STAMPS AS BELOW.

	LION PASSANT.	ANCHOR.	DATE LETTER.	QUEEN'S HEAD.	MAKER'S MARK.	MAKER'S NAME.	ARTICLES AND OWNERS.
1849-50	🦁	⚓	A	👑	N·M	Nathaniel Mills.	
1850-1	,,	,,	B	,,	{ E·S	,, ,, Edward Smith.	
1851-2	,,	,,	C	,,	,,	,, ,,	
1852-3	,,	,,	D	,,		Nathl. Mills, as 1849.	
1853-4	,,	,,	E	,,		... ...	
1854-5	,,	,,	F	,,		... ...	
1855-6	,,	,,	G	,,	G·U	George Unite.	
1856-7	,,	,,	H	,,		... ...	
1857-8	,,	,,	I	,,		... ...	
1858-9	,,	,,	J	,,		... ...	
1859-60	,,	,,	K	,,	G·U	George Unite.	
1860-1	,,	,,	L	,,		... ...	
1861-2	,,	,,	M	,,		... ...	
1862-3	,,	,,	N	,,		J. H. & Co., as on page 414.	
1863-4	,,	,,	O	,,		... ...	
1864-5	,,	,,	P	,,	J·M·&·C	Names registered after 1850 not disclosed.	
1865-6	,,	,,	Q	,,		... ...	
1866-7	,,	,,	R	,,		... ...	
1867-8	,,	,,	S	,,	J·G	... ...	
1868-9	,,	,,	T	,,		... ...	
1869-70	,,	,,	U	,,		... ...	
1870-1	,,	,,	V	,,		... ...	
1871-2		,,	W	,,	J·T	Crown and 18 instead of lion passant.	
1872-3	,,	,,	X	,,		... ...	
1873-4	,,	,,	Y	,,		... ...	
1874-5	,,	,,	Z	,,		... ...	

TABLE V.

	LION PASSANT.	ANCHOR.	DATE LETTER.	QUEEN'S HEAD.	MAKER'S MARK.
1875-6	🦁	⚓	a	👑	TP&S
1876-7	„	„	b	„	„
1877-8	„	„	c	„	H&T
1878-9	„	„	d	„	
1879-80	„	„	e	„	
1880-1	„	„	f	„	
1881-2	„	„	g	„	
1882-3	„	„	h	„	H&T
1883-4	„	„	i	„	„
1884-5	„	„	k	„	
1885-6	„	„	l	„	
1886-7	„	„	m	„	
1887-8	„	„	n	„	
1888-9	„	„	o	„	
1889-90	„	„	p	„	N&H
1890-1	„	„	q	„	TWD
1891-2	„	„	r	„	N&H
1892-3	„	„	s	„	JMB
1893-4	„	„	t	„	SWS
1894-5	„	„	u	„	L.G
1895-6	„	„	v	„	T·H
1896-7	„	„	w	„	HM
1897-8	„	„	x	„	HH&Cᵒ JHW
1898-9	„	„	y	„	AᴱJZ
1899 1900	„	„	z		J.S SS

TABLE VI.

DATE.	An-chor.	Lion Passant.	Date Letter.	Maker's Mark.
1900-1	⚓	🦁	a	E & CoLᵈ
1901-2	„	„	b	HWI:
1902-3	„	„	c	IS G
1903-4	„	„	d	L & Cᵒ
1904-5	„	„	e	H&F
1905-6	„	„	f	
1906-7	„	„	g	
1907-8	„	„	h	
1908-9	„	„	i	
1909-10	„	„	k	
1910-1	„	„	l	
1911-2	„	„	m	
1912-3	„	„	n	
1913-4	„	„	o	
1914-5	„	„	p	
1915-6	„	„	q	
1916-7	„	„	r	R&TW
1917-8	„	„	s	
1918-9	„	„	t	
1919-20	„	„	u	
1920-1	„	„	v	
1921-2	„	„	w	
1922-3	„	„	x	
1923-4	„	„	y	
1924-5	„	„	z	

The Birmingham Assay Office will not disclose the names of silversmiths registered after 1850.

The twenty-year cycle for Birmingham commencing with 1925-6 and continuing to 1945-6 is distinguished by date letters in Roman capitals, in a shield resembling that for London, 1875-6.

SUPPLEMENTARY LIST OF ADDITIONAL MARKS OF GOLDSMITHS.

Impressed at Birmingham, not illustrated in the preceding tables.

DATE.	MARK.	MAKER'S NAME.	ARTICLES AND OWNERS.
1776-7	JA&S	Jos. Adams & Son.	Pierced sugar-tongs : Messrs. Crichton.
1778-9	E·S	Edward Sawyer.	Do. do. : Do. do.
1783-4	S P	Samuel Pemberton.	Do. do. : Do. do.
1804-5	W	···· ··· ···	Caddy spoon : Mr. P. Phillips.
1806-7	H&Co.	··· ··· ···	Do. do. : Do. do.
1807-8	M	··· ··· ···	Do. do. : Do. do.
1811-2	W	··· ··· ···	Do. do. : Do. do.
1814-5	J L	··· ··· ···	Do. do. : Do. do.
1820-1	T N	Thos. Newbold.	Musical snuff-box : Mr. A. J. Grimes.
1822-3	S P	··· ··· ···	Caddy spoon : Mr. P. Phillips.
1826	T&K	Geo. Tye & Jas. Kilner.	Fox-mask box : Messrs. Crichton.
1832-3	G T	Geo. Tye.	Do. do. : Do. do.
1876-7	TT &Co	··· ··· ···	Church plate in several Cornish parishes.
1862-3	J H & Co	··· ··· ···	Church plate : Lanlivery.
1892-3	H W	··· ··· ···	Church plate in several Cornish parishes.

HALL MARKS ON BIRMINGHAM GOLD WARES

THE MARKS HERE GIVEN ARE FOR THE SEVERAL CLASSES OF GOLD WARES
ASSAYED AT BIRMINGHAM.

22 Carat	👑	22	⊡	V
18 ″	″	18	″	″
15 ″	15	·625·	″	″
12 ″	12	5	″	″
9 ″	9	375	″	″

The date-letter for 1920-
is a small Roman **V**
as here illustrated.

CHAPTER XI

Marks on Sheffield Silver

The Sheffield Assay Office was established in 1773.

TABLE I.

	LION PASSANT	CROWN	DATE LETTER	KING'S HEAD (from 1784)	MAKER'S MARK	MAKER'S NAME.
1773-4	[lion]	[crown]	[letter]		R&M&Co / SR&Co / MF&Co	Rich'd. Morton & Co. / S. Roberts & Co. / Mat'w. Fenton & Co.
1774-5	"	"			GA&Co	Geo. Ashforth & Co.
1775-6	"	"			IW&Co	John Winter & Co.
1776-7	"	"			W-D	Wm. Damant.
1777-8	"	"			MF RC	Tudor and Leader. / Fenton Creswick & Co.
1778-9	"	"			I-S	John Smith ?
1779-80	"	"			"	" "
1780-1	"	"			N-S&Co	Nath'l. Smith & Co.
1781-2	"	"			MF RC	Fenton Creswick & Co.
1782-3	"	"			IW&Co	John Winter & Co.
1783-4	"	"			DH&Co / IP&Co	Danl. Holy & Co. / John Parsons & Co.
† 1784-5	"	"		[king's head]	"	" "
‡ 1785-6	"	"			R-M	Richd. Morton & Co.
1786-7	"	[crown]		[king]	IP&Co	John Parsons & Co.
1787-8	"	"			"	" "
1788-9	"	"			ITY&Co	John Younge & Sons.
1789-90	"	"			RS	R. Sutcliffe & Co. (?)
1790-1	"	"			IP&Co	John Parsons & Co.
* 1791-2	"	"			ITY&Co	John Younge & Sons.
1792-3	[lion]	[crown]			IP&Co	John Parsons & Co.
1793-4	"	"			TL	Thos. Law.
1794-5	"	"			IG&Co	John Green & Co.
1795-6	"	"			ITY&Co	John Younge & Sons, as above.
1796-7	"	"			GE&Co	Geo. Eadon & Co.
1797-8	"	"			T-LAW	T. Law.
1798-9	"	"			SR&Co / GC&Co	Saml. Roberts, jr. / Geo. Cadman & Co.

TABLE II.

	LION PASSANT	CROWN	DATE LETTER	KING'S HEAD	MAKER'S MARK	MAKER'S NAME.
1799 / 1800	[lion]	[crown]	E	[king]	ILA&Co / IG&Co	John Love & Co. / John Green & Co.
1800-1	"	"	N	"	GA&Co / IG&Co	Geo. Ashforth & Co. / John Green & Co.
1801-2	"	"	H	"	TW&Co	Thos. Watson & Co.
* 1802-3	"	"	M	"	TL DL / R-M	Thos. & Danl. Leader. / Richd. Morton & Co.
1803-4	"	"	F	"	N-S&Co	Nathan Smith & Co.
1804-5	"	"	G	"	IE&Co	Jas. Ellis & Co.
† 1805-6	"	"	B	"	AG&Co	Alexr. Goodman & Co.
1806-7	"	"	A	"	ITY	J. T. Younge & Co.
1807-8	"	"	S	"	WT&Co	W. Tucker & Co.
1808-9	"	"	P	"	TB&Co	Thos. Blagden & Co.
1809-10	"	"	K	"	IR&Co	John Roberts & Co.
* 1810-1	"	"	L	"	GE&Co	Geo. Eadon & Co. / John Roberts & Co., as 1809-10 above.
‡ 1811-2	"	"	C	[king]	"	
1812-3	"	"	D	"	ST N&H	Smith, Tate & Co. (Nicholson & Holt).
1813-4	"	"	R	"	I-K-I-W&Co	Kirkby, Waterhouse & Co.
* 1814-5	"	"	O	"	I-L	John Law
1815-6	"	"	T	"	JE&Co	J. Ellis & Co. (?)
1816-7	"	"	T	"	IW	John Watson.
1817-8	"	"	X	"	I-&-T-S	John and Thos. Settle.
1818-9	"	"	I	"	SCY&Co	S. C. Younge & Co.
* 1819-20	[lion]	"	V	"	I-K-W&CO / TJC	Thos. and Jas. Creswick / Kirkby, Waterhouse & Co.
GEO. IV 1820-1	"	"	Q	"	G C&Co / ST H&T	G. Cooper & Co. / Smith, Tate, Hoult & Tate.
1821-2	"	"	Y	"	JL	Joseph Law
1822-3	"	"	Z	"	IG&Co	John Green & Co.
1823-4	"	"	U	"	W-B	Wm. Briggs.

*†‡ See notes on p. 150.

TABLE III.

	LION PASSANT	CROWN	DATE LETTER	KING'S HEAD	MAKER'S MARK	MAKER'S NAME.
1824-5	⬡	♛	a	◈	SCY&Co / WB&Co	S. C. Younge & Co. / Wm. Blackwell & Co.
1825-6	,,		b	,,	I&IW&Co	Waterhouse, Hodson & Co.
*1826-7	,,	,,	c	,,	BH&H	Battie, Howard & Hawksworth. }
1827-8	,,		d		TJ NC	T. J. & N. Creswick.
1828-9	,,	,,	e		BH&H	Battie, Howard & Hawksworth. }
1829-30	,,		f	,,	IS HW	John Settle & Henry Williamson. }
WM. IV. 1830-1	,,		g	,,	TJ NC	T. J. & N. Creswick.
1831-2	,,	,,	h	◉	JB	Jas. Burbury.
1832-3	,,	,,	k		S&N / A&O	Stafford & Newton. / Atkin & Oxley.
1833-4	,,	♛	l	,,	TJ NC / WA&Co	T. J. & N. Creswick. / Wm. Allanson & Co.
1834-5	,,		m	,,	I&IW&Co	Waterhouse, Hodson & Co.
1835-6	,,	♛	P	◉	H&H	Howard & Hawksworth.
1836-7	,,	,,	q	,,	...	...
VICT. 1837-8	,,	,,	r	,,	HW&Co	Hy. Wilkinson & Co.
1838-9	,,	,,	S	,,	HW&Co	,, ,, ,,
1839-40	,,	,,	t	,,	SH	Samuel Harwood.
1840-1	,,	◉	u	,,		,, ,,
1841-2	,,	,,	v	,,		,, ,,
1842-3	,,		x	,,	HE&Co	Hawksworth, Eyre & Co.
1843-4	,,	,,	Z	,,		...

*Additional examples for the year 1826–7:

⬡ ♛ C ◈   JN WN F·R   Makers' mark of J. Nowill
,,   ,,   ,, W. Nowill.
,,   ,,   ,, T. Rodgers.

TABLE IV.

	CROWN	DATE LETTER	LION PASSANT	QUEEN'S HEAD	MAKER'S MARK	MAKER'S NAME.
*1844-5	♛	A	⬡	◉	HE&Co	Hawksworth, Eyre & Co.
1845-6	,,	B	,,	,,	...	... ...
1846-7	,,	C	,,	,,	...	... ...
1847-8	,,	D	,,	,,	...	... ...
1848-9	,,	E	,,	,,	...	... ...
1849-50	,,	F	,,	,,		Hawksworth, Eyre & Co.
1850-1	,,	G	,,	,,	...	... ...
1851-2	,,	H	,,	,,	...	... ...
1852-3	,,	I	,,	,,	...	... ...
1853-4	,,	K	,,	,,	...	... ...
1854-5	,,	L	,,	,,	...	... ...
1855-6	,,	M	,,	,,	...	... ...
1856-7	,,	N	,,	,,	...	... ...
1857-8	,,	O	,,	,,	...	... ...
1858-9	,,	P	,,	,,	...	... ...
1859-60	,,	R	,,	,,	MH&Co	Martin Hall & Co.
1860-1	,,	S	,,	,,	...	... ...
1861-2	,,	T	,,	,,	...	... ...
1862-3	,,	U	,,	,,	HH	Harrison Bros. & Howson.
1863-4	,,	V	,,	,,	...	... ...
1864-5	,,	W	,,	,,	FBro	Fenton Bros.
1865-6	,,	X	,,	,,	HA	Hy. Archer & Co.
1866-7	,,	Y	,,	,,	RM SH	Martin Hall & Co., Ltd.
1867-8	,,	Z	,,	,,	...	... ...

* WA ⬡ ◉ A◈   A further example of the marks for 1844–5. Candlesticks: Windsor Castle.

Makers' mark of W. Allanson & Co.

TABLE V.

	CROWN.	LION PASSANT.	DATE LETTER.	QUEEN'S HEAD.	MAKER'S MARK.	MAKER'S NAME.
1868-9	👑	🦁	A	👑	RM EH	Martin Hall & Co., Ltd.
1869-70	,,	,,	B	,,	,,	,, ,,
1870-1	,,	,,	C	,,	...	... ...
1871-2	,,	,,	D	,,		... ...
1872-3	,,	,,	E	,,		... ...
1873-4	,,	,,	F	,,	IH	John Harrison & Co., Ld.
1874-5	,,	,,	G	,,		... ...
1875-6	,,	,,	H	,,		... ...
1876-7	,,	,,	J	,,		... ...
1877-8	,,	,,	K	,,		... ...
1878-9	,,	,,	L	,,		... ...
1879-80	,,	,,	M	,,		... ...
1880-1	,,	,,	N	,,		... ...
1881-2	,,	,,	O	,,		... ...
1882-3	,,	,,	P	,,		... ...
1883-4	,,	,,	Q	,,		... ...
1884-5	,,	,,	R	,,		... ...
1885-6	,,	,,	S	,,		... ...
1886-7	,,	,,	T	,,		... ...
1887-8	,,	,,	U	,,		... ...
1888-9	,,	,,	V	,,	J·K·B	Hawksworth, Eyre & Co., Ltd.
1889-90	,,	,,	W	,,	WB JA	W. Briggs & Co.
1890-1	,,	,,	X	,,	RM EH	Martin Hall & Co., Ltd.
1891-2	,,	,,	Y	,,	J·D&S	Jas. Dixon & Sons.
1892-3	,,	,,	Z		H·S	Henry Stratford.

TABLE VI.

	CROWN.	LION PASSANT.	DATE LETTER.	MAKER'S MARK.	MAKER'S NAME.
1893-4	👑	🦁	a	JD &S	James Deakin & Sons.
1894-5	,,	,,	b	JR	John Round & Son, Ltd.
1895-6	,,	,,	c	JD WD	Jas. Deakin & Sons.
1896-7	,,	,,	d	M&W	Mappin & Webb.
1897-8			e	WF AF	Fordham & Faulkner.
1898-9		,,	f	H.W	Lee & Wigfull.
1899 1900	,,	,,	g	HA	Atkin Brothers.
1900-1	,,	,,	h	W&H	Walker & Hall.
EDW. VII. 1901-2	,,	,,	i	R&B	Roberts & Belk.
1902-3	,,	,,	k	GH	Harrison Bros. & Howson.
1903-4	,,	,,	l		... ...
1904-5	,,	,,	m		... ...
1905-6	,,	,,	n		... ...
1906-7	,,	,,	o		... ...
1907-8	,,	,,	p		... ...
1908-9	,,	,,	q		... ...
1909-10	,,	,,	r		... ...
1910-1	,,	,,	s		... ...
1911-2	,,	,,	t		... ...
1912-3	,,	,,	u		... ...
1913-4	,,	,,	v		... ...
1914-5	,,	,,	w		... ...
1915-6	,,	,,	x		... ...
1916-7	,,	,,	y		... ...
1917-8	,,	,,	z		... ...

TABLE VII.

FOUR STAMPS AS BELOW.

DATE.	CROWN.	LION PASSANT.	DATE LETTER.	MAKER'S MARK.	MAKER'S NAME.	ARTICLES AND OWNERS.
1918-9	[crown]	[lion]	a	TB &S	Thos. Bradbury & Sons.	Various articles of plate.
1919-20	,,	,,	b	W & H	Walker & Hall.	Do. do. do.
1920-1	,,	,,	c	,,	,, ,,	Do. do. do.

Notes for p. 147.

1779-80	[marks]				John Younge & Co.	Pierced cruet: Mr. H. D. Ellis.
1796-7	[marks]				Makers' mark of Henry Tudor & Thos. Leader.	

*From 1780 to 1853 the crown was often impressed in the same stamp with the date letter.

†The King's head for this year is an oval stamp.

‡1811-12. [marks] The outline of the King's head stamp has varied in the same year, being oval in some cases and indented in others. The marks here illustrated are very small, and occur on dessert knives and forks: Messrs. Crichton.

SUPPLEMENTARY LIST OF MARKS OF GOLDSMITHS

Impressed at Sheffield, not illustrated in the preceding tables, from 1773 to 1905.

DATE.	MARKS.	MAKER'S NAME.	DATE.	MARKS.	MAKER'S NAME.	DATE.	MARKS.	MAKER'S NAME.
1773	W·H I·R	W. Hancock & J. Rowbotham.	1784	T·F&C⁰	T. Fox & Co.	1822	A·H	A. Hadfield.
	WB &C⁰	W. Birks & Co.	1788	P·S	P. Spurr.	1824	CHS	C Hammond & Co
			1789	W·J	W. Jervis.	1825	RG	R. Gainsford.
"	TL LAW	T. Law.	1790	RS	R. Sporle.	1828	GH	G. Hardesty
"		" "	1791	I·B	J. Bailey.	1829	D&S	J Dixon & Son.
"	WB &C⁰	W. Birks & Co.	"	MF &C⁰	M. Fenton & Co.	1833	JM	J Mappin & Son.
"	I·R	J. Rowbotham ?		L·P &C⁰	? Luke, Proctor & Co.	1836	K&W	Kitchen & Walker.
"	JL	J. Littlewood.	1792			1840	L&M	Lee & Middleton.
"	SO	Name not traced.	1796	G·A &C⁰	G. Ashforth & Co.	"	WK &C⁰	Walker, Knowles & Co.
"	IK&C⁰	John Kay & Co.	1797	CP	C. Proctor.	1843	W&S	Waterhouse & Co
"	JN WN	J. Nowill. W. Nowill.	"	EG	E. Goodwin.	1844	BW&A	Badger Worrall & Co.
1774	I·M	J. Mappin.	"	IC	J. Creswick.	1846	R&S	Roberts & Slater.
"	W·M &C⁰	W. Marsden & Co.	"	HT&C⁰	Mark of Henry Tudor & Co.	1847	P·P &C⁰	Padley, Parkins & Co.
"	SR	S. Roberts.	1798	GG&C⁰	Goodman, Gainsford & Co.	1853	JC NC	J. & N. Creswick.
1775	IR·C⁰	J. Rowbotham & Co.	"	SK&C⁰	S. Kirkby & Co.	1856	WS HS	W. & H. Stratford.
"	R·K	R. Kippax.	1799	RJ	R. Jewesson.	1857	F&A	Fenton & Anderton.
"	IM&C⁰	J. Mappin & Co.	1801	TP	T. Poynton.	1858	WH	W. Hutton.
1776	T·H	T. Hoyland.	1804	TL	Name not traced.	"	WS GS	W. & G. Sissons.
"	IT	J. Tibbitts.	"	IS	J. Staniforth.	1859	MB	Mappin Bros.
1777	IH C⁰	J. Hoyland & Co.	1807	WT&C⁰	W. Tucker & Co.	"	EM&C⁰	Elkington Mason & Co.
"	IH&C⁰	" "	1808	JW	J. Watson.	1861	WWH	W W. Harrison.
			1810	G·W	G. Wostenholme	1862	W&H	Walker & Hall.
1778	S·W	S. Warburton.	1811	IS TS	J. Staniforth & Co.	1863	LB	Levesley Bros.
"	DH	D. Holy.	"	RG	R. Gainsford.	1864	MCB&C⁰	Mappin & Webb.
1779	M&T	Madin & Trickett	1813	I·R	J. Rogers.	1866	WA MD	W. & M. Dodge.
1780	Y·G&H	Young, Greaves & Hoyland.	1817	RG	R. Gainsford.	1867	J·H·S	J. Slater & Son.
"	N·S	N. Smith & Co.	1818	B·R	B. Rooke & Son.	1868	CT TL	Levesley Bros.
1781	I·D	J. Dewsnap.	"	W·W	W. Wrangham	1869	AB	A. Beardshaw.
			1820	T·J&N·C	T. J. & N. Creswick.	1905	I·E &·S	Name not traced.
1783	S·K	S. Kirkby.	1822	T&I·S	T. & J. Settle.			

CHAPTER XII

Marks on Lincoln Plate

TABLE I.

FROM ABOUT 1560 TO ABOUT 1650.

(THE DATES ARE APPROXIMATE EXCEPT TO THE EXTENT THAT THE INSCRIBED DATES MAY BE RELIED ON.)

DATE (ABOUT).	MARKS.	ARTICLES AND OWNERS.
1560		Apostle spoon (St. Jude). The three fleur-de-lys grouped, are in the bowl: the three in line, on back of stem.
"		Hexagonal seal-top spoon: Messrs. Crichton.
"		Elizabethan seal-top spoon: Mr. J. W. Usher, Lincoln.
1569		Com. cups, dated 1569 and 1570 (maker's mark only visible): Osbournby, and ten other parish churches in Lincolnshire.
c. 1590		Seal-top spoon:
1617		Seal-top spoon, pricked 1617: Mr. J. H. Walter, Drayton, Norfolk.
1624		Com. cup and paten, inscribed "Ex Dono Petri Harison Anno 1624": St. Audoen's, Dublin.
1628		Seal-top spoon, pricked "Ianu. 4, 1628": Mr. J. H. Walter.
1633		Do. do., do. 1633: Messrs. Crichton.
1639		Do. do., do. 1639 Do. do.
1640		Do. do., do. 1640: Mr. W. Boore.
1640-50		Puritan spoon: Mr. J. H. Walter.
"		Struck thrice on small porringer: Mr. R. G. Westmacott.
"		Communion plate: Hintlesham.

TABLE II.
FROM ABOUT 1650 TO ABOUT 1706.

(THE DATES ARE APPROXIMATE EXCEPT TO THE EXTENT THAT THE INSCRIBED DATES
MAY BE RELIED ON).

DATE. (ABOUT).	MARKS.	ARTICLES AND OWNERS.
1640-50		Communion cup : St. Margaret's, Ipswich.
,,		Do. do. : Noted by Mr. J. H. Walter.
,,		Seal-top spoon : Mr. J. H. Walter.
,,		Do. do. : Mr. H. D. Ellis.
1642		* (Timothy Skottowe ?) Beaker : Mr. Wm. Minet. F.S.A.
1650		,, ,, (?) ⎰ Beaker : Mr. A. D. George. ⎱ Mug found in Norwich : submitted by Mr. J. H. Walter. Puritan spoon ; S. Ken. Museum. Tankard : The Goldsmiths & Silversmiths & Co.
,,		Mark stamped thrice on Com. cup : Wherwell, Hants.
1650-6		,, ,, ,, ,, plain flat-stemmed spoon: Messrs. Christie.
1660		* Puritan spoons : Mercers' Company, and S. Kensington Museum.
,,		Do. do. : The Author's Collection.
1686		Trifid spoon, dated 1686 : Mr. A. W. Stone.
1690		Trifid spoon, pricked 169⁰ : South Kensington Museum.
,,		Rat-tail spoon, flat stem : Goldsmiths' Company, London.
,,		Do. do., pricked 1690 : Mr. E. W. Colt.
1706		Communion paten inscribed " Given to the Holy Trinity Church, Goodramgate, 1706 " : Holy Trinity Church, Goodramgate, York.

CHAPTER XIII

Marks of the Minor English Guilds

HULL

DATE.	TOWN MARK.	MAKER'S MARK.	TOWN MARK.	MAKER'S MARK.	MAKER'S NAME.
1580		PC			Peter Carlille.
1587		LC	H		James Carlille.
1621		IC	RR	HB	,, ,,
1629	H	RR	H		Robt. Robinson.
1635		RR	,,		,, ,,
1638	H	CW	H		Chr. Watson.
1651		IB			James Birkby.
1666		EM			Edwd. Mangie } or Mangy. }
1666-70		IG		DATE? LETTER. E	Name not traced.
1670-80	,,	,,		K	,, ,,
† ,,		EM		A	Edwd. Mangie } or Mangy. }
1680	,,	M			,, ,,
,,	,,	EM	,,	D	,, ,,
1680-97		KM	,,	E	Kath. Mangy.
,,		KM			,, ,,
,,	,,	EM	,,	F	Edwd. Mangy.
1689	,,	TH	,,		Thos. Hebden.
1690-7		KM			Kath. Mangy.
1697		KM			,, ,,
1706		AB	,,		Abm. Barachin.

† 1670   Date-letter on porringer : Messrs. Gilder & Son.

EXAMPLES OF ROCHESTER MARKS.

DATE.	MARKS.	ARTICLES AND OWNERS.
1560		Elizabethan communion cup : Snave Church, Kent.
c. 1640		Mark stamped in bowl, and thrice on stem of seal-top spoon : Mr. H. D. Ellis.

EXAMPLES OF LEWES MARKS

c. 1590		On stems of seal-top spoons : Mr. H. D. Ellis, and Mr. J. H. Walter. The town mark alone is stamped once in the bowl of each spoon.
c. 1637		Seal-top spoon, engraved on the seal end with the date 1637, and the initials D. A. and D. C.: Mr. J. E. Couchman, Hurst-Pierpoint.

EXAMPLES OF LEICESTER MARKS.

DATE.	MARKS.	ARTICLES AND OWNERS.
1540		Spoon, with "·Dyamond" point at end of stem : Mr. E. W. Colt.
1590		Maidenhead spoon : Mr. J. H. Walter.
1600		Seal-top spoon : Mr. H. D. Ellis. The same mark, with the addition of L.R. in monogram, on a seal-top spoon : Mr. Letts.
,,		Seal-top spoon : Mr. H. D. Ellis.
1575 to 1600		Communion cups : Thurnby, Welham, and 15 other Churches in Leicestershire.
1630		Seal-top spoon, pricked 1631 : Mr. H. D. Ellis.
,,		Do. do. : Messrs. Christie.

EXAMPLES OF SHREWSBURY MARKS.

(THE DATES ARE, OF COURSE, APPROXIMATE.)

DATE.	MARKS.	ARTICLES AND OWNERS.
1530		Maidenhead spoon : Mr. H. D. Ellis.
1560		Apostle spoon : Mr. J. H. Walter, Drayton, Norfolk.
,,		Communion cups at Tugby and Saxton, Leicestershire.

EXAMPLES OF KING'S LYNN MARKS.

DATE.	MARKS.	ARTICLES AND OWNERS.
1632		Communion cup and paten cover (inscribed : " Elizabeth Wilton gave 40s. and Mary Griffin gave 10s. towered this bowle for the parrish Church of Middleton in Norfolke Anno Dom. 1632 ") : Middleton near King's Lynn.
1635		Communion cup (inscribed : " The Quest of Thomas Clarke to the Church of Barmar) : Bagthorpe near King's Lynn.
1640		{ Communion paten : St. Nicholas Chapel, King's Lynn. ,, cup of slender shape on baluster stem : St. Ethel-dreda's, Southgate, Norwich.

EXAMPLES OF TAUNTON MARKS.

DATE (ABOUT).	MARKS.	ARTICLES AND OWNERS.
1645		Apostle spoons : Mr. E. W. Colt and Dunn-Gardner Collection.
,,		Do. do. : Mr. Crichton.
,,		Do. do. : Mr. S. Phillips.
1660		Seal-top spoon : Mr. A. Trapnell.
1676-82		{ Paten, dated 1676 : Wooton Courtney, Somerset. { Spoon, flat stem, foliated end, pricked " 1682 " : South Kensington Museum.
1689		Apostle spoon, engraved 1689 : Messrs. Crichton.

EXAMPLES OF SHERBORNE MARKS

DATE.	MARKS.	ARTICLE SAND OWNERS.
Mark of Richard Orenge (probably).		{ Communion cup and paten cover (dated 1574): Gillingham; and much other church-plate in Dorset; also on an apostle spoon (St. Matthew) noted by the Author.
Marks of Richard Orenge.		Communion cup of 1603: Charlton-Horethorne, Sherborne.

EXAMPLES OF POOLE MARKS

DATE.	MARKS.	ARTICLES AND OWNERS.
c. 1540		In bowls of maidenhead spoon: Messrs. Crichton.
,,		Seal-top spoon: Messrs. Crichton.
c. 1560		Apostle spoon (St. Paul)
c. 1580		Apostle spoon (St. Mathias): Mr. F. W. Kell.
,,		Seal-top spoon: Sir E. Marshall Hall, K.C.
c. 1620		{ Apostle spoon: Mr. J. H. Walter. Do.　do.: Holburne Museum, Bath. Do.　do., and seal-top spoon: Sir E. Marshall Hall, K.C.

EXAMPLES OF SALISBURY MARKS.

DATE.	MARKS.	ARTICLES AND OWNERS.
c. 1596		Seal-top spoon (one of seven found near Salisbury), date 1596 pricked on seal end.
,,		Two seal-top spoons (part of above seven); one pricked 1595 and EH, the other 1621 and IE.
c. 1620		Seal-top spoon (one of above seven); has 1621 and $\frac{MA}{WE}$ pricked on seal end.
,,		Do.　do.　do.　do.　; has 1621 and $\frac{BE}{IE}$ pricked thereon.
c. 1627		Silver-gilt Vishnu-topped spoon; pricked "S.W.L.P. 1627": Messrs. Christie.
c. 1629		Seal-top spoon (one of above seven): has 1629 and $\frac{I. I.}{B. E}$ pricked on seal end.
,,		Do.　do.　do.　do.　; has "$\frac{IS}{EE}$ 1629" pricked on seal end.

SEALS OF THE BOROUGH OF BARNSTAPLE

BARNSTAPLE MARKS.

DATE (ABOUT).	MARKS.	MAKER'S NAME.	ARTICLES AND OWNERS.
1568-1601	IC	John Coton.	Chalice: Abbotsham,
c. 1570-75	M	Thos. Mathew.	
1576	T MATEV	,, ,,	{ Communion cup, dated 1576: St. Genny's, Bude. Lion-sejant spoon: Messrs. Christie.
1578	D COTON	J. Coton.	Com. cup : Stoke-Rivers, near Barnstaple.
1580	MATEV	T. Mathew,	Seal-top spoons : Mr. W. Boore.
,,	IC	J. Coton.	{ Communion cup: Tresmere. Spoon with cherub's head: Mr. J. H. Walter.
1584	I COTON	,, ,,	Communion cup: Morwenstow, Bude.
c. 1650	I.P	John Peard	Tankard :
1670-80	IP I·P IP	,, ,,	Spoon with flat stem: From the Temple-Frere Collection,
1680	IP	,, ,,	{ Porringer of about 1680 but pricked 1703 : Noted by the Author. Com. paten and flagon : St. Ewe, Cornwall.
1687	IP	,, ,,	Trifid spoon, pricked 1687 : Noted by the Author.
1695	I·P	,, ,,	Trifid spoon, pricked 1695 : Noted by the Author.

EXAMPLES OF PLYMOUTH MARKS.

DATE.	MARKS.	ARTICLES AND OWNERS.
c. 1600		In bowls of two spoons with Vishnu knops: Noted by the Author. Apostle spoon: Dr. Wilfred Harris.
1690-5		Spoon, flat stem, trifid end: Messrs. Crichton.
1695-9	P JM Britannia	Spoon, flat stem, foliated end, embossed ornamentation, dated 1699: Mr. J. H. Walter.
,,	JM Starling	Spirally fluted mug, riband handle: Mr. J. H. Walter.
c. 1694	HM Sterling	Flat stem spoon, with trifid end, pricked 1694: Messrs. Page, Keen, and Page, Plymouth.
1698 to 1700	Rowe Plmo Britan Row St Now Ply	The "Eddystone Lighthouse" salt belonging to Miss Rous, of Cwrt-yr-Ala, Glam. Flat-top tankard: Mr. Crichton.

EXAMPLES OF BRISTOL MARKS.

DATE.	MARKS.	ARTICLES AND OWNERS.
c. 1730	R·G A	Straining spoon: Temple Church, Bristol.
c. 1731	,, B ,, ,, ,,	Milk-jug: Mr. Crichton.
c. 1780-90	FEL COO SALMON	Reeded-edged gravy spoon, with oval (not pointed) bowl and pointed oval end to stem: Noted by the Author.

EXAMPLE OF COLCHESTER MARKS.

DATE.	MARKS.	ARTICLE AND OWNER.
c. 1723		Marks of R. Hutchinson, on punch ladle engraved T M HA IM : Mr. Fredk. Bradbury. 1723 17 23

EXAMPLES OF TRURO MARKS.

DATE (ABOUT).	MARKS.	ARTICLES AND OWNERS.
1560 1600		In bowl of apostle spoon : The Author's Collection.
,,		{ Massive seal-top spoon : Do. do. { Also on many spoons in other collections.
,,	,,　　　,,	Seal-top spoons : Mr. H. D. Ellis and others.
1600		Baluster-topped spoon : Messrs. Crichton.
1620		TR in monogram in bowl, the other marks on stem of spoon with lion-sejant terminal : Mr. H. D. Ellis.
,,		An anchor (one of the Saltash bearings or devices) in bowl, the pig mark on stem, of spoon with baluster and seal top : Mr. H. D. Ellis.
,,		Seal-top spoon : The Author's Collection.
1630	,,	Spoon : Mr. Du Cane.

EXAMPLE OF DORCHESTER MARKS.

Mark of Lawrence Stratford, of Dorchester.		{ Communion cup and paten cover (dated 1574) : West Purley ; and (dated 1575) : Bothenhampton ; and communion plate in many other Dorset churches.

EXAMPLES OF DEVON AND CORNWALL LOCAL MAKERS' MARKS.

DATE. (ABOUT).	MARKS.	ARTICLES AND OWNERS.
1576-80		Communion cups at St. Levan, Sancreed, Morvah, St. Ives, St. Hilary, Wendron, and St. Anthony, West Cornwall.
,,		Mark resembles a bunch of grapes. Communion cup : St. Columb Minor, Cornwall.
1580		Chalice of Exeter pattern : Wembworthy, Devon.
? c. 1600		Patens : St. Anthony-in-Meneage, and several other parishes in West Cornwall.

DEVON AND CORNWALL LOCAL MAKERS' MARKS (*continued*).

DATE, (ABOUT).	MARKS.	ARTICLES AND OWNERS.
c. 1600-30		Stamped twice on communion cup : St. Erth, Cornwall.
,,		Communion cup and paten : St. Eval, Cornwall.
,,		Paten : St. Hilary, Cornwall. The larger mark is on the flat part of paten, and the smaller mark on foot.
,,		Paten : Kenwyn, Cornwall.
,,		Spirally-fluted porringer : Gerrans, Cornwall.
,,		Embossed spoon, flat stem, trifid end : Mr. J. H. Walter.
1610		Com. cup and paten : North Hill Church, Cornwall.
1610-50		Do. do. do. cover : Treaeglos, Cornwall.
1630		{ Do. do. : Liskeard, Cornwall. { Apostle spoon : Mr. J. H. Walter.
1641		Com. cup and paten, dated 1641 : St. Ives, Cornwall.
$\frac{1650}{1700}$		{ Do. do. do. do. cover : St. Wenn. { Do. do. : St. Erwun, Cornwall.
1675		Paten (inscribed : " Mr. Abraham Heiman of this towne gave this plate to the Church in the year '75 ") : Bideford.
1680-5		Spoon, flat stem, trifid end, pricked 1684 : Mr. J. H. Walter.
1690		ID conjoined, stamped thrice on paten : West Putford, Devon.
1695		Communion cup and paten, dated 1695 ; also on flagon, dated 1712 : Paul Church, Cornwall.
,,		Struck thrice on beaker : St. Ervan, Cornwall.
1700		The R H stamped thrice, the B once, on com. plate with engraved date 1701 : Mevagissey, Cornwall. Probably mark of Richard Holin of Truro, who registered his mark at Exeter in 1704. The B may indicate Britannia standard.
1715		Probably mark of Richard Plint of Truro. Com. paten (dated 1719) St. Enoder Also com. cup and paten (dated 1728), St. Clement, Truro.

EXAMPLE OF GATESHEAD MARKS.

c. 1680		On a tankard and a mug inscribed " Ex dono XXX." : Sir Robert Mowbray, Bart.

EXAMPLES OF CARLISLE MARKS.

(THE DATES ARE APPROXIMATE.)

DATE.	MARKS.	ARTICLES AND OWNERS.
1571		Communion cups: Bolton, Ireby and Lazonby, Cumb., and Cliburn, and Long Marton, Westmor.
1630		Seal-top spoon: Mr. H. D. Ellis.
,,		Spoon, slipped in the stalk: Mr. W. Boore.
1670		Do. flat stem, foliated end: The Goldsmiths' Company, London.

EXAMPLES OF LEEDS MARKS.

DATE.	MARKS.	ARTICLES AND OWNERS.
1650 TO 1702		Communion cup: Almondbury, Yorks, and other Yorkshire plate. Paten, dated 1702: Harewood, Yorks; and other Yorkshire plate.
,,	,, ,,	The TS in monogram mark stamped thrice on communion cup: Darrington, Yorks.
1660		Maker perhaps R. Williamson of York. Maker's mark struck once, the fleece twice, on flat-topped tankard: Judge A. Clearwater, New York.
1680	,,	Trifid spoon: Mr. J. H. Walter.
1690		Do. do. made by Arthur Mangey (see above): Mr. J. H. Walter.
,,	,,	Beaker: Mr. D. T. Davis.

THE CHANNEL ISLANDS, CALCUTTA AND JAMAICA.

The preceding pages contain all the known place marks used in Great Britain except those employed in the Channel Islands. In Guernsey, 1690–1730 a silversmith stamped his wares with **GH** surmounted by what resembles an eye, fringed above, a harp lying on its side, and the letter R (old English) in a shield. The other marks, they are very few, are initials only, and do not, in the absence of especial knowledge, enable one definitely to assign them. An exception is the mark of T.DG over the letters J. LG, which we know was a mark used on the Isle of Jersey *circa* 1830.

The British firms of Pillar & Co. and Hamilton & Co. made silver in Calcutta in the first two decades of the last century. The former's mark was a date letter A similar to that for London, 1796–7, a lion passant, and the letter P over & Co. Hamilton & Co. identified their products with an elephant in an oval shield, a covered ewer with handles, the letters "H & Co." in a square block, and the letter A in a pyramid. This description will enable the reader to dispense with illustrations.

One piece of silver is known to have come from Jamaica, W. I. It is marked with a leopard's head crowned, in a plain shield, concave at top, J. EWAN in a rectangle, and a lion passant in a shield straight at the top and rounded at the sides and base.

CHAPTER XIV
Unascribed British Marks

The place and time of origin of the examples upon which the following marks have been found cannot be determined accurately.

DATE (ABOUT).	MARKS.	DATE (ABOUT).	MARKS.	DATE (ABOUT).	MARKS.
		1570·7		1590	
1500		"		"	
"		"		"	
1510		"		1600	
1520		1570-80		"	
1530		"		"	
"		"		"	
1550		"		"	
"		1576		"	
1560		1580		"	
"		"		"	
1570		1590		"	
"		"		"	
"		"		"	
1570		"		"	

DATE (ABOUT).	MARKS.
1600	
"	
"	
1600-50	
1609	
1610	
"	
"	
"	
"	
"	
"	
"	
"	
1620	
"	
"	
"	
"	
"	
"	

DATE (ABOUT).	MARKS.
1620	
1623	
1625	
1630	
"	
"	
"	
"	
"	
"	
"	
"	
"	
1630-5	
"	
"	
"	
"	
"	
"	

DATE (ABOUT).	MARKS.
1630-5	
"	
"	
"	
"	
"	
1637	
"	
1638	
1640	
"	
"	
"	
"	
"	
"	
"	
"	
"	
"	
"	

DATE (ABOUT).	MARKS.	DATE (ABOUT).	MARKS.	DATE (ABOUT).	MARKS.
1640				1674	
"		1650		1675	
"		"		"	
"		"		1677	
"		1658		"	
1640-8		1660		1680	
1640-50		"		"	
"		"		"	
"		"		"	
"		"		"	
1650		1660-70		"	
"		"		"	
"		1667		"	
"		1670		"	
"		"		"	
"		1670-4		"	
"		"		"	
"		1674		"	
"		"		"	
"		"		"	
"				"	
"				"	

DATE (ABOUT).	MARKS.	DATE (ABOUT).	MARKS.	DATE (ABOUT).	MARKS.
1686		1685		1695	
"		1687		"	
"		1690		"	
"		"		"	
1680-5		"		1700	
"		"		"	
"		"		1700-5	
"		1690-1		"	
"		1690-5		1700-40	
"		"		1702	
"		"		1706-9	
"		"		"	
"		"		"	
"		"		1710	
"		"		"	
"		"		1720-5	
"		"		1720-30	
"		"		1725-30	
1682		"		"	
1684-5		1690-9		"	
"		"		1730	
"		1693			

DATE (ABOUT).	MARKS.
1730	
,,	
,,	
,,	
1730-4	
1730-40	
,,	
,,	
,,	
,,	
,,	
,,	
1740	
1750	
1750-60	
c. 1760	

CHAPTER XV
Marks on Edinburgh Plate

❖ ❖ ❖HERE were no marks struck on Scotch silver before
❖ T ❖ 1457. In that year a statute was enacted which required
❖ ❖ ❖ the maker and the deacon of the guild to affix their
marks to each piece before it was offered for sale. The records, of
Edinburgh at least, have been so well preserved that it is possible
to place each piece of silver made subsequent to that year within
a period limited by the working life of the silversmith or the
incumbency of the deacon. In 1681, the Edinburgh Goldsmiths'
Incorporation adopted a variable annual date letter, abolished
the office of deacon and substituted an assay master whose mark
fixed his responsibility for each piece struck. In 1759, the use of
the thistle as an assay master's mark took the place of the initials which the assay master had used up to that time.

The "Britannia Standard" act of William and Mary was not
applied to Scotland and the practice of making silver of the higher
standard never prevailed in the northern province.

In 1836 a British statute designated the thistle as the sterling
mark and the castle as the guild mark for Edinburgh.

The date in parentheses indicates the year of the workman's admission to the guild.

TABLE I.

DATE.	MAKER'S NAME.	MAKER'S MARK	TOWN MARK CASTLE	DEACON'S MARK
1552-62	Alex. Auchinleck			
1563-4	Henry Thompsone (1561)		,,	
c. 1570	(*Mark indistinct.*)		,,	
1576	Adam Craige			
1585-6	John Mosman (1575)		,,	
1590-1	Adam Allane, jr. (1589)			
1591-2	James Craufuird			
1591-4	David Gilbert (1590)			
,,	James Craufuird (1591)			
1596/1600	Hugh Lindsay (1587)		,,	
1609-10	Gilbert Kirkwood (1609)		,,	
1611-3	Robert Denneistoun (1597)			
,,	George Craufuird, jr. (1606)		,,	,,
1617-9	Do. do.	,,		
,,	John Lindsay (1605)		,,	,,
,,	George Robertsone (1616)		,,	,,
,,	Thos. Thompson (1617)		,,	,,
c. 1617	Hew. Anderson		,,	
1613-21	Gilbert Kirkwood (1609)			
1616-35	George Robertsone (1616)		,,	
1633	Adame Lamb (1619)		,,	,,
,,	Thos. Kirkwood (1631)		,,	,,
1633 (?)	(*Mark indistinct.*)			

TABLE II.

DATE.	MAKER'S NAME.	MAKER'S MARK.	TOWN MARK CASTLE.	DEACON'S MARK.
1637-9	Jon Scott (1621) Adm.			
1640-2	Thos. Clyghorne (1606)			
1642	Patrick Borthwick (1642)		,,	
1643	Jon Scott (1621)			,,
,,	Nicoll Trotter (1635)		,,	,,
1644-6	George Cleghorne (1641)		,,	
,,	Andro Denneistoun (1636)		,,	,,
,,	Thos. Clyghorne (1606)		,,	,,
1644	{John Myln or / Jas. McAulay		,,	,,
1649	Andro Burrell (1642)		,,	
1648-57	Peter Neilsone (1647)		,,	,,
1650	Thos. Scott (1649)		,,	,,
1651-9	Robert Gibsoune (1627)		,,	
1657	John Wardlaw (1642)		,,	,,
1660	Edwd. Cleghorne (1649)		,,	
1665-7	Wm. Law (1662)		,,	
,,	Andrew Law (c. 1665)		,,	,,
1665	Alexr. Reid		,,	
1669-75	Alexr. Scott (1649)		,,	
1674	James Cockburne (1669)		,,	,,
1663-81	Alexr. Scott (1649)		,,	
1675-7	George Rolland (1675)		,,	
1677	Alexr. Reid (3rd) (1677)		,,	,,

TABLE III.

MAKER'S NAME.	MAKER'S MARK.	TOWN MARK. CASTLE.	ASSAY MASTER'S MARK.	DATE LETTER.	DATE.
Alexr. Reid (1660) *Adm.*					
Edwd. Cleghorne (1649)					1681-2
Andrew Law (c. 1665)		,,			1682-3
Wm. Law (1662)		,,	,,		1683-4
Thos. Yorstoun (1673)		,,	,,		1684-5
John Lawe (1661)		,,	,,		1685-6
James Penman (1673)		,,	,,		
Do. do.	,,	,,	,,		1686-7
James Cockburne (1669)		,,	,,		1687-8
George Scott (1677)		,,	,,		1688-9
Wm. Scott (1686)		,,	,,		WM. & MY. 1689-90
James Cockburne (1669)		,,	,,		1690-1
Robert Bruce (1687)		,,	,,		1691-2
Robert Inglis (1686)		,,	,,		1692-3
James Sympsone (1687)		,,	,,		1693-4
Geo. Yorstoune (1684)		,,	,,		1694-5
Alexr. Forbes (1692)		,,	,,		WM. III. 1695-6
James Sympsone ? (1687)		,,			1696-7
(*Not identified*).		,,	,,		1697-8
Thos. Ker (1694)			,,		1698-9
Alexr. Kincaid (1692)		,,	,,		1699 1700
Colin McKenzie (1695)		,,	,,		1700-1
Geo. Scott, jr. (1697)		,,	,,		1701-2
Mungo Yorstoun (1702)		,,	,,		ANNE. 1702-3
Thos. Cleghorne (1689)		,,	,,		1703-4
James Sympson (1687)		,,	,,		1704-5
Patrick Murray (1701)					

TABLE IV.

MAKER'S NAME.	MAKER'S MARK.	TOWN MARK. CASTLE.	ASSAY MASTER'S MARK.	DATE LETTER.	DATE.
Patrick Murray (1701) *Adm.*					1705-6
James Tait (1704)					
Walter Scott (1701)		,,	,,		1706-7
Wm. Ged (1706)		,,	,,		1707-8
John Penman, jr. (1703)		,,			
Harry Beathune (1704)		,,	,,		1708-9
John Seatoune (1688)		,,	,,		1709-10
James Mitchellsone (1706)		,,	,,		1710-1
Patrick Turnbull (1689)		,,	,,		1711-2
Robert Ker (1705)		,,	,,		1712-3
Robert Inglis (1686)		,,	,,		1713-4 GEO. I.
Mungo Yorstoun (1702)					1714-5
,, ,,		,,	,,		1715-6
Thos. Ker (1694)		,,	,,		
Harry Beathune (1704)		,,	,,		1716-7
John Seatoun (1685)		,,	,,		
Chas. Dickson (as 1721)		,,	,,		1717-8
Chas. Blair (1707)					
Wm. Ure (1715)					,,
James Mitchellsone (1706)		,,	,,		1718-9
Mungo Yorstoun (1702)		,,	,,		1719-20
Alexr. Sympsone (1710)		,,	,,		
Jas. Inglis (1720)		,,			,,
,, ,,		,,	,,		1720-1
David Mitchell (1700)		,,	,,		
Chas. Dickson (1719)		,,	,,		1721-2
James Clarke (1710)		,,			
Colin Campbell (1714)		,,	,,		1722-3
Ken'th McKenzie (1714)		,,	,,		1723-4
Chas. Blair (1707)		,,	,,		
Alexr. Edmonstoune (1721)		,,	,,		1724-5
Archd. Ure (1715)		,,	,,		1725-6
James Taitt (1704)		,,	,,		1726-7 GEO. II.
Harry Beathune (1704)		,,	,,		1727-8
Patrick Graeme (1725)		,,	,,		1728-9
Wm. Aytoun (1718)		,,			} 1729-30
Wm. Jameson (1729)					

James Cockburne				1682-3	John Borthwick
James Penman, as 1685				1687-8	,,
Colin McKenzie, as 1700-1				1697-8	James Penman.

Colin Campbell				1711-2	Edward Penman.
... ...				1717-8	,,
James Ker				1723-4	
Thos. Mitchell				1724-5	,,

TABLE V.

MAKER'S NAME.	MAKER'S MARK.	TOWN MARK. CASTLE.	ASSAY MASTER'S MARK.	DATE LETTER	DATE.
James Anderson (Adm. 1729)	IA	castle	AU	A	1730-1
Hugh Gordon (1727)	HG	,,	,,	B	1731-2
George Forbes (1731)	GF	,,	,,	C	1732-3
John Main (1729)	IM	,,	,,	D	1733-4
Edw'rd Lothian (1731)	EL	,,	,,	E	1734-5
John Rollo (1731) (afterwards Lord Rollo)	IR	,,	,,	F	1735-6
Hugh Penman (1734)	HP	,,	,,	G	1736-7
Alexander Farquharson (1734)	AF	castle	,,	H	1737-8
James Ker (1723) Dougal Ged (1734)	IK GED	,,	,,	I	1738-9
James Ker (1723) ,, ,, (1737)	IK	,,	,,	K	1739-40
Ebenr. Oliphant (1737)	EO	,,	GED	L	1740-1
Law'ce Oliphant (1737)	LO			M	1741-2
William Aytoun (1718)	WA				
Robert Gordon (1741)	RG	,,	EL	N	1742-3
Edwd. Lothian (1731)	EL	,,	,,	O	1743-4
Chas. Dickson (1738)	CD	castle	HG	P	1744-5
Ebenr. Oliphant (1737)	EO	,,	,,	Q	1745-6
John Kincard (1726)	IK	,,	,,	R	1746-7
(Not identified.)	CL	,,	,,	S	1747-8
William Gilchrist (1736)	WG	,,	,,	T	1748-9
Edward Lothian (1731)	EL	,,	,,	U	1749-50
Robert Lowe (1742)	LOW	,,	,,	U	1750-1
Ebenr. ,, Oliphant (1737)	EO	,,	,,	W	1751-2
James McKenzie (1747)	IM	,,	,,	X	1752-3
James Weems (1738) John Edmonston (1755)	IW IE	,,	,,	Y	1753-4
Wm. Davie (1740)	WD	,,	,,	Z	1754-5

George Forbes	GF		1737-8	...
Robt. Hope	HOPE		1743-4	...
Wm. Aytoun	WA	HG	1744-5	Hugh Gordon.

TABLE VI.

MAKER'S NAME.	MAKER'S MARK.	TOWN MARK. CASTLE.	ASSAY MASTER'S MARK.	DATE LETTER
Ker & Dempster.	KD	castle	HG	A
Rbt. Gordon (Adm. 1741)	RG	,,	,,	B
Wm. Taylor (1753) John Clark (1751)	WT CLARK	,,	,,	C
Lothian & Robertson. James Welsh (1746)	L&R IW	,,	,, THISTLE	D
James Gilsland (1748)	IG	,,	,,	E
Alexr. Aitchison (1746) Jas. Somervail (1754)	AIT IS	,,	,,	F
John Robertson (1758) Wm. Dempster (1742)	JR WD	,,	,,	G
,, John Welsh (1742)	IW	,,	,,	H
John Taylor (1760) James Hill (1746)	IT IH	,,	,,	I
Milne & Campbell?	M&C	,,	,,	K
Rbt. Clark (1763) Wm. Drummond (1760)	RC WD	,,	,,	L
John Stirling? (1757)	IS	,,	,,	M
Benjn. Tait (1763) Gillsland & Ker.	TAIT G&K	,,	,,	N
Patk. Robertson (1751)	PR	,,	,,	O
"Daniel Ker." (1761) (not identified.)	DK JB	,,	,,	P
James Gilsland (1748)	IG	,,	,,	Q
Wm. & Jno. Taylor. Wm. Davie (1740)	WT IT WD	,,	,,	R
,, ,, Alexr. Gairdner (1754) James Welsh (1746)	AG IW	,,	,,	T
... ...		,,	,,	U
Wm. Davie (1740)	WD	,,	,,	V
James Dempster (1775)	ID	,,	,,	X
Patk. Robertson (1751)	PR	,,	,,	Z
James Hewitt (1750)	IH	,,	,,	U

... ...	MW	CF	1759-60
Wm. Ker. Wm. Taylor?	KER WT	G	1761-2
... ...	PR	R	1767-8
... ...	DE	R	1771-2

TABLE VII.

MAKER'S NAME.		MAKER'S MARK.	TOWN MARK CASTLE	THISTLE	DATE LETTER	DATE.
& P. Cunningham.		W&PC	[castle]	[thistle]	A	1780-1
...vid Downie	Adm. (1770)	DD	,,	,,	B	1781-2
...s. Howden	(1781)	FH	,,	,,	C	1782-3
...ot. Bowman	(1780)	RB	KING'S HEAD.	,,	D	1783-4
...x. Edmonston	(1779)	AE	[king's head]	,,	E	1784-5
...vid Marshall	(1782)	DM	,,	,,	F	1785-6
...nes Dempster	(1775)	ID	[mark]	,,	G	1786-7-8
...os. Duffus	(1780)	TD	,,	,,	H	1788-9
...x. Gairdner	(1754)	AG	,,	,,	IJ	1789-90
...es Douglas	(1785)	JD				
& P. Cunningham.		WCPC	,,	,,	K	1790-1
...Christie	(1791)	GC	,,	,,	L	1791-2
...x. Zeigler	(1782)	AZ	,,	,,	M	1792-3
...er Mathie	(1774)	PM	,,	,,	N	1793-4
...a. Robertson	(1789)	WR	,,	,,	O	1794-5
...x. Henderson	(1792)	AH	,,	,,	P	1795-6
...Christie	(1791)	GC	,,	,,	Q	1796-7
...Spence	(1783)	AS				
& P. Cunningham.		WPC	[mark]	,,	R	1797-8
...s. Duffus	(1780)	TD	,,	,,	S	1798-9
...Graham & Co.?		AG&C	,,	[castle]	[thistle]	T	1799 / 1800
& P. Cunningham.		WPC				
...Zeigler	(1798)	IZ	,,	,,	U	1800-1
...Howden	(1781)	FH	,,	,,	V	1801-2
...Craw.		MC	[castle]	,,	W	1802-3
...Auld	(1788)	WA	,,	,,	X	1803-4
...n Cunningham	(1800)	SC	,,	,,	Y	1804-5
(Not identified).		M&R	,,	,,	Z	1805-6

TABLE VIII.

MAKER'S NAME.	MAKER'S MARK.	KING'S HEAD	TOWN MARK CASTLE	THISTLE	DATE LETTER	DATE.
R. Green or R. Grierson.	RG	[head]	[castle]	[thistle]	a	1806-7
Cunningham & Simpson.	PC&S					
(Not identified).	D&M	,,	,,	,,	b	1807-8
Do. do.	IH	,,	,,	,,	c	1808-9
George Fenwick.	GF	,,	[castle]	,,	d	1809-10
John McDonald.	IMD					
Robt. Gray & Son (of Glasgow).	R&S	,,	,,	,,	e	1810-1
Math. Craw.	MC	,,	,,	,,	f	1811-2
Alexr. Henderson.	AH	,,	,,	,,	g	1812-3
J. McKay.	JM	,,	,,	,,	h	1813-4
Frs. Howden.	FH	,,	,,	,,	i	1814-5
R. K. (a Perth maker). Wm. Zeigler.	WZ					
Js. & Wm. Marshall.	J&WM	,,	,,	,,	j	1815-6
Chas. Dalgleish.	CD				k	1816-7
J. McKay.	JM	,,	,,	,,	l	1817-8
Do. do.						
Redpath & Arnot.	R&A	,,	,,	,,	m	1818-9
J'n'th'n Millidge ?	JM	,,	,,	,,	n	1819-20
Frs. Howden.	FH	,,	[castle]	[thistle]	o	GEO. IV. 1820-1
Do. do.		,,	,,	,,	p	1821-2
Redpath & Arnot.	R&A	,,	,,	,,	q	1822-3
Alexr. Zeigler.	AZ	[head]	,,	,,	r	1823-4
Marshall & Sons.	MSS	,,	[castle]	,,	s	1824-5
J. McKenzie ?	MC	,,	,,	,,	t	1825-6
J. McKay.	JM	,,	[castle]	,,	u	1826-7
Leon'd Urquhart.	LU	,,	,,	,,	v	1827-8
(Not identified).	WC	,,	,,	,,	w	1828-9
J. McKay.	JM	,,	,,	,,	x	1829-30
Do. do.		,,	,,	,,	y	WM. IV. 1830-1
Peter Sutherland.	PS	,,	,,	,,	z	1831-2
Cunningham & Simpson	PC&S					1808-9
(Not identified).	GMH		P			1821-2

TABLE IX.

MAKER'S NAME.	MAKER'S MARK.	KING'S HEAD.	TOWN MARK CASTLE.	THISTLE.	DATE LETTER	DATE.
Marshall & Sons.	M&S	●	●	●	A	1832-3
Jas. Nasmyth.	JN	,,	,,	,,	B	1833-4
(*Not identified*).	GB	,,	,,	,,	C	1834-5
Elder & Co.	E&Cᵒ	,,	,,	,,	D	1835-6
R. & R. Keay, of Perth.	R&RK	,,	,,	,,	E	1836-7
J. McKay.	JMᶜ	,,	,,	,,	F	VICTORIA. 1837-8
A.D. (see the Arbroath Marks).		,,	,,	,,	G	1838-9
Jas. Howden & Co.	JH&Cᵒ	,,	,,	,,	H	1839-40
Jas. Nasmyth & Co.	JN&Cᵒ	QUEEN'S HEAD. ,,	,,	,,	I	1840-1
Geo. Jameson, of Aberdeen.	GJ	●	,,	,,	K	1841-2
Marshall & Sons.	M&S	,,	,,	,,	L	1842-3
... ...		,,	,,	,,	M	1843-4
McKay.	JMᶜ	,,	,,	,,	N	1844-5
... ...		,,	,,	,,	O	1845-6
D G as Canongate c. 1836 (page 514).		,,	,,	,,	P	1846-7
Marshall & Sons.	M&S	,,	,,	,,	Q	1847-8
J. Hay.	JH	,,	,,	,,	R	1848-9
Mackay & Chisholm.	M&C	,,	,,	,,	S	1849-50
Do. do.		,,	,,	,,	T	1850-1
... ...		,,	,,	,,	U	1851-2
... ...		,,	,,	,,	V	1852-3
... ...		,,	,,	,,	W	1853-4
Chas. Robb.	CR	,,	,,	,,	X	1854-5
J. Hay.	JH	,,	,,	,,	Y	1855-6
(*Not identified*).	RN	,,	,,	,,	Z	1856-7

TABLE X.

MAKER'S NAME.	MAKER'S MARK.	QUEEN'S HEAD.	TOWN MARK CASTLE.	THISTLE.	DATE LETTER
J. & W. Marshall.	J&WM	●	●	●	A
Jonthn. Millidge?	JM	,,	,,	,,	B
(*Not identified*).	JU	,,	,,	,,	C
Alex. Hay.	A·H	,,	,,	,,	D
J. Asherheim.	JA	,,	,,	,,	E
R. L. Christie. J. E. Vernon.	RLC JEV	,,	,,	,,	F
Wm. Crouch. D. Blackley. W. J. McDonald.	WC DB WJM'D PMC WM	,,	,,	,,	G
Wm. Marshall. Elder & Co.	DMᶜ E&Cᵒ				H
J. Smith or Scott. D. & J. Sanderson. Cockburn & McDonald.	JM JS D&JS COCKBURN	,,	,,	,,	I
Geo. Edwards & Son.	GE &S	,,	,,	,,	K
J. Hamilton & Son.	J HAMON GEO. ST				L
George Laing. Walter Neil. Wm. Carstairs. Carlisle & Watt. W. Fraser.	GL WN WC C&W WF	,,	,,	,,	M
Jas. Aitchison.	AITCHISON	,,	,,	,,	N
J. Johnston. Jas. Hamilton.	JJ HAMILTON JH&Cᵒ M&GS				O
John Crichton.	J CRICHTON				P
M. Crichton.	JH&C MC JG&C				Q
Robb & Whittet	R&W J&WM	,,	,,	,,	R
C. or J. Gray.	GRAY				S
Mackay & Chisholm.	M&C	,,	,,	,,	T
J. Crichton.	JC	,,	,,	,,	U
Hamilton & Inches.	H&I	,,	,,	,,	V
... ...		,,	,,	,,	W
					X
					Y
					Z
... ...	WM				

TABLE XI.

MAKER'S NAME.	MAKER'S MARK.	QUEEN'S HEAD.	TOWN MARK. CASTLE.	THISTLE.	DATE LETTER	DATE.
... ...	CS				a	1882-3
Wm. Knaggs.	WK	,,	,,	,,	b	1883-4
Hamilton & Inches.	H&I	,,	,,	,,	c	1884-5
... ...	,,	,,	,,	,,	d	1885-6
Mackay & Chisholm,	M&C	,,	,,	,,	e	1886-7
Jas. Duncan.	J·D	,,	,,	,,	f	1887-8
Milne of Aberdeen.	MILNE A H D N	,,	,,	,,	g	1888-9
W. Crouch & Sons.	WC&S	,,	,,	,,	h	1889-90
Hamilton & Inches.	H&I		,,	,,	i	1890-1
J. Crichton & Co.	J&C°		,,	,,	k	1891-2
Jas. Duncan.	J D		,,	,,		
Brook & Son.	B&S		,,	,,	l	1892-3
J. Crichton & Co.	J&C°		,,	,,	m	1893-4
Lewis Cohen.	L.C		,,	,,	n	1894-5
Latimer & Sons.	L & SONS					
Jas. Duncan.	J D					
D. Crichton.	D.C		,,	,,	o	1895-6
J. Crichton & Co.	J&C°		,,	,,	p	1896-7
McDonald & Horne.	M&H					
J. Hardy & Co.	H&C° C&K		,,	,,	q	1897-8
W. Crouch & Sons.	WC&S		,,	,,	r	1898-9
W. & J. Milne.	W&JM					1899
Hamilton & Inches.	H&I		,,	,,	s	1900
Thos. Johnston.	T·J		,,	,,	t	1900-1
Young & Tatton.	Y&T					
Jas. Robertson.	JR		,,	,,	u	EDW. VII. 1901-2
Brook & Son.	B&S		,,	,,	v	1902-3
... ...		,,	,,		w	1903-4
... ...		,,	,,		x	1904-5
... ...		,,	,,		y	1905-6
... ...		,,	,,		z	1906-7

TABLE XII.

MAKER'S NAME.			TOWN MARK. CASTLE.	THISTLE.	DATE LETTER.	DATE.
..	...	...	🏰	🌿	**A**	1907-8
...	...	...	"	"	**B**	1908-9
...	...	...	"	"	**C**	1909-10
...	...	...	"	"	**D**	1910-1
...	...	...	"	"	**E**	1911-2
...	...	...	"	"	**F**	1912-3
...	...	...	"	"	**G**	1913-4
...	...	...	"	"	**H**	1914-5
...	...	...	"	"	**I**	1915-6
...	...	...	"	"	**K**	1916-7
...	...	...	"	"	**L**	1917-8
...	...	...	"	"	**M**	1918-9
...	...	...	"	"	**N**	1919-20
...	...	...	"	"	**O**	1920-1
...	...	...	"	"	**P**	1921-2

CANONGATE GOLDSMITHS' MARKS.

FROM ABOUT 1680 TO ABOUT 1836.

(The dates are approximate, except to the extent that the inscribed dates may be relied on.)

DATE (ABOUT).	MARKS.	MAKER'S NAME.	ARTICLES AND OWNERS.
1680	GC 🦄 XI·D "	... ...	Spoon : Edinburgh Museum of Antiquities.
"	GC 🦄 KI·D	... ...	Spoon, with flat stem, dated 1689 : Edinburgh Museum of Antiquities.
"	MZ 🦄 MZ	... ...	Two com. cups, carried off 1689, recovered 1697 : Flisk.
1696	G·Z G·Z	... ...	Two com. cups, dated 1696 : Bolton, Haddington.
1700	P XI ASN	... ...	Wine taster : Messrs. Crichton.
"	P FIS XI XX	... ...	Do. do. do.
1760	CM 🦄 CM	... ...	Table-spoon,† "double drop" back of bowl : Glasgow Exhibition, of 1901.
1763	WC ., WC	... ...	Two com. cups, dated 1763 : Auchtertool.
1780-90	F GIG GA	... ...	Oil lamp, which may also have been used as a candlestick : Mr. G. Glass. Also stag's head over R, on fork : Mr. Clement Gadsby.
	PC 🦄 PC	... ...	Table-spoon (fiddle pattern) : Rev. J. Carr.
1790	🦄 K $	... ...	Tea-spoon (fiddle pattern) : The Marquess of Breadalbane.
TO	🦄 K HINCHSLIFFE M *	M. Hinchsliffe.	Tea-spoons (fiddle pattern) : The Marquess of Breadalbane and the Author.
1820	🦄 e ⚓ IP	... ...	Tea-spoon : Mr. Geo. Henderson.
	🦄 ᛗ 🦄 ᛗ	... ...	Table-spoon (fiddle pattern) : Mr. Chisholm.
1836	ᛉ K ⚓ DG	David Greig (?)	Toddy ladle (fiddle pattern) : Mr. Dudley Westropp.

CHAPTER XVI

Marks on Glasgow Plate

The Glasgow goldsmiths were incorporated with other metal workers under the name of "hammermen" in 1536.

A date letter was probably adopted in 1681, as it was in Edinburgh, but its use was discontinued about 1710 and was not regularly used again until 1819. The letter S which is frequently found on early pieces probably stands for sterling. The assay office was established by statute of George III in Glasgow in the year 1819.

TABLE I.

DATE.	MAKER'S MARK.	TREE, FISH & BELL.	MAKER'S MARK.	DATE LETTER	MAKER'S NAME.
1681-2	TM	(tree)	TM	a	Thos. Moncrur (1665)
1682-3	...	...	...	b	... ...
1683-4	B	(tree)	B	c	Robt. Brook (1673)
1684-5				d	... ...
1685-6	"	"	"	e	Robert Brook (1673)
1686-7				f	... ...
1687-8				g	... ...
1688-9				h	... ...
1689-90	S	(tree)	S	i	Jas. Stirling (1686)
1690-1	"	"	"	k	Do. Do.
1691-2				l	... ...
1692-3				m	... ...
1693-4				n	... ...
1694-5	B	(tree)	B	o	Robt. Brook (1673)
1695-6				p	... ...
1696-7	B	"	B	q	Robert Brook (1673)
1697-8				r	... ...
1698-9	WC	(tree)	WC	s	Wm. Clerk (1693)
1699 / 1700	B	(tree)	B	t	Robert Brook (1673)
1700-1	IL	(tree)	IL	u	John Luke*
1701-2	IL	"	IL	v	James Luke (1692)
1702-3				w	... ...
1703-4				x	... ...
1704-5	TC / IL	"	TC / IL	y	Thos. Cumming (1682) / John Luke, jr. (1699)
1705-6	"	"	"	z	Do. do. do.

TABLE II.

DATE (ABOUT.)	MAKER'S MARK.	TREE, FISH & BELL.	MAKER'S MARK.	LETTER.	MAKER'S NAME.
1706-7				A	... ...
1707-8	IL	(tree)	IL	B	John Luke, jr. (1699)
	"	"	"	D	Do. do. "
1709-10	WC	(tree)	WC	"	William Clerk (1693)
1709-20	IF	(tree)	IF		John Falconer (1709)
"	JL	"	JL		James Lockhart (1707)
1717-49	IB	"	IB		Johan Got-helf-Bilsings (1717)
1728-31	"	"	"	S	Do. do. "
1725-35	RL	"	RL	S	Robert Luke (1721)
1743-52	IG	(tree)	IG	S	James Glen (1743)
"	GLN	"	GLN	"	Do. do. "
1747-60	ST		ST	S	Saml. Telfer (1747)
1756-76	DW	"	DW	S	David Warnock (1756)
"		"		S	(No maker's mark).
1757-80	IC	(tree)	IC		John Campbell (1757)
"	JL		JL		(Not identified.)
"	J·S	(tree)	J·S	"	Do. do.
1758-65	WN	"	WN		Wm. Napier (1758)
"	B&N	"	B&N	S	Bayne & Napier.

TABLE III.

DATE (ABOUT).	MAKER'S MARK.	TREE, FISH & BELL.	MAKER'S MARK.	LETTER.	MAKER'S NAME.
1763-70	AG	✹	AG		Adam Graham (1763)
,,	,,	,,	,,	E	Do. do.
,,	,,	,,	,,	F	Do. do.
1773-80	IT	S	IT	S	James Taylor (1773)
1776-80	M&C	✹		O	Milne & Campbell.
,,	M&C	✹	M&C	O	Do. do.
,,	RG	✹	RG		Robert Gray (1776)
,,	RG	✹	RG	S	Do. do. ,,
1783	T&H	✹	T&H		Taylor & Hamilton.
,,	J·Mᶜ	✹	J·Mᶜ	,,	James McEwen (1783)
1777-90	WL	,,	WL	,,	Wm. Love (1777)
1782-92	J·W	✹	J·W		James Wright (1782)
1785-95	ID	✹	ID	S	John Donald (1785)
,,	,,	,,	,,	O	Do. do. ,,
1781 1800	MF	✹	MF	S	Patrick McFarlane (1781)
		LION RAMPANT.			
1811-3	Mᶠ	✹			Archibald McFadyen (1811)

The town mark is usually found between the duplicated makers' marks, both of which are struck with the same punch.

TABLE IV.

DATE (ABOUT).	TREE, FISH & BELL.	LION RAMPANT.	DATE LETTER.	KING'S HEAD.	MAKER'S MARK.	MAKER'S NAME.
1819-20	✹	✹	A	✹	B.SCOTT M&R	B. Scott. (Not identified.)
GEO. IV. 1820-1	✹	,,	B	,,	LFN JD	Luke F. Newlands (1816) Jas. Downie (1812)
1821-2	,,	,,	C	,,	RG &S	Robt. Gray & Son (1819)
1822-3	,,	,,	D	,,	RD	Robt. Duncan (1813)
1823-4	,,	,,	E	,,	JB	John Bruce (1815)
1824-5	,,	,,	F	,,	M&S	(Not identified.)
1825-6	,,	,,	G	,,	AM	Alexr. Mitchell (1822)
1826-7	,,	,,	H	,,	AMᴰ	Angus McDonald (1824)
1827-8	,,	,,	I	,,	PA	Peter Arthur (1808)
1828-9	,,	,,	J	,,	EB	Edwd. Bell (1827)
1829-30	,,	,,	K	,,	JB CO	Jas. Burrell & Co. (1825)
WM. IV. 1830-1	,,	,,	L	,,	DR	Danl. Robertson (1829)
1831-2	,,	,,	M	,,		John Mitchell (as 1835-6 below).
1832-3	,,	,,	N	✹	RG &S	Robt. Gray & Son (1819)
1833-4	,,	,,	O	,,	PA	Peter Arthur (1808)
1834-5	,,	,,	P	,,	DCR	D. C. Rait (1832)
1835-6	,,	,,	Q	,,	JM	John Mitchell (1834)
1836-7	,,	,,	R	,,	DCR JW	D. C. Rait (1832) (Not identified.)
VICT. 1837-8	,,	,,	S	,,	WP	W. Parkins (1835)
1838-9	,,	,,	T	,,	RG &S	Robt. Gray & Son (1819)
1839-40	,,	,,	U	,,	,,	Do. do. ,,
1840-1	,,	,,	V	,,	JM	John Mitchell (1834)
1841-2	,,	,,	W		HM	*Henry Muirhead (1838)
1842-3	,,	,,	X		HD	*Henry Downs (1831)
1843-4	,,	,,	Y		DCR	*D. C. Rait (1832)
1844-5	,,	,,	Z		CB	*Chas. Bryson (1834)
1823			P·G			Philip Grierson.
1826		✹	JL	✹		John Law.

TABLE V.

Year	Tree, Fish & Bell	Lion Rampant	Date Letter	Queen's Head	Maker's Mark	Maker's Name		
1845-6	🐟	🦁	A	👑	WB	Walter	Baird	(1845)
1846-7	,,	,,	B	,,	RG&S	Robt.	Gray & Son	(1819)
1847-8	,,	,,	C	,,		...	...	...
1848-9	,,	,,	D	,,	JR	John	Russell	(1845)
1849-50	,,	,,	E	,,	PAJr	Peter	Aitken, jr.	,,
1850-1	,,	,,	F	,,	J&WM	J. & W.	Mitchell	(1834)
1851-2	,,	,,	G	,,		...	...	...
1852-3	,,	,,	H	,,	RG&S	Robt.	Gray & Son (second mark)	(1819)
1853-4	,,	,,	I	,,		...	...	...
1854-5	,,	,,	J	,,	AM	A.	McMillan	(1837)
1855-6	,,	,,	K	,,	RS	R.	Stewart	(1842)
1856-7	,,	,,	L	,,		...	...	...
1857-8	,,	,,	M	,,	AMcD	A.	McDonald	(1845)
1858-9	,,	,,	N	,,	WA&S	W.	Alexander & Son	
1859-60	,,	,,	O	,,		...	...	...
1860-1	,,	,,	P	,,		...	...	...
1861-2	,,	,,	Q	,,		...	...	...
1862-3	,,	,,	R	,,	JM	J.	Murray	(1862)
1863-4	,,	,,	S	,,		...	...	...
1864-5	,,	,,	T	,,		...	...	...
1865-6	,,	,,	U	,,		...	...	...
1866-7	,,	,,	V	,,		...	...	...
1867-8	,,	,,	W	,,		...	...	...
1868-9	,,	,,	X	,,		...	...	...
1869-70	,,	,,	Y	,,		...	...	...
1870-1	,,	,,	Z	,,		...	...	...

TABLE VI.

Year	Tree, Fish & Bell	Lion Rampant	Date Letter	Queen's Head	Maker's Mark
1871-2	🐟	🦁	A	👑	
1872-3	,,	,,	B	,,	
1873-4	,,	,,	C	,,	
1874-5	,,	,,	D	,,	
1875-6	,,	,,	E	,,	
1876-7	,,	,,	F	,,	
1877-8	,,	,,	G	,,	
1878-9	,,	,,	H	,,	
1879-80	,,	,,	I	,,	
1880-1	,,	,,	J	,,	
1881-2	,,	,,	K	,,	
1882-3	,,	,,	L	,,	
1883-4	,,	,,	M	,,	
1884-5	,,	,,	N	,,	
1885-6	,,	,,	O	,,	
1886-7	,,	,,	P	,,	
1887-8	,,	,,	Q	,,	
1888-9	,,	,,	R	,,	
1889-90	,,	,,	S	,,	
1890-1	,,	,,	T	,,	
1891-2	,,	,,	U	,,	
1892-3	,,	,,	V	,,	
1893-4	,,	,,	W	,,	
1894-5	,,	,,	X	,,	
1895-6	,,	,,	Y	,,	
1896-7	,,	,,	Z	,,	

FOR MAKERS' MARKS SEE LIST ON FOLLOWING PAGES.

TABLE VII.

	TREE, FISH & BELL.	LION RAMPANT.	DATE LETTER.	MAKER'S MARKS.
1897-8			A	
1898-9	,,	,,	B	
1899 1900	,,	,,	C	
1900-1	,,	,,	D	
EDW. VII. 1901-2	,,	,,	E	
1902-3	,,	,,	F	
1903-4	,,	,,	G	
1904-5	,,	,,	H	
1905-6	,,	,,	I	
1906-7	,,	,,	J	
1907-8	,,	,,	K	
1908-9	,,	,,	L	
1909-10	,,	,,	M	
C. 1910-1	,,	,,	N	
1911-2	,,	,,	O	
1912-3	,,	,,	P	
1913-4	,,	,,	Q	
1914-5	,,	,,		R
1915-6	,,	,,	,,	S
1916-7	,,	,,	,,	T
1917-8	,,	,,	,,	U
1918-9	,,	,,	,,	V
1919-20	,,	,,	,,	W
1920-1	,,	,,	,,	X
1921-2	,,	,,	,,	Y

CHAPTER XVII

Marks of the Minor Scotch Guilds

ABERDEEN

TABLE I.

DATE (ABOUT).	MAKER'S MARK.	MAKER'S NAME.
1600-25	AB	... ...
"	,, ...	... ...
"	AB ...	... ...
1650	M ABD M	Thomas Moncrur (1649)
"	W ABD TM	Do. do. ,,
"	W VM ABD W	Walter Melvil (1650)
1660-70	AB AB	(Not identified.)
1670-7	WS VS	Wm. Scott (1666)
1672-8	AG AG	Alexr. Galloway (1671)
1690	AB	(Not identified.)
1691-7	GW ABD	Geo. Walker (1685)
1703	GW ABD	Do. do. ,,
1708-14	GR ABD GR	Geo. Robertson (1708)
1710-20	GR GR C	Do. do. ,,
1718-27	IW IW	John Walker (1713)
1730	J WALKER	Do. do. ,,
"	GC GC	George Cooper (1728)
"	AF B	Alexr. Forbes (1728)
"	GC	George Cooper (1728)
"	... ...	Do. do. ,,
1734-51	JA	Jas. Abercrombie (1734)
1748-67	CA ABD	Coline Allan (1748)
1750	CA ABD	Do. do. ,,
1763-70	IW	James Wildgoose (1763)
"	IW ABD	Do. do. ,,

TABLE II.

DATE (ABOUT).	MAKER'S MARK.	MAKER'S NAME.
1760	BL ABD	(Not identified.)
"	BL BL	Do. do.
	IG ABD	Jas. Gordon (1766)
1766-79	IG ABD	Do. do.
	"	Do. do.
1772-7	AT ABD	Alexr. Thompson (1772)
	JL ABD	Jas. Law (1777)
1777-8	" "	Do. do.
	IL	Do. do.
	IL ABD	John Leslie (1782)
1782-96	IL ABD	Do. do.
	IL	Do. do.
	"	Do. do.
	JS ABD	Jas. Smith (1783)
1783-90	JS ABD	Do. do.
	JS	Do. do.
1785-95	PR ABD	(Not identified.)
1786 to 1818	NG	Nathl. Gillet (1786)
	"	Do. do.
	NG	Do. do.
1790 to 1800	NG Z	Do. do.
	N	Do. do.
	E	James Erskine (1796)
1796 to 1820	"	Do. do.
	JE	Do. do.
	JE	Do. do.
	R&S ABD	(Not identified.)

ABERDEEN (Continued).
TABLE III.

DATE (ABOUT).	MAKER'S MARK.	MAKER'S NAME.
1800	WB	(Not identified.)
	DOUGLAS ID	J. Douglas (?)
	JA AB	John Allan (1797)
	J.A	Do. do.
	ID	J. Douglas (?)
1800	I·D	'Do. do.
TO	GB ABD	(Not identified.)
1830	GB AB GB AB	Do. do.
	G.B ABDN	Do. do.
	WJ ABD WJ	Do. do.
	WJ ABD WJ	Do. do.
	A A A	Do. do.
1820	IB ABD	Do. do.
1830	WJ A B D	Do. do.
1841	GJ ABDN	Geo. Jamieson
1850	WW ABDN	(Not identified.)
	WW ABD WW	Do. do.
1871	GS ABD	Do. do.

EXAMPLES OF ARBROATH MARKS

DATE (ABOUT).	MARKS.
1830	AD
1838	AD
1830-9	AD AD
"	AD

STIRLING.

ELGIN

DATE (ABOUT).	MAKER'S MARK	MAKER'S NAME.
1728		Wm. Livingston.
1730		E. R........
1754		James Humphrey.
1760		{ (E on its back and LN for Elgin). James Humphrey
1770		.. ..
		Chas Fowler.
1790		Do. do.
to		Do. do.
1820		W. F.........
1830		Thos. Stewart (see Inverness, p. 549).

AYR

Seventeenth Century

WICK

End of the Eighteenth Century

GREENOCK

DATE (ABOUT).	MAKER'S MARK.	MAKER'S NAME.
1750		W. L.........
		Jonas Osborne, of Glasgow.
1765		Do. do.
		Do. do.
		Do. do.
		James Taylor, of Glasgow.
1780		G. B.........
		W. C.........
"		M. C.........
1790		B. C.........
"		N. H.........
1800		J. H.........
"		R. N.........
"		P. H.........
		John Heron.
		Do. do.
1800		Thos. Davie.
		Do. do.
		John Heron.
		J. & G. Heron ?
1800 TO 1830		Do. do.
		W. H. T.........
1820		Do. do.
"		Peterhead and Greenock mark.

BANFF

DATE (ABOUT).	MAKER'S MARK.	MAKER'S NAME.
1680	VS ABC	Wm. Scott.
1698	VS BAN D	Do. do.
1720	VS — VS ◊	Wm. Scott, junr.
1725	PS ♥ PS BAN	Patk. Scott.
1732-41	PG BAF B	Patrick Gordon.
1750	AS BAF AS	Alexr. Shirras.
1775	BA IA	John Argo.
1780	JA BANF	Do. do.
1785	WB BANF	Wm. Byres.
1795	R IK ⌇ B	John Keith.
"	B IK ◉ H	Do. do.
1800-20	ℬ IK F	Do. do.
"	ℬ IK BANF ◉	Do. do.
"	ℬ IK	Do. do.
"	IK BANF	Do. do.
"	IK B H	Do. do.
"	◯ ▦ ▽	Do. do.
"	S·A ◗	(Not identified.)
1820	GE B	Geo. Elder.*
1835	BA ✿ McQ	John McQueen.
1850	WS H B	Wm. Simpson.
"	" "	Do. do.

DUNDEE

DATE (ABOUT).	MAKER'S MARK.	MAKER'S NAME.
1628	AL ♦ AL	Alexr. Lindsay (1628)
1631	RG ♦	Robt. Gairdine (mentioned 1683)
1643	RG ✿ RG	Do. do.
1648	RG ♦ RG	Do. do.
1667	TL ✿ TL	Thos. Lindsay (1662)
1722	CD ✿ CD E	Chas. Dickson (1722)
1730	IS ✿ IS M	John Steven (mentioned 1764)
1742	AI ,, AI K	Alexr. Johnston (1739)
1764	JS ✿	John Steven (1764)
1776	WS ,, WS ⊡	Wm. Scott (1776)
"	,, ,, M	Do. do.
	AC ✿ C ▦	Alexr. Cameron (1818)
	EL ,, D ,,	Edwd. Livingstone (1809)
	CAMERON ,, C ,, DUNDEE	Alexr. Cameron (1818)
	RN ✿ ⊡ ▦	Robt. Naughton ? (see Inverness, p. 549)
1800	T·S ,, ,,	Thos. Stewart ? (see Inverness, p. 549)
TO	WC ,, ,,	Wm. Constable. (1806)
1840	RH S ✿ ⌂ ⊡ DUNDEE	(Not identified.)
	EL ✿ EL III	Edwd. Livingstone (1809)
	WK ▦ ✶	(Not identified.)
	DM ✿ DM	David Manson (1809)
	DM ,, DM	Do. do.
1809	WY ✿ D ✿	Wm. Young (1809)

PERTH

DATE (ABOUT).	MAKER'S MARK.	MAKER'S NAME.
1675		W. M......
1680		Robert Gardiner (1669)
1687		Do. do. do.
1710		William Scott, of Banff
1750		... ...
1772		James Cornfute (1772)
1780		T. F......
,,		Robert Keay (1791)
,,		J. J.
1791		Robert Keay (1791)
1800		William Ritchie (1796)
1810		John Sid (1808)
,,		R. & R. Keay
1815		David Greig (c. 1810)
1816		Charles Murray (1816)
,,		(No maker's mark.)
,,		R. McG.
,,		I. H.
1820		Robert Greig (1817)
1830		Robert Keay, jr. (1825)
,,		A. M......
,,		John Pringle (1827)
,,		Robert Keay, jr. (1825)
,,		John Pringle (1827)
1830 TO 1850		J. K......
		R. D......
1856		David Greig, jr.

INVERNESS

DATE (ABOUT).	MAKER'S MARK.	MAKER'S NAME.	DATE (ABOUT).	MAKER'S MARK.	MAKER'S NAME.
1640	MK INS	M. K......	1800	J&N INS	Jameson & Naughton.
1643	,, ,, T	Do. do.	,,	MAC MAS ,,	—— Macmas.
1680	MR INS	M. R......	..	D F INS	Donald Fraser.
1708	M ,, M	M. L......	1810	CJ INS CJ	Charles Jamieson.
1715	M ,,	—— M......	,,	,, ,, ,,	Do. do.
1720	RI INS A	R I......	,,	J.McR INS	J. McR.
1730	IB FB	John Baillie (and another)	1815	RN INS J RN	Robt. Naughton.
,,	IB FB A	Do. do.	,,	RN J	Do. do.
1740	IB INS	John Baillie	1820	AM INS OO	Alexr. MacLeod.
,,	TB INS	Thos. Baillie	,,	AM·L INS	Do. do.
1770	A·S INS	Alexr. Stewart	1830	TS INS	Thos. Stewart.
1780	RA C INS	Robert Anderson	,,	D·F INS	Donald Fraser.
1790	A·S INS	Alexr. Stewart, jr.	,,	A·S INS	Alexr. Stewart.
,,		(No maker's mark.)	1840		... ...
,,	H&C A	* Hamilton & Co.	1857	F BROS	Ferguson Brothers.
,,	JA ,, A	J. A.	1880	F&M INVS	Ferguson & MacBean.
,,	T&C	T. & Co.			
,,	AS	Alexr. Stewart, jr.			
1800	CJ INS	Chas. Jamieson			

ST. ANDREWS

PG X PG

About 1671

TAIN

LATE EIGHTEENTH CENTURY

MARKS.	ARTICLES AND OWNERS.
H·R S·O·B *A*	Table-spoon : The Marquess of Breadalbane, K.G.
H·R TAIN S·O·B *L*	Tea-pot : Mr. Willoughby Farr.
A·S TAIN	Toddy ladle : The Marquess of Breadalbane, K.G.
RW ,,	Dinner fork : Do. do.
W·I·*TAIN* ,,	Tea-spoon : Do. do.

MONTROSE

DATE (ABOUT).	MARKS.	MAKER'S NAME.	ARTICLES AND OWNERS.
1670	WL	Wm. Lindsay (probably).	Table-spoon, pricked 1672, Mr. A. W. Stone.
1671	WL	Wm. Lindsay.	{ Com. cups, " gifted 1671 ": Forfar. Spoon with flat stem : Mr. W. Boore.
	,, ,, ,, E	Do. do.	Com. cup, " given 1688 " : Laurence-kirk, Montrose.
1680-3	WL	Do. do.	Com. cups, " gifted 1680 ": Bervie, and (1683) Aberlemno.
1710	X H	... ...	Wavy-end spoon : Mr. J. H. Walter.
1752	T·I B	Thos. Johnston.	{ Com. cups : Marykirk, Montrose. Table-spoon : Mr. H. Dawson.
1788	BL	Benj. Lumsden (admitted 1788).	Dessert-spoon : The Marquess of Breadalbane, K.G.
1811	WM	Wm. Mill (1811)	Tea-spoon : Do. do.

CHAPTER XVIII
Unascribed Scotch Marks

THE DATES APPENDED—WHICH ARE CONJECTURED APPROXIMATELY—ARE SUCH AS THE CHARACTER OF THE ARTICLE AND STYLE OF THE WORK IN EACH CASE SUGGEST.

DATE (ABOUT).	MARKS.	ARTICLES AND OWNERS.
1500		Possibly an Inverness mark. Spoon with "wrythen" knop: Lord Breadalbane.
1690		Folding rat-tail spoon: Museum of Antiquities, Edinburgh.
1700		Fork, with seal at end: Do. do. do.
"		Small quaich: Lord Breadalbane.
1720		Plaid brooch: Do. do.
1730		Taper stand, etc.: Windsor Castle. (? Chas. Alchorne, ent. 1729.)
1750		Dessert-spoons: Lord Breadalbane.
"		Salt-box: Mr. Dudley Westropp.
"		Small bowl: Messrs. Crichton.
"		Large soup ladle: The Marquess of Breadalbane, K.G.
"		Small quaich: Mr. Nyberg.
"		*{Bonbonnière: The Marquess of Breadalbane, K.G. {Table-spoons: Lord Newlands.
1760		Tea-spoons: The Marquess of Breadalbane, K.G.
"		Tea-spoon: Do. do.
"		Two-handled tray: Mr. A. J. Davis.
1770		Table-spoon: The Marquess of Breadalbane, K.G.
"		Dessert-spoon: Messrs. Mackay & Chisholm.

* Lord Breadalbane suggests that these marks emanate from some place near Glasgow.

DATE (ABOUT).	MARKS.	ARTICLES AND OWNERS.
1780	JW	Sugar tongs : The Marquess of Breadalbane, K.G.
,,	CF	Tea-spoon :　　　Do.　　　do.
1790	R&S	Sauce ladle :　　　Do,　　　do.
,,	AR	(Perhaps Dundee marks).　Each mark struck twice on table-spoons : Messrs. Crichton.
,,	LM	Dessert-spoons : Messrs. Crichton.
,,	F⚫G	Fiddle-pattern forks : Noted by Mr. Dudley Westropp.
1800	T·H	*(Perhaps Dundee marks) Marrow scoop : Lord Breadalbane.
,,	EW	†Shell-pattern caddy spoon : Lord Breadalbane.
,,	RR	Small tea-spoon　　　　: Do.　　do.
,,	RB	Salt-spoon　　　　　: Do.　　do.
,,	CM	Table-spoon and mounts of shell snuff-box : The Marquess of Breadalbane, K.G.
1816	1816 F·D	‡ Pepper caster : Messrs. Crichton.
1800-20	O JG	*Perhaps John Glenn of Montrose.　Half a dozen tea-spoons : Lord Breadalbane.
,,	H·I	*Dozen fiddle-pattern table-spoons : Lord Breadalbane.
,,	WV AM	* Dozen fiddle-pattern tea-spoons　:　Do.　　do.

* These are believed to be the marks of travelling goldsmiths, called " Tinkers ".
† It has been suggested that these are Leith marks.
‡ It is with considerable hesitation that this line of marks is included.　The work, however, not appearing to be continental, as suggested by the striking of the full date " 1816," the marks have been placed here as " doubtful " Scotch because of the thistle.

CHAPTER XIX

Marks on Dublin Plate

Highly skilled goldsmiths worked in Ireland when Saxon kings reigned in England. Names of goldsmiths of the Twelfth Century have been preserved. The Dublin Goldsmiths Company was chartered in 1637.

TABLE I.

	HARP CROWNED.	DATE LETTER.	MAKER'S MARK.	.MAKER'S NAME.
CHAS. I. 1638-9		A		James Vanderbeck,
1639-40		B		John Thornton. / Edwd. Chadsey.
1640-1	,,	C		John Thornton.
1641-2	,,	D		Wm. Cooke.
1642-3		E		... ...
1643-4		F		... ...
1644-5		G		... ...
1645-6		H		... ...
1646-7		I		John Burke (or John Banister).
1647-8		K		... ...
1648-9 COMWTH.		L		... ...
1649-50		M		... ...
1650-1		N		... ...
1651-2		O		... ...
1652-3		P		... ...
1653-4		Q		... ...
1654-5		R		... ...
1655-6		S		Daniel Bellingham.
1656-7	,,	T		Joseph Stoaker (or John Slicer).
1657-8		U		... ...

TABLE II.

	HARP CROWNED.	DATE LETTER.	MAKER'S MARK.	MAKER'S NAME.
1658-9		a		... ...
				Joseph Stoaker.†
1659-60		b		Do. do.
CHAS. II. 1660-1		c		... ...
1661-2		d		... ...
1662-3		e		... ...
1663-4		f		Joseph Stoaker.†
1664-5	,,	g		Abel Ram.‡
1665-6		h		... ...
1666-7		i		... ...
1667-8		k		... ...
1668-9		l		... ...
1669-70		m		... ...
1670-1		n		... ...
1671-2		o		Joseph Stoaker.†
1672-3		p		... ...
1673-4		q		... ...
1674-5		r		... ...
1675-6		s		... ...
1676-7		t		... ...
1677-8		u		... ...

 1639-40 George Gallant.

191

TABLE III.

	HARP CROWNED.	DATE LETTER.	MAKER'S MARK.	MAKER'S NAME.
1678-9		A		... ...
	(harp)	B	TB	Timothy Blackwood.‡
1679-80			SM	Samuel Marsden.
			IK	James Kelly.
			AG	Andrew Gregory.
1680-1	(harp)	C	,,	Do. do.
			IP	John Phillips.
			WL	Wm. Walter Lucas or Lewis.
1681-2	,,	D	ES	Edwd. Swan.
1682-3	,,	E	IK	James Kelly.
1683-4		F		... ...
JAS. II. 1685-6-7	,,	G	IF	John Farmer.
			IC	John Cuthbert.
			RN	Robert Nevill.
			IH	John Humphrys.
1688 to 1692	(harp)	H	DK	David King.
			RS	Robt. Smith (warden 1701).
		I		
WM. III. 1693-4-5	(harp)	K	IW	Joseph Walker.
			WD	Wm. Drayton.
			WM	Wm. Myers.
			AS	Ant'ny Stanley.
			B	Thos. Bolton.
1696-9	,,	L	IP	John Phillips.
			DK	David King.
			IW	Joseph Walker.
			IH	John Humphrys.
			AS	Anth'y Stanley.

TABLE IV.

	HARP CROWNED.	DATE LETTER.	MAKER'S MARK.	MAKER'S NAME.
1699 / 1700	(harp)	P	EW	Ant'ny Stanley (as 1693-4-5.) Edward Workman.
1700-1	,,	Q	S	Alexr. Sinclair.
1701-2	(harp)	D	IW	Joseph Walker.
			B	... ... Thomas Boulton.
ANNE. 1702-3	(harp)	P	B	Do. do.
1703-4	,,	M	,,	Do. do.
1704-5-6	(harp)	R	HM	Henry Matthews.
			IW	Joseph Walker.
1706-7-8	(harp)	S	DK	David King.
			EB	Edward Barrett.
			B	Thomas Bolton.
1708-9-0	,,	T	,,	Do. do. (*Maker's mark indistinct*)
1710-1-2	(harp)	U	DK	David King. (*Maker's mark indistinct*)
1712-3-4	(harp)	W	EW	Edward Workman.
			WR	Walter Archdall.
			JC	John Clifton.
GEO I. 1714-5	,,	Y	WA	Wm. Archdall.
1715-6	(harp)	Y	IT	John Tuite.†
			IC	John Cuthbert, jun.
			IW	Joseph Walker. David King (as 1706 above).
1716-7		Z		... ...
1703-4	(harp)	B	RN	... ...
(1712)	(harp)	T	FG	Francis Gerard (oval)

TABLE V.

	HARP CROWNED.	DATE LETTER.	MAKER'S MARK.	MAKER'S NAME.
1717-8		J	W	Joseph Walker.
			CT	Christr. Thompson.
			WC	Wm. Clarke (of Cork).
			IH	John Hamilton.
"		"	Sa	John Savage?
			TP	Thos. Parker.
1718-9	"		EC	Erasm's Cope.
1719-20			HD	Henry Daniell.
			HC	John Clifton, jr.
"				John Clifton, sr.
1720-1		A	IH	John Hamilton.
				Do. do.
1721-2	"	B	TS	Thos. Sutton.
1722-3	"	C		John Clifton, sr.
			EB	Edwd. Barrett.
			RH	Robert Harrison.
1723-4	"	D	TW	Thos. Walker.
			WD	Wm. Duggan.
			TS	Thos. Slade.
1724-5		E	IT	John Taylor.
			B	Thos. Bolton.
				Mathw. Walker.
1725-6	"	F	MH	Michl. Hewitson.
				Mathw. Walker.
1726-7	"	G	NV	Noah Vialas.
			PK	Philip Kinnersly.
			RC	Robert Calderwood.
GEO. II. 1727-8		H	IK	John King.
			WC	Wm. Clarke (of Cork).
			IR	John Robinson.
1728-9	"	I	BC	Bolton Cormick.
			RC	Robert Calderwood.
1729-30		K	IM	John Moore.
			WA	Wm. Archdall.
1730-1	"	L	DK	David King.

TABLE VI.

	HARP CROWNED.	DATE LETTER.	HIBERNIA.	MAKER'S MARK.	MAKER'S NAME.
1731-2		L		EF	Esther Forbes.
				EC	Erasmus Cope?
1732-3	"	M		AL	Anthony Lefebure.
				JD	James Douglas.
				WW	Wm. Williamson.
1733-4	"	N	"	CL	Charles Lemaitre.
				IT	John Taylor.
				WT	Wm. Townsend.
1734-5		O		CL	Chas. Leslie.
				TW	Thos. Williamson.
				BM	Barth Mosse.
1735-6	"	P	"	AB	Alexr. Brown.
				IW	John Williamson.
				IW	John Wilme.
1736-7	"	Q	"	AG	Andrew Goodwin.
				IT	James Taylor.
1737-8	"	R	"	DK	David King?
				SW	Samuel Walker.
1738-9	"	S	"	MW	Matthew Walker.
				AG	Andrew Goodwin.
1739-40	"	T	"	FW	Francis Williamson.
				IW	John Walker.
1740-1	"	U	"	IM	John Moore.
				AR	Alexr. Richards.
1741-2-3		W	"	ID	Isaac D'Olier.
			"	IL	John Laughlin.
				CL	Christr. Locker.
1743-4	"	Y	"	RH	Robt. Holmes.
				Let	John Letablere.
				IW	James Whitthorne.
1745	"	B	"	M	John Moore.
1746	"	Z	"	IW	Jas. Whitthorne. (see 1745).

TABLE VII.

	HIBERNIA.	DATE LETTER.	HARP CROWNED.	MAKER'S MARK.	MAKER'S NAME.
*1747		A		WW CF	Wm. Williamson. C. Fox.
1748	,,	B	,,	WW WB	Will. Walsh. Will. Beates.
1749		C		IC IL	John Christie. John Laughlin.
1750		D	,,	M·B ID	Mathias Brown. Isaac D'Olier.
1751-2	,,	E		IP WR	John Pittar. William Ring.
1752-3	,,	F	,,	MH	Mich'el Homer.
1753-4	,,	G	,,	W·T AR	Wm. Townsend. Alexr. Richards.
1754-5	,,	H	,,	CS	Christr. Skinner.
1757	,,	I	,,	A	Matt'w Alanson.
1758	,,	K		D·P MS	Daniel Popkins. (Not identified.)
1759	,,	L		SW IP	Saml. Walker. J'nth'n. Pasley.
GEO. III. 1760	,,	M	,,	R·C	Robt. Calderwood.
1761	,,	N		GH TJ	Geo. Hill. Thos. Johnston.
1762	,,	O		A	Do. do. Matt'w Alanson.
1763	,,	P	,,	DP	David Peter.
1764	,,	Q	,,	WC WH	Wm. Currie. Wm. Homer.
1765	,,	R	,,	FI IC	Francis Jones. Joseph Cullen.
1766		S		MC IL F&K	M. Cormick & J. Locker. French & Keating.
1767	,,	T		JW RW	John West. Richd. Williams.
1768		U	,,	R·T ID	Richd. Tudor. Jer'm'h D'Olier.
1769		W		J·S IG	John Shields. James Graham.
1770	,,	X		IL CH	John Locker. Christr. Haines.
1771		Y		TK JL	Thos. Kinsela. John Lloyd.
1772	,,	Z	,,	CT CM	Chas. Townsend. Chas. Mullin.

* This Hibernia stamp was also used 1752-3-4

TABLE VIII.

	HIBERNIA.	DATE LETTER.	HARP CROWNED.	MAKER'S MARK.	MAKER'S NAME.
1773		A		JW	John Walker.
1774	,,	B	,,	WH I·C	Wm. Hughes. John Craig.
1775		C		A·B RW	Ambrose Boxwell. Richd. Williams.
1776	,,	D		CT MW	Chas. Townsend. Matthew West.
1777		E		HA DK SW	Hay Andrews. Darby Kehoe. Stephen Walsh.
1778	,,	F	,,	MH JP	Michael Homer. John Pittar.
1779	,,	G		I·I MK	Jos. Jackson. Michael Keating.
1780	,,	H		MW J·B	Michael Walsh. John Bolland.
1781	,,	I	,,	IK I·I TJ	John Kelly. Jos. Jackson. Thomas Jones.
1782	,,	K	,,	W·W	Wm. Ward.
1783		L		H	John Laughlin, jr.
1784	,,	M		RW W·T MW	Robert Wyke. Wm. Thompson. Matthew Walsh.
1785	,,	N	,,	CH W·S	Christr. Haines. Wm. Supple.
1786	,,	O	,,	WJ L&B	Wm. Johnson. (Not identified.)
* 1787		P		JP MW	John Pittar. Matthew West.
* 1788	,,	Q		MK I·S	Michael Keating. John Stoyte.
* 1789	,,	R		WL RW	Wm. Law. Robt. Williams.
1790	,,	S	,,	AC A·N	Arthur Clark. Arthur O'Neill.
* 1791	,,	T	,,	BT TJ	Benjn. Tait. Thos. Jones?
* 1792	,,	U	,,	RS WB IK	Robt. Smith. Wm. Bond. James Keating.
* 1793	,,	W	,,	MK JP	Michael Keating. John Power.
* 1794		X		GW L&B	George West. (Not identified.)
1795	,,	Y	,,	I·L	John Laughlin, jr.
* 1796		Z		IE GW FB	James England. Geo. Wheatley. Fredk. Buck.

*The date-letters D & G have been also found without the pellet in its shield, which is occasionally rounded.

IRISH SILVER OF THE PERIOD 1755-1765

TABLE IX.

	HIBERNIA.	DATE LETTER.	HARP CROWNED.	KING'S HEAD.	MAKER'S MARK.	MAKER'S NAME.
1797	[Hibernia]	A	[harp]		J·R / JD	John Rigby. / Geo. West (as 1794.)
1798	,,	B	,,		J·K / JD	John Keene. / John Daly.
1799	,,	C	,,		I·K WEST / IS	James Keating.† / James Scott.
1800	,,	D	,,		J·K / WP	John Kearns. / Walter Peter.
1801	,,	E	,,		IC / JP	Jas. Connor. / John Power.
1802	,,	F	,,		RS / WH	Richd. Sawyer. / Wm. Hamey.
1803	,,	G	,,		O/A·N / IB	Arthur O'Neil. / J. Brady.
1804	,,	H	,,		R·B / DE	Robt. Breading. / Danl. Egan.
1805	,,	I	,,		W·D / DM	Wm. Doyle. / (Not identified.)
1806	,,	K	,,	KING'S HEAD.	S·N / T·K·W / W·W	Samuel Neville, / Tudor & Whitford. / Wm. Ward.
1807	,,	L	,,	[head]	GB	Gust'v's Byrne.
1808	,,	M	,,	,,	C·T/I·W / S·N	Terry & Williams (of Cork). / Saml. Neville.
1809	,,	N N	,,	[head]	JJ / RB	Joseph Johnson. / Robt. Breading.
1810	[Hibernia]	O O	[harp]	,,	I·L·B / T·R	Jas. Le Bass. / (Not identified.)
1811	,,	P	,,	,,	C·S / W·N	Chas. Stewart. / W. Nowlan.
1812	,,	Q	,,	,,	HAMY R·S / PM	{W. Hamey & R. Smith.} / P. Moore.
1813	,,	R	,,	,,	WR / J·P	Wm. Rose. / John Pittar.
1814	,,	S	,,	,,	I·S / LAW / I·N	Jas. Scott. / Wm. Law. / John Nicklin.
1815	,,	T	,,	,,	PG / SB	Phineas Garde (Cork). / S. Bergin.
1816	,,	U	,,	,,	DE / RC	Danl. Egan. / Randall Cashell.
1817	,,	W	,,	,,	J·M / WC / NWB / T·R	James Moore. / W. Cummins. / Sir N. W. Brady. / T. Read.
1818	,,	X	,,	,,	LB	J. Buckton.
1819	,,	Y	,,		I·L·B / IF WEST	Jas. Le Bass. / Jas. Fry.†
GEO. IV. 1820	,,	Z	,,		JS / EM	J. Salter (Cork). / Edwd. Murray.

TABLE X.

	HIBERNIA.	DATE LETTER.	HARP CROWNED.	KING'S HEAD.	MAKER'S MARK.	MAKER'S NAME.
1821	[Hibernia]	A	[harp]	[head]	MW&S / WM	M. West & Sons. / Wm. Morgan.
1822	,,	B	,,	,,	EC / I·B	E. Crofton. / J. Buckton.
1823	,,	C	,,	,,	LAW / EP	Wm. Law. / Edwd. Power.
1824	,,	D	,,	,,	IF / SN / SB	Jas. Fray. / Saml. Neville. / Saml. Beere.
1825-6		E e	,,	[head]	WT / R·G	Wm. Teare.? / Richd. Garde (Cork).
1826-7	,,	F	,,	,,	W&C° / J·S	Ald'm'n West (& Co.). / J. Smith.
1827-8	[Hibernia]	G	,,	[head]	CM / DR	Chas. Marsh. / J. Read.
1828-9	[Hibernia]	H	[harp]	[head]	TWY† / HF / IN	Edwd. Twycross. / Hy. Flavelle. / L. Nowlan.
1829-30	[Hibernia]	I I	[harp]	[head]	CM / M·G (D.&W.)	Chas. Marsh. / D. Moulang & W. Gibson.
WM. IV. 1830-1	[Hibernia]	K	[harp]	[head]	S&G / E·J	Smith & Gamble. / Edmd. Johnson.
1831-2	[Hibernia]	L	[harp]	[head]	R·S / TF / PM	Richd. Sawyer, jr. / T. Farnett. / P. Moore.
1832-3	,,	M	,,	,,	HF / TM	Hy. Flavelle. / Thos. Meade.
1833-4	[Hibernia]	N N	[harp]		E·J / LN	Edmd. Johnson. / L. Nowlan?
1834-5	[Hibernia]	O O	,,	[head]	WS / PW	Wm. Sherwin. / P. Weeks?
1835-6	[Hibernia]	P P	,,	,,	I·M	J. Moore.
1836-7	,,	Q Q	,,	,,	WS / R·G	Wm. Sherwin. / Richd. Garde (Cork).
VICT. 1837-8	,,	R R	,,	,,	IL / S&G	Josiah Low. / Smith & Gamble.
1838-9	,,	S	,,	[head]	H&F	Hughes & Francis.
1839-40	[Hibernia]	T	[harp]	,,	PW	Peter Walsh.
1840-1	,,	U U	,,	,,	E&J·J / LN	E. & J. Johnson, / L. Nowlan.
1841-2	[Hibernia]	V	,,	,,	GA	G. Alcock.
1842-3	[Hibernia]	W	[harp]	,,	IW / I·L·B	John Warren. / Jas. Le Bass.
1843-4	,,	X	,,	,,	IF / GW	J. Francis. / Geo. West?
1844-5	[Hibernia]	Y	[harp]		MN	Michl. Nowlan.
1845-6	[Hibernia]	Z	[harp]	[head]	JG / JJ20	J. Gamble. / ‡ Joseph Johnson.

‡The tax on silver plate enacted in England in 1784 did not apply in Ireland until after the Act of Union (1800) and does not appear to have been enforced until 1807.

TABLE XI.

	HIBERNIA.	DATE LETTER.	HARP CROWNED.	QUEEN'S HEAD.	MAKER'S MARK.	MAKER'S NAME.
1846-7		a			JJ	Joseph Johnson.
1847-8	,,	b	,,	,,	J·M / TM	J. Mahoney. / Thos. Mason.
1848-9	,,	c	,,	,,	CC / WL / RS	C. Cummins, jr. / Wm. Lawson. / R. Samuel.
1849-50	,,	d	,,	,,	D&W	Donegan & Co.
1850-1	,,	e	,,	,,	J·G / HF	J. Gamble. / Henry Flavelle.
1851-2	,,	f f	,,	,,	IN / AC	Joseph Needham. / Ann Cummins.
1852-3	,,	g g	,,	,,	GARDNER / JS	— Gardner. / J. Smyth.
1853-4	,,	h h	,,	,,	RS / T&W	R. Sherwin. / Topham & White.
1854-5	,,	j	,,	,,	M·K	Michael Keating.
1855-6	,,	k	,,	,,	CC	C. Cummins.
1856-7	,,	l	,,	,,	W·A	W. Atcheson.
1857-8	,,	m	,,	,,	D&W / A·J	Donegan & Co. / Arthur Johnson.
1858-9	,,	n	,,	,,	J.R.N / NEILL	J. R. Neill. / Do. do.
1859-60	,,	o	,,	,,	S·L·B	Samuel Le Bass.
1860-1	,,	p	,,	,,	WP / W&IP	Wm. Percival. / W. & I. Percival.
1861-2	,,	q	,,	,,	EP	E. Powell.
1862-3	,,	r	,,	,,	JK / EJ·JJ	J. ⅟ Keating. / E. & J. Johnson.
1863-4	,,	s	,,	,,	J·S	John Smyth.
1864-5		t	,,	,,	IS / RYAN&C	J. Scriber. / Ryan & Co.
1865-6	,,	u	,,	,,	I·W / WATERHOUSE / F·M	Jas. West. / Waterhouse & Co. / Francis Martin.
1866-7	,,	v	,,	,,	AH / BRUNKER DUBLIN	A. Hutton. / Thos. Brunker.
1867-8	,,	w	,,		P·D / WL	Patk. Donegan. / Wm. Lawson.
1868-9	,,	x	,,	,,	EJ / M·T	Edmd. Johnson, jr. / Mars. Trench.
1869-70	,,	y	,,	,,	W·L	Wm. Lawson.
1870-1	,,	z	,,	,,	TDB	T. D. Bryce.

TABLE XII.

FROM JUNE, 1871, TO JUNE, 1896—TWENTY-FIVE YEARS.

FIVE STAMPS TILL 1890, THENCEFORWARD FOUR, AS BELOW: The date marks being plain block letters in plain shields.

	HIBERNIA.	DATE LETTER.	HARP CROWNED.	QUEEN'S HEAD.	MAKER'S MARK.	MAKER'S NAME AND DATE OF REGISTRATION OF MARK.		
1871-2		A			J·W W·R	J. Weir	Wickham. & Rogers.	(1871). "
1872-3	"	B	"	"	J·D	John	Donegan.	(1872).
1873-4	"	C	"	"	EGAN CORK	Wm.	Egan & Son (of Cork).	"
1874-5	"	D	"	"	I·C	Ignatius	Cummins.	(1874).
1875-6	"	E	"	"	McDB	McDowell	Bros.	(1875).
1876-7	"	F	"	"	McDB	Do.	do.	"
1877-8	"	G	"	"	W&S	West	& Son.	(1877).
1878-9	"	H	"	"	J·R	J.	Redmond.	(1876).
1879-80	"	I	"	"	W&S	West	& Son.	(1879).
1880-1	"	K	"	"	O·C &D	O'Connor	& Dillon.	(1880).
1881-2	"	L	"	"	E·JOHNSON E·J	Edmond Do.	Johnson. do.	(1881). (1882).
1882-3	"	M	"	"	W·C H·H	Wm. Henry	Carty. Hopkins.	(1881). (1883).
1883-4	"	N	"	"	D·M	Danl.	Moulang.	"
1884-5	"	O	"	"	W&L	Winder	& Lamb.	"
1885-6	"	P	"	"	F·B³	Frengley	Bros.	(1885).
1886-7	"	Q	"	"	A&C⁰	Austin	& Co.	(1886).
1887-8	"	R	"	"	M·A J·E·P	M. Jas. E.	Anderson. Pim.	(1887). "
1888-9	"	S	"	"	T·B F·H	Thomas Fredk.	Barton. Hill.	(1871). (1889).
1889-90	"	T	"	"	W·Q J·F	Wm. Joseph	Quinlan. Fray.	(1888). (1889).
1890-1	"	U	"		H·L·S	Henry L.	Stewart (of Limerick).	"
1891-2	"	V	"		S·D·NEILL	Sharman D.	Neill (of Belfast).	(1890).
1892-3	"	W	"		H&H MOSLEY	Hopkins Jas. C.	& Hopkins. Mosley (Waterford). Harris (Coventry).	(1883). (1892). (1893).
1893-4	"	X	"		C·H E·J	Edmond	Johnson.	"
1894-5	"	Y	"		C·H·L K&G R·D	Chas. Howard Kane Richard	Lawson. & Gunning Dillon (Waterford).	(1894). " "
1895-6	"	Z	"		C·L C&S	Charles Chancellor	Lamb. & Son.	(1893). (1895).

TABLE XIII.

	HIBER-NIA.	DATE LETTER.	HARP CROWNED.	MAKER'S MARK.	MAKER'S NAME AND DATE OF REGISTRATION OF MARK.		
1896-7		A		{ R&W JM	Richards John	& Walsh. Morton.	(1895). (1896).
1897-8	,,	B	,,	G	Gibson,	Ltd. (Belfast).	(1897).
1898-9	,,	C	,,	{ RK M&C	Robert Moore	Knaggs. & Co.	(1898). ,,
1899		D		RV	Robert	Valentine.	,,
1900	,,	D	,,	W.J.G LAWSON DUBLIN	W. J. Chas. Howard	Gethings. Lawson.	,, (1900).
1900-1	,,	E	,,	LAW	Langley Archer	West.	,,
EDW. VII. 1901-2	,,	F	,,	{ H&T M°C&D	Henderson McCutcheon	& Thompson (Belfast). & Donaldson (Belfast).	(1901).
1902-3	,,	G	,,	W&S	West	& Son.	(1902).
1903-4		H		JEB	J. E.	Byrne (Belfast).	(1909).
1904-5	,,	I	,,	JAMESON	——	Jameson.	,,
1905-6	,,	K	,,	R LTD	Russell	Ltd. (Manchester).	,,
1906-7	,,	L	,,	A DUFFNER TIPPERARY	A.	Duffner (Tipperary).	(1907).
1907-8	,,	M	,,	FS LR	Finnegans	Ltd. (Manchester).	(1912).
1908-9	,,	N	,,	E&Co	Elkington	& Co. (Birmingham).	,,
1909-10	,,	O	,,	W.E&SNS LTD	W. Egan	& Sons (Cork).	(1910).
1910-1	,,	P	,,	N	——	Neill (Belfast).	(1906).
1911-2	,,	Q	,,	A M	Youghal Art Metal Works Co.		,,
1912-3	,,	R	,,	FALLER,GALWAY	——	Faller (Galway).	,,
1913-4	,,	S	,,	J M°D	J.	McDowell.	,,
1914-5	,,	T	,,	C.CROMER LIMERICK	C.	Cromer (Limerick).	(1907).
1915-6	,,	U	,,	& W.W	Wakeley	& Wheeler (London).	(1909).

TABLE XIV.

FOUR STAMPS AS BELOW.

	HIBER-NIA.	DATE LETTER.	HARP CROWNED.	MAKER'S MARK.	MAKER'S NAME AND DATE OF REGISTRATION OF MARK.		
1916-7		A		W·S	Will	Stokes.	(1910).
1917-8	,,	B	,,	WALDRON SKIBBEREEN	M.	Waldron (Skibbereen).	,,
1918-9	,,	C	,,	JR	Jas.	Ramsay (Dundee).	(1912).
1919-20	,,	D	,,	R S	R.	Sharman.	(1908).
1920-1	,,	E	,,	L&C	Crichton	Bros. (London).	(1912).

SUPPLEMENTARY MARKS.

DATE.	MARKS.			MAKER'S NAME.	ARTICLES AND OWNERS.
1663-4				Abel Ram.	Spoon, with flat stem, trefoil end: National Museum, Dublin.
1708-10				Philip Tough.	Cylindrical tankard, domed top: Mr. Nyburg.
1715-6				Wm. Archdall.	Small salver: Mr. Arthur Irwin Dasent.
1731				——— Sutton?	Tankard: Noted by Mr. Dudley Westropp.
1739				Robert Holmes.	Table-spoon, Hanoverian pattern: Mr. Dudley Westropp.
1740				Will. Walsh.	Do. do.: Do. do.
				Jane Daniell.	Salver: Mr. Arthur Irwin Dasent.
,,	,,	,,	,,	——— Sutton	{ Sauce boat, with date-letter Ꜳ as in Table VI.: Mr. Dudley Westropp.
c. 1750					{ No date letter (but date about 1750), Paten: Donabate. The communion cup pertaining to it is dated 1751. Also on soup ladle with D for 1750: Noted by Mr. Dudley Westropp.

The following marks and dates are copied from the Dublin Assay Book.

1660		Andrew Edwards.	1704	**IG**	John Garrett.
1704	**AV**	Abraham Voisin.	,,	**IW**	James Walker.
,,	**RS**	Robert Smith.			

Supplementary List of Dublin Silversmiths.

TABLE I.

DATE.	MARK.	MAKER'S NAME.
1636	I W	John Woodcocke.
1663-4	F C	Francis Coffee or Clifton.
1679	E S	Edward Swan.
1680	E S	" "
"	L S	Lawrence Salmon.
"	I S	John Seager.
1685	I P	John Phillips.
1685-7	I C	John Cuthbert.
1696-7	D M	(Not identified.)
1698	A S	A. Stanley?
1699	C M P	Cyriac Mallory.
"	G L	George Lyng.
1700	A M	Alexr. Mackay.
1701-2	T S	Thos. Sumpner.
"	A S	... ...
1702-3	E B	Edward Barrett.
"	H	Thos. Hartwell.
1703-4	D	... ...
"	K	David King.
1706	R F	Robt. Forbes.

TABLE II.

DATE.	MARK.	MAKER'S NAME.
1706	B	Thos. Bolton.
1710	H S	Henry Sherwin.
1710-2	B	Thos. Bolton?
"	P	J. Pennyfather or J. Palet?
1712-4	E D	" ... ...
1715	G S	Geo. Smart.
"	E D	Ed. Dowdall.
1715-6	M	Mark Twelves.
1716-7	Z I W	... ...
1717-8	W B	W. Bell.
1718-9	T W	Thos. Walker.
1719-20	A W	Arthur Weldon.
1720	I R	Thos. Racine.
1722-3	E F	Ed. Fitzgerald.
1723-4	D W S	... ...
1724-5	P K	Phillip Kinnersly.
1725-6	S A	John Sale.
"	R P	Robt. Pilkington.
"	M C	Matt. Copeland.

TABLE III.

DATE.	MARK.	NAME OF MAKER.
1725-6	M B	Mary Barrett.
"	T W	Thos. Wheeler.
1726-7	P R	Peter Racine.
1728-9	S C	... ...
1729	E F	Esther Forbes.
"	U S	Thos. Sutton.
1730-1	G C	George Cross.
"	G C	Geo. Cartwright.
"	D M	Dorothy Monjoy.
1731	A	Matthew Alanson.
1732-3	E C	Erasmus Cope.
1734	I G	John Gumly.
1735	D	Isaac D'Olier.
1736-7	T M	Thos. Maculla?
"	A	Anthony Lefebure.
"	R W	Ralph Woodhouse.
"	D S	... ...
1737-8	I F	John Freebough.

Supplementary List of Dublin Silversmiths.—*Continued.*

TABLE IV.

DATE.	MARK.	NAME OF MAKER.
1737-8	TD	Thos. de Limarest.
1740-1	PD	Peter Desenard.
"	MR	... ...
"	I·C	Jas. Champion ?
"	PD	... ...
"	I·L	John Letablere.
"	T·B	Thos. Burton.
"	SU	Thos. Sutton.
c. 1740	H3	? Henry Jago.
1743-4	WB	Wm. Bonynge.
"	R·C	Robt. Calderwood.
1745	GB	George Beere.
"	RG	Robt. Glanville.
1746	I·H	John Hamilton ?
"	W·F	Wm. Faucett ?
"	B·S	Bart'mew Stokes.
"	WW	Wm. Walsh.
c. 1750	IT	Joseph Taafe.
1751	NM	Nathan Murray.
"	I*P	J. Pittar.
"	W·B	Wm. - Betagh.

TABLE V.

DATE.	MARK.	MAKER'S NAME.
1752	ER	Edward Raper.
1754	O R·C	Robt. Calderwood or Cope.
"	H*W	Hy. Waldron.
1757	M·F	Michael Fowler.
1758	WW	Wm. Williamson.
"	CS	Christr. Skinner.
c. 1760	H*W	See 1754 above.
1762	I·M	John Moore, Jr.
1764	I·D	John Dawson.
"	FI	... ...
1766	RV	Ralph Vizard ?
1767	W*F	Wm. French.
c. 1767	WT	Wm. Townsend.
1768	IW	Jno. Williamson.
"	B·W	Benj. Wilson.
"	A·T	Abraham Tuppy.
1769	WT MC	... ...
"	GH	George Hall.
1770	KAR	John Karr.
1776	I·B	... ...
1779	IL	John Locker ?
"	MS	... ...

TABLE VI.

DATE.	MARK	MAKER'S NAME.
1780	HO	Hugh O'Hanlon or Owen Hart ?
c. 1780	O C	Owen Cassidy.
"	AB	Alex. Barry ?
1780-5	BD	Barnaby Delahoyde ?
1785	D·E	Dan. Egan ?
1792	MH	Michael Homer ?
1795	IASK	J. R. Ash.
c. 1795	I·W	... ...
c. 1797	TT	Thos. Tudor.
1798	IB	John Brooks ?
1800	ST	Saml. Teare.
1800-1	JB	John Bolland.
"	G&PW	... ...
1802	JD	John Daly ?
1807	C&W	Clarke & West.
"	ÆR	Æneas Ryan.
1810	RS	Richard Sawyer.
"	IT	John Teare.
1811	JK RF	... ...
1812	JH	J. Henzell ?
"	JK	... ...
1815	RW	Richard Whitford.

The following marks of Dublin goldsmiths have been reproduced from a pewter plate preserved in the Dublin Assay Office. The marks were in use 1765–1812.

RA	Robt.	Atkinson?	JSB			WG	
ET			EB			LT	
RID	Richard & Jeremiah	D'Olier.	CF			WS	Will.	Stafford?
GM			JN	Joseph	Nixon.	IE	John	Ebbs.
JA	John	Austin.	RB	Robert	Breading.	TA	
JC	John	Clarke.	RH			EC BC	
TF	Thos.	Farley.	JE	Joshua	Emerson.	GN	George Nangle.
II	Joseph	Jackson.	SR	Saml.	Reily (Cork).	IH	James Hadmill.
TS			RL			G·ALLEY	Geo. Alley.
WD	Will.	Digby?	GT	Geo.	Thompson.	IK	James Kenzie.
JK	John	Keene.	JJ	James	Jones.	IA	Jerome Alley?
G&B			PM			LD	John Dalrymple.
TW	Thos.	Williamson.				WS	
WB	Will	Beere.	M:CL	Mark	M'Cloughlin.	PS	
TP			WFG	Wm.	Fitzgerald (Limerick).	TM	Thos. Martin.
JC	John	Coleman.	HL			WJ	Will. Johnson.
MB	Michael	Byrne.	TN			AT	Alex. Ticknell.
WP	Walter	Peter.	AN	Ambr'se	Nicklin.	JO	John Osborne.
CD	Chas.	Dowdall.	M·N			HN	Henry Nicholson.
T·C	Thos.	Cooksey.	HM			RT	
J·J	James	Jones.	NICOLSON	J.	Nicolson (Cork).	WS	
IP			JA			S·R	Saml. Reily (Cork).
GW			WK	Wm.	Keene.	H&H	Hopper & Hannay.
CC	Christr.	Clarke?	JJ	James	Jones?	JG	
IW	Jacob	West.	IN			TH	Thos. Hunt?
IM			LM	La'rence	Martin (Kilkenny).	GN	George Nangle.
LA			C·G			PF	

Marks found on a pewter plate, *continued*, 1765–1812.

MARK.	NAME.	MARK.	NAME.	MARK.	NAME.
LH		W.W		FB	Fredk. Buck.
W·H	Will. Hughes?	BT	Benjn. Tait.	ST	Samuel Taylor.
CK		PW	Peter Wingfield.	RC	Randall Cashell?
WG	Will. Gethin?	TA	Thos. Adams.	W·H	Wm. Hannay?
I·T	John Tweedie?	HM		I·C	
R·S	Robt. O'Shaughnessy (Limerick).	TR	Thos. Rourke.	JL	John Lloyd.
I·H	James Hewitt?	DP		E&B	
IW	John West?	RC	Randall Cashell?	WF	Will French.
J·R	J'n'th'n Robinson?	GIBSON	Joseph Gibson (Cork).	W·W	Will Ward.
SLY	Thos. Sly.	GR			
G&PW		JJ	Joseph Johnson.	AM	Arthur Murphy.
MS		JC	James Campbell?	W·L	
TE		D·P		R·D	
I·M	James Mills?	ID	Isaac Davis?	BP	
WL	Wm. Law?	MW&S	Matt. West & Son.	J·T	
WH	Will. Hamey?	I·C	Jas. Connor?	I·G	
T·B	Thos. Baker?	BB		WH	
W·F		SINGLETON	—— Singleton.	IB	John Bolland?
FR		T·T	Thomas Townsend.	TSW	

THE FOLLOWING MARKS, WHICH ARE STAMPED ON A COPPER-PLATE OF LATER DATE, RANGE FROM ABOUT 1813 TO ABOUT 1850.

MARK.	NAME.	MARK.	NAME.	MARK.	NAME.
WG		GF		LK	
TK JF		TT		GW WM	
TK		CM		GA	
HL	Henry Lazarus.	IH WHT	Wm. H. Townsend.	JT	John Townsend.
DM		SB	S. Bergin.	W·N	Wm. Nelson.
S&W		J·MOORE	James Moore.	K&F	
J·M & E·M		WC		RE	
IM	J. Moore.	FM &S		TO	
BOYLE	—— Boyle.	LEE		GRAYS	—— Grays.
EM	Edwd. Murphy.	RWS	R. W. Smith.	PG	
				IS	

CHAPTER XX
Marks on Cork Plate

No date letter was ever used at Cork. The dates are approximate.

TABLE I.

DATE (ABOUT).	MAKER'S MARK.	MAKER'S NAME.
1662		James Ridge.
1663		(Not identified).
1670		Walter Burnett.
1673		James Ridge.
1679		Richard Smart.
1680		Samuel Pantaine.
,,		Walter Burnett.
,,		(Both marks repeated).
,,		John Hawkins.
1691		Do. do.
1683		Robert Goble.
1686		Do. do.
1690		Do. do.
1692		Caleb Webb.
,,		Robert Goble.
1696		Do. do.
,,		Walter Burnett.
,,		Robert Goble.
,,		Do. do.
1697		Charles Bekegle.
1700		Robert Goble.
,,		Anthony Semirot.
1705		Robert Goble.
1709		William Clarke.

TABLE II.

DATE (ABOUT).	MAKER'S MARK.	MAKER'S NAME.
1709		Adam Billon.
1702-29		George Brumley.
1709		John Wigmore.(?)*
1710		Wm. Clarke.
,,		Robert Goble.
1710-20		John Rickotts
1712		Robert Goble.
1715-25		Robert Goble, Junr
,,		... ...
,,		William Clarke.
,,		,, ,,†
1719		Caleb Rotheram.
,,		William Clarke. ‡
1720		,, ,,
,,		Bernald Baldwin.
,,		... ...
1720-30		}... ...
,,		}Wm. Newenham.
,,		Edward Dunsterfield.
1720-34		William Newenham.
,,		,, ,,
,,		(Not identified—perhaps not Cork).
1722		... ...

TABLE III.

DATE (ABOUT).	MAKER'S MARK.	MAKER'S NAME.
1724	THO·LILLY STERLING	} Thomas Lilly.
1725-6	R M STERLING	Reuben Millard.
1730	WN STERLING	Wm. Newenham.
,,	WN STERLING	,, ,,
1730-40	W*B STERLING	William Bennett.
,,	I H STERLING I H	John Harding?
,,	CR STE RLING CR	Caleb Rotheram.
,,	STERLING I·H	John Harding?
,,	R·G	Robt. Goble, jr.?
,,	CP CP CP	Christr. Parker.
1720-37	W·MARTIN	William Martin.
,,	W·MARTIN	Do. do.
,,	W·M	Do. do.
,,	R·M	Reuben Millard.
1730-40	WB STERLING WB	William Bennett or Wm. Bentley.
1731	T·BULL	Thomas Bull.
1740	G·H STERLING	George Hodder.
,,	G·H G·H	Do. do.
,,	WB WB	William Bennett or Wm. Bentley.
1740-50	RA	... ...
,,	AS STERLING	} Anthony Semirot.
1745-70	STARLING G*H	George Hodder.
,,	GH STERLING GH	Do. do.
,,	STARLING GH	} Do. do.
,,	G*H GH GH G+H	*Do. do.

TABLE IV.

DATE (ABOUT).	MAKER'S NAME.	MAKER'S NAME.
c. 1750	STERLING SB	} Stephen Broughton.
1750-70	R·P STERLING	Robt. Potter.
,,	II L·IRISH II	John Irish.
,,	H STERLING	Do. do. (?)
1757-80	MD DERMOTT	Michael McDermott.
,,	MD STER	Do. do.
,,	MD STERLING MD	Do. do.
,,	WR ,,	William Reynolds.
,,	WR ,,	Do. do.
,,	WR	Do. do.
,,	WR STERLING	Do. do.
,,	,, STERLING	Do. do.
,,	WR	Do. do.
,,	WR WR	Do. do.
,,	WR WR	Do. do.
,,	McD STERLING	Michael McDermott.
,,	MD ,,	Do. do.
1760	L*R STARLING L*R	... ...
,,	LA STERLING LA	... ...
1760-80	WALSH SW STERLING	} Stephen Walsh.
,,	C·B STERLING	Croker Barrington.
,,	SW WALSH STERLING	} Stephen Walsh.
,,	SW STERLING	Do. do.
,,	WALSH STERLING	} Do. do.
,,	SW WALSH STERLING	Do. do.
,,	SW ,,	Do. do.
,,	SM ,,	Stephen Mackrill.

TABLE V.

DATE (ABOUT).	MAKER'S MARK.	MAKER'S NAME.
1760-80	STERLING DMC	} Daniel McCarthy?
,,	DMC STER	Do. do.
,,	STARLING C·B	Croker Barrington.
,,	C·B DOLLAR	Do. do.
1760-85	IH STERLING	John Illery.*
1765-95	CT ,, CT	Carden Terry.
1770	IRH STER	John Irish.
,,	TA STERLING TA	... ...
,,	McD Sterling	Michael McDermott.
,,	MD STERLING	Do. do.
1770-88	STER JWS STER	} John Whitney (free 1775).
1770-99	IN STERLING	John Nicolson.
,,	IN STERLING	Do. do.
,,	IN ,,	Do. do.
,,	,, NICOLSON	Do. do.
1777 1820	PW STERLING	Peter Wills.
1780	C·T STERLING	Carden Terry.
,,	IH STERLING IH	John Humphreys.†
,,	I·H ,,	Do. do.
,,	JK STERLING	Joseph Kinselagh.
,,	I·H STERLING	John Hillery.*
,,	C·T STERLING	Carden Terry.
,,	SC STERLING	(Not identified.)
,,	SR ,,	Samuel Reily.
,,	JSN ,,	Jno. & Sam. Nicolson.
,,	IC STIRLING	} Thomas Cumming.

TABLE VI.

DATE (ABOUT).	MAKER'S MARK.	MAKER'S NAME.
1770-80	WM STERG	W. Morrisey.
1770-99	NICOLSON STERLING	John Nicolson.
1777 1810	S·R STERLING	Samuel Reily.
,,	S·R STERLING	Do. do.
,,	SR STERLG	Do. do.
,,	REILY STERLING	Do. do.
1783-95	W·ROE STERLING	} William Roe.
,,	TG STERLING TG	... ...
1786-95	T·H STERLING	Thos. Harman.
1787-95	TC STERLG TC	Tim. Conway.
1787	TD STERLING	Thomas Donnallan.
1787-95	IS ,,	John Sheehan.
,,	IG STERLING	Joseph Gibson.
1787-99	R·S STERLING	Richard Stevens.
,,	R·S STERLING	Do. do.
,,	I·S ,, I·S	John Sheehan.
,,	STERLING SHEEHAN	Do. do.
,,	SHEEHAN STERG	Do. do.
,,	SHEEHAN STERLING	} Do. do.
,,	R·S STERLING	} Richard Stevens.
1790 1800	JMcN STERLING	} (Not identified.)
,,	RI STERLING	} Do. do.
1795	WT STERLG	Wm. Teulon.
,,	W·T STERLING	Do. do.
,,	★ WT STERLING	Do. do.
,,	,, STERLG	Do. do.

TABLE VII.

DATE (ABOUT).	MAKER'S MARK.	MAKER'S NAME.
1795		John Supple.
,,	WT STERLING	William Teulon.
,,	WT STERLING	Do. do.
,,	HSM STERLING	(Not identified.)
,,	WT ,,	William Teulon.
,,	TJB STERLING	(Not identified.)
1791	IW ,,	John Warner.
1780-99	,, STIRLING	Do. do.
1795	IW STERLING	John Williams.
,,	I·W STER	James Warner.
,,	I·W STERLING	Do. do.
,,	I·W STERLG	Do. do.
,,	STERLING TOLLAND STERLING	—— Tolland.
1796	I·H STERLING	James Heyland.
,,	RD STERLING	... ...
,,	HEYLAND STERLING	} James Heyland.
,,	J·K STERLING	Jos. Kinselagh.
,,	JMᵈ	... ...
1800	IT TOLEKEN	John Toleken.
,,	TWM STERLING	(Not identified.)
1800-20	{ GIBSON STERLING GIBSON }	Joseph Gibson.
,,	WHELPLEY STERLING	John Whelpley.
,,	,, WHELPLY	Do. do.
,,	K ,, WHELPLY	Do. do.

TABLE VIII.

DATE (ABOUT).	MAKER'S MARK.	MAKER'S NAME.
1800-20	GIBSON STERLING	Joseph Gibson.
,,	HEYLAND ,,	William Heyland.
,,	,, TOLEKEN	John Toleken.
1795 / 1807	T&W ,,	{ Carden } Terry & { John } Williams.
1805	SG STERLING	Samuel Green.
1805-14	SG STERLING SG	} Do. do.
,,	C·T ⚓ I·W STERLING	Terry & Williams.
,,	T.MONTJOY ,,	Thomas Montjoy.
,,	IN NN ,,	John & } Nicolson. Nicholas
1807-21	CT IW STERLING	{ Carden } Terry & { Jane } Williams.
1808-20	·CORBETT· STERLING	Daniel Corbett.
1809-30	JS STERLING	James Salter.
,,	R·G ,,	Richard Garde.
1810	T·MONTJOY STERLING	Thos. Montjoy.
,,	CONWAY STERLING	} James Conway.
,,	IE STERLING	John Egan.
,,	P.W STERLING	Peter Wills.
1810-20	WS STERLING	—— Steele?
,,	I SOLOMON STERLING	Isaac Solomon.
,,	IS STERLING	John Seymour.
,,	I·SOLOMON ,,	Isaac Solomon.
,,	FS ,,	(Not identified.)
,,	PG STERLING	Phineas Garde.
1810-40	IS ,,	{ Isaac } Solomon, or { John } Seymour.
1812	GARDE STERLING	Phineas Garde.
1820	SEYMOUR STERLING	John Seymour.
1820-40	KM ,,	Kean Mahony.
,,	EH ,,	Edward Hawkesworth.
1824	O·BRIEN STERLING	Francis O'Brien.
,,	MAHONY STERLING	} Kean Mahony.
1838	M&B STERLING	(Not identified.)

CHAPTER XXI

Marks of the Minor Irish Guilds

YOUGHAL.

DATE (ABOUT).	MAKER'S MARK.	MAKER'S NAME.
1620		Morrish Lawless.
„		John Sharpe.
1644		John Green.
1650		Do. do.
1683		Bartholomew Fallon of Galway.
1702		(*Not identified*, but possibly Bartholomew Fallon as above.)
1712		Edward Gillett.
1720	„	Austin Beere.

GALWAY.

DATE (ABOUT).	MAKER'S MARK.	MAKER'S NAME.
1648		R. Joyes, sen. (?)
1666-1684		... ...
1695		Richard Joyes.
1700		Do. do.
„		... ...
„		... ...
1720		... ...
1725		Richard Joyes.
1730		Mark Fallon.
„		Do. do.
1743-5		... ...

BELFAST (?)

DATE (ABOUT).	MAKER'S MARK.	MAKER'S NAME.
1780		... ...
„		... ...
1790		Matthew Bellew ?
1800		... ...
„		... ...

208

LIMERICK.

TABLE I.

DATE (ABOUT).	MAKER'S MARK.	MAKER'S NAME.
1710		J. Buck, senr. (?)
1718	AB	Adam Buck.
1730-40	IB STERLING	Jonathan Buck. (free 1731)
"	STERLING IB	Do. do.
1730-62	STERLING	Do. do.
"	IB	Do. do.
"	STERLING IB	Do. do.
"	STERLING IB	Do. do.
1730-75	STERLING	Joseph Johns.
"	STERLIN	Do. do.
"		Do. do.
1749-50	I·I	? Joseph Johns.
1750	S·I STARLING	Samuel Johns.
1760-85	GM STERLING	George Moore.
"	GM STARLING	Do. do.
1768-80	GFG STERLING GFG	Garret Fitzgerald.
1770	GM	George Moore.
1780	TW	(Not identified.)
"	TW STERLING	Do. do.
1784	P·C P·C	Patrick Connell.
"	P·C STER P·C	Do. do.

TABLE II.

DATE (ABOUT).	MAKER'S MARK.	MAKER'S NAME.
1784	P·C STER P·C	Patrick Connell.
"	STERLING	Do. do.
"	MFG MFG	Maurice Fitzgerald.
"	MFG MFG MFG	Do. do.
"	MFG STERLING	Do. do.
"	STER TB STER	Thomas Burke.
"	TB STERLING TB	Do. do.
"	TB STER TB	Do. do.
"	TB STERLING	Do. do.
"	TB STERLING	Do. do.
"	MW STERLING	Matt. Walsh.
"	MW STERLING	Do. do.
1786	DL STERLING DL	Daniel Lysaght.
"	DL STERLING	Do. do.
"	DL	Do. do.
1798	WW STER WW	Wm. Ward.
1800	WFG STERLING WFG	Wm. Fitzgerald.
"	WFG STERLING	Do. do.
"	RS RS	Robt. O'Shaughnessy.
"	RS STERLS	Do. do.
"	WW WW	Will. Ward.
"	WW STERLING	Do. do.
"	M·C	... ...
1810-20	S★P STERLING	Samuel Purdon.
"		Do. do.
1800-13	IP	John Purcell.

Unascribed Irish Provincial Marks

DATE (ABOUT).	MAKER'S MARK.
1611	
1650	C K
1652	N
1666	
1673	ES
1680	IH
"	HC · HC
1682	WH
"	
1690	MK
1700	W · W
1705	I·B
1710	WS
"	W
1720	IR
1720-40	MC
1726	AV
"	CM
1750	
1756	IS·I
1760	EC
"	CK · H
1780	G·M
"	I·F
"	WG

Unascribed Marks English, Scotch, or Irish

DATE (ABOUT).	MAKER'S MARK.
1574	
1590	COK
1660	
1680	SW
"	RW
1700	GB
"	A
1730	R · StG
1740-50	WD · A·D · WD
"	CA · CW
1770	I·S
1780	T·B·BROWN · HX
1800	H·FOSTER

Index

TO THE MARKS OF ENGLISH, SCOTCH, AND IRISH SILVERSMITHS

Marks comprising two or more letters are indexed under the first letter of the pair or group. Marks composed of intertwined letters are indexed under each letter appearing in the monogram. Devices accompanied by initials are indexed under the first initial letter. Marks difficult to identify by a short description must be looked for among the marks themselves. Such marks are few and appear only among the very earliest. Later, initials or names were always used. Marks appearing in the form of a cross, e. g., C $\overset{\text{B}}{\underset{\text{D}}{\text{L}}}$ are indexed under the first of the horizontal line letters (in this case under C).

GLOSSARY

Affrontée	Facing the spectator.
Annulet	A ring borne as a charge (*see* Charge).
Bendwise	Lying in the direction of the bend or bends (of a shield or escutcheon).
Charge	Any figure borne on an escutcheon.
Couped	Cut evenly across. Opposed to Erased.
Dimidiated	Cut in half.
Erased	Represented as having been torn across leaving ragged projections.
Incuse	Cut in. Opposed to "in relief."
Moline	A description of ends of a figure divided and turned backward.
Mullet	A five- or six-pointed star.
Palewise	Divided into four or more equal parts by vertical lines.
Pattée	Spreading toward the extremity, e. g., the arms of a Maltese cross.
Saltire	A cross, both members of which lie diagonally, as a St. Andrew's cross. Any bearing set obliquely to the sides of an escutcheon.
Slipped	A twig or branch represented as torn from the stalk so as to leave a strip of the bark still clinging to it.

C & S, 197.

CS, 201.

CS
H } 33.

CT, 50, 59, 193, 194, 206.

CT or TC (in monogram), 51, 54, 60, 170, 171.

CT, 92.

CTF
GF } 32, 33, 105.

CT & IW, 207.

CT
IW } 195, 207.

C
TW } 93.

Cup, a, covered, 24, 37, 39.

CV, 69, 73.

CW, 30, 56, 94, 95, 96, 98, 108, 154, 204, 210.

C
W } 54, 164.

C & W, 174, 201.

C enclosing W, 44, 79.

CY (in monogram), 53.

D, 24, 25, 36, 42, 47, 107, 115, 165, 200.

D, 28, 42, 60, 62, 90.

DA, 61, 63, 67, 70, 71, 72, 74, 78.

Dagger, hand grasping, 182.

Dagger between the letters ID, 28, 61.

DB, 60, 61, 95, 174, 191.

D & B, 131.

DC, 27, 55, 58, 80, 82, 121, 128, 165.

D & C, 33.

D enclosing C, 26, 43, 47, 48.

DC, 85.

DC, 175.

DCF, 90.

DCR, 179.

DD, 128.

DD (linked), 190.

DD, 173.

DD (interlaced), 177.

DD
TB } 128.

DE, 67, 68, 172, 195, 201.

DE BA, 65.

DERMOTT, 205.

DF, 2, 34, 187.

DF
INS } 187.

DG, 26, 47, 58, 62, 86, 177, 186.

DG (in monogram), 170.

DH, 29, 83, 91, 151.

DH (in monogram), 170.

DH & Co., 147.

DH, 86.

DH
CH } 33.

DH RH, 30, 93.

DI, 49, 65, 66, 80.

DI or ID (in monogram), 165.

Di, 77, 78.

D & JS, 174.

DK, 75, 172, 189, 192, 193, 194.

D enclosing K, 200.

DL, 55, 82, 83, 128, 209.

D
LG } 152.

DM, 30, 94, 185, 195, 197, 200, 203.

DM (in monogram), 171.

D & M, 173.

DM, 90, 173.

DMC, 206.

DmcG, 174.

DO, 67, 68.

DOLLAR, 206.

DOUGLAS, 183.

Dove, holding an olive branch, 43; holding an olive branch below HN, 27, 53.

DP, 31, 88, 90, 102, 194, 203.

DP in monogram, 170.

DP, 194.

DPW, 90.

DR, 27, 51, 52, 53, 54, 57, 130, 131, 164, 179.

Dragon between letters TF, 45.

Dragons' heads (3) each holding a crosslet in its mouth, 156.

DS, 88, 90, 166.

DS (in monogram), 120.

D & S, 151.

DS
BS } 101.

DS BS IS, 102.

DS
RS } 93.

DS
RS } 99.

DS RS, 29, 30, 94, 96.

DSK, 167.

DT, 78.

Du, 133.

DUFFNER A
TIPPERARY } 198.

DUN
DEE } 185.

DU
NH } 100.

DV, 164.

DV, 27.

DW, 27, 48, 50, 63, 77, 81, 84, 102.

D & W, 196.

D enclosing W, 152.

DW, 56, 86.

DW, 85, 89.

CHAPTER XXII

Early American Silver

❖ ❖ ❖HE earliest "American" silversmith was the Englishman,
❖ T ❖ John Hull, who became the first mint master in Boston,
❖ ❖ ❖ in 1652. Hull, his contemporaries and successors, Dix-
well, Dummer, Coney, Winslow, David Jesse, and many others,
were all prominent in the civic life of the colonies. It is fortunate
for us that during most of the Colonial period very high artistic
standards prevailed in England, for the fashions of the new
country were faithfully modelled upon those prevailing in the old.

A higher standard of intelligence seemed to prevail among the
Colonial silversmiths, and it is generally conceded that the average quality of their production was higher than that in England.

In spite of the apparent temptation to fabricate early American
silver with forged names or marks, instances of that practice
must be extremely rare. Offences of that sort are very apt to
reach the courts and the newspapers, and the writer, though for
many years interested in the subject, has never heard of a case
or seen one instance of deliberate forgery.

Conditions of life were singularly stable in the American
colonies, continuing so even during the throes of the Revolution-
ary War. Specimens of the handiwork of New England silversmiths would only be exposed to destruction when they drifted
into the possession of Southern families whose personal belong-
ings were, in many instances, destroyed during the Civil War.
Consequently, a large part of the products of New England and
New York silversmiths has been handed down to us.

New York had a group of silversmiths whose work in the first half of the Eighteenth Century was clearly distinguishable from that of their New England contemporaries because of its Dutch and French characteristics.

At the close of the Eighteenth Century, such distinctions seem to have disappeared, and we can only distinguish the place of origin of American silver at that period by its marks. One exception to this statement may be made. In 1810–1820, the silversmiths of Philadelphia had an objectionable habit of soldering moulded or stamped silver strips with a stereotyped decoration around the necks and bases of pieces belonging to tea and coffee sets.

After spinning and stamping silver came into general use, about 1840, the factory supplanted the silversmith. One or two silversmiths have continued to turn out handwrought silver up to the present time, but their work is not "Early Americana."

In the very early Colonial days our silversmiths closely followed the fashion of marking employed by their English fellow craftsmen; they used their initials with some symbol. A little later, the use of a symbol became less frequent and it became more common for the workman to impress his entire name, with or without his initials. In the last quarter of the Eighteenth Century that practice had become almost universal, as had also the use of Roman letters, frequently all capitals. Unless otherwise specified, the reader will know that that type was employed.

In nearly every case, the American silversmiths used Roman capitals to designate their ware. In some cases, both capitals and small letters were employed: "John Brown," for example. The marks given in the following tables will show the form used, without any qualifications being necessary except the word "script," where that type had been employed by the silversmiths.

The author has been enabled to give some twenty-five or thirty or more marks than have hitherto been published in books on this subject.

The following list has been compiled from different sources. Some of the names and the respective locations of those bearing them have been gleaned from directories and the columns of old newspapers. The term "silversmith" is often inaccurately applied in both mediums and at this time it is not always possible to distinguish between the retailer and actual worker in silver. Many silversmiths, beginning with the Nineteenth Century, stamped the names of the retailer upon their wares. The custom still prevails. Hence even where the name appearing here has been taken from a piece of silver, it may have designated a dealer. Of course this caution does not apply to pieces marked with initials only or a symbol (device).

I have thought it wise to make the list as comprehensive as possible, and though that course excludes the possibility of strict discrimination, it does enable one at least to fix the period and place of production and does not present any difficulty in regard to those silversmiths whose work is the most highly prized.

Abbreviations: D means that the name appeared in the local directory of the year given: *c.* stands for *circa;* F for Freeman; when two dates are shown (1735–1815), they represent the birth and death year of the silversmith; hyphen followed by date (e.g. –1815) signifies the date of the demise; one date followed by hyphen (e.g., 1735–), the date of birth. A date alone, if unqualified, means that the subject was working at that period.

Follows a key to the descriptive words used in connection with the marks:

KEY TO TERMS USED

CARTOUCHE

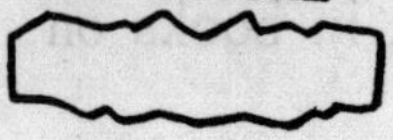

WAVY-LINED
OBLONG

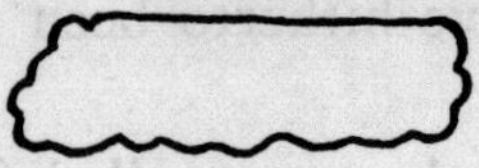

RECTANGLE

CARTOUCHE

HEART

SHAPED
RECTANGLE

SHAPED
SHIELD

OVAL

ENGRAILED
RECTANGLE

SHIELD

BOX

SERRATED
RECTANGLE

SQUARE

SHAPED OVAL

HOLLOW
LETTER

STAR

OBLONG

SCROLL

DOUBLE
CIRCLE

QUATREFOIL

RIBBON

RADIANT
SUN

SHAPED
CARTOUCHE

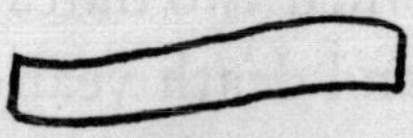

TREFOIL

238

A SPOUT-CUP BY JOHN CONEY (BOSTON, 1655-1722)
The property of Major Cortlandt Parker, U. S. A.

CHAPTER XXIII
American Silversmiths and Their Marks

SILVERSMITHS	MARKS	LOCATIONS	PERIOD
Aaron, Joseph	†	Philadelphia	1798
Abbott, John W.	JABBOT in rectangle	Portsmouth, N. H.	1839
Ackerman, David		New York City	1818
Ackley, Francis W.	F.ACKLEY in rectangle	" " "	1797
Acton, George		" " "	1795
Adam, J.	JA (script) in oval and J Adam (script) in shaped rectangle; I·ADAM in *shaded* rectangle	Alexandria, Va.	1800
Adam, John B.		New Orleans, La.	1822
Adams, John	J A (script) conjoined in rectangle	{ Alexandria, Va. Dist. of Col.	1829
Adams, Jonathan		Philadelphia	1783
Adams, Pygan	PA in shaped rectangle and P.A. in rectangle	New London, Conn.	1736
Adams, William	W.ADAMS and NEW YORK, each in serrated rectangle	New York City	1830
Adgate, William		Norwich, Conn.	1767
Adriance, E.	E.ADRIANCE, ST.LOUIS, in two rectangles	St. Louis, Mo.	1820
Aiken, George	G.Aiken in oval; G.Aiken (script) in cartouche	Baltimore, Md.	1815
Ainsworth, Michael		Fred'k Co., Va.	1755
Aitken, John	I Aitkin (script) in rectangle and JAIKEN in rectangle	Philadelphia	1785
Aitkins, W.		Baltimore, Md.	1802
Aldis, Charles		New York City	1814
Alexander, A.		Philadelphia	1802
Alexander, Samuel	S·ALEXANDER in rectangle and a bird in kite	"	1797
Alford, Samuel		"	1840
Alford, Thomas		"	1762
Allen, C.	C ALLEN in rectangle	Not traced	c. 1760
Allen, James		Philadelphia	1720
Allen, Joel		Middletown, Conn.	1787
Allen, John	IA in cartouche, IA in oval, IA in shaped rectangle	Boston, Mass.	1692
Allen, John		Philadelphia	1814
Allen, Richard		"	1816
Allen, Robert		"	1776
Allen, Thomas		Boston, Mass.	1758
Allen & Edwards	🔲🔲 ‡	" "	1700

†Where no mark is given, the maker used his name or initials.

‡I desire to express my obligation to Mr. Stephen G. C. Ensko for his courteous permission to reproduce the facsimiles of American makers' marks on this and the following pages; they have been taken from *American Silversmiths and Their Marks*. Mr. Ensko's book contains a very great number of such facsimiles and is on sale in his shop at 682 Lexington Avenue, New York City.

SILVERSMITHS	MARKS	LOCATIONS	PERIOD
Allison, Peter	†	New York City	1791
Alstyne, Jeronimus		" " "	1789
Anderson, William	WA in oblong	" " "	1746
Andras, William	ANDRAS in rectangle	" " "	1795
Andras & Richard	A & R in rectangle	" " "	1797
Andreas, Abraham		Bethlehem, Pa.	1780
Andrew, John	I·ANDREW in rectangle; J.Andrews (script) in cartouche	Salem, Mass.	1769
Andrews, Abraham		Philadelphia	1795
Andrews, Henry		"	1795
Andrews, Joseph	I ANDREWS in rectangle and NOR-FOLK in rectangle; J· ANDREWS in shaped rectangle	Norfolk, Va.	1800
Andrews, Jeremiah		Philadelphia	1776
Anthony, Joseph		"	1764
Anthony, Joseph, Jr.	J. Anthony (script) in shaped rectangle; J A (script) in rectangle	"	1783
Anthony, Joseph & Sons		"	1810
Anthony, L. D.		Providence, R. I.	1805
Anthony, M. H. & T.		Philadelphia	1814
Anthony, Michael H.		"	1810
Anthony, Thomas		"	1810
Anthony, William		New York City	1800
Anwyl, Kenrick		Baltimore, Md.	1780
Archie, John		New York City	1759
Armstrong, Allen	A·Armstrong and Phia' each in script and rectangle	Philadelphia	1806
Armstrong, John		"	1810
Armstrong, William		"	1750
Arnold, Thomas	TARNOLD, T A, TA, each in rectangle	"	1760
Ashmead, William		"	1797
Atherton, Nathan		"	1825
Atkinson, Isaac		"	1825
Atlee, Charles		"	1837
Atterbury, J.		New Haven, Conn.	1799
Austen, David		Philadelphia	1837
Austin, Benjamin		Portsmouth, N. H.	1775
Austin, Ebenezer	AUSTIN in cartouche, E A in rectangle	Hartford, Conn.	1764
Austin, Ebenezer J.	E.J.AUSTIN in rectangle	Boston, Mass.	1790
Austin, John		Philadelphia	1802
Austin, Josiah	I·Austin (script) in rectangle, I·A in rectangle, and I·AUSTEN in rectangle	Charlestown, Mass.	1739
Austin, Nathaniel	N·A· and AUSTIN, each in rectangle	Boston, Mass.	1760
Austin & Boyer	I·Austin in oblong, Boyer in cartouche	" "	1750
Avery, John	IA and IAVERY in rectangle	Preston, Conn.	1760
Avery, John, Jr.		" "	1776
Avery, Robert Stanton		" "	1792
Avery, Samuel		" "	1786
Avery, William		" "	1786
Avery, Willis & Billis		Salisbury, N. Y.	1820
Ayres, S.	S.AYERS-LEX.K. on riband	Lexington, Ky.	1805

†Where no mark is given, the maker used his name or initials.

SILVERSMITHS	MARKS	LOCATIONS	PERIOD
Babcock, Samuel	Babcock (script) in shaped rectangle	Middletown, Conn.	1812
Bacall, Thomas	†	Boston, Mass.	1836
Backus, Delucine	D Backus in shaped oval and DBACKUS in shaped rectangle	New York City	1792
Baielle, Lewis		Baltimore, Md.	1799
Bailey, Benjamin		Boston, Mass.	1820
Bailey, E. E. & S. C.	EE & SC above BAILEY in rectangle	Portland, Me.	1825
Bailey, Edward		Baltimore, Md.	1779
Bailey, Henry	H·B in rectangle, anchor, sheaf of wheat, and star, each in square	Boston, Mass.	1780
Bailey, John	J·Bailey (script) in shaped rectangle, NYORK in rectangle	New York City Philadelphia	1762 1785
Bailey, Loring	L·B in rectangle	Hingham, Mass.	1780
Bailey, Robert H.		Woodstock, Vt.	1825
Bailey, Simon A.		New York City	1789
Baily, W.	WBAILY in engrailed rectangle; bird in cartouche	New York City	c. 1810
Baker, Anson		" " "	1821
Baker, E.	E.BAKER in rectangle	" " "	1761
Baker, George	G.BAKER in shaped rectangle	Providence, R. I.	1825
Balch, Ebenezer	E. BALCH in oval cartouche	Hartford, Conn.	1744
Balch & Fryer		Albany, N. Y.	1784
Baldwin, Ebenezer	BALDWIN in rectangle and in hollowed letters without rectangle	Hartford, Conn.	1810
Baldwin, Jabez	BALDWIN incised	Boston, Mass.	1813
Baldwin, Jedediah	J.Baldwin in rectangle	Portsmouth, N. H.	1793
Baldwin, Stanley S.	STANLEY S.BALDWIN in rectangle and NY in rectangle	New York City	1820
Baldwin & Baker		Providence, R. I.	1817
Baldwin & Co.		Newark, N. J.	1830
Baldwin & Jones	*BALDWIN & SONS* in rectangle *BALDWIN & SONS* in scroll	Boston, Mass. "	1813 1813
Ball, Henry	J·BALL in rectangle and	New York City	1833
Ball, John	{JOHN / BALL} in cartouche	Boston, Mass.	1765
Ball, William	BALL in oval; W·BALL in a shaped cartouche; WB in a box	Philadelphia	1759
Ball, Tompkins & Black		New York City	1839
Bancker, Adrian	AB in oval and AB in shaped oval	" " "	1731
Bangs, John		Cincinnati, Ohio	1825
Barberet, Théon		New Orleans, La.	1822
Barbier, Peter		Philadelphia	1823
Bard, Conrad	C.BARD 205 ARCH ST in rectangle	"	1825
Bard, J.		"	1800
Bard & Hoffman		"	1837
Bardeer, Connard		"	1831
Bardick, George	G·B in rectangle	"	1790
Bardick, John		"	1805
Bardon, Stephen		"	1785
Baria, William		New York City	1805
Barnes, Abraham		Boston, Mass.	1716
Barret, James		Norwich, Conn.	1717
Barrett, James		New York City	1805
Barrett, S.		Nantucket, Mass.	1800

†Where no mark is given, the maker used his name or initials.

SILVERSMITHS	MARKS	LOCATIONS	PERIOD
Barrington & Davenport	B & D in serrated rectangle	Philadelphia	1806
Barrows, James M.	J.M.BARROWS in rectangle	Tolland, Conn.	1828
Barry, Standish	BARRY in shaped rectangle and NO.92 in rectangle	Baltimore, Md.	1790
Bartholomew, Joseph	†	Philadelphia	1833
Bartholomew, Roswell		Hartford, Conn.	1804
Bartholomew, Joseph		Philadelphia	1833
Bartlett, Edward		Philadelphia	1833
Bartlett, N.	N·BARTLETT in rectangle	Concord, Mass.	1760
Bartlett, Samuel	S.B script in rectangle and S·BARTLETT in rectangle	Boston, Mass.	1775
Barton, Erasmus		New York City	1810
Bartram, William		Philadelphia	1769
Basset, Francis	BASSET in rectangle and sheaf of wheat in rectangle	New York City	1764
Batchellor, N.		" " "	1825
Bay, A. S.		" " "	1786
Bayley, Alexander		" " "	1790
Bayley, S. H.		" " "	1790
Bayley, Simeon A.	BAYLEY in rectangle, in shaped rectangle, and sheaf of wheat in shaped rectangle	" " "	1791
Bayley, S. & A.		" " "	1790
Bayley & Douglas	DB & AD in rectangle, lion in rectangle and 11? in rectangle	" " "	1798
Bayly, John		Philadelphia	1755
Baysset, Joseph		New Orleans, La.	1822
Beach, A.	A·BEACH in serrated rectangle	Hartford, Conn.	1823
Beach, Isaac		New Milford, Conn.	1788
Beach, Ives & Co.		New York City	1820
Beach, Miles	BEACH in rectangle, M·B in rect. and MB in oval	Litchfield, Conn.	1763
Beach & Sanford	B & S, in rectangle	Hartford, Conn.	1785
Beach & Ward	B & W in rectangle	Hartford, Conn.	1789
Beal, Caleb	BEAL in rectangle	Boston, Mass.	1796
Beam, Jacob C.		Philadelphia	1818
Beck, Thomas		"	1773
Becker, Fredrick		New York City	1736
Becker, Philip		Lancaster, Pa.	1764
Bedford, John	I Bedford (script), in shaped rectangle	Fishkill, N. Y.	1781
Beebe, James W.	J.W.BEEBE in rectangle	New York City	1835
Beebe, Stanton		Providence, R. I.	1824
Beecher, Clement		Meriden, Conn.	1801
Beecher, C. & Co.		" "	1820
Belin, Lewis		Philadelphia	1818
Belknap, Samuel		Boston, Mass.	1789
Belliard, François		New Orleans, La.	1822
Belloni, Louis J.		New York City	1835
Belloni & Durandeau		" " "	1835
Benedict, A. C.	A.C.BENEDICT without rectangle	" " "	1840
Benedict, J.		" " "	1830
Benedict & Son		" " "	1840
Benedict & Squire	BENEDICT & SQUIRE in rectangle	" " "	1825
Benjamin, Barzillai		New Haven, Conn.	1799

†Where no mark is given, the maker used his name or initials.

SILVERSMITHS	MARKS	LOCATIONS	PERIOD
Benjamin, Benjamin	BB in rectangle and B. Benjamin in rectangle	New Haven, Conn.	1825
Benjamin, Everard	E· BENJAMIN in an oblong	" " "	1828
Benjamin, John	I·B in rectangle	Stratford, Conn.	1752
Benjamin, Samuel C.	†	New Haven, Conn.	1819
Benjamin, Solomon		Baltimore, Md.	1817
Bennet, James		New York City	1773
Bennett, Jacob		Philadelphia	1839
Bentley, Thomas	BENTLEY in rectangle, TB in oval, U in rectangle, and sheaf of wheat in vertical oval	Boston, Mass.	1786
Bentson, Peter		Philadelphia	1718
Berard, Andrew		"	1797
Berard, E.	E BERARD in shaped cartouche	"	1800
Berkenbush, Charles H.		New York City	1825
Berry, William		" " "	1805
Besley, Thauvet	B surmounted by a crown, both incised	" " "	1727
Besselievre, Thomas		Philadelphia	1831
Best, Joseph		"	1723
Bevan, Richard		Baltimore, Md.	1804
Bigelow, John	JOHN BIGELOW in rectangle	Boston, Mass.	1830
Bigelow & Bros.	BIGELOW & BROS. in rectangle	" "	1840
Biggs, Joseph		New York City	1830
Bigotut, S.		" " "	1800
Bijotal, Silvian A.		" " "	1795
Billings, A.	A · B I L L I N G S in long rectangle	Preston, Conn.	1780
Billings, Daniel	D.Billings (script) in long oval	" "	1795
Bingham, John		Newark, N. J.	1664
Binneau, Theodore		Philadelphia	1820
Bird, Conard		"	1831
Bissbrown, Thomas		Albany, N. Y.	1790
Black, James	J.B in rectangle, repeated	Philadelphia	1795
Black, John		"	1811
Black, William		New York City	1833
Blackman, Frederick S.	F.S.Blackman without rectangle	Danbury, Conn.	1832
Blackman, F. S. & Co.	F.S.B & CO. in rectangle	" "	1840
Blackman, John C.		" "	1829
Blackman, John S.	J.S.B in oval	" "	1798
Blakslee, William		Newtown, Conn.	1820
Blakslee, Ziba		" "	1790
Blanchard, Asa	A · BLANCHARD in rectangle and A· BLANCHARD in long oval	Lexington, Ky.	1810
Blauvelt, John W.		New York City	1835
Bleasom & Reed	BLEASOM & REED NASSAU, without rectangle	Nassau, N. H.	1830
Bliss, Jonathan		Middletown, Conn.	1800
Blondell, Anthony		Philadelphia	1797
Blondell & Descuret		"	1798
Blowers, John	BLOWERS in oblong; Blowers (script) in oval cartouche	Boston, Mass.	1731
Boehler, Andreas W.		New York City	1784

†Where no mark is given, the maker used his name or initials.

SILVERSMITHS	MARKS	LOCATIONS	PERIOD
Boehme, Charles L.	CLBoehme (script) in rectangle and Sterling (script) in shaped rectangle	Baltimore, Md.	1804
Boelen, Henricus	HB conjoined in cartouche; HB conjoined in shield	New York City	1705
Boelen, Jacob	IB in cartouche with escalloped top, I has two radiating arms, forming cross	" " "	1698
Boelen, Jacob	†	" " "	1754
Boemper, Abraham		Bethlehem, Pa.	1780
Bogardus, Everadus	E B in rectangle	New York City	1698
Bogert, Albert		" " "	1815
Bogert, Nicholas J.	N.J.BOGERT in rectangle	" " "	1801
Bolton, James		" " "	1789
Bonjean, Victor		New Orleans, La.	1822
Bontecou, Timothy	TB: without rectangle	New Haven, Conn	1735
Bontecou, Timothy, Jr.	TB in oval	" " "	1744
Boone, Jeremiah	IBOONE in serrated rectangle	Philadelphia	1791
Bordeaux, Augustine		"	1798
Boss and Kindell		New York City	1794
Bosworth, Samuel	BOSWORTH in rectangle	Buffalo, N. Y.	1835
Botsford, Gideon B.	G. B. BOTSFORD in rectangle	Woodbury, Conn.	1797
Boudar, Joseph		New York City	1800
Boudinot, Elias	EB; and BOUDINOT, each in rectangle	Philadelphia	1743
Boudo, Louis	L⁵BOUDO in rectangle	Charleston, S. C.	1819
Boullien, Mousier		Philadelphia	1811
Bourdet, Stephen		New York City	1730
Boutier, John	J.BOUTIER in oblong	" " "	1805
Boutelle, James		Worcester, Mass.	1787
Bouvar, Joseph		Philadelphia	1797
Bower, C.		"	1831
Bowne, Samuel	S:Bowne in rectangle	New York City	1799
Boyce, Geradus	G:BOYCE, G.B, NY, each in rectangle	" " "	1814
Boyce, James		" " "	1825
Boyce, Jared		" " "	1820
Boyce, John	J.B & NY, each in rectangle	" " "	1801
Boyce & Jones	B & J in rectangle; N YORK in rectangle	" " "	1825
Boyd, Joseph W.	J.W.B. in rectangle	" " "	1820
Boyd, William		Albany, N. Y.	1800
Boyd & Hoyt		" " "	1830
Boyd & Mulford		" " "	1840
Boyer, Daniel	DB Boyer DB BOYER	Boston, Mass.	1766
Brabant, Isaac		Savannah, Ga.	1750
Bradbury, Theophilas	BRADBURY and 1825, each in rectangle; Bradbury in rectangle; rose, figure, B in cartouches	Newburyport, Mass.	1815
Bradbury & Brother		" "	1810
Bradley, Abner	Cross mark in circle and A.BRADLEY in rectangle	New Haven, Conn.	1774
Bradley, Luther		" " "	1798
Bradley, Phineas	PB in rectangle	" " "	1776
Bradley, Richard		Hartford, Conn.	1825
Bradley, Zebul	Z. BRADLEY in serrated rectangle	New Haven, Conn.	1801

†Where no mark is given, the maker used his name or initials.

SILVERSMITHS	MARKS	LOCATIONS	PERIOD
Bradley & Bunce	†	Hartford, Conn.	1830
Bradley & Merriman	B&M in cartouche	New Haven, Conn.	1826
Brady, E.	E·BRADY in shaped rectangle; BRADY in rectangle	New York City	1825
Brady, William V.		" " "	1835
Brainerd, Charles		Hartford, Conn.	1809
Bramhall, S.	S.BRAMHALL in rectangle	Plymouth, Mass.	1863
Brasher, A.	ABRASHER in rectangle	New York City	1790
Brasher, Ephraim	EB in rectangle, EB in oval, and Brasher in rectangle	" " "	1766
Brasher, E. & Co.	E·B & CO in rectangle	" " "	1790
Brasher & Alexander		" " "	1800
Bray, Henry		Philadelphia	1799
Breed, John		Colchester, Conn.	1773
Breed, William	WBreed (script) in rectangle; WB in a heart; W B (script) in rectangle	Boston, Mass.	1750
Brenton, Benjamin	BB in rectangle	Newport, R. I.	1731
Brevoort, John	B in trefoil, IBV in shaped rectangle, IV	New York City	1715 1775
Brewer, Charles	C BREWER in shaped rectangle; same in rectangle; C Brewer (script) in cartouche	Middletown, Conn.	1810
		" "	1810
Brewer & Co.		" "	1803
Brewer & Mann		Norwich, Conn.	1797
Brewster, Abel			
Bridge, John	I BRIDGE in wavy oblong and BRIDGE in cartouche	Boston, Mass.	1751
Brigden, C.	C.B in shaped rectangle, C·B in cartouche, and C·B in rectangle; BRIGDEN in shaped rectangle	" "	1770
Brigden, Timothy		Albany, N. Y.	1813
Brigden, Zachariah	Z·B in rectangle, Z.Brigden in cartouche	Boston, Mass.	1734 1787
Bright, Anthony		Philadelphia	1739
Brinkley, William		New York City	1802
Brinton, Gordon & Quick		Boston, Mass.	1780
Britton, Isaac		Philadelphia	1811
Britton, Jacob		"	1807
Broadhurst, Samuel		New York City	1724
Brock, John	I BROCK, NEW YORK, each in rectangle	" " "	1833
Brock, L.	L.BROCK, in rectangle with serrated ends, NEW YORK in rectangle	" " "	1830
Brookhouse, Robert	RB (script) in oval	Salem, Mass.	1750
Brooks, Samuel	Brooks in rectangle with escalloped ends	Philadelphia	1793
Brothears, Michael		"	1772
Brower, S. D.		Albany, N. Y.	1834
Brower, S. & B.	S. & B. BROWER in rectangle	" " "	1810
Brower & Rusher	B&R in rectangle	New York City	1834
Brown, Alexander		Philadelphia	1840
Brown, D.	D.BROWN in rough rectangle	"	1811
Brown, Ebenezer		Boston, Mass.	1793
Brown, Henry		Philadelphia	1777

†Where no mark is given, the maker used his name or initials.

SILVERSMITHS	MARKS	LOCATIONS	PERIOD
Brown, James	†	Philadelphia	1785
Brown, Jesse		"	1813
Brown, John		"	1785
Brown, Robert	R.BROWN in oblong with curved ends and 10 oz 13 in oval	Baltimore, Md.	1830
Brown, Samuel C.	S.BROWN in rectangle	New York City	1820 1825
Brown & Houlton		Baltimore, Md.	1799
Brown, Liberty		Philadelphia	1801
Browne & Seal		"	1810
Bruff, Charles O.	C.O.B. in rectangle	New York City	1763
Bruff, Joseph		Philadelphia	1767
Brush, Edward		New York City	1774
Bryan, Philip	BRYAN, rough capitals in rectangle	Philadelphia	1802
Buché, Peter		New York City	1795
Buchoz, I. R.		" " "	1835
Buckley, J. B.		Philadelphia	1807
Buckley & Anderson		"	1804
Buddy, Daniel		"	1769
Buel, Abel	BUEL in serrated rectangle and A.B. in fringed oval	New Haven, Conn.	1763
Buel, D. H.		Hartford, Conn.	1825
Buel, John		New Haven, Conn.	1789
Buel, Samuel	S.B in square	" " "	1777
Buel & Greenleaf		" " "	1798
Buel & Mix		" " "	1783
Bull, Caleb		Hartford, Conn.	1840
Bull, Epaphras		Boston, Mass.	1813
Bull, G. W.	G.W.BULL in rectangle	Farmington, Conn.	1840
Bull, Martin		" "	1775
Bull & Morrison		Hartford, Conn.	1780
Bumm, Peter		Philadelphia	1814
Bumm & Shepper		"	1819
Bunker, Benjamin		Providence, R. I.	1810
Burdick, William S.		New Haven, Conn.	1810
Burdock, George		Philadelphia	1791
Burdock, Nicholas		"	1797
Burgalie, J. P.		New York City	1799
Burger, David I.	D·I· BURgER in a shaped cartouche	" " "	1805
Burger, John	BURGER in rectangle; NEW YORK in rectangle	" " "	1786
Burger, John	*Burger* in shaded rectangle; *N.York* in rectangle	" " "	1786
Burger, Thomas		" " "	1805
Burnham, Robert		" " "	1790
Burkloe, Samuel		Philadelphia	1795
Burnap, Daniel		East Windsor, Conn.	1782
Burnet, Samuel		Newark, N. J.	1796
Burnet & Ryder	B and R (script initials in capitals) in rude rectangle	Philadelphia	1795
Burnett, Charles A.	C.A.B. in rectangle and C.A. Burnett in rectangle	Alexandria, Va.	1793
Burns, Anthony		Philadelphia	1785

---

†Where no mark is given, the maker used his name or initials.

SILVERSMITHS	MARKS	LOCATIONS	PERIOD
Burns, James	†	Philadelphia	1810
Burns, John H.		New York City	1835
Burot, Andrew		Baltimore, Md.	1819
Burr, A. C.	A.C.BURR in rectangle	Providence, R. I.	1815
Burr, Christopher A.		" " "	1810
Burr, C.A. & Co.		" " "	1820
Burr, Ezekiel	E BURR in rectangle and E.BURR in oval; E. Burr (script) in oval	" " "	1815
		" " "	1793
Burr, E. & W.		" " "	1793
Burr, William		" " "	1815
Burr & Lee		Boston, Mass.	1823
Burrill, Joseph			
Burrill, Samuel	S:Burrill in rectangle; S:Burrill in shaped rectangle; S·B in oval; S·B dots above in cartouche, and S·B in heart	Boston, Mass.	1733
Burrill, Samuel, Jr.		" "	1829
Burrill, Theophilus		New London, Conn.	1736
Burrows, William		Philadelphia	1831
Burt, Benjamin	BENJAMIN in a cartouche; BURT BURT and B·BURT each in a rectangle.	Boston, Mass.	1750
Burt, John	JOHN italic capitals in oval; IB with BURT a pellet below and crown above in a cartouche. I BURT in cartouche	" "	1712
Burt, Samuel	SAMUEL in a cartouche; SB in a BURT square.	" "	1746
Burt, William	W.BURT in a rude oblong; W BURT in rectangle	" "	1747
Burton, Jacob		Philadelphia	1839
Bushnell, Phineas		Guilford, Conn.	1762
Bussey, Benjamin	B B in rectangle	Dedham, Mass.	1778
Bussey, Thomas		Baltimore, Md.	1799
Buswell, Jason		Portsmouth, N. H.	1839
Butler, Henry W.		Philadelphia	1833
Butler, James	IB crowned in shield; IB; IB crowned in cartouche; J.BUTLER in rectangle	Boston, Mass.	1734
Butler, John	I B in circle and J BUTLER in oblong	Portland, Me.	1765
Butler, N.		Utica, N. Y.	1800
Butler, N. H.		Philadelphia	1837
Butler & Little		Portland, Me.	1759
Byrne, James	*J. Byrne* in shaped cartouche	New York City	1789
Byrne, James		Philadelphia	1780
Cady, Samuel		New York City	1792
Cady & Backus		" " "	1792
Calder & Co.		Albany, N. Y.	1830
Caldwell, E.		New York City	1800
Cammon, Alexander	A·C in square	Albany, N. Y.	1813
Camoin——		Philadelphia	1797
Camp, Elias		Bridgeport, Conn.	1825
Campbell, Christopher	CAMPBELL in rude rectangle	New York City	1808

†Where no mark is given, the maker used his name or initials.

SILVERSMITHS	MARKS	LOCATIONS	PERIOD
Campbell, John W.	†	New York City	1814
Campbell, R.		Baltimore, Md.	1824
Campbell, Thomas	T CAMPBELL in rectangle	New York City	1770
Campbell, W.		Philadelphia	1765
Canavillo, Antonio		New York City	1825
Canavillo, S.		" " "	1825
Candee, Lewis B.		Woodbury, Conn.	1825
Candell, Charles	C C (script capitals) in rectangle	New York City	1795
Canfield, Samuel	CANFIELD in oval	Middletown, Conn.	1780
Canfield & Brother		Baltimore, Md.	1830
Canfield & Foot		Middletown, Conn.	1798
Cann, John		New York City	1835
Cant, Godfrey		" " "	1796
Caralin, Pierce		" " "	1804
Carbin, Theodore		Philadelphia	1758
Cario, Michael		New York City	1728
Cario, William	W.CARIO in shaped oblong; W.CARIO in engrailed rectangle	" " "	1742
Cariolle——		New Orleans, La.	1822
Carlile, Abraham	A. Carlile (script) in rectangle	Philadelphia	1791
Carman, John		"	1771
Carman, John		New York City	1800
Carman, Samuel		"	1807
Carpenter, Joseph		Norwich, Conn.	1769
Carrel, Daniel		Philadelphia	1806
Carrel, John & Daniel	CARREL in rectangle	"	1785
Carribec, Peter		"	1795
Carroll, James		New York City	1825
Carson, Thomas		Albany, N. Y.	1815
Carson & Hall		" "	1813
Cary, Lewis	L.CARY in engrailed scroll ending with rosettes	Boston, Mass.	1815
Case, George		E. Hartford, Conn.	1779
Casey, Gideon	G:CASEY in shaped rectangle	South Kingston & Newport, R. I.	1754
Casey, Samuel	S:Casey in rectangle	South Kingston & Newport, R. I.	1745
Cashell, Randall H.		Philadelphia	1807
Cassedy, Andrew		Philadelphia	1840
Caston, Françoise		New York City	1804
Cerneau, John		" " "	1823
Cerneau, Joseph		" " "	1807
Cerneau & Co.		" " "	1811
Chadwick, Thomas		Philadelphia	1809
Chamberlain, Wilson		Portsmouth, N. H.	1839
Champlin, John		New London, Conn.	1768
Chandler, Stephen		New York City	1812
Chapin, Aaron		Hartford, Conn.	1790
Chapin, Alexander		Hartford, Conn.	1838
Chase, J. D.		New York City	1820
Chase & Easton		Brooklyn, N. Y.	1837
Chat, Claudius		Philadelphia	1793
Chaudrons, Simon		"	1798

†Where no mark is given, the maker used his name or initials.

SILVERSMITHS	MARKS	LOCATIONS	PERIOD
Chaudrons, S. & Co.	†	Philadelphia	1807
Chaudrons & Rasch		"	1812
Chene, Daniel		New York City	1786
Cherry, James		Philadelphia	1824
Chevalier, Clement E.		"	1816
Chevalier & Tanguay		"	1816
Childs, George H.		"	1828
Chitrey, Peter	P. Chitrey in oval	New York City	1814
Chittenden, Beriah		New Haven, Conn.	1787
Chitten, Ebenezer	EC in square; EC in oval; E. Chitten-den in rectangle	" " "	1747
Church, Joseph		" " "	1818
Church, Ralph		Buffalo, N. Y.	1832
Church & Rogers		New Haven, Conn.	1825
Churchill, Jesse	CHURCHILL in rectangle; I. CHURCHILL in rectangle	Boston, Mass.	1794
Churchill & Treadwell	{CHURCHILL & TREADWELL} in rectangle	Hartford, Conn.	1794
Churchwell, Charles		Philadelphia	1781
Clapp, Philip		New York City	1802
Clapp & Riker		" " "	1802
Clark, Andrew		" " "	1744
Clark, C & G.		Boston, Mass.	1833
Clark, Charles		" "	1798
Clark, Curtis		New York City	1823
Clark, George C.	G.C.CLARK in rectangle	Providence, R. I.	1824
Clark, George D.	G.D.CLARK in rectangle	Baltimore, Md.	1826
Clark, Henry		Philadelphia	1813
Clark, I.		Boston, Mass.	1754
Clark, I. & H.	I&H·CLARK	Portsmouth, N. H.	1821
Clark, J. H.	J. H. CLARK in rectangle	New York City	1812
Clark, Joseph	CLARK ICLARK IC	Danbury, Conn.	1791
Clark, Levi	CLARK in rectangle; NORWALK in rectangle	Norwalk, Conn.	1823
Clark, Metcalf B		Boston, Mass.	1835
Clark, Peter G.		New Haven, Conn.	1810
Clark, Richard		New York City	1795
Clark, Samuel		Boston, Mass.	1673
Clark, Thomas	T.Clark in shaped cartouche	" "	1770
Clark, William	WC in oval cartouche	Bridgeport, Conn.	1774
Clark & Anthony		New York City	1790
Clark & Brother		Norwalk, Conn.	1825
Clark & Coit		Norwich, Conn.	1820
Clarke, Jonathan	IC in square; J Clarke (script) in oval; J.CLARKE in rectangle	Newport, R. I.	1734
Cleveland, Aaron	AC in octagon; A CLEVELAND in oblong with curved ends	Norwich, Conn.	1820
Cleveland, Benjamin	B CLEVELAND in long oval pinched to separate initial from name	" "	1760
Cleveland, William	Cleveland and WC, each in rectangle	" "	1815
Cleveland & Post	C & P in rectangle	" "	1815
Cline, Charles		Philadelphia	1829

†Where no mark is given, the maker used his name or initials.

SILVERSMITHS	MARKS	LOCATIONS	PERIOD
Cobb, Ephraim	E.Cobb in oval and EC in rectangle; E COBB in rectangle.	Boston, Mass.	1729
Coburn, John	I·C in square; IC in square; and J CO-BURN in rectangle.	" "	1750
Coddington, John	IC in a turnip- or beet-shaped cartouche	Newport, R. I.	1711
Codman, Willard	†	Boston, Mass.	1839
Coe & Upton		New York City	1840
Coen, Daniel B.		" " "	1787
Coffman, William		Philadelphia	1839
Coggeswell, H.	H. COGGSWELL in rectangle	Boston, Mass.	1760
Cohen, Barrow A.		New York City	1825
Cohen, William		Alexandria, Va. Dist. of Col.	1833
Coignard, Louis		New York City	1805
Coit, E.	E.COIT and PURE COIN, each in rectangle	Norwich, Conn.	1820
Coit, Thomas C.	T.C.C (script) in rectangle	" "	1812
Coit & Mansfield	C & M in an oblong; same in a hexagon	" "	1816
Cole, Ebenezer		New York City	1818
Cole, Jacob		Philadelphia	1785
Cole, John		Boston, Mass.	1686
Coleman, B.	B.COLEMAN in rectangle	Burlington, N. J.	1785
Coleman, C. C.		" " "	1835
Coleman, John		New York City	1814
Coleman, Nathaniel	N. COLEMAN in rectangle; NC in oval	Burlington, N. J.	1786
Coleman, S.	S. COLEMAN in rectangle	" " "	1805
Coley, Simeon		New York City	1767
Coley, William	W. COLEY (script) in shaped oval	" " "	1801
Collet, J. B.		" " "	1805
Collette, Lambert		Buffalo, N. Y.	1835
Collins, Arnold	AC in heart; AC in shield; AC in square	Newport, R. I.	1690
Collins, W. & L.		New York City	1830
Colner, John		" " "	1818
Colonel, John		Philadelphia	1804
Colton, Levi		New York City	1825
Colton, Oren		" " "	1818
Colton & Baldwin		" " "	1819
Colton & Collins		" " "	1832
Coney, John		Boston, Mass.	1676
Connor, John H.	J H CONNOR in serrated rectangle	New York City	1835
Conyers, Joseph		Boston, Mass.	1708
Conyers, Richard		" "	1688
Cook, John	I COOK in rectangle; .COOK in an oval; JCOOK in rectangle	New York City	1795
Cook & Co.		New York City	1797
Cooke, Joseph		Philadelphia	1785
Cooke & Co.		"	1785
Coolidge, Joseph, Jr.	COOLIDGE in shaped oval‡	Boston, Mass	1773

†Where no mark is given, the maker used his name or initials.
‡A shaped oval follows the upper and lower contour of letters.

SILVERSMITHS	MARKS	LOCATIONS	PERIOD
Cooper,——	†	Philadelphia	1816
Cooper, B.		New York City	1814
Cooper, B. & J.		" " "	1810
Cooper, John		" " "	1814
Cooper, Joseph		" " "	1770
Copp, Joseph		New London, Conn.	1754
Copp, Nathaniel P.		Albany, N. Y.	1834
Corley, William		New York City	1811
Cornelison, Cornelius		" " "	1711
Cornelius, Christian	C CORNELIUS in rectangle	Philadelphia	1810
Cornell, Walter	CORNELL in rectangle	Providence R. I.	1780
Corrin, Josiah		Philadelphia	1823
Courcelle, Hilaire		New Orleans, La.	1822
Couvertie, Louis	L'COUVERTIE in rectangle	" " "	1822
Coverly, Thomas	T:COVERLY in rectangle	Newburyport, Mass.	1760
Cowell, William	WC in oval; W.COWELL in cartouche; WC surmounted by star and pellets in a shaped shield; WC in scroll; WC in rectangle	Boston, Mass.	1703
Cowell, William, Jr.	W:COWELL in shaped rectangle; W.COWELL in shaped oval; W COWELL (script) in cartouche	Boston, Mass.	1736
Cowan, William D.	W.COWAN in shaped rectangle	Philadelphia	1808
Cox, John		"	1818
Craft, Stephen		New York City	1811
Craig, James		Williamsburg, Va.	1750
Crandall, Benjamin		Providence, R. I.	1824
Crandall, Benjamin		Portsmouth, N. H.	1839
Crane, Stephen M.		New York City	1813
Cranston, Samuel		Newport, R. I.	1684
Crawford, John	J.CRAWFORD in rectangle J (script) Crawford (italics) in rectangle	New York City	1815
Crittenden, Newton E.		Cleveland, Ohio	1839
Crone, Henry		" "	1780
Crosby, Jonathan	JC in double circle	Boston, Mass.	1769
Cummings, David B.		Philadelphia	1811
Currier & Trott	*Currier & Trott*, in rectangle	Boston, Mass.	1836
Currin, Joseph		Philadelphia	1829
Curry, John	J.CURRY in rectangle; J in square with rounded lower corners; and PHILA in rectangle	"	1831
Curry & Preston	CURRY & PRESTON in serrated rectangle; C & P in square	"	1831
Curtis, Candee & Styles	CURTIS, CANDEE & STYLES IN rectangle	Woodbury, Conn.	1831
Curtis, Daniel		" "	1825
Curtis, Joel		Wolcott, Conn.	1810
Curtis, Lewis	L.Curtis in rectangle	Farmington, Conn.	1795
Curtis, Thomas		New York City	1835
Curtiss & Candee		Woodbury, Conn.	1826
Curtiss & Duning	CURTISS & DUNING in scroll	" "	1828
Curtiss, Candee & Stiles	Name in capitals in rectangle	" "	1825
Curtiss & Stiles		" "	1835

---

†Where no mark is given, the maker used his name or initials.

SILVERSMITHS	MARKS	LOCATIONS	PERIOD
Cushman, Isaac	†	Boston, Mass.	1823
Cutler, A.	A.CUTLER, BOSTON, each in rectangle	" "	1820
Cutler, E.	E. CUTLER in rectangle	New Haven, Conn.	1820
Cutler, Richard		" "	1760
Cutler, Richard, Jr.		" " "	1800
Cutler, Richard & Sons		" " "	1800
Cutler, Silliman, Ward & Co.		" " "	1767
Cutler, William		" " "	1806
Cutter, William		Portland, Me.	1823
Dagget, Henry		New Haven, Conn.	1763
Dallon, John		Philadelphia	1791
Dally, Philip		New York City	1780
Dally & Halsey		" " "	1787
Dane, Thomas	T.DANE in cartouche	Boston, Mass.	1745
Daniels, Charles W.		Troy, N. Y.	1836
Dargee, John		New York City	1810
Daubayson, Victoire		Philadelphia	1820
Dauce, Simon		"	1798
Davenport, Robert		"	1808
Davenport, Samuel		Milton, Mass.	1741
Daverne, John		Baltimore, Md.	1799
David, John	I DAVID in rectangle; DAVID in rectangle; ID in oval	Philadelphia	1763
David, John, Jr.	J:D in oval; JD in square; JD in oval	"	1785
David, Lewis A.		"	1823
David, Peter	P.D in cartouche; PD in oval	"	1738
David & Dupuy		"	1792
Davis, E.	ED in rectangle; E DAVIS in oblong; E DAVIS in oval; E D in rectangle with a lion passant		
Davis, Elias		Newburyport, R. I.	1775
Davis, Joshua G.	IDAVIS in serrated rectangle	Boston, Mass.	1796
Davis, T. A.	T.A.DAVIS in rude rectangle	Boston, Mass.	1824
Davis, William		" "	1823
Davis & Babbitt		Providence, R. I.	1820
Davis & Brown	DAVIS & BROWN in rectangle	Boston, Mass.	1802
Davis & Watson	D & W (script) in rectangle, probably dealers only	" "	1815
Davison, Brazillai		Norwich, Conn.	1765
Davison, Charles	C.DAVISON in serrated rectangle	" "	1805
Davy, Adam		Philadelphia	1795
Dawes, William		Boston, Mass.	1766
Dawson, John		New York City	1769
Dawson, William		Philadelphia	1793
Deane, James		New York City	1760
Deas, David		Philadelphia	1831
Decker, J.		New York City	1830
Delagrow, Andrew		Philadelphia	1795
Delano, Jabez		New Bedford, Mass.	1784
Delarue, John		New Orleans, La.	1822

†Where no mark is given, the maker used his name or initials.

SILVERSMITHS	MARKS	LOCATIONS	PERIOD
Delauney, Jean	†	New York City	1805
Demilt, Andrew	DEMILT in rectangle; N.YORK in rectangle	New York City	1805
Demmock, John		Boston, Mass.	1798
Demorsy, Jean		New Orleans, La.	1822
Demort, John		New York City	1810
Demort, Lucien		" " "	1810
Denise, J. & T.	J:D and JD, each in square	" " "	1798
Dennis, Ebenezer		Hartford, Conn.	1782
Dennis, George Jr.		Norwich, Conn.	1770
Dennis & Fitch		Troy, N. Y.	1836
De Perrizang, Otto		New York City	1786
De Peyser, William		" " "	1732
De Riemer, Cornelius B.		Ithaca, N. Y.	1804
De Riemer, Jacob R.		New York City	1830
De Riemer, Pieter	P D R in oval; P D R in rectangle	" " "	1769
De Riemer & Mead		Ithaca, N. Y.	1831
Deshon, Daniel	〇〇	New London, Conn.	1719
Desquet & Tanguy		Philadelphia	1805
Desuret, Lewis		Philadelphia	1799
Deverell, John	DEVERELL in oblong	Boston, Mass.	1785
Dexter, John		Marlboro, Mass.	1756
Dickerson, H. & Co.		Philadelphia	1815
Dickerson, John		Morristown, Mass.	1778
Dickinson, Jonathan		Philadelphia	1794
Dickinson & Robinson		"	1796
Dimmock, John		New York City	1801
Dimond, Isaac M		" " "	1830
Dixwell, Basil		Boston, Mass.	1732
Dixwell, John	ID in oval; ID (small) in oval	" "	1702
Doane, Joshua	DOANE in cartouche; DOANE in rectangle	Providence, R. I.	1720
Dobbs, Adam			
Dobleman, Frederick		Philadelphia	1813
Doblemar, F. F. G.		"	1810
Dodge, Benjamin		Boston, Mass.	1836
Dodge, Ezekiel		New York City	1792
Dodge, Ezra		New London, Conn.	1787
Dodge, John	J.DODGE in oval	New York City	1790
Dodge, Nehemiah	N DODGE in serrated rectangle	Providence, R. I.	1795
Dodge, Seril	S DODGE in serrated rectangle, preceded and followed by star	" " "	1793
Doler, Daniel		Boston, Mass.	1765
Donalon, John W.		" "	1823
Donovan, William		Philadelphia	1784
Dontremei, C.		"	1805
Doolittle, Amos	A D in oval	New Haven, Conn.	1775
Doolittle, Enos		Hartford, Conn.	1781
Doran, John		Cincinnati, Ohio	1826
Dorgy, Peter		Philadelphia	1816
Dorsey, Joshua	I.DORSEY in rectangle	Philadelphia	1793
Dorsey, Samuel		"	1804

†Where no mark is given, the maker used his name or initials.

SILVERSMITHS	MARKS	LOCATIONS	PERIOD
Dorsey, Simon	†	Philadelphia	1820
Dorson, Joshua		"	1802
Doster, Michael		"	1831
Douglas, Alexander		New York City	1792
Douglas, Cantwell		Baltimore, Md.	1799
Douglas, Robert	R.D in double lined square	New London, Conn	1766
Douglass, James		New York City	1800
Douglass, J. W.	J. Douglass (script) framed in outline shaped by name	Philadelphia	1791
Douglass, John		"	1840
Douglass & Heckman		"	1837
Doutiemer, Gille		"	1791
Dowig, Christopher		"	765
Dowig, George		Baltimore, Md.	770
Downes, J.	J.DOWNES in rectangle; J. Downes in shaped cartouche	Philadelphia	1770
Downing, G. R.	G R D and N.YORK, each in rectangle	New York City	1810
Downing, & Phelps	D & P in rectangle	" " "	1810
Drewry, George	G D in rude square	Philadelphia	1763
Drinker, John		New York City	1835
Drown, T. P.	T. P. DROWN in rectangle	Newburyport, Conn.	1790
Drowne, Benjamin		Portsmouth, N. H.	1800
Drowne, Samuel	S D, small cross between letters in shaped frame and S Drowne, small cross between S and Drowne, in rectangle	" " "	770
Drowne, Shem		Boston, Mass.	1749
Drumont, Antoine		New York City	1808
Dubois, Abraham	A. DUBOIS in oblong	" " "	1775
Dubois, A., Sr. & Jr.		" " "	1803
Dubois, Joseph	I. DUBOIS in oblong; J.DUBOIS in rectangle	" " "	1790
Dubois, Tunis	T.D.DUBOIS in rectangle; T.D.D. in rectangle sheaf of wheat in oblong	" " "	1797
Dubois & Co.		" " "	1803
Duché, Benne R.		" " "	1795
Duché & Donard		Philadelphia	1820
Dudley, Benjamin		Birmingham, Ga.	1768
Duffel, James	I.DUFFEL in rectangle		1801
Dummer, Jeremiah	J D, pellet between letters and star below in a heart. I D, star below in a heart "star" may be a fleur-de-lis.	Boston, Mass.	1680
Dumourier, Joseph		Philadelphia	1816
Dumoutet, John B.	DUMOUTET in scroll	"	1793
Dundas, Pratt			1837
Dunkerly, Joseph		Boston, Mass.	1787
Dunlevy, Robert		Philadelphia	1831
Dunn, Cary	C.DUNN in oval; eagle in kite; N. YORK in rectangle	New York City	1764
Dunn, David		" " "	1835
Dunn & Son		" " "	1787
Dunscomb, Dennis		" " "	1765
Duon, H.		Baltimore, Md.	1819

†Where no mark is given, the maker used his name or initials.

SILVERSMITHS	MARKS	LOCATIONS	PERIOD
Dupuy, Daniel	D:D in rectangle; DD in double circle; DD in cartouche; D.DUPUY in rectangle	Philadelphia	1746
Dupuy, Daniel, Jr.	†	"	1782
Dupuy, John		"	1770
Dupuy, John & Daniel, Jr.		"	1783
Dupuy & Sons	D D D, each in apple-shaped cartouche	"	1784
Durand, John		New York City	1835
Durandeau, John		" " "	1835
Dutens, Charles J.		Philadelphia	1751
Dutens & Harper		"	1755
Duyckinck, Daniel		New York City	1798
Dwight, Timothy	T.D with six dots below, in heart	Boston, Mass.	1671
Eagles & Morris		New York City	1799
Eames, Joshua		Boston, Mass.	1828
Easton, James		Nantucket, Mass.	1828
Easton, Nathaniel		" "	1780
Easton & Sanford	EASTON & SANFORD in rectangle; E&S in rectangle	" "	1830
Eastwick, Thomas		Boston, Mass.	1743
Eaton, Timothy		Philadelphia	1793
Eayres, Thomas	EAYRES in rectangle	Boston, Mass.	1781
Edgar, John		New York City	1807
Edmechat, Claude		" " "	1790
Edwards, Andrew		Boston, Mass.	1796
Edwards, Calvin		Ashby, Mass.	1710
Edwards, John	I E in quatrefoil; IE crowned, fleur-de-lis below in a shaped shield	Boston, Mass.	1691
Edwards, Joseph	⟦Edwards⟧ ⟦IE⟧ ⟦IE⟧ ⟦IE⟧ ⟦Edwards⟧	" "	1707–1777
Edwards, Joseph, Jr.		" "	1761
Edwards, Samuel	S E, pellet between letters, small cross below and crown above, all enclosed in shield (shaped)	" "	1730
Edwards, Thomas		New York City	1731
Edwards, Thomas	T.Edwards (script); T.E in rectangle; TE shaped rectangle; TE with crown in shaped rectangle; T E, crowned in a shield	Boston, Mass.	1725
Elderkin, Alfred		Killingsworth, Conn.	1792
Elderkin, Elisha		New Haven, Conn.	1777
Elderkin & Staniford		Windom, Conn.	1790
Elliott, John A.		Sharon, Conn.	1815
Elliott, Joseph		New Castle, Del.	1768
Ellis, Lewis W.		Philadelphia	1837
Ellison, Peter		New York City	1792
Ellsworth, David		Windsor, Conn.	1772
Eltonhead, Thomas		Baltimore, Md.	1835
Emery, Stephen	EMERY in a cartouche; S.EMERY in rectangle; S.EMERY in shaped oval; S E in rectangle	Boston, Mass.	1746

†Where no mark is given, the maker used his name or initials.

SILVERSMITHS	MARKS	LOCATIONS	PERIOD
Emery, Thomas K.	T.Emery (script) in shaped rectangle; T.K.EMERY (large) in a rectangle	New York City	1802
Emery & Co.	†	" "	1798
England, George		New York City	1800
England, William		Philadelphia	1717
Eoff, Garret	G.Eoff in rectangle; G Eoff in rectangle; bird in circle	New York City	1803
Eoff & Connor		" " "	1833
Eoff & Howell	EOFF & HOWELL in rectangle	" " "	1805
Eoff & Moore		" " "	1835
Epps, Ellery		Boston, Mass.	1808
Equer & Aquimac		New York City	1816
Erwin, Andrew		Philadelphia	1837
Erwin, Henry	H.ERWIN in rectangle; same in wav bordered rectangle	" "	1817
Erwin, John	J.ERWIN in rectangle	New York City	1815
Esteva, Hayacinth		" " "	1804
Etting, Benjamin		" " "	1769
Evans, Henry	HENRY EVANS in rectangle	" " "	1820
Evans, John	EVANS in an engrailed "near" rectangle	" " "	1816
Evans, Robert	EVANS in engrailed rectangle; R.E in rectangle; RE in rectangle; R.EVANS in rectangle; R.E. in rectangle; EVANS in oblong	Boston, Mass.	1765
Everitt, Jesse		New York City	1811
Eversten, John		Albany, N. Y.	1813
Ewan, John	J. EWAN in engrailed rectangle	Charleston, S. C.	1800
Faber, William		Philadelphia	1828
Faber & Hoover		"	1837
Fagaler, George M.			1808
Fairchild, James L.		New York City	1830
Fairchild, Joseph		New Haven, Conn.	1824
Fairchild, Robert	R.FAIRCHILD in rectangle; RF in oblong; R.F in cartouche; RF in oval	Durham, Conn.	1724
Faris, Charles	Chas Faris (script) in oval	" "	1790
Farley, Charles	C. FARLEY in rectangle	Portland, Me.	1812
Farnam, Henry	H. FARNAM in rectangle	Boston, Mass.	1799
Farnam, R. & H.	R & H FARNAM in rectangle	" "	1807
Farnum, Rufus	R. FARNUM in rectangle	" "	1796
Farnam, Thomas	Th: Farnam in rude rectangle	" "	1836
Farnam & Ward	FARNAM & WARD in rectangle	" "	1810
Farr, John C.	J.C: Farr in rectangle; JOHN C FARR in shaded ribbon	" "	1813
Farrington, John		" "	1826
Farrington & Hunnewell	FARRINGTON & HUNNEWELL in rectangle	" "	1830
Fellows, Abraham	FELLOWS in rectangle	Newport, R. I. & Albany, N. Y.	1826
Fellows, John F.		Portsmouth, N. H.	1824
Fellows & Storm	FELLOWS & STORM in rectangle	Albany, N. Y.	1839
Ferguson, John		Philadelphia	1802

†Where no mark is given, the maker used his name or initials.

SILVERSMITHS	MARKS	LOCATIONS	PERIOD
Ferrier, John	†	New Orleans. La.	1802
Ferris, Benjamin		New York City	1816
Fielding, George	G F in oval	" " "	1731
Fields, Samuel		Philadelphia	1816
Finch, Hiram		Albany, N. Y.	1840
Finewell, Samuel		New York City	1835
Fireng, J. P.	J.P.FIRENG in rectangle; BURLING-TON with N.J. below each in rectangle	Burlington, N. J.	1810
Fisher, James		New York City	1821
Fisher, Thomas	T. FISHER in shaped cartouche	Philadelphia	1797
Fitch, Allen		New Haven, Conn.	1808
Fitch, D. M.		" " "	1840
Fitch, John	J.FITCH in rectangle, followed by two birds in squares	Trenton, N. J.	1780
Fitch & Hobart		New Haven, Conn.	1811
Flagg, Josiah		Boston, Mass.	1765
Fletcher, Charles		Philadelphia	1817
Fletcher, Thomas	T.FLETCHER in oblong	Boston, Mass.	1810
		Philadelphia	1830
Fletcher & Bennett		"	1837
Fletcher & Gardiner	F & G in rectangle; dog(?) in circle; P in circle	"	1815
Fling, George		"	1749
Flott, Lewis		Baltimore, Md.	1817
Folloppe, A. A.		Boston, Mass.	1808
Folsom, John		Albany, N. Y.	1781
Foote, William		Middletown and East Haddam, Conn.	1796
Forbes, Abraham G.	A G F in crude oblong; A F in square; N.YORK in rectangle	New York City	1769
Forbes, Benjamin G.		" " "	1817
Forbes, Collins V. G.	CVGF in rectangle	" " "	1816
Forbes, C.V.G.& Son	FORBES & SON in rectangle	" " "	1835
Forbes, G. & J. W.		" " "	1810
Forbes, Garret	G FORBES in rectangle; IWF over a square and compass in shaped rectangle; anchor, star, head, C, each in circle	" " "	1808
Forbes, John W.		" " "	1802
Forbes, William	W.F. in rectangle; eagle in square and NEW YORK in ribbon; W.FORBES in rectangle; N.Y. in rectangle	" " "	1830
Forbes, William G.	W.G. Forbes (script) in shaped oval; W G FORBES in shaded rectangle	" " "	1773
Force, Jabez W.	J.W.FORCE in rectangle	" " "	1819
Ford, Samuel		Philadelphia	1797
Forest, Alexander		Baltimore, Md.	1802
Forman, Benoni B.		Albany, N. Y.	1813
Fortune, Anthony		Philadelphia	1767
Foster, Abraham		"	1816
Foster, G.		Salem, Mass.	1838
Foster, Hiram		Philadelphia	1817

†Where no mark is given, the maker used his name or initials.

SILVERSMITHS	MARKS	LOCATIONS	PERIOD
Foster, John	J.FOSTER in rectangle; bird in oval; wheat stack in oval	New York City	1811
Foster, Joseph	J.FOSTER FOSTER	Boston, Mass.	1798
Foster, Samuel	†	" "	1676–1702
Foster, N. & T.		Newburyport, R. I.	1823
Foster, Thos.	T.FOSTER in rectangle	?	c.1825
Fourniquet, Louis	Fourniquet in shaped rectangle	New York City	1795
Fourniquet & Wheatley		" " "	1817
Fowler, Gilbert		" " "	1825
Fradgley, Thomas		" " "	1797
Francis, Julius C.		Middletown, Conn.	1807
Francis, Nathaniel	N.FRANCIS in rectangle	New York City	1804
Franciscus, George		Baltimore, Md.	1776
Frank, Jacob		Philadelphia	1785
Franks, William		"	1839
Fraser, William		"	1735
Freeman, William		"	1839
Frinth, James		"	1840
Frobisher, Benjamin C.	FROBISHER in oval; B. C. Frobisher in rectangle	Boston, Mass.	1834
Frost & Mumford	F & M in wavy lined rectangle	Providence, R. I.	1810
Frotheringham, Ebenezer		Boston, Mass.	1756–1814
Fryer, John W.		Albany, N. Y.	1784
Fueter, Daniel C.	D C F in a shaped rectangle; and N over YORK, in a shaped rectangle	New York City	1756
Fueter, Lewis		" " "	1775
Fuller, Alexander		" " "	1811
Furt, Peter		Boston, Mass.	1720
Gafkins, J.		Providence, R. I.	1832
Gaither, Greenberg		Dist. of Col.	1834
Gale, John L.	J.L.G. in rectangle; J.L.GALE in rectangle	New York City	1818
Gale, John S.	J. GALE in rectangle	" " "	1820
Gale, William	W.G. in rectangle; head in square; tulips in cup-shaped cartouche	" " "	1821
Gale, William, Jr.	Wm.GALE JR in rectangle	" " "	1823
Gale, William & Son	W.GALE & SON, W.G.&S. in oblong; diamond with 1825 in angles	" " "	1823
Gale, Wood & Hughes	G. W. & H in rectangle	" " "	1835
Gale & Mosely	G & M in serrated rectangle	" " "	1830
Gale & Stickler	G & S in rectangle	" " "	1823
Gale & Willis		" " "	1840
Gallop, Christopher		Ledyard, Conn.	1790
Galt, Samuel		Williamsburg, Va.	1749
Gardiner, Baldwin	B.G in rectangle; animal in oval and head in oval; B.GARDINER in rectangle	New York City	1829
Gardiner, B. & Company	B G & CO in rectangle	" " "	1825
Gardiner, John	IG J.GARDINER	New London, Conn.	1734
Gardiner, Sidney		Philadelphia	1810

†Where no mark is given, the maker used his name or initials.

SILVERSMITHS	MARKS	LOCATIONS	PERIOD
Gardner, John J.	J:Gardner in rectangle	Boston, Mass.	1730–1776
Garllow, Shavelier	†	Philadelphia	1813
Garner, John		Cincinnati, Ohio	1825
Garren, Anthony		Philadelphia	1813
Garret, P.	P. GARRET in rectangle	"	1811
Garret, T. C. & Co.	T.C.GARRET & Co. in rectangle	"	1815
Garrison, John		New York City	1825
Garrow & Dorsey		Baltimore, Md.	1800
Gaskins, W. W.	W W G in rectangle	Norfolk, Va.	1806
Gatham, William		Philadelphia	1802
Gay, Charles		Baltimore, Md.	1779
Gay, Nathaniel		Boston, Mass.	1664
Gee, Joseph		Philadelphia	1785
Geffroy, Nicholas	N.GEFFROY in escalloped rectangle	Newport, R. I.	1782
Geley, Peter		Philadelphia	1793
Gelston, George S.	G. S. GELSTON in rectangle	New York City	1833
Gelston, Ladd & Co.	GELSTON, LADD & CO. in rectangle	" " "	1836
Gelston & Co.		" " "	1837
Gelston & Gould		Baltimore, Md.	1819
Gelston & Treadwell		New York City	1836
Georgion, Bernard		Philadelphia	1794
Georgeon & Philipe		"	1794
German, Greenberg D.		"	1814
German, Joseph		Baltimore, Md.	1819
Germon, John	🅸🅶	Philadelphia	1788
Gero, Francis		"	1818
Gerrish, Timothy	GERRISH in serrated rectangle; T. Gerrish (script)	Portsmouth, N. H.	1753–1813
Gethen, John		Philadelphia	1811
Gethen, William	W.GETHEN in rectangle	"	1797
Getty, James		Williamsburg, Va.	1772
Getz, Peter	P.Getz in rectangle	Lancaster, Pa.	1782
Ghiselin, Caesar	C G in heart; star; C G in rude oval; C G in rude hexagon	Philadelphia	1695
Ghiselin, William	W.G in rectangle; GHISELIN in rectangle	"	1751
Gibbs, Daniel		Boston, Mass.	1716
Gibbs, John	J GIBBS in rude oval	Providence, R. I.	1790
Gibbs, John F.		" "	1803
Giffing, Christopher	C Giffing, N. Y. in rectangle	New York City	1816
Gilbert, Samuel	S G in square	Hebron, Conn.	1798
Gilbert, Wm.	Gilbert (script) and N. York (script) both in rectangles; GILBERT in rectangle; WG in rectangle with N.YORK in rectangle	New York City	1765
Gilbert, William W.	W. Gilbert (script) in rude rectangle; W G in box	" " "	1783
Gilbert & Cunningham		" " "	1839
Gill, Caleb	GILL in rectangle	Hingham, Mass.	1790
Gill, Leavitt		" "	1810
Gilman, John W.	I.W.G. incised	Exeter, N. H.	1792
Giquel, John B. F.		New Orleans, La.	1822
Girard, Francis		Philadelphia	1817

†Where no mark is given, the maker used his name or initials.

SILVERSMITHS	MARKS	LOCATIONS	PERIOD
Giraud, Henry	†	New York City	1805
Girrad, Henry		" " "	1805
Girreaun, Stephen		Philadelphia	1785
Glidden, Joseph	J G, crowned fleur-de-lis below in shield	Boston, Mass.	1607–1780
Goelet, Philip	P G in rude square; P G in oval	New York City	1731
Goforth, Jeremiah		Philadelphia	1700
Goldthwaite, Joseph		Boston, Mass.	1727
Gombach, John		Philadelphia	1802
Goodhue, John	J.GOODHUE in rectangle	Salem, Mass.	1840
Gooding, Henry	GOODING in double-lined rectangle	Boston, Mass.	1833
Gooding, Joseph		" "	1815
Goodwin, Allyn		Hartford, Conn.	1811
Goodwin, Benjamin	B:GOODWIN in rectangle	Boston, Mass.	1756
Goodwin, H. & A.	GOODWIN in an oblong	Hartford, Conn.	1811
Goodwin, Horace		" "	1811
Goodwin, Ralph		" "	1828
Goodwin & Dodd		" "	1812
Gordon, A. & J.		New York City	1798
Gordon, Alexander S.	GORDON in escalloped rectangle	" " "	1795
Gordon, G.	G.Gordon in oblong	" " "	1800
Gordon, James		" " "	1795
Gordon, James S.		Philadelphia	1769
Gorham, Jabez		Providence, R. I.	1814
Gorham, John		New Haven, Conn.	1814
Gorham, Miles	M.G. in rectangle; M. GORHAM in rectangle	" " "	1778
Gorham, Richard		" " "	1799
Gorham & Webster	Gorham & Webster (script) in rectangle	Providence, R. I.	1831
Gough, James		Boston, Mass.	1769
Gould, J.	J.GOULD and 10–15 in rectangles with curved ends	Baltimore, Md.	1825
Gould, John		Philadelphia	1840
Gould, Stowell & Ward		Baltimore	1840
Gould & Ward		"	1835
Govert, James		Philadelphia	1802
Gowen, William	W.G. in rectangle; W.GOWEN in rectangle	Charlestown, Mass.	1777
Graham, Daniel		West Suffield, Conn.	1789
Grant, Thomas	T. GRANT in rectangle	Marblehead, Mass.	1752
Grant, William, Jr.	W. Grant (script) in shaped rectangle and WG in oval	Philadelphia	1785
Gravelle, René L.		"	1813
Graves, Thomas		Cincinnati, Ohio	1828
Gravier, Nicholas		New Orleans, La.	1822
Gray, G.	G.GRAY in escalloped rectangle	Portsmouth, N. H.	1839
Gray, John		New London, Conn.	1692
		Boston, Mass.	1720
Gray, Robert	R.Gray, script in rectangle	Portsmouth, N. H.	1830
Gray, Samuel	S:GRAY in rectangle; GRAY in rectangle	Boston, Mass.	1705
Green, James		New York City	1805

†Where no mark is given, the maker used his name or initials.

SILVERSMITHS	MARKS	LOCATIONS	PERIOD
Green, Benjamin	B:GREEN in rectangle	Boston, Mass.	1712–1748
Green, Rufus	R: GREEN in rectangle; R:GREEN in shaped rectangle	" "	1707–1717
Greene, William & Co.	†	Providence, R. I.	1815
Greenleaf, David	GREENLEAF in wavy-lined rectangle	Bolton, Mass. Norwich & Hartford, Conn.	1737
Greenleaf, David, Jr.	D.Greenleaf	Hartford, Conn.	1766
Greffin, Peter		Philadelphia	1801
Griffen, P.		Albany, N. Y.	1825
Griffen & Hoyt	GRIFFEN & HOYT in shaped rectangle; anchor, eagle, and star, each in circle	" "	1830
Griffing, C.		New York City	1825
Grifith, David		Boston, Mass.	1789
Grigg, William	GRIGG and W.GRIGG, each in shaped rectangle; Grigg (script) in shaped cartouche	New York City	1765
Grignon, Benjamin		Boston, Mass.	1685
Grignon, René	RG, crown above and dog below in very rudely drawn shield	Norwich, Conn.	1690
Grimke, John P.		Charleston, S. C.	1744
Griscom, George		Philadelphia	1791
Griselm, Caesar		"	1700
Griswold, Gilbert	W. GRISWOLD in rectangle	Middletown, Conn.	1825
Guercy, Dominick		New York City	1795
Guerin, Anthony		Philadelphia	1791
Guille, Noah		Boston, Mass.	1701
Gunn, Enos	E. GUNN in rectangle	Norwich, Conn.	1792
Gurley, William	W.G in rectangle	Norwich, Conn.	1804
Gurnee, Benjamin		New York City	1820
Gurnee, B. & S.		" " "	1833
Gurnee & Co.		" " "	1820
Hackle, William		Baltimore, Md.	1776
Haddock, Henry		Boston, Mass.	1836
Haddock & Andrews		" "	1838
Hadwen, William		Nantucket, Mass.	1816
Haggenmacher, J. H. & Co.		Philadelphia	1836
Haines, Abraham		New York City	1801
Hall, Abijah		Albany, N. Y.	1813
Hall, Brower & Co.		" "	1836
Hall, Charles		Lancaster, Pa.	1765
Hall, David	D H in cartouche; D HALL in rectangle	Philadelphia	1765
Hall, Drew		New York City	1789
Hall, Green		Albany, N. Y.	1813
Hall, Hewson & Merrifield		" "	1840
Hall, Ivory		Concord, N. H.	1801
Hall, Joseph	I HALL Hall	Albany, N. Y.	1781
Hall & Brower		" "	1830

†Where no mark is given, the maker used his name or initials.

SILVERSMITHS	MARKS	LOCATIONS	PERIOD
Hall & Hewson	H & H in rectangle, head and eagle and D in cartouches	Albany, N. Y.	1819
Hallam, John	†	New London, Conn.	1773
Halsey, Jabez	HALSEY I·HALSEY	New York City	1789
Halstead, Benjamin	Halstead (script) in shaped cartouche	" " "	1764
Halstead & Son		" " "	1799
Ham, George		Portsmouth, N. H.	1810
Hamill, James	J.HAMILL, N.Y. in rectangle	New York City	1816
Hamill & Co.		" " "	1817
Hamilton, James		Annapolis, Md.	1766
Hamilton, John		New York City	1798
Hamlin, Cyrus		Portland, Me.	1831
Hamlin, William	W.H. in rectangle followed by crescent moon open to left; WH in rectangle with crescent moon open to right	Middletown, Conn.	1791
Hammersley, Thomas	T.H in square; T H; TH (script) in oval	New York City	1756
Hancock, John	J HANCOCK in oblong; J.HANCOCK in rectangle	Boston, Mass.	1760
Handle, John		Philadelphia	1839
Hanks, Benjamin		Windham, Conn.	1777
Hannah, W. W.	W. W. HANNAH, heavy, crude capitals, unframed	New York City	1840
Hanners, George	G. HANNERS in rectangle; G H, crown above and pellet below, in shield; G.H in an oval.	Boston, Mass.	1718
Hansell, Robert			1823
Harache, Pierre		Williamsburg, Va.	1691
Harding, N. & C.	N. HARDING in rectangle; N. Harding in rectangle	New York City	1830
		Boston, Mass.	1830
Harding, Newill	N HARDING in rectangle; N HARDING in oblong	" "	1822
Harding, N. & Co.	N.H & Co in rectangle	" "	1830
Hardwood, John		Philadelphia	1816
Hardy, Stephen	HARDY in oblong with clipped corners	Portsmouth, N. H.	1802
Harland, Thomas	HARLAND in rectangle	Norwich, Conn.	1735
Harland, Thomas, Jr.		" "	1777
Harpel, Thomas W.		Philadelphia	1813
Harper, Alexander		"	
Harper, David		"	
Harper, Thomas W.		"	1813
Harris, George		New York City	1802
Harris, H.		Albany, N. Y.	1820
Harris & Stanwood	H in circle, & in diamond; S in circle, connected HARRIS & STANWOOD in rectangle	Boston, Mass.	1835
Hart, Eliphaz	E. HART in rectangle; E H in square	Norwich, Conn.	1812
Hart, John		Philadelphia	1776
Hart, John J.		New York City	1820
Hart, Judah	J·Hart	Berlin, Conn.	1777
Hart, William		Philadelphia	1818
Hart & Bliss		Middletown, Conn.	1803

†Where no mark is given, the maker used his name or initials.

SILVERSMITHS	MARKS	LOCATIONS	PERIOD
Hart & Brewer	†	Middletown, Conn.	1800
Hart & Wilcox	HART & WILCOX in rectangle	Norwich, Conn.	1805
Hartford, George		Philadelphia	1794
Hartin & Bargi		Bound Brook, N. J.	1766
Hartley, Samuel		Philadelphia	1818
Hartman, Philip		"	1813
Haskell, Barnabus		Boston, Mass.	1833
Hastier, John		New York City	1726
Hastier, Marquette	M H in square	" " "	1771
Hastings, B. B.		Cleveland, Ohio	1835
Haugh, Samuel	S H in square	Boston, Mass.	1675
Haverstick, William		Philadelphia	1781
Hawley, Noah		New York City	1816
Haws, John		Philadelphia	1837
Hayden & Gregg	HAYDEN & GREGG in rectangle	New York City	1840
Hayes & Colton		Newark, N. J.	1831
Hays, Andrew		" "	1769
Hays & Myers	HAYS & MYERS in rectangle; H & M in oblong	" "	1770
Head, Joseph		Philadelphia	1798
Healy		Boston, Mass.	1773
Heath, John	HEATH	Newark, N. J.	1761
Heck, Ludwig	L H in square	Lancaster, Pa.	1760
Hedges, David, Jr.	HEDGES in rudely drawn rectangle	New York City	1880
Heguenburg, Charles, Jr.		New Haven, Conn.	1809
Hempsted & Chandler		New York City	1811
Henchman, Daniel	Henchman in rectangle; D.H in rectangle	Boston, Mass.	1751
Hendriks, Ahasuerus	A H conjoined in an asymmetric circle; AI in oval; A.H in oval	New York City	1675
		" " "	1815
Henry, Felix		New Haven, Conn	1781
Hequenbourg, Charles, Jr.		New York City	1816
Herbert, Timothy B.		Philadelphia	1804
Herils, Francis		New York City	1768
Heron, Isaac		" " "	1731
Heurtin, William	W H in rectangle		
Hews, Abraham, Jr.	A. HEWS Jr. in rectangle	Boston, Mass.	1838
Hewson, John D.		Albany, N. Y.	1815
Heyer, William B.	W.B.HEYER in rectangle; W.B.HEYER in shaped rectangle	New York City	1798
Heyer & Gale	W.B.HEYER in rectangle; & in rectangle; J.GALE in an oblong	" " "	1807
Higbie & Crosby	HIGBIE & CROSBY in oblong	Boston, Mass.	1820
Hildebur, ——	HILDEBUR in oval	Philadelphia	1790
Hill, James		Boston, Mass.	1770
Hill & Waddill		Petersburg, Va.	1780
Hilldrup, Thomas		Hartford, Conn.	1774
Hiller, Benjamin	B H two crescents below, in shaped rectangle; B H in cartouche	Boston, Mass.	1711
		" "	1745
Hiller, Joseph		Philadelphia	1814
Hilton, William		"	
Hind, John			1760

†Where no mark is given, the maker used his name or initials.

SILVERSMITHS	MARKS	LOCATIONS	PERIOD
Hinsdale, Epaphras	HINSDALE in crude rectangle	New York City	1796
Hitchborn, Daniel	†	Boston, Mass.	1773
Hitchborn, Samuel		" "	1752
Hitchcock, Eliakim (or Hitchborn, Eliakim)	E H, cross between in rectangle; E H in rectangle	New Haven, Conn.	1776
Hobarth, Joshua	J.HOBARTH in oblong with rounded ends	" " "	1813
Hobbs, Nathan	HOBBS in rectangle	Boston, Mass.	1824
Hodge, John	J. HODGE in rectangle with HADLEY in rectangle	Hadley, Mass.	1771
Hoffman, Frederick		Philadelphia	1819
Hoffman, James M.	J. M. HOFFMAN in rectangle	"	1804
Holland, Littleton	L. HOLLAND in rectangle, STER in rectangle, A, head, and a web in cartouches	Baltimore, Md.	c.1804
Hollingshead, John		Philadelphia	1768
Hollingshead, William	W H (fancy script) in shaped cartouche	"	1762
Holmes, Adrian B.	A. Holmes in rectangle	New York City	1801
Holmes, Israel		Waterbury, Conn.	1793
Holmes, J.		New York City	1816
Holmes, William		" " "	1801
Holton, David		Baltimore, Md.	1804
Holton, John		Philadelphia	1794
Holyoke, Edward	HOLYOKE in rude rectangle	Boston, Mass.	1817
Homes, William	W. HOMES in rectangle; HOMES in rectangle, W.H in rectangle	" "	1763
Homes, William, Jr.	W. Homes in oval	" "	1789
Hoover, Henry		Philadelphia	1816
Hoover, Joseph E.		"	1837
Hopkins, Jesse		Waterbury, Conn.	1787
Hopkins, Joseph		" "	1766
Hopper, Samuel		Philadelphia	1835
Hosford, Harley		New York City	1820
Hotchkiss, Hezekiah		New Haven, Conn	1754
Houlton, John		Philadelphia	1797
Houtzell, Jacob		"	1801
How, David		Boston, Mass.	1790
Howard, Abraham		Salem, Mass.	1810
Howard, John		Philadelphia	1819
Howard, Thomas		"	1620
Howard, William		Boston, Mass.	1800
Howe, G. C. & Co.		New York City	1815
Howe, George C.	GEO. C. HOWE in oblong; anchor, star, and eagle in separate ovals	" " "	1810
Howe, Otis		Boston, Mass.	1788
Howell, G. W.	G W Howell (script) in rectangle,	" "	1790
Howell, James		Philadelphia	1811
Howell, Paul	I.Howell (script) in shaped cartouche P. HOWELL in rectangle; Howell (script) in shaped rectangle	New York City	1810
Howell, Silas W.	S. W. Howell (script) in rectangle same in shaped rectangle	Albany, N. Y.	1798

†Where no mark is given, the maker used his name or initials.

SILVERSMITHS	MARKS	LOCATIONS	PERIOD
Howell & Arnold	†	Albany, N. Y.	1797
Hoyt, George B.	GEO. B. HOYT in rectangle	New York City	1840
Hoyt, Henry E.	HENRY HOYT in rectangle	" " "	1820
Hoyt, S.	S. HOYT in rectangle	" " "	1840
Hubbal, William		Dist. of Col.	1834
Hughes, Christopher & Co.		Baltimore, Md.	1773
Hughes, Edmund		Hampton, Conn.	1804
Hughes, Henry		Baltimore, Md.	1781
Hughes, J.	J. HUGHES in rectangle	Middletown, Conn.	1798
Hughes & Bliss		" "	1806
Hughes & Francis		" "	1807
Hulbeart, Philip	P H in shaped square	Philadelphia	1761
Hull, John		Boston, Mass.	1645
Hull & Sanderson		" "	1652
Humbert, Augustus		New York City	1818
Humphreys, Richard	R H (script) in shaped cartouche; R H in rectangle; R.H in oval, R.HUmphreys (script) in shaped cartouche	Philadelphia	1771
Humphreys, Thomas		"	1814
Hunlock, Bouman		"	1752
Hunnewell, George W.		Boston, Mass.	1836
Hunt, Edward		"	1717
Hunt, William		"	1819
Huntington, Phil	P H in square; Huntington in shaped rectangle	Norwich, Conn.	1791
Huntington, Roswell		" "	1763
Hurd, Benjamin (son of Jacob Hurd)	B H, arrow between, in a rectangle	Roxbury, Mass.	1739
Hurd, Isaac		" "	1754
Hurd, Jacob		Boston, Mass.	1702
Hurd, Nathaniel	N.Hurd in rectangle; N. Hurd, very small, in cartouche	" "	1729
Hurst, Henry	H H in a shield	" "	1665
Husband, John	Probably the I H (script) in shaped rectangle given in *American Church Silver*, page 81	Philadelphia	1796
Huston, James		Baltimore	1799
Hutchins, Jacob	HUTCHINS in rude oblong	New York City	1774
Hutton, George		Albany, N. Y.	1799
Hutton, Isaac	Spray or bird in circle; HUTTON in oblong; first figure repeated and ALBANY in rectangle	" "	1790
Hutton, I & G.		" "	1799
Hutton, John		New York City	1720
Hutton, John S.		" " "	1684
Hyde & Goodrich	HYDE & GOODRICH in rectangle; N.O. in rectangle	New Orleans, La.	1830
Hyde & Nevins	Hyde & Nevins in rectangle	New York City	1798

†Where no mark is given, the maker used his name or initials.

SILVERSMITHS	MARKS	LOCATIONS	PERIOD
Iago, Henry	†	New York City	1745
Ingraham, Joseph		Portland, Me.	1785
Inman, Benjamin		Philadelphia	1816
Isaacks, Michael		New York City	1765
Jacks, James		Charleston, S. C.	1795
Jacks, William		Philadelphia	1798
Jackson, Daniel	D I in cartouche; DJACKSON in oblong	New York City	1783
Jackson, James		Baltimore, Md.	1775
Jackson, John	JACKSON in oblong	New York City	1731
Jackson, Joseph		Baltimore, Md.	1804
Jacob, Moses		Philadelphia	1775
Jacobs, Abel	A JACOBS in rectangle	Baltimore, Md.	1816
Jacobs, George	G. JACOBS in long oval	" "	1802
Janvier, Louis		Charleston, S. C.	1744
Jarvis, Munson	M:J in box; M.J in box	Stamford, Conn.	1763
Jenckes, John C.	J.JENCKES incised; JCJENCKES in an oblong	Providence, R. I.	1795
Jenckes & Co.		" "	1798
Jenkins, John		Philadelphia	1777
Jennings, Jacob		New London, Conn.	1750
Jennings, Jacob, Jr.		" " "	1800
Jesse, David		Boston, Mass.	1691
Johannes, John M.		Baltimore, Md.	1835
John, ——	JOHN in an oblong		c. 1760
Johnson, C.		Albany, N. Y.	1825
Johnson, John		Pittsburgh, Pa.	1815
Johnson, Maycock W.	M.W.JOHNSON in engrailed rectangle	Albany, N. Y.	1815
Johnson, Samuel	S J in oblong	New York City	1783
Johnson & Ball		Baltimore, Md.	1785
Johnson & Reat	JOHNSON & REAT in shaped oval	" "	1810
Johonnot, William B.		Middletown, Conn.	1810
Jones, Ball & Co.		Boston, Mass.	1835
Jones, Ball & Poor		" "	1840
Jones, E.		Baltimore, Md.	1820
Jones, George B.		Boston, Mass.	1839
Jones, James		Philadelphia	1815
Jones, John	J. JONES in oblong	Boston, Mass.	1810
Jones, John B.	J. B. JONES in oblong and PURE COIN in rectangle	" "	1782
Jones, William	W.I in square	Marblehead, Mass.	1715
Jones, William		New York City	1820
Jones & Ward		Boston, Mass.	1815
Jordan, Peter		Philadelphia	1823
Joubert, P.		"	1807
Judah, ——		New York City	1774
Kay, Amos	A K in square; the K resembles H	Boston, Mass.	1725
Keeler, A.	KEELER in rectangle; lower line engrailed	New London, Conn.	1800
Keeler, Joseph		" " "	1807
Keeler, Thaddeus	T KEELER in oblong	Boston, Mass.	1823

†Where no mark is given, the maker used his name or initials.

SILVERSMITHS	MARKS	LOCATIONS	PERIOD
Keiff, Joseph	†	Philadelphia	1831
Keith, T. & W	T. & W. KEITH in rectangle	New York City	1805
Keley, Grael		Boston, Mass.	1823
Kelly, Allen		Providence, R. I.	1810
Kelley, E. G. & J. H.		" "	1820
Kendle, Charles		New York City	1807
Kendrick, William	W. KENDRICK, LOUISVILLE, incised	Louisville, Ky.	1840
Kennedy, Mathew		Philadelphia	1825
Kenrick, Anwyl		Maryland	1775
Ketchum, James		New York City	1807
Kettell, Thomas	T. K in rectangle	Charlestown, Mass.	1781
Keyworth, Robert	R. KEYWORTH in rectangle	Washington, D. C.	1830
Kiersteade, Cornelius	C K in cartouche; C K in rectangle; C.K in oval; C K, a diamond and two pellets below in shield	New York City	1753
		New Haven, Conn.	1722
Kimberly, William	W K in rectangle; Kimberly in shaped rectangle	New York City	1790
King, Joseph		Middletown, Conn.	1770
Kingston, John		New York City	1775
Kinney, Thomas	T K in rectangle; T K in partially engrailed rectangle	Norwich, Conn.	1825
Kip, Benjamin		New York City	1702
Kippen, George	G.KIPPEN in rectangle	Middletown, Conn.	1790
		Bridgeport, Conn.	1825
Kirby, William		New York City	1783
Kirk, Samuel		Baltimore, Md.‡	1816
Kirk & Smith		Baltimore, Md.	1818
			1820
Kirtland, Joseph P.		Middletown, Conn.	1796
Kitchen, Andrew		Philadelphia	1835
Kline, Bartholomew		"	1837
Kline, B. & Co.		"	1837
Kneeland, I.		Boston, Mass.	1698
Krause, John S.		Bethlehem, Pa.	1805
Kucher, Jacob		Philadelphia	1806
Kumbel, William		New York City	1780
Lachaise, Peter		New York City	1794
Ladd, William F.	WM F. LADD in rectangle; NEW YORK in rectangle	" " "	1830

†Where no mark is given, the maker used his name or initials.

‡Pursuant to an act of the Maryland Legislature, the local government of Baltimore, in 1814, passed a law which interdicted the use of a lower standard of silver than 11 oz. troy to the pound of metal, and appointed an assayer who signified his approval of pieces submitted to him by affixing a dominical letter, arbitrarily chosen, and a head of the goddess of liberty. The office was abolished in 1830 and a law was substituted requiring the gold or silversmith to stamp the quality of his wares. The use of the head was discontinued in 1823. The letters and the years represented by each are: A, 1815; G (and F), 1816; E, 1817, D, 1818, C, 1819, B (and A) 1820; G, 1821; F, 1822; E, 1823; C (and D), 1824; B, 1825; A, 1826; G, 1827; F (and E), 1828; D, 1829.

SILVERSMITHS	MARKS	LOCATIONS	PERIOD
Laforme, Antoine	†	Boston, Mass.	1836
Laforme, Bernard		" "	1836
Laforme, F. J.		" "	1835
Lainecourt, Stephen		New York City	1800
Lakeman, E. K.		" " "	1800
Lamar, Benjamin	B L in oval, LAMAR in oblong	Philadelphia	1775
Lamar, Mathias		"	1796
Lamesiere, Peter		"	1811
Lamothe, John		New Orleans, La.	1822
Lamothe, Pierre & Sons	Lamothe (script) in shaped oblong	New Orleans, La.	1822
Lampe, John		Baltimore, Md.	1787
Lamson, J.	J. LAMSON in rectangle		1790
Lane, Aaron	A L in oval	Elizabeth, N. J.	1780
Lang, Edward	E D in cartouche; LANG in oblong	Salem, Mass.	1763
Lang, Jeffery	J.LANG J.LANG	" "	1730
Lang, Richard	R LANG in rectangle	" "	1754
Langer, Joseph		Philadelphia	1811
Lansing, Jacob	J·L I·L	Albany, N. Y.	1736
Laperouse, John B.		New Orleans, La.	1832
Laroussebierre, Peter		New York City	1797
Lashing, Peter		" " "	1805
Lathrop, Rufus		Norwich, Conn.	1755
Latruit, John P.		Washington, D. C.	1833
Lawrence, Josiah H.		Philadelphia	1817
Lawrie, Robert O.		"	1840
Leach, Charles	C.L in engrailed rectangle; LEACH in oblong	Boston, Mass.	1765
Leach, John		" "	1780
Leach, Nathaniel		" "	1789
Leach, Samuel	S.L in square	Philadelphia	1741
Leach & Bradley		"	1832
Leacock, John	I·L I·LEACOCK I·L	"	1751
Leacock, Peter		"	1750
Le Blanc, Lewis		"	1815
Ledell, Joseph		"	1797
Le Dorc,——		"	1797
Lee, S. W.	S.LEE in oblong; teapot in cartouche; wheat stack in cartouche	Providence, R. I.	1815
Lefevre, F.		Philadelphia	1818
Lefevre, John F.		"	1806
Lefevre & Gravelle		"	1811
Legare, Francis		Boston, Mass.	1657
Lemaire, Baptiste		Philadelphia	1804
Lemaire, Mathias		"	1781
Lench, Peter		New York City	1805
Lendigree, M.		" " "	1814
Lent, John		" " "	1787
Leonard, Allen		" " "	1830
Leret, Peter	P. Leret in oblong	Baltimore, Md.	1787
Le Roux, Bartholomew	BR (LR conjoined) in a cartouche	New York City	1700
Le Roux, Charles	C L in box; C L in rectangle	" " "	1725

†Where no mark is given, the maker used his name or initials.

SILVERSMITHS	MARKS	LOCATIONS	PERIOD
Le Roux, John	[mark] [mark]	New York City	1723
Lescure, Edward	†	Philadelphia	1822
Le Telier, John	[LETELIER] [mark]	"	1770
Letourneaux, M.		New York City	1797
Lively, ——		Baltimore, Md.	1788
Leverett, Knight	K LEVERETT in rectangle; K L in rectangle; K L in straight-topped shield; K Leverett (script) in oblong	Boston, Mass.	1724
Levis, William		Philadelphia	1810
Lewin, Gabriel	G L in square	Baltimore, Md.	1771
Lewis, Harvy	H. LEWIS in rectangle	Philadelphia	1811
Lewis, Isaac	[I.LEWIS] [I.LEWIS]	Ridgefield, Conn.	1796
Lewis, Tunis		New York City	1805
Lewis & Smith	Lewis & Smith (script) in shaped oblong	Philadelphia	1806
Lightfoot, James		New York City	1749
Linch, Peter		" " "	1805
Lincoln, Elijah	E.LINCOLN in rectangle	Hingham, Mass.	1818
Lincoln & Foss	LINCOLN & FOSS in rectangle	Boston, Mass.	1829
Lincoln & Read	LINCOLN & READ in rectangle	" "	1835
Lindner, George		Philadelphia	1837
Lingley, Henry		New York City	1810
Link, Peter		Philadelphia	1811
Lintot		New York City	1762
Little, Paul		Portland, Me.	1760
Little, William	W L in rectangle	Newburyport, Mass.	1775
Lockwood, A.	A. LOCKWOOD in oblong	" "	1810
Lockwood, James		New York City	1799
Lofland, Purnel		Philadelphia	1810
Logan, Adam	A.LOGAN in rectangle	New York City	1803
Logan, James		Philadelphia	1810
Long, Andrew		"	1837
Long, William		"	1807
Longly, Henry	H.LONGLY (script) in shaped oblong	New York City	1810
Lord, Benjamin		Pittsfield, Mass.	1796
Lord, Jabez C.	J. LORD in oblong	New York City	1823
Lord, Joseph		Philadelphia	1815
Lord & Smith		New York City	1823
Loring, Elijah	E.Loring (last four letters in script) in shaped cartouche; E.Loring in cartouche	Barnstable, Mass.	1773-1818
Loring, Henry		Boston, Mass.	1794
Loring, Joseph	[I.Loring] [I.Loring]	Hull, Mass.	1743
		Boston, Mass.	1810
Loud, Asa		Hartford, Conn.	1792
Low, Ball & Co.		Boston, Mass.	1840
Low, Francis		" "	1827
Low, John J. & Co.	J.J.LOW & CO. in rectangle	" "	1828
Low, John S.		Salem, Mass.	1821
Lower, Joseph	LOWER in rectangle	Philadelphia	1806

†Where no mark is given, the maker used his name or initials.

SILVERSMITHS	MARKS	LOCATIONS	PERIOD
Lowner, Jacob	†	Philadelphia	1833
Lowner, William		"	1833
Lownes, Edward	E.LOWNES in rectangle and tree in oval; E.LOWNES in wavy rectangle	"	1806
Lownes, J. & J. H.		"	1816
Lownes, Joseph		"	1796
Lownes, Josiah H.		"	1819
Lownes & Erwin		"	1816
Loyer, Adrian		Savannah, Ga.	1760
Lucet, James		New York City	1802
Luls, Lambert		" " "	1804
Lusada, Benjamin		" " "	1797
Luscomb, John G.		Boston, Mass.	1823
Lussaur, John		New York City	1791
Lyell, David		" " "	1699
Lynch, John	J.LYNCH in oblong and [J.LYNCH]	Baltimore, Md.	1796
Lynde, Thomas	T.LYNDE in oval cartouche	Worcester, Mass.	1748
Lyng, John	[IBL]	Philadelphia	1734
Lyng, John Burt	I B L in rectangle; LYNG in engrailed rectangle, followed by N.YORK in rectangle	New York City	1761
Lynn, Adam		Alexandria, Va.	1796
Mabrid & Co.		New York City	1787
MacFarland, John	J : M : FARLAND in oblong; J M 'F oblong	Boston, Mass.	1796
Machon, Austin		Philadelphia	1759
Main, David		Stonington, Conn.	1773
Mainwaring, Thomas		West New Jersey	1664
Mairot, Jean C.		New Orleans, La.	1822
Mann, Alexander		Middletown, Conn.	1804
Mannerback, L.		Reading, Pa.	1820
Manning, Daniel		Boston, Mass.	1823
Manning, Joseph		New York City	1823
Manning, Samuel		Boston, Mass.	1823
Mansfield, Elisha H.		Norwich, Conn.	1816
Mansfield, John		Charlestown	1634
			1674
Mansfield, Thomas		Philadelphia	1804
Marble, Simeon	S.MARBLE in oblong	New Haven, Conn.	1806
Marchand, Evariste		New Orleans, La.	1822
Marquand, Frederick	F. MARQUAND in shaped rectangle; F.M in rectangle; Lion in cartouche; F and C in separate rectangles	New York City	1823
Marquard, Isaac		" " "	1810
Marquand & Brother		" " "	1825
Marquand & Co.		" " "	1810
Marshall, Joseph		Philadelphia	1818
Marshall, Thomas		Troy, N. Y.	1839

†Where no mark is given, the maker used his name or initials.

SILVERSMITHS	MARKS	LOCATIONS	PERIOD
Marshall & Tempest	†	Philadelphia	1813
Martin, Abraham W.		New York City	1835
Martin, Peter	P.MARTIN in oblong	" " "	1756
Mather & North	MATHER & NORTH in double ruled rectangle	New Britain, Conn.	1825
Matlack, William		Philadelphia	1828
Maverick, Peter R.		New York City	1780
Maysenhoelder, C.		Philadelphia	1824
McClymon, J. C.		New York City	1805
McConnell, Hugh	McCONNELL in oblong	Philadelphia	1813
McConnelly, H.		"	1811
McCormick, John		"	1837
McCrea, Robert		"	1785
McDaniel, Peter		New York City	1743
McDonald, Daniel		Philadelphia	1828
McDonnough, Patrick		"	1811
McDonough, John		"	1775
McFarland, John	J.M'F. in oblong; J. M'FARLAND in oblong	Boston, Mass.	1796
McFee, John		Philadelphia	1793
McFee, M.		"	1769
McFee & Reeder	M & R (& is very minute) in rectangle	"	1797
McGraw, Daniel		Chester, Pa.	1772
McIntire, James		Philadelphia	1840
McIntosh, John		Ft. Stanwix, Pa.	1761
McKliment, John		New York City	1804
McLawrence, John		" " "	1818
McMahon, John		Philadelphia	1804
McMaster, John		"	1805
McMullen, James		"	1814
McMullen, William		"	1791
McMullin, John		"	1796
McMullin & Black	McMuLLin & BLack in rectangle	"	1811
McPherson, Robert		"	1831
Meade, Adriance & Co.	MEADE & ADRIANCE in rectangle, ST. Louis in oblong	St. Louis, Mo.	1831
Mecom, John		New York City	1770
Mecum, George		Boston, Mass.	1836
Merchant, J.	J.MERCHANT in oblong	New York City	1795
Merkler, John H.		" " "	1788
Merrifield, Thomas V. Z.		Albany, N. Y.	1840
Merriman, C.		New York City	1825
Merriman, Marcus	M.M in engrailed oval; M.M. between parallel curves, convexed on upper sides and closed at ends; M.M in oblong; eagle, M, and wheat shock each in square	Cheshire, Conn. New Haven, Conn.	1762 1787

†Where no mark is given, the maker used his name or initials.

SILVERSMITHS	MARKS	LOCATIONS	PERIOD
Merriman, Reuben	†	Litchfield, Conn.	1827
Merriman, Samuel	S.Merriman in rectangle	Cheshire, Conn.	1794
Merriman, Silas		New Haven, Conn.	1760
Merriman & Bradley	M & B, tree above the &, in circle on rectangle; M & B, bird above the &, in circle on rectangle	" " "	1817
Merriman, Marcus & Co.	M M&CO in escalloped rectangle; staff of wheat in circle	" " "	1806
Merriman & Tuttle		" " "	1802
Merrow, Nathan		East Hartford, Conn.	1783
Michaels, James		New York City	1820
Miksch, John M.	I·M·MIKSCH	Bethlehem, Pa.	1775
Miles, John		Philadelphia	1785
Milhe, Stephen		"	1780
Millar, James		Boston, Mass.	1832
Millard, George		Philadelphia	1816
Miller, William	MILLER in rectangle; Miller in script capitals in oblong	"	1810
Miller & Son		"	1833
Millner, Thomas	T M in heavy capitals in cartouche; T M in oblong	Boston, Mass.	1690
Millon, Peter		New York City	1820
Milloudon, Phillippe		Philadelphia	1811
Mills, Edmund		"	1785
Mills, Edward		"	1794
Mills, John		"	1793
Milne, Edmund	E.MILNE in oblong; E M in oval cartouche; EM in a rude square	"	1757
Milné, F.		New York City	1800
Milne, Thomas		" " "	1795
Minott, Samuel	S M in box; M (script) in box; Minott in oblong; Minott (script) in rectangle	Boston, Mass.	1732
Minott & Austin (Samuel & Joseph)	Minnot and I A in rectangles	" "	1760
Minott & Simpkins (Samuel & William)	Minott (script) in rectangles and WS in rectangle	" "	1750
Minshall, William		Philadelphia	1773
Mitchell, Phineas		Boston, Mass.	1812
Mitchell, William	W. MITCHELL, rude capitals on scroll	" "	1820
Mix, James		Albany, N. Y.	1817
Mobbs, William		Buffalo, N. Y.	1835
Moffat, Charles H.		New York City	1830
Moffat, John L.		" " "	1815
Mood, Joseph	J MOOD and J MOOD in wavy-lined oblong; J&P MOOD in engrailed oblong	Philadelphia	1806
Moore, Charles		"	1804
Moore, John C.	J.C.M. in rectangle, followed by star, anchor, and M in rude circles	New York City	1835
Moore, John L.	J.L.M. in rectangles; J.L. MOORE in rectangle	" " "	1835

†Where no mark is given, the maker used his name or initials.

SILVERSMITHS	MARKS	LOCATIONS	PERIOD
Moore, Robert	†	——Maryland	1778
Moore, Thomas		Philadelphia	1805
Moore & Brewer		New York City	1835
Moore & Brown		" " "	1833
Moore & Ferguson		Philadelphia	1801
Morgan, John		"	1813
Mormagea, Michael		"	1816
Morris, John		New York City	1796
Morris, Sylvester		" " "	1797
Morris, William H.		" " "	1759
Morrison, Israel		Philadelphia	1823
Morse, David		Boston, Mass.	1798
Morse, Hazen		" "	1815
Morse, J. H.	J. H. MORSE in rectangle	" "	1792
Morse, Moses	M. MORSE in rectangle	" "	1816
Morse, Nathaniel	N M crowned, bird? below in a shield; N M in a rectangle	" "	1709
Morse, Stephen	MORSE in rectangle	" "	1764
Moseley, David	D Moseley, in rectangle; D M in rectangle; D Moseley (script) in rectangle	" "	1774
Moseley, Joseph		New York City	1830
Moses, Jacob	MOSES in oblong	Birmingham, Ga.‡	1768
Moses, M.		Boston, Mass.	1830
Moshore, John		New York City	1905
Moss, Isaac N.		Derby, Conn.	1781
Mott, John & William	MOTT'S in wavy-lined rectangle	New York City	1789
Mott, J. S.	J MOTT in rectangle	" " "	1790
Mott, W. & J. S.		" " "	1789
Moulinar, John	🔲🔲🔲	" " "	1744
Moulton, Abel	A.MOULTON in rectangle	Newburyport, Mass.	1815
Moulton, Ebenezer S.	E. S. Moulton (script) in oblong; MOULTON incised	Boston, Mass.	1796
Moulton, Enoch	E. MOULTON in rectangle, straight-lined on top and serrated on 3 sides	Portland, Me.	1801
Moulton, Joseph, I	J.M. in an engrailed rectangle; 🔲🔲🔲 J. MOULTON incised 🔲🔲🔲	Newburyport, Mass.	1680
Moulton, Joseph, II	MOULTON in heavy capitals	" "	1740
Moulton, Joseph, III		" "	1813
Moulton, William, I	W.MOULTON in rectangle; MOULTON in a rectangle; MOULTON incised	" "	1710
Moulton, William, II	W M in rectangle; MOULTON in rectangle	" "	1720
Moulton, William, III	MOULTON in rectangle	" "	1772
Moulton & Bradbury		" "	1796
Moulton & Davis		" "	1824
Mulford, John H.		Albany, N. Y.	1835
Mumford, H. G.		Providence, R. I.	1813

†Where no mark is given, the maker used his name or initials.

‡The town is correctly located in Georgia; it now has a population of 100.

SILVERSMITHS	MARKS	LOCATIONS	PERIOD
Munroe, James	[MUNROE] and JAMES MUNROE and PURE COIN in rectangles	Barnstable, Mass.	1824
Munson, Amos	†	New Haven, Conn.	1776
Munson, Cornelius		Wallingford, Conn.	1742
Murdock, James	[J.Murdock] [I.M.] [I.M.] [J.Murdock]	Philadelphia	1779
Murphy, James	J. MURPHY in oblong	"	1823
Musgrave, James	Musgrave (script) in shaped cartouche	New York City	1810
Myer, H. B.	H B Myer in oblong	" " "	1810
Myers, Albert		Philadelphia	1837
Myers, John	[I.MYERS] [I.Myer]	"	1796
Myers & Jacob		"	1839
Myers, Myer	MM (script) in oval; MM in rectangle; MM in cartouche; Myer (script) in shaped cartouche	New York City	1746
Mygatt, Comfort S.		Danbury, Conn.	1763–1823
Mygatt, David	D.MYGATT in escalloped rectangle	" "	1777–1822
Mygatt, Eli		" "	1742–1807
Mysendhender, ——		Philadelphia	1813
Nagles, John		Philadelphia	1748
Neuill, Richard		Boston, Mass.	1674
Neuss, Jan	I N, spray? below in a heart; the I is barred	Philadelphia	1698
Nevill, Richard		Boston, Mass.	1764
Newberry, Edwin C.		Mansfield, Conn.	1828
Newhall, Dudley		Salem, Mass.	1730
Newkirke, Joseph	I.N in oval; I.N. in rectangle	New York City	1716
Newman, Timothy H.	Newman (script) in cartouche	?	1799
Nichols, Bassett	NICHOLS in rectangle; anchor, star, and head in ovals	Providence, R. I.	1815
Nichols, William S.	W.S.N in rectangle; NICHOLS in rectangle	Newport, R. I.	1808
Nicherson, Baty		Harwich, Mass.	1825
Nixon, Richard		Philadelphia	1820
Noble, Joseph		Portland, Me.	1823
Norcross, Nehemiah		Boston, Mass.	1796
Norris, George		Philadelphia	1779
North, William B.	W.B.N in rectangle	"	1808
North & Co.		New York City	1823
Northee, David I.	D.I.NORTHEE in a rectangle; D N in rectangle	Salem, Mass.	1775
Northey, Abijah	A N in rectangle	" "	
Norton, Andrew		Goshen, Conn.	1787
Norton, Benjamin		Boston, Mass.	1810
Norton, C. C.	C C NORTON in rectangle	Hartford, Conn.	1820
Norton, Samuel		Hingham, Mass.	1795
Norton, Thomas	T N in rectangle	Farmington, Conn.	1796
Norton & Pitkin	C.C.NORTON in rectangle; & in rectangle; W. PITKIN in rectangle	Hartford, Conn.	1825

†Where no mark is given, the maker used his name or initials.

SILVERSMITHS	MARKS	LOCATIONS	PERIOD
Norwood, Richard	†	New York City	1774
Noyes, John	IN IN	Boston, Mass.	1695
Noyes, Samuel		Norwich, Conn.	1770
Noyes, N. & T. F.		?	
Nuttall, Joseph		——, Maryland	1778
Oakes, Frederick	OAKES in rectangles; OAKES in oblong	Hartford, Conn.	1825
Oakes & Spencer	O & S in rectangle	" "	1814
Obrihim, Joseph		Annapolis, Md.	1784
Odell, Lawrence		New York City	1830
Oertelt, Charles E.		Philadelphia	1831
Ogier, John		New York City	1791
Ogilvie, Gabriel		" " "	1791
Oliver, Andrew		Boston, Mass.	1722
Oliver, Daniel	D. OLIVER in a rectangle	Philadelphia	1805
Oliver, Peter	P.O in heart	Boston, Mass.	1682–1712
Olivier, Peter	P.O in engrailed rectangle	Philadelphia	1797
Olmstead, Nathaniel	N OLMSTEAD in rectangle, followed by bird in cartouche and P (probably a workman's mark) in cartouche	New Haven, Conn.	1826
Onclebagh, Garret	GBO, letter in each leaf of trefoil	New York City	1698
Osgood, J.		Salem, Mass.	1817
Osthoff, Andrew		Pittsburgh, Pa.	1815
Otis, John		Barnstable, Mass.	1706
Otis, Jonathan	J.Otis (script) in oblong; Otis in cartouche; I.O in a cartouche; Otis (small script) in cartoon; Otis (large) in rectangle	Newport, R. I.	1791
Ott, Daniel		New York City	1792
Ott, George	G. Ott (script) in oblong, Ott (script) in rectangle	Norfolk, Va.	1806
Overin, Richard		New York City	1702
Owen, Jesse	J SE E. OWEN in rectangle	Philadelphia	1794
Owen, John	I.OWEN in rectangle; OWEN in rectangle	"	1804
Paddy, Samuel		Boston, Mass.	1659
Painter, John		Philadelphia	1735
Palmer, James		New York City	1815
Palmer & Bachlader		Boston, Mass.	1815
Palmer & Clapp		New York City	1823
Palmer & Hinsdale		" " "	1815
Pancoast, Samuel		Philadelphia	1785
Paradice, William A.		"	1799
Paraset, William		"	1811
Parham, William		"	1785
Parie, Joseph		"	1811
Parisen, Otto	Parisen in rectangle	New York City	1763
Parisien, Otto W.		" " "	1791
Parisien, O. & Son	O P D P in oblong	" " "	1789
Parker, Daniel	D: P in rectangle ; D : PARKER in rectangle	Boston, Mass.	1727–1786

†Where no mark is given, the maker used his name or initials.

SILVERSMITHS	MARKS	LOCATIONS	PERIOD
Parker, George	G. PARKER in rectangle	Baltimore, Md.	1800
Parker, Isaac	I PARKER in rectangle	Deerfield, Mass.	1780
Parker, Richard	†	Philadelphia	1785
Parker, William H.		New York City	1835
Parkman, C.	C.PARKMAN in an oblong	Boston, Mass.	1790
Parkman, John	PARKMAN in oblong	" "	1748
Parkman, Thomas	T. PARKMAN in serrated rectangle	" "	1793
Parks, John		New York City	1791
Parmele, James		Durham, Conn.	1763–1828
Parmele, Samuel	S:Parmele (surname in script) in shaped cartouche; S.P in cartouche; S P in oval; S. Parmele (script) in oblong	Guilford, Conn.	1737–1803
Parry, Martin	PARRY in rectangle	Portsmouth, N. H.	1760
Parry, Rowland		Philadelphia	1795
Parry & Musgrave		"	1793
Parsons, ——	PARSONS in rectangle	"	1770
Pascal, William		"	1675
Paterson, George		New York City	1835
Pattit, Thomas		" " "	1796
Patton, Thomas		Philadelphia	1824
Paulgreen, Quam		"	1798
Paxson, John A.		"	1810
Peabody, John	J.PEABODY in rectangle	Enfield, Conn.	1799
Peale, Charles W.		Philadelphia	1765
Pear, Edward	E P in serrated square	Boston, Mass.	1836
Pearce, W.	{ W PEARCE / Va / Norfolk } in oval	Norfolk, Va.	1820
Pearse, Samuel		New York City	1783
Pearson, John	J.Pearson (script) in rectangle; I P in cartouche	" " "	1796
Peck, Lawrence M.		Philadelphia	1837
Peck, Timothy		Middletown, Conn.	1786
Pedosy, S.		Philadelphia	1810
Peiri, Joseph		"	1811
Pelletreau, Elias	E P in square	New York City / Southampton, L. I.	1750
Pelletreau, John		"	1785
Pelletreau, Maltby		New York City	1813
Pelletreau, William S.	W.S.P. in escalloped rectangle; W. S. PELLETREAU in an oblong	" " "	1807
Pelletreau & Upson		" " "	1818
Pepper, Henry I.	H.I.PEPPER in rectangle	Philadelphia	1828
Perkins, Houghton		Boston, Mass.	1762
Perkins, Isaac		Charlestown, Mass.	1707
Perkins, Jacob	I P crowned in shield	Newburyport, Mass. / Philadelphia	1768 / 1790
Perpignan, Peter		"	1809
Perpignan & Varnier		"	1800
Perraux, Peter	P.P in cartouche; PP in square	"	1797
Perret, Augusta		New York City	1801
Perret & Sandoz		" " "	1810

†Where no mark is given, the maker used his name or initials.

SILVERSMITHS	MARKS	LOCATIONS	PERIOD
Perry, Thomas	†	Westerly, R. I.	
Peters, James		Philadelphia	1821
Peters, R.		"	1807
Petit, Matthew	M.P in rectangle	New York City	1811
Pettit, Thomas		" " "	1791
Phelps, Jedediah		Great Barrington, Vt.	1781
Philip & Yver		Philadelphia	1796
Phillips, James D.	JAˢ D.PHILLIPS in rectangle	Cleveland, Ohio	1829
Phillips, Samuel		Salem, Mass.	1680
		Boston, Mass.	1721
Phyfe, William		" "	1836
Pickering, Charles		Philadelphia	1683
Pierce, Hart		New York City	1835
Pierce, John	PIERCE in an oblong	Boston, Mass.	1810
Pierce, O.	O·PIERCE in rectangle	" "	1824
Pierpont, Benjamin	B* PIERPONT, in a shaped oblong; BP very small in rectangle; PIERPONT in an oblong; B PIERPONT in cartouche	Roxbury, Mass.	1730–1797
Pierson, Phillip		New York City	1798
Pinchin, William		Philadelphia	1779
Pinto, Joseph		New York City	1758
Pitkin, Henry	H P, hollow block letters in cartouche	Hartford, Conn.	1811
Pitkin, James F.		East Hartford, Conn.	1834
Pitkin, John O.		" " "	1826
Pitkin, J. O. & W.	J. O. & W. PITKIN in rectangle	Hartford, Conn.	1826
Pitkin, Walter	W. PITKIN in rectangle, followed by a star, rooster, and P, in crudely made circles	" "	1808
Pitkin, William J.	WM J. PITKIN in rectangle	" "	1820
Pitkin, William L.	WM.L.PITKIN in rectangle	" "	1825
Pitkin & Norton	W.PITKIN, C C NORTON in rectangles	" "	1825
Pitman, Benjamin	B. PITMAN in rectangle; Pitman in rectangle	Providence, R. I.	1825
Pitman, John K.		" "	1805
Pitman, Sanders	PITMAN in rectangle; Pitman in rectangle	" "	1732–1804
Pitman, William R.		New Bedford, Mass.	1835
Pitman & Dodge		Providence, R. I.	1790
Pitman & Dorrance		" "	1795
Pitts, Richard	PITTS (script) in cartouche	Philadelphia	1741
Pitts, A.		"	1790
Plain, Edward		New York City	1835
Planquet, Gregory		" " "	1797
Platt, George W.		" " "	1820
Platt, James		" " "	1835
Platt, N. C.		" " "	1820
Platt & Brother	PLATT & BROTHER in rectangle; G.W. & N.C. PLATT in rectangle	" " "	1816
Poincignon, Francis		Philadelphia	1796
Poincy, Peter		"	1813
Pointe, James		"	1813

†Where no mark is given, the maker used his name or initials.

SILVERSMITHS	MARKS	LOCATIONS	PERIOD
Pointe & Tanguy	†	Philadelphia	1811
Poissenot, N. J.		"	1806
Poissonier, Francis		"	1795
Poland, P.		"	1837
Polgrain, Quom		"	1797
Polhamus, J.		New York City	1802
Pollard, William	W.P in rectangle; W.P in cartouche	Boston, Mass.	1690
Poncet, Lewis		Baltimore, Md.	1790
Pons, Thomas	PONS in rectangle; PONS in engrailed oblong	Boston, Mass.	1757–1817
Poor, Nathaniel		" "	1829
Porter, F. W.	F.W.PORTER in oblong	New York City	1820
Porter, Henry C.		" " "	1820
Porter, H. C. & Co.	H. PORTER & CO. in rectangle	" " "	1830
Portram, Abraham	AP, fleur-de-lis below, in a heart; AP in a heart	" " "	1727
Post, Samuel		New London	1783
Potter, J. O. & J. R.		Providence, R. I.	1810
Potwine, John	IP (separated by a diamond shaped pellet) in a rectangle; IP with a pellet between the letters in a shield with shaped top; I:Potwine in a shaped cartouche; I·Potwine in an oblong. When the name is used the initials are in Roman capitals, the other letters in *script*.	Hartford, Conn.	1698–1792
Potwine & Whiting		" "	1761
Poupard, Jas.		Boston, Mass.	1751
Powell, C. F.		" "	1746
Powelson, Chas.		Albany, N. Y.	1840
Pratt, Henry		Philadelphia	1730
Pratt, Nathan	N.PRATT in rectangle	Essex, Conn.	1772–1842
Pratt, Phineas		Lyme, Conn.	1747–1813
Pratt, Seth		" "	1764
Price, Benjamin		Boston, Mass.	1767
Price, John		Lancaster, Pa.	1764
Prince, Job		Milford, Conn.	1680–1764
Putnam, Edward		Salem, Mass.	1710
Putnam, Rufus		Albany, N. Y.	1814
Quaritus, Frederick		New York City	1835
Quincy, Daniel		Boston, Mass.	1684
Quintard, Peter	PQ in cartouche; Pq in rectangle; P.Q in rectangle	New York City	1731
Rabeth, Jas.		New York City	1835
Rait, David		" " "	1835
Rait, Robert	R.RAIT in rectangle	" " "	1830
Rasch, Anthony	ANTY RASCH in oblong; Sterling above the word silver, in rectangle	Philadelphia	1807
Rasch & Willig		"	1819
Ravee, Xavier		"	1796
Reed, A. G. & Co.		Nassau, N. H.	1835

†Where no mark is given, the maker used his name or initials.

SILVERSMITHS	MARKS	LOCATIONS	PERIOD
Reed, Isaac	†	Stamford, Conn.	1776
Reed, Isaac & Son	I.REED & SON in rectangle	" "	1810
Reed, Lewis		New York City	1810
Reed, Osman	O.REED PHILA in rectangles	Philadelphia	1840
Reeder, Abner	A.REEDER in rectangle	"	1797
Reeder, John		"	1835
Reeves, Enos	REEVES in rectangle	Charleston, S. C.	1775
Reeves, Stephen	S.Reeves (script) in shaped rectangle	Burlington, N. J.	1767
Revere, Edward		Boston, Mass.	1796
Revere, J. W.		" "	1798
Revere, Paul‡		" "	1735–1818
Revere, Paul, Sr.		" "	1702–1754
Revere, 3d, Paul		" "	1795
Revere, Thomas	T R in rectangle	" "	1789
Revere & Son		" "	1796
Reynolds, Theodore J.		Philadelphia	1835
Rice, Henry P.	H.P.RICE in rectangle	Albany, N. Y.	1815
Rice, Joseph T.	Rice (script)in cartouche	Baltimore, Md.	1785
Rice, Joseph T.	Joseph T. Rice (script) in rectangle and Albany (script) in rectangle; J.T.Rice (script) in rectangle	" "	1835
Rich, Obadiah	O.RICH and BOSTON, each in rectangle; O.RICH * BOSTON*	Boston, Mass.	1824
Richard, Augustus		Philadelphia, Pa.	1818
Richard, Stephen	SR in square; S.RICHARDS in rectangle	" "	1793
Richards, Samuel	SRichard, in shaped oblong; S.RICHARD in rectangle	New York City	1828

---

†Where no mark is given, the maker used his name or initials.

‡To distinguish the marks of the two Paul Reveres is often a matter of difficulty unless one has some extraneous evidence of the origin of the silver of which provenance is sought.

The following statemets should help:

Revere, Senior, alone used the marks: P'REVERE in a rectangle and (2d) P. Revere, italic script, in a rectangle, and (3d) P R in a crowned shield.

Paul Revere, Jr., used the mark REVERE in a rectangle; his fathern ever did; he also used P. R script in a rectangle, sometimes in conjunction with REVERE.

The following marks are also attributed to Paul Revere, the son: P R in a rectangle; P R incised; and REVERE in a rectangle. The points of the V are joined to the two Es.

One should know that tea or coffee *sets* were not made in the lifetime of the elder Revere. This often will prove a decisive factor, as the younger Revere made a number of tea sets.

Writing upon this subject to the author, Judge A. T. Clearwater says: "Paul Revere, the patriot, ordinarily used the mark REVERE, although there are authenticated pieces upon which he used the marks of P. R. but they are rare. There are, as well, pieces made by the elder Revere which were finished, particularly as to the engraving, by the son. They also are "unusual." Upon such pieces it might be possible that both silversmiths would place their marks.

Mr. Charles O. Cornelius, replying to an inquiry upon this subject, was kind enough to give me an opinion which agrees with that of Judge Clearwater.

Another help lies in the fact that the initial mark of the father appears in a crowned shield, while that of the son is in a rectangle or simply incised. Writing to the author upon this subject, Mr. Henry Davis Sleeper says:

"My intensive experience for many years collecting Paul Revere silver leads me to believe that the very large majority of the silver done by him or in his shop during his life, was marked REVERE with a pellet before it, in a rectangle, and the father's marked exactly as you have it, P. REVERE or P. R. . . . All of the twenty-three pieces of silver, many of them large ones, which I gave to the Boston Museum have a pedigree as I acquired pieces only of which I could get complete proof as to ownership from the first to the final owner . . . were all under Revere, the son's time, and were all marked REVERE with a pellet in a rectangle. I have also several pieces of Revere, Senior, all of which are marked P. R. or P. REVERE."

SILVERSMITHS	MARKS	LOCATIONS	PERIOD
Richards, Thos.	†	New York City	1815
Richards, W.		Philadelphia	1813
Richards, W. & S. R.		"	1818
Richards & Williamson	RICHARDS & WILLIAMSON in rectangle	"	1798
Richardson, Francis	FR in a heart	"	1718
Richardson, Joseph	JR and IR in rectangles	"	1730
Richardson, Joseph, Jr.	J.R. in a square	"	1777
Richardson, J. & N.	I.NR (N and R conjoined) in a cartouche	"	1785
Richardson, Richard		"	1793
Richmond, Franklin	F.RICHMOND in rectangle	Providence, R. I.	1815
Richmond, G. & A.		" "	1815
Ridgeway, James		Boston, Mass.	1789
Ridgeway, John	J:RIDGEWAY in rectangle	" "	1807
Ridout, George	G R in rectangle	New York City	f. 1745
Ried, Johan		Philadelphia	1810
Rielly, Bernard		New York City	1835
Riggs, Richard	RIGGS in rectangle; Riggs in shaped cartouche; RR in cartouche	Boston, Mass.	1814
Riker, Peter	P. RIKER in oblong	New York City	1797
Riker & Alexander		" "	1800
Ritter, Michael		" " "	1786
Roath, Roswell W.		Norwich, Conn.	1826
Robbins, Elisha		Philadelphia	1831
Robert, Christopher	⬭CR⬭	New York City	1731
Roberts, Frederick		Boston, Mass.	1770
Roberts, Michael		New York City	1786
Roberts & Lee		Boston, Mass.	1772
Robertson, Alexander		Philadelphia	1740
Robertson, Robert		"	1777
Robinson, Anthony W.	A ROBINSON in rectangle	"	1798
Robinson, Benjamin		"	1818
Robinson, Israel		"	1840
Robinson & Harwood		"	1814
Rockwell, Edward	ROCKWELL in rectangle; ROCK-WELL in engrailed rectangle	New York City	1807
Rockwell, R.			
Rockwell, Thomas	Rockwell in oblong	Norwalk, Conn.	1775
Rodier, Peter G.		New York City	1825
Roe, W.	W.ROE in rectangle; W ROE in oblong cartouche with a wheat sheaf (horizontal) in an oblong	Kingston, N. Y.	1805
Roff, ——		New York City	1813
Roe & Stollenwerck	W.ROE & STOLLENWERCK	" " "	1800
Rogers, Augustus		Boston, Mass.	1830
Rogers, Daniel	D.ROGERS in oblong	New York City	1835
Rogers, Daniel		Newport, R. I.	1750
Rogers, Joseph	I.R in cartouche; I.R in oval	" "	1760
Rogers Wm.	Wm. ROGERS HARTFORD in rectangles	Hartford, Conn.	1801–1873

†Where no mark is given, the maker used his name or initials.

SILVERSMITHS	MARKS	LOCATIONS	PERIOD
Rollingson, Wm.	†	New York City	1783
Romney, John		" " "	1770
Roosevelt, Nicholas	N.R (diagonal line through R) in rudely drawn oval N.R (diagonal line through R in oblong)		
Rose, Anthony		New York City	1755
Roshore, John		" " "	1792
Roshore & Prime		" " "	1825
Ross, Robert		Federika, Del.	1789
Round, John		Portsmouth, N. H.	1634
Rouse, Anthony		Philadelphia	1807
Rouse, Michael		Boston, Mass.	1711
Rouse, William	WR with two pellets in shaped oval; WR, star, and three pellets in cartouche; WR with two crosses in cartouche	" "	1660
Royalston, John		" "	1770
Russel, Daniel	DR in outlined leaf	Newport, R. I.	1721
Russel, John H.	[mark]	New York City	1792
Russel, Jonathan	.RUSSELL in irregular rectangle	Ashford, Conn.	1804
Russelier, Peter		New York City	1794
Russell, Moody	MR in oval; MR in cartouche	Barnstable, Mass.	1715
Ryerson, Lou	L.Ryerson (script) in shaped rectangle	York, Pa.	1760
Sackett & Williard		Providence, R. I.	1815
Sadd, Hervey	H.SADD in rectangle	New Hartford, Conn.	1798
Sadtler, Philip	P. Sadtler (script) in rectangle	Baltimore, Md.	1819
Saint Martin, Anthony		Philadelphia	1796
Sanderson, Benjamin	B S in two rectangles	Boston, Mass.	1617
Sanderson, Robert	R S, with sun above; RS with moon above; RS with stars above, each in rectangle	" "	1638
Sanderson, Robert, Jr.		" "	1638
Sanderson, William		New York City	1799
Sandford, F. S.		Nantucket, Mass.	1828
Sandford, William		" " "	1817
Sandoz, Philip A.		Philadelphia	1814
Sandoz & Brother		New York City	1811
Sands, Stephen		" " "	1774
Sanford, Isaac		Hartford, Conn.	1785
Sardo, Michael		Baltimore, Md.	1817
Sargeant, Ensign	E.SARGEANT in rectangle	Boston, Mass.	1820
Sargeant, Jacob	J SARGEANT in rectangle; head in circle; sheaf of wheat in rectangle; HARTFORD in rectangle	Hartford, Conn.	1785
Savage, Edward		Philadelphia	1794
Savage, Thomas	T S with star below, in shield	Boston, Mass.	1689
Savage, Thomas, Jr.		" "	1719
Sawin, Silas	SS in rectangle; SS in oval	" "	1823
Sawin, Silas W.		New York City	1835
Sawyer, H. L.	H.L. SAWYER in rectangle	" " "	1840
Sayre, Joel	J.SAYRE in rectangle	" " "	1802

†Where no mark is given, the maker used his name or initials.

SILVERSMITHS	MARKS	LOCATIONS	PERIOD
Sayre, John	I.SAYRE in rectangle; I.Sayre (script) in shaped rectangle; spread eagle in rectangle	New York City	1796
Sayre & Richards	S & R in oval; S & R in rectangle	" " "	1802
Scarret, Joseph		Philadelphia	1797
Schaats, Bartholomew	B S in square; B S in heart with cross below letters	New York City	1708
Schaffield, Jeremiah	†	Philadelphia	1785
Schanck, Garret	G.SCHANCK in rectangle, m in rectangle, sheaf of wheat in square	New York City	1791
Schanck, John	J.SCHANCK in rectangle; m in rectangle; the m is workman's mark	" " "	1797
Schofield, Solomon		Albany, N. Y.	1815
Scott, John B.		New York City	1820
Scrymageour, James		" " "	1835
Scwind, John		" " "	1790
Seal, William	W. SEAL in rectangle	Philadelphia	1816
Sears, Matthew		New York City	1835
Sebastien, Jeanne L.		" " "	1814
Segn, George		Philadelphia	1820
Selkirk, William		New York City	1817
Sell, J.		" " "	1800
Senemand, John B.		Philadelphia	1798
Seveignes, Jacques		New Orleans, La.	1822
Sevrin, Lewis		Philadelphia	1837
Sexnine, Simon		New York City	1722
Seymour, Joseph		" " "	1835
Sharp, W.		Philadelphia	1835
Shaw, Edward G.		"	1825
Shaw, John A.	J. SHAW in rectangle; I.A.SHAW in wavy-lined rectangle	Newport, R. I.	1819
Shaw & Dunlevey		Philadelphia	1833
Shepherd, Robert	R Shepherd (script) in shaped rectangle	Albany, N. Y.	1805
Shepherd & Boyd	S & B in rectangle; SHEPHERD & BOYD in an oblong	" "	1810
Shepherd, Robt.	R. Shepherd (script) in shaped rectangle	" "	1805
Shepper, John D.		Philadelphia	1818
Shethar, Samuel		Litchfield, Conn.	1801
Shethar & Gorham		New Haven, Conn.	1806
Shethar & Thompson		Litchfield, Conn.	1801
Shields, Caleb		Baltimore, Md.	1773
Shields, Thomas	T S in rectangle; TS in rectangle with curved end	Philadelphia	1768
Shipman, Nathaniel	NS in rectangle; N.SHIPMAN in rectangle	Norwich, Conn.	1790
Shiving, Godfrey		Philadelphia	1779
Shoemaker, Charles		New York City	1825
Shoemaker, Joseph	J.SHOEMAKER in rectangle	Philadelphia	1793
Shonnard, George		New York City	1797
Shopshire, Robert		Baltimore, Md.	1778
Shreve, Benjamin		Boston, Mass.	1834
Sibley, Clark		New Haven, Conn.	1801

†Where no mark is given, the maker used his name or initials.

SILVERSMITHS	MARKS	LOCATIONS	PERIOD
Sibley, J.	J.SIBLEY in rectangle	New Haven, Conn.	1810
Sibley & Marble	S & M in rectangle	" " "	1801
Silliman, Hezekiah	†	" " "	1767
Sime, William		Birmingham, Ga.	1768
Sime & Moses		" "	1768
Simes, William	W.S in rectangle; W.SIMES in rectangle; W.SIMES in engrailed rectangle	Portsmouth, N. H.	1794
Simmons, Andrew		Philadelphia	1796
Simmons, Anthony	A.Simmons (script) in rectangle; A.S. in oblong	"	1797
Simmons, James	J. Simmons (script) in rectangle	New York City	1815
Simmons, Joseph		Philadelphia	1828
Simmons, J. & A.	J. & A. SIMMONS in rectangle; J. & A. S in rectangle	New York City	1805
		" " "	1816
Simmons, Peter		Philadelphia	
Simmons, S.	S.SIMMONS in rectangle	"	1797
Simmons & Alexander	SIMMONS & ALEXANDER in shaped rectangle	"	1798
Simpkins, Thomas B.	T.B.Simpkins (script) in irregular rectangle	Boston, Mass.	1749
Simpkins, William	W. Simpkins in plain cartouche; W.SIMPKINS in cartouche; W S in rectangle; Simpkins (script) in cartouche	"	1726
Singleton & Young		New York City	1800
Sixte, Joseph A.		Philadelphia	1837
Sixte, Vincent B.		"	1837
Skerry, George W.		Boston, Mass.	1837
Skinner, Abraham		New York City	1756
Skinner, Elizer		Hartford, Conn.	1826
Skinner, Matt	MATT SKINNER in oblong	Philadelphia	1752
Skinner, Thomas	T S in cartouche; SKINNER in oblong	New York City	1733
Slidell, Joshua		" " "	1765
Sloan, William		Hartford, Conn.	1794
Smith, Christian		Philadelphia	1820
Smith, David	D.SMITH in rectangle	——, Va.	1778
Smith, Ebenezer		Brookfield, Conn.	1775
Smith, George		Philadelphia	1831
Smith, George O.		New York City	1825
Smith, I.	I.S in rectangle	Boston, Mass.	1742
Smith, Jacob		Philadelphia	1809
Smith, James		New York City	1794
Smith, James		Philadelphia	1807
Smith, John		"	1819
Smith, Joseph	I.SMITH in rectangle	Boston, Mass.	1789
Smith, Joseph		Philadelphia	1804
Smith, J. & T.		Baltimore, Md.	1817
Smith, Levin H.		Philadelphia	1837
Smith, Robert	R.E.SMITH in rectangle	"	1820
Smith, Samuel		"	1785
Smith, William		New York City	1770
Snyder, George		Philadelphia	1816

†Where no mark is given, the maker used his name or initials.

SILVERSMITHS	MARKS	LOCATIONS	PERIOD
Solomon, Samuel	†	Philadelphia	1811
Sonnier, Joseph		"	1811
Souque, Michael		New York City	1794
Soumain, Samuel		Philadelphia	1754
Soumaine, Simeon	S S in rectangle	New York City	1719
Sowerlt, Anthony	Sowerlt, script in cartouche	Philadelphia	1823
Sparrow, Henry		"	1811
Spear, Isaac		Boston, Mass.	1836
Spencer, George		Essex, Conn.	1810
Spencer, James		Hartford, Conn.	1793
Squire, S. P.	S. P. SQUIRE in rectangle	New York City	1835
Squire & Lander	SQUIRE & LANDER incised	" " "	1840
Stacy, P.	P. STACY in rectangle	Boston, Mass.	1819
Stall, Joseph		Baltimore, Md.	1804
Staniford, John	J S in cartouche; Staniford (script) in shaped oblong	Windham, Conn.	1789
Stanton, Daniel	D. Stanton in oblong	Stonington, Conn.	1755
Stanton, Enoch		" "	1745
Stanton, Zebulon	Z S in rectangle; STANTON in rectangle	" "	1753
Stanwood, Henry B.	Henry B. Stanwood in rectangle	Boston, Mass.	1739
Staples, John J.	J.J.S in rectangle; IIS in oval	New York City	1788
St. Cyr, S. L.		New Orleans, La.	1822
Stebbins, E. & Co.		New York City	1825
Stebbins, T. E.	T.STEBBINS in oval; STEBBINS in rectangle	" " "	1810
Stebbins & Howe	STEBBINS & HOWE in rectangle	" " "	1815
Stedman, Alexander		Philadelphia	1793
Steele, John		Annapolis, Md.	1710
Stephanis, Gothelf		New York City	1791
Stephen, Thomas H.		Philadelphia	1839
Stephens, George	G. S in cartouche	New York City	1790
Steven, George		" " "	1719
Stevens & Lakeman	STEVENS & LAKEMAN in rectangle	Salem, Mass.	1825
Stewart, C. W.		New York City	1840
Stewart, John	Stewart (script) in oval cartouche	" " "	1791
Stickler, John		" " "	1823
Stickney, Jonathan, Jr.	I.STICKNEY in rectangle	Newburyport, Mass.	1796
Stickney, M. P.	M. P. STICKNEY in rectangle	" "	1820
Stiles, Benjamin		Woodbury, Conn.	1831
Stillman, Alexander		Philadelphia	1806
Stillman, E.	E.Stillman in oblong oval	Stonington, Conn.	1825
Stillman, Richard	R.STILLMAN in rectangle	Philadelphia	1805
Stilman, William		Hopkinton, R. I.	1788
Stinson, William		New York City	1813
Stockerman & Pepper	STOCKERMAN & PEPPER in rectangle	Philadelphia	1840
Stockman, Jacob		" "	1828
Stodder & Frobisher	STODDER & FROBISHER in rectangle	Boston, Mass.	1817
Stollenwerck & Brother	Stollenwerck, italics in cartouche	New York City	1805
Stollenwerck & Co.	Stollenwerck & Co. in shaped cartouche	" " "	1800
Stone, Adam		Baltimore, Md.	1804

---

†Where no mark is given, the maker used his name or initials.

SILVERSMITHS	MARKS	LOCATIONS	PERIOD
Stone & Osborn	†	New York City	1796
Strom, A. G.	A.G.STROM in engrailed rectangle	Albany, N. Y.	1830
Strom & Son	STROM & SON, script in a shaped rectangle	Albany, N. Y.	1835
Storrs, N.	N.STORRS in rectangle	New York City	1825
Storrs & Cooley	S & C in shaped cartouche, diamond centre	" " "	1832
Stout, Samuel		Princeton, N. J.	1779
Stoutenburgh, Tobias,	T S B in crude rectangle	New York City	1731
Stow, John		Wilmington, Del.	1772
Strong, John		——, Md.	1778
Strong, William		Philadelphia	1807
Stuart, H.		New York City	1808
Stuart, John	Stuart (script) in oval	Providence, R. I.	1720
Stuckert, Isaac		Philadelphia	1809
Sullivan. D. & Co.	D. SULLIVAN & CO in wavy-lined rectangle	New York City	1820
Supplee, Jacob		Philadelphia	1791
Sutherland, George		Boston, Mass.	1810
Sutton, Robert		" "	1820
Swan, Caleb		" "	1775
Swan, Robert	R : SWAN in rectangle	Philadelphia	1799
Swan, William	Swan (script) in cartouche	Worcester, Mass.	1736
Sweetser, Henry P.		" "	1768
Symmes, John		Boston, Mass.	1766
Syng, Daniel		Lancaster, Pa.	1734
Syng, Philip	P S in rectangle	Philadelphia	1715
Syng, Philip, Jr.	P S in double circle, followed by star in cartouche	"	1727
Taber, William		"	1835
Tanguy, John	J TANGUY in rectangle	"	1801
Tanguy, J. & P.		"	1808
Tanguy, Peter		"	1810
Tanguy, Repiton		"	1806
Tanner, John		Newport, R. I.	1740
Targee, John	I.T in rectangle; calyx of lily (?); I T (script) in shaped cartouche	New York City	1794
Targee, J. & P.	1 & P T, a letter *a* and three four unrecognizable objects in cartouches; I.P.TARGEE in rectangle	" " "	1811
Targee, Peter		" " "	1811
Targee, William		" " "	1807
Taylor, George W.		Philadelphia	1824
Taylor, John		New York City	1801
Taylor, Najah		" " "	1793
Taylor, Thomas		Providence, R. I.	1727
Taylor, William		Philadelphia	1772
Taylor & Hinsdale	T & H in rectangle; head, lion, and a workman's mark (G?) in cartouche	New York City	1801
Taylor & Lawrie		Philadelphia	1837
Tempest, Robert		"	1814

†Where no mark is given, the maker used his name or initials.

SILVERSMITHS	MARKS	LOCATIONS	PERIOD
Ten Eyck, Jacob	I T in cartouche (I barred); ITE (TE in monogram) in box	Albany, N. Y.	1728
Ten Eyck, Koenraet	K T E (T E in monogram) in cartouche	New York City	1699
Terry, Geer	G TERRY in oblong	Enfield, Conn.	1802
Terry, John	†	New York City	1820
Terry, L. B.	L.B. TERRY in rectangle	Enfield, Conn.	1810
Terry, William‡	Wm.TERRY in an oblong	" "	1785
Thaxter, Joseph B.		Hingham, Mass.	1815
Theofile, William		New Orleans, La.	1822
Thibault, Felix		Philadelphia	1814
Thibault, Francis		"	1800
Thibault, Francis & Felix	.THIBAULT in rectangle	"	1807
Thibault, Frederick		"	1818
Thibault, Fred'k & Felix		"	1813
Thibault Bros.	THIBAULT	"	1810
	BROTHERS in rectangle	"	1810
Thibault & Co.		"	1797
Thomas, Thomas		New York City	1784
Thomas, Walter		" " "	1769
Thomas, William		Trenton, N. J.	1775
Thompson, D. B.	D.B.Thompson in rectangle	Litchfield, Conn.	1825
Thompson, Isaac	I. THOMPSON in rectangle	" "	1801
Thompson, James		Brooklyn, N. Y.	1834
Thomson, Peter		Philadelphia	1835
Thomson, James		New York City	1834
Thomison, Peter		Boston, Mass	1817
Thomson, William	W.Thomson (script) in shaped oblong	New York City	1810
Thornton, Henry		Providence, R. I.	1824
Tiley, James	I.TILEY in oblong cartouche	Hartford, Conn.	1765
Tingley, Samuel	S I (script) in cartouche; N York (script) in shaped cartouche; I. Tingley (script) in shaped cartouche	New York City	1767
Tisdale, B. H.	B H TISDALE in rectangle; B H Tisdale (script) in rectangle	Providence, R. I.	1824
Titcomb, Francis	F. TITCOMB in rectangle	Newburyport, Mass.	1813
Tompkins, Edmund		Waterbury, Conn.	1779
Touzell, John	J.TOUZELL in oval cartouche	Salem, Mass.	1756
Towson, Obadiah		Philadelphia	1819
Tracy, Erastus		Norwich, Conn.	1791
Tracy, Gordon		" "	1787
Tripler, Christian		New York City	1794
Troll, William		Philadelphia	1810
Troth, James		Pittsburgh, Pa.	1800
Trott, J. P. & Son	I.P.T. & Son in rectangle	New London, Conn.	1820
Trott, John P.	J.P.T. in engrailed rectangle; J:P TROTT in oval cartouche	" " "	1769
Trott, Jonathan	J. TROTT in oval; J Trott (script) in oval	Boston, Mass.	1760
Trott, Jonathan, Jr.		New London, Conn.	1800
Trott, Thomas	T.T in rectangle; T:T crowned in rectangle	Boston, Mass.	1722

---

†Where no mark is given, the maker used his name or initials.

‡This may be the "Wilbert" Terry referred to by Ensko. Terry silver spoons, straight sided, in the author's collection are plainly marked as above. The period is 1785.

SILVERSMITHS	MARKS	LOCATIONS	PERIOD
Trott & Brooks	T & B in rectangle	New London, Conn.	1798
Trott & Cleveland	T & C in oblong	" " "	1792
Truax, Henry R.	H R T in rectangle	Albany, N. Y.	1815
Trumbul, Richard	†	Boston, Mass.	1767
Tucker, Daniel		Portland, Me.	1781
Tucker, John W.		New York City	1803
Turner, James	I.T in oval	Boston, Mass.	1744
Tuthill, Christopher		Philadelphia	1730
Tuttle, Bethuel		New Haven, Conn.	1802
Tuttle, William		" " "	1821
Tyler, Andrew	A TYLER in oblong	Boston, Mass.	1715
Tyler, D. M.	D.M.TYLER in rectangle	" "	1810
Tyler, David	D T in shield; D T in cartouche	" "	1781
Tyler, George	G T in square	" "	1761
Ubelin, Frederick		Philadelphia	1773
Ufford & Burdick	U & B in rectangle	New Haven, Conn.	1812
Underhill, Andrew	A.U in oval; A UNDERHILL in rectangle	New York City	1780
Underhill, Thomas	T U in square	" " "	1787
Underhill & Vernon	T.V in rectangle; I.V in cartouche	" " "	1787
Underwood, John		Philadelphia	1797
Vail, Elijah		Troy, N. Y.	1836
Vaissiere, Victor		New York City	1816
Valet, Peter		" " "	1787
Vallee, Antoine		New Orleans, La.	1822
Van Bergen, John		Albany, N. Y.	1813
Van Beuren, Peter	VB in monogram crowned in circle	New York City	1797
Van Beuren, William	W.V.B in cartouche	" " "	1790
Vanderbrugh, Cornelius		" " "	1677
Vanderhan, J.	I V (script) capitals in cartouche	Philadelphia	1740
Vanderspiegel		New York City	1701
Vanderspiegel, Johannes	S S IV in cartouche; IV in trefoil; IVS in rectangle; IVS in cartouche P	" " "	1687
Van Dyke, Peter	P V D in oblong; V D in trefoil; P V D in oval; P.V.D in oval	" " "	1705
Van Dyke, Richard	R V D in cartouche	" " "	1750
Van Horn, David		Philadelphia	1801
Van Ness & Waterman	V & W in oblong	New York City	1835
Van Riper, Tunis		" " "	1813
Van Veghten, Henry		Albany, N. Y.	1760
Van Vleit, B. C.	BVANVLEIT incised	Poughkeepsie, N. Y.	1840
Van Voorhis, Daniel	D.V.VOORHIS in rectangle; bird in diamond; D V VOORHIS in rectangle; D V in rectangle with a bird in a kite; D V in cartouche with bird in kite	New York City	1779
Van Voorhis & Coley		" " "	1786
Van Voorhis & Schanck	V V & S in rectangle with bird in kite	" " "	1791

---

†Where no mark is given, the maker used his name or initials.

SILVERSMITHS	MARKS	LOCATIONS	PERIOD
Van Voorhis & Son	†	New York City	1798
Varney, John		Philadelphia	1795
Veazie, Joseph		Providence, R. I.	1815
Vergereau, Peter	P V in cartouche; P.V in cartouche	New York City	1720
Vernon, J. & Co.		" " "	1798
Vernon, John	I.V in oval; I V in oval; conventional battle-ax and two other figures in cartouche	" " "	1787
Vernon, N. & Co.	N.VERNON & CO in serrated rectangle	Charleston, S. C.	1800
Vernon, Nathaniel	N.VERNON in rectangle; NV in rectangle	" "	1798
Vernon, Samuel	S V a small device below, all in a heart	Newport, R. I.	1714
Vernon & Park		Pittsburgh, Pa.	1815
Vilant, William	W V, a swallow beneath, in heart	Philadelphia	1725
Villard, R. H. L.	*Villard* in rectangle	Georgetown, Dist. of Col.	1833
Vincent, Richard		Baltimore, Md.	1799
Vinton, David	D.V in rectangle	Providence, R. I.	1790
Wachner, F. W.		New York City	1819
Waddill, Noel		Petersburg, Va.	1778
Waglin, Thomas		Philadelphia	1837
Wagstaff, Thomas		New York City	1791
Wait & Wright		Philadelphia	1837
Waldron, D.	D WALDRON in oblong	New York City	1789
Walker, George	G. WALKER in oblong	Philadelphia	1797
Walker, Hannah	H WALKER in serrated oblong; PHIA in oblong	"	1816
Walker, John, Jr.		"	1798
Walker, W. & G.		"	1795
Walker, William	W. WALKER in oblong	"	1793
Waller, John		"	1763
Wallis, Thomas		"	1804
Walton, Daniel		"	1808
Walworth, Daniel		Middletown, Conn.	1785
Ward, Ambrose		New Haven, Conn.	1767
Ward, Bartholomew & Brainard		Hartford, Conn.	1809
Ward, Billious	B.W in shaped cartouche; BW in cartouche; BW in oval	Guilford, Conn.	1750
Ward, James	WARD and HARTFORD, each in rectangle; JW in oval followed by HARTFORD as above	Hartford, Conn.	1789
Ward, John	WARD 67 MARKET ST	" "	1805
Ward, John		Philadelphia	1808
Ward, Richard		Boston, Mass.	1815
Ward, Samuel L.		" "	1830
Ward, Timothy		Middletown, Conn.	1766
Ward, William	W.W. in rectangle; W.Ward in a shaped cartouche	Guilford, Conn.	1730
Ward, William		Litchfield, Conn.	1757

†Where no mark is given, the maker used his name or initials.

SILVERSMITHS	MARKS	LOCATIONS	PERIOD
Ward & Bartholomew	WARD & BARTHOLOMEW in rectangle; Hart ford in rectangle W & B in rectangle	Hartford, Conn.	1804
Ward & Cox	†	" "	1811
Ward & Gavett		" "	1813
Ward & Hughes	W & H in rectangle; 1846 in the apexes of a diamond	Middletown, Conn.	1805
Ward & Miller		Philadelphia	1822
Ward & Rich		Boston, Mass.	1830
Wardin, Daniel		Bridgeport, Conn.	1811
Warner, Andrew E.	A E WARNER in serrated rectangle, followed by 11 in rectangle; AE W in cartouche	Baltimore, Md.	1811
Warner, Andrew E. Jr.‡		" "	1837
Warner, A. E. & T. H.	T.&A.E.WARNER in rectangle; followed by STERLING in rectangle	" "	1805
Warner, Caleb	C.WARNER in rectangle and PURE SILVER COIN in a shaped rectangle	Portsmouth, N. H.	1805
Warner, D.	D.WARNER in wavy-lined rectangle	Ipswich, Mass.	1810
Warner, Joseph		Philadelphia	1811
Warner, Joseph	J. Warner in rectangle	Wilmington, Del.	1768
Warner, Samuel	SW in rectangle	Philadelphia	1797
Warner, Thomas H.	T.WARNER in rectangle‡	Baltimore, Md.	1805
Warner & Fellows		Portsmouth, N. H.	1824
Warren, Benjamin		Philadelphia	1809
Waters, Samuel	S.WATERS in cartouche	"	1790
Watkins, James		New York City	1819
Watling, James		Philadelphia	1837
Watson, E.	E. WATSON in rectangle; E:Watson (script) in oblong	Boston, Mass.	1821
Watson, J.	J. WATSON in rectangle	Philadelphia	1820
Watson & Brown	WATSON & BROWN in rectangle	"	1820
Watts, J. & W.		"	1829
Watts, James		"	1835
Watts, John W.		New York City	1794
Waynes, Richard		Philadelphia	1750
Weathers, Michael		New York City	1794
Weaver, Emmor T.	WEAVER (script) on ribbon	Philadelphia	1808
Webb, Barnebus		Boston, Mass.	1762
Webb, Charles		Philadelphia	1738
Webb, Robert		"	1798
Webb, James		Baltimore, Md.	1817
Webb & Boon		Philadelphia	1785
Webster, Henry L.	H.L.WEBSTER in rectangle	Providence, R. I.	1831
Wedge, S.		Baltimore, Md.	1804
Weeden, Peleg		North Kingstown, R. I.	1803
Welles, A. & G.	A & G WELLES in rectangle	Boston, Mass.	1804
Welles, Andrew		Hebron, Conn.	1804
Welles, George I.	WELLES; BOSTON; in rectangles	Boston, Mass.	1804

---

†Where no mark is given, the maker used his name or initials.
‡See footnote under Kirk.

SILVERSMITHS	MARKS	LOCATIONS	PERIOD
Welles & Co.	WELLES & CO. in rectangle	Boston, Mass.	1810
Welles, James M.	†	New York City	1835
Wells, L. & C.		" " "	1798
Wells, L. & H.		" " "	1794
Wells, Lemuel	L W in rectangle	" " "	1790
Wells, William		Hartford, Conn.	1828
Wendover, John	J.W in cartouche; J W in shield	New York City	1694
Wenman, Barnard	B.WENMAN in rectangle; B W in rectangle followed by N YORK in rectangle	" " "	1789
West, Benjamin	B.WEST in rectangle	Boston, Mass.	1770
West, Charles		" "	1830
West, Joseph		Philadelphia	1797
Weston, Benjamin		"	1797
Westphal, Charles W.	C. WESTPHAL in rectangle	"	1802
Whartenby, John		"	1829
Whartenby, Thomas	T.W in box; WHARTENBY in oblong	"	1811
Whartenby & Bunn		"	1816
Wheatley, Frederick G.		New York City	1805
Wheaton, Calvin	C. WHEATON in engrailed rectangle	Providence, R. I.	1791
White, Alfred		Boston, Mass.	1807
White, Amos	A.WHITE in rectangle; WHITE in rectangle	East Hadden, Conn.	1770
White, Edward	E:WHITE in rectangle	Ulster Co., N. Y.	1757
White, George L.		Cincinnati, Ohio	1822
White, Peregrine	P. WHITE in rectangle	Woodstock, Conn.	1774
White, Peter		Norwalk, Conn.	1738
White, Samuel		New York City	1805
White, Silas	S. WHITE in rectangle	" " "	1791
White, Stephen		" " "	1805
White, William		Philadelphia	1805
White, William J.		New York City	1835
White, William W.	Wm. W. WHITE in rectangle	" " "	1835
Whiteman, Ira		" " "	1761
Whiting, B.	B:WHITING in rectangle	Norwich, Conn.	1755
Whiting, Charles	C W in cartouche; WHITING in rectangle	" "	1749
Whiting, S.		" "	1700
Whitlock, Thomas B.	Whitlock (script) in oblong	New York City	1805
Whitlock, William H.	Wm. H. WHITLOCK in rectangle	" " "	1805
Whitney, Amos		" " "	1800
Whitney, E.	E. WHITNEY in rectangle; WHITNEY in an oblong	" " "	1805
Whitney & Hoyt	WHITNEY & HOYT in rectangle	" " "	1808
Whiton, Ezra	E.WHITON (script) in oval cartouche	Boston, Mass.	1836
Whittaker & Green		Providence, R. I.	1825
Whittemore, William	Whittemore in oblong	Portsmouth, N. H.	1730
Wickham, Daniel H.		New York City	1835
Willcox, Alvan		New Haven, Conn.	1805
Willcox, Cyprian		" " "	1827
Williams, Alexander		Philadelphia	1807
Williams, Charles M.		New York City	1825
Williams, Deodat		Hartford, Conn.	1776

†Where no mark is given, the maker used his name or initials.

SILVERSMITHS	MARKS	LOCATIONS	PERIOD
Williams, John	†	Philadelphia	1793
Williams, Samuel		"	1796
Williams, Stephen		Providence, R. I.	1799
Williams, W. A.	W. A. WILLIAMS in rectangle	Washington, D. C.	1829
Williams, W. W.		" "	1829
Williamson, Samuel	S.W in rectangle; S W in oval; WIL-LIAMSON in rectangle	Philadelphia	1794
Willig, George		"	1819
Willis, J.		Boston, Mass.	1820
Willis, Stilman	S. WILLIS in oblong	" "	1823
Wills, Henry		New York City	1774
Wilmot, Samuel	WILMOT in engrailed rectangle; S. WILMOT in rectangle	New Haven, Conn.	1798
Wilmot, T. T.	T. T. Wilmot in rectangle	" " "	1810
Wilmot & Stilliman		" " "	1800
Wilson, Albert		Troy, N. Y.	1834
Wilson, Hosea	H.WILSON in rectangle	Philadelphia	1812
		Baltimore, Md.	1819
Wilson, James		Trenton, N. J.	1769
Wilson, John		Philadelphia	1770
Wilson, R. & W.	R & W W in rectangle; R & W WIL-SON rectangle	"	1825
Wilson, Robert	R.W in an oval	New York City	1805
Wilson, S.		Philadelphia	1805
Wilson, S. & S.	S & Wilson in engrailed rectangle; and S & Wilson, with S reversed in engrailed rectangle	"	1805
Wilson, Thomas		"	1837
Wilson, William		"	1829
Wiltberger, Christian	CWiltberger, (script) in a shaped cartouche	"	1793
Wiltberger & Alexander		"	1797
Winslow, Edward	E W, a trefoil (?) below all in a cartouche; E W in rectangle; E W in a double circle	Boston, Mass.	1702
Winsor, William		" "	1759
Wishart, Alexander		New York City	1808
Wishart, Daniel		" " "	1825
Wishart, Hugh	H.WISHART in rectangle; WISHART in an oblong	" " "	1784
Wishart, William		" " "	1800
Wolf, Francis H.		Philadelphia	1829
Wolf, James G.		"	1831
Wolfe & Wriggins	WOLFE & WRIGGINS in oblong	"	1837
Wood, Benjamin B.	B.WOOD in oval cartouche	New York City	1805
Woodcock, Bancroft	S W in oval; .WOODCOCK in long oval	Wilmington, Del.	1754
Woodruff, Enos		Cincinnati, Ohio	1820
Woodruff & White		" "	1829
Woods, Freeman	Woods (script) in shaped cartouche F.W. (script) in cartouche	New York City	1791
Woodward, Antipas	A W in rectangle; Woodward in rectangle	Middletown, Conn.	1791

†Where no mark is given, the maker used his name or initials.

SILVERSMITHS	MARKS	LOCATIONS	PERIOD
Woodward, Charles	†	New York City	1825
Woodward, Eli		Boston, Mass.	1812
Wool, Jeremiah W.		New York City	1791
Wriggin & Co.		Philadelphia	1831
Wriggins, Thomas		"	1837
Wright, Alexander		——, Maryland	1776
Wright, John F.		Philadelphia	1831
Wyatt, Joseph		"	1797
Wyer, Eleazer, Jr.	E. WYER in rectangle	Boston, Mass.	1773
Wyer & Farley	WYER & FARLEY in oblong	Portland, Me.	1828
Wyer & Noble		" "	1823
Wynkoop, Benjamin	W K in a heart B	New York City	1675-1729
Wynkoop, Cornelius		" " "	1726
Wynkoop, Jacobus		" " "	1765
Yeomans, Elijah		Hadley, Mass.	1771
Yettons, Randell		Philadelphia	1739
Young, Alexander	A.YOUNG in rectangle	Camden, S. C.	1800
Young, Ebenezer		Hebron, Conn.	1778
Young, Levi		Bridgeport, Conn.	1827
Young, William		Philadelphia	1761

†Where no mark is given, the maker used his name or initials.

of the bottom of the piece and on the under side. It was then taken to the Farmer-general, and he, or his representative, placed the "charge" mark as near as possible to the other two. The piece was then carried away and finished, the workman taking care not to obliterate the marks. If the bottom of the piece was "belled" out the marks would be deformed but not effaced.

After the work was completed it was again taken to the Farmer-general who placed upon it his little "punch of discharge," after having collected the tax computed upon its weight. This mark, unlike the others, was placed upon the edge or rim of the piece. The piece was now ready for the market.

Until 1784 the date letter was the same for all of France. That system was then superseded by one that gave to each town a distinctive letter and provided for the use of date latters by all of them but Paris. That was allotted a crowned P with the date between the crown and the P. 1785 would be represented by the figures 85. They are so minute that they escape notice unless one exercises care or possesses extraordinary acuity of vision.

The marks of charge and discharge were employed until the law of April, 1791, abolished all the taxes on silver. The law November, 1797, re-imposed the duty but it was levied with the imposition of the first stamp, which denotes both the standard and the payment of the duty.

There are two other marks besides those mentioned above that find a place in the law of November 19, 1797:

1. The punch *de hasard*.

2. The punch variously called *recense*, verification, and recognition.

The punch *de hasard* was applied to ancient pieces that for some reason (age would be one) had not been marked.

The *recense* mark was a confirmatory mark which testified to the genuineness of the stamps already upon the piece and the purported standard. It is not clear as to whether the *recense* could or could not be demanded by a private individual uncertain as to the genuineness of a recent purchase or to settle a dispute. The ordinance of Louis Philippe (April, 1838), which required the *recense*, was a precautionary device against counterfeiting and was employed under some secret system. There were a hundred and thirty-eight of these devices used. They were struck on a *bigorne* anvil in the manner I have described elsewhere. With the head of Minerva we frequently find as an assay mark the head of a woman, in full face with neck exposed; she looks to the right and there is a letter P at the left side of the neck. The P is the Paris mark. Boivin says that there is a variation of this mark with a figure 1 (denoting the higher standard) replacing the P. He is clearly in error. Apart from the fact that I have never seen such a mark, we know that the assay mark never, of itself, indicated the standard. It only guaranteed that the silver was of the quality represented by the standard mark. In other words, the woman's head just described would be the same on a piece bearing the Minerva head with the figure 1 as it would be on a piece bearing the lower standard mark, a head of Minerva with the numeral 2.

CHAPTER XXV

Marks on Paris Plate

DATE LETTERS

a	1461	x	1504	s	1546	p	1589	M	1632
b	1462	y	1505	t	1547	q	1590	N	1634
c	1463	z	1506	v	1548	r	1591	O	1635
d	1464	a	1507	x	1549	s	1592	P	1636
e	1465	b	1507	y	1550	t	1593	Q	1637
f	1466	c	1508	z	1551	v	1594	R	1638
g	1467	d	1509	a	1552	x	1595	S	1639
h	1468	e	1510	b	1553	x	1596	T	1640
i	1469	f	1511	c	1554	z	1597	V	1641
k	1470	g	1512	d	1555	a	1598	X	1642
l	1471	h	1513	e	1556	b	1599	Y	1643
m	1472	i	1514	f	1557	c	1600	Z	1644
n	1473	k	1515	g	1558	d	1601	A	1645
o	1474	l	1516	h	1559	e	1602	B	1646
p	1475	m	1517	i	1560	f	1603	C	1648
q	1476	n	1518	k	1561	g	1604	D	1649
r	1477	o	1519	l	1562	h	1605	E	1650
s	1478	p	1520	m	1563	i	1606	F	1651
t	1479	q	1521	n	1564	k	1607	G	1652
v	1480	r	1522	o	1565	l	1608	H	1653
x	1481	s	1523	p	1566	m	1609	I	1654
y	1482	t	1524	q	1567	n	1610	K	1655
z	1483	v	1525	r	1568	o	1611	L	1656
a	1484	x	1526	s	1569	p	1612	M	1657
b	1485	y	1527	t	1570	q	1613	N	1658
c	1486	z	1528	v	1571	r	1614	O	1659
d	1487	a	1529	x	1572	s	1615	P	1660
e	1488	b	1530	y	1573	t	1616	Q	1661
f	1489	c	1531	z	1574	v	1617	R	1662
g	1490	d	1532	a	1575	x	1618	S	1663
h	1491	e	1533	b	1576	y	1619	T	1664
i	1492	f	1534	c	1577	z	1620	V	1665
k	1493	g	1535	d	1578	A	1621	X	1666
l	1494	h	1536	e	1579	B	1622	Y	1667
m	1495	i	1537	f	1580	C	1623	Z	1668
n	1496	k	1538	g	1581	D	1624	A	1669
o	1497	l	1539	h	1582	E	1625	B	1670
p	1498	m	1540	i	1583	F	1626	C	1671
q	1499	n	1541	k	1584	G	1627	D	1672
r	1500	o	1542	l	1585	H	1628		
s	1501	p	1543	m	1586	I	1629		
t	1502	q	1544	n	1587	K	1630		
v	1503	r	1545	o	1588	L	1631		

VINCENT FORTIER (Louis xiv)
1672 — 1680

D	1672	I	1677
E	1673	K	1678
F	1674	K	1679
G	1675	K	1680
H	1676		

PAUL BRION de SAUSSOY (Louis xiv)
1680 — 1684

K	1680	N	1682
L	1680	O	1683
M	1681	P	1684

ÉTIENNE RIDEREAU (Louis xiv)
1684 — 1687

P	1684	R	1686
Q	1685	S	1687

JACQUES LÉGER (Louis xiv)
1687 — 1691

S	1687	X	1690
T	1688	X	1691
V	1689		

PIERRE POINTEAU (Louis xiv).
1691 — 1698

X	1691			B	1695
Y	1692			C	1696
Z	1693			D	1697
A	1694			E	1698

PERRINE (Louis xiv).
1698 — 1703

E	1698			H	1701
F	1699			I	1702
G	1700			K	1703

ÉTIENNE BALIGNY (Louis xiv).
1703 — 1713

K	1703			Q	1709
L	1704			R	1710
M	1705			S	1711
N	1706			T	1712
O	1707			V	1713
P	1708				

FLORENT SOLLIER.
1713 — 1717

(Louis xiv).				(Régence).	
V	1713			Z	1716
	1714			A	1717
Y	1715				

ÉTIENNE DE BOURGES (Régence).
1717 — 1722

A	1717	D	1720
B	1718	E	1721
C	1719	F	1722

CHARLES CORDIER.
1722 — 1726

(Régence).

		(Louis xv).	
		G	1723
		H	1724
F	1722	I	1725
		K	1726

JACQUES COTTIN (Louis xv).
1726 — 1732

K	1726	O	1730
L	1727		1731
M	1728	Q	1732
N	1729		

HUBERT LOUVET (Louis xv).
1732 — 1738

Q	1732	V	1736
R	1733	X	1736
S	1734		1738
T	1735		

ROBIN (Louis xv).
1738 — 1744

	1738	A	1740
		B	1742
	1739	C	1743
		D	1744

ANTOINE L'ECHAUDEL (Louis xv)
1744 — 1750

D	1744		
E	1745	H	1748
F	1746	I	1749
G	1747	K	1750

JULIEN BERTHE (Louis xv).
1750 — 1756

K	1750	O	1754
L	1751	P	1755
M	1752		1756
N	1753		

ELOI BRICHARD (Louis xv).
1756 — 1762

	1756		
R	1757	V	1760
S	1758	X	1761
T	1759	Y	1762

JEAN-JACQUES PREVOST (Louis xv).
1762 — 1768

Y	1762		
Z	1763		C 1766
A	1764		D 1767
B	1765		E 1768

JULIEN ALATERRE (Louis xv).
1768 — 1774

E	1768		H 1771
F	1769		I 1772
G	1770		K 1773
			L 1774

J.-B. FOUACHE (Louis xvi).
1774 — 1780

L	1774		P 1778
M	1775		Q 1779
N	1776		
O	1777		R 1780

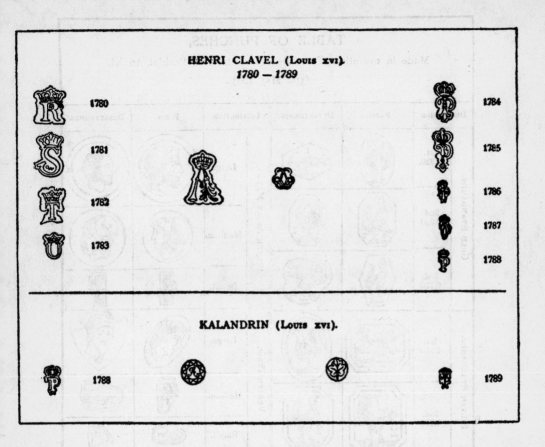

HENRI CLAVEL (Louis xvi)
1780 — 1789

1780   1784
1781   1785
1782   1786
1783   1787
        1788

KALANDRIN (Louis xvi).

1788   1789

The Decree of 9 November, 1797, also provided for the verification of pieces of silver of foreign or of undetermined origin; in the latter case the pieces were termed *de hasard*, and the mark is so designated.

DISTINCTION		PARIS.	DEPARTMENTS.
FOREIGN.	Large.		
	Small.		
HAZARD.			

TABLE OF PUNCHES,

Made in execution of the Decree of the 11th Prairial, An XI.

(31st May 1803).

At this epoch there were two small assay marks for gold: the first for articles with garniture; the other without.

Note.—The use of these punches ceased on the 16th of August 1819. The same day they were replaced by those of the Standard and Assay drawn in the following tables. The punches of the Ingots and the Argué were not renewed.

Note.—The above table is according to Markham & Chaffers.

DECREE OF 9TH NOVEMBER, 1797.	DECREE OF 1ST SEPTEMBER, 1809

Higher standard mark for silver (.950). The numeral is also found on the left side of the cock.

Higher standard mark for silver.

Lower standard mark for silver (.800).

Lower standard mark for silver (.800).

The assay office mark for large pieces of silver; sometimes the figures are inverted.

Assay office marks for large pieces of silver.

Assay office mark for small pieces of silver.

Assay office mark for small pieces of silver.

Confirmation (recense) mark of the assay office on pieces of silver made during the period current with the time of stamping. Modern pieces.

Recense marks of the assay office.

Confirmation mark for old pieces of silver.

This head often appears on silver marked with the head of Minerva. See table of marks under the Decree of 1835.

Note.—The above marks are according to Boivin.

It seems that the recense mark was originally designed to settle the question of authenticity. It was affirmative. In England the procedure was different. There was no confirmation, but, if the marks were forged, or fraudulent (i.e. substituted) they would be erased. At a later period the Paris Assay Office used the recense mark to check frauds upon the revenue and compelled all silversmiths to re-submit their marked wares so that this mark might be applied to those found genuine.

TABLE OF PUNCHES,

Made in execution of the Royal Ordinance of 22nd October 1817.

DISTINCTION.		PARIS.	DEPARTMENTS.	DISTINCTION.		PARIS.	DEPARTMENTS.
GOLD STANDARDS.	1st. 0.920			SILVER ASSAY.	Large.		
	2nd. 0.840				Medium.		None for the Departments.
	3rd. 0.750				Small.		See the Table of Divisional Punches.
SILVER STANDARDS.	1st. 0.950			VERIFICATION.	Large.		
	2nd. 0.800				Small.		See the Table of Divisional Punches.
GOLD ASSAY.	Large.			FOREIGN.	Large.		
	Small.		See the Divisional Punches.		Small.		

REMARKS.—1. In the figure of the large punch of Assay of gold and silver, and of Verification, is engraved the number of the Department as shown in the list of Assay Offices. 2. The numeral indicative of each standard is engraved in the figure of the punches which serve to standard the works of gold and silver.

Note.—The above table is according to Markham & Chaffers.

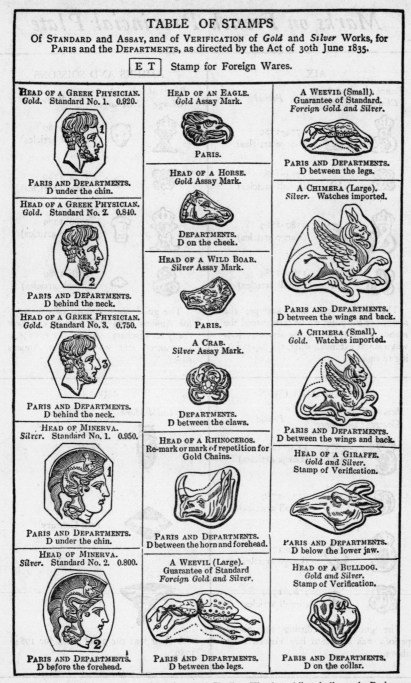

TABLE OF STAMPS

Of Standard and Assay, and of Verification of *Gold* and *Silver* Works, for Paris and the Departments, as directed by the Act of 30th June 1835.

| E T | Stamp for Foreign Wares. |

Head of a Greek Physician.
Gold. Standard No. 1. 0.920.

Paris and Departments.
D under the chin.

Head of a Greek Physician.
Gold. Standard No. 2. 0.840.

Paris and Departments.
D behind the neck.

Head of a Greek Physician.
Gold. Standard No. 3. 0.750.

Paris and Departments.
D behind the neck.

Head of Minerva.
Silver. Standard No. 1. 0.950.

Paris and Departments.
D under the chin.

Head of Minerva.
Silver. Standard No. 2. 0.800.

Paris and Departments.
D before the forehead.

Head of an Eagle.
Gold Assay Mark.

Paris.

Head of a Horse.
Gold Assay Mark.

Departments.
D on the cheek.

Head of a Wild Boar.
Silver Assay Mark.

Paris.

A Crab.
Silver Assay Mark.

Departments.
D between the claws.

Head of a Rhinoceros.
Re-mark or mark of repetition for Gold Chains.

Paris and Departments.
D between the horn and forehead.

A Weevil (Large).
Guarantee of Standard
Foreign Gold and Silver.

Paris and Departments.
D between the legs.

A Weevil (Small).
Guarantee of Standard.
Foreign Gold and Silver.

Paris and Departments.
D between the legs.

A Chimera (Large).
Silver. Watches imported.

Paris and Departments.
D between the wings and back.

A Chimera (Small).
Gold. Watches imported.

Paris and Departments.
D between the wings and back.

Head of a Giraffe.
Gold and Silver.
Stamp of Verification.

Paris and Departments.
D below the lower jaw.

Head of a Bulldog.
Gold and Silver.
Stamp of Verification.

Paris and Departments.
D on the collar.

Note.—The above table is according to Markham and Chaffers. The dotted lines indicate the Paris punches.

CHAPTER XXVI

Marks on French Provincial Plate

AIX

Punch of Charge	Punch of Discharge	Period
		1774–1780 (Large articles)
		1774–1780 (Small articles)
		1780–1789 (Large articles)
		1780–1789 (Small articles)

The above were state stamps; the stamps of the guild which guaranteed the standard (.958) during the above periods was a single extended wing, the top pointing to right.

AMIENS AND SOISSONS

Punch of Charge	Punch of Discharge	Period
		1774–1780 (Large articles)
		1774–1780 (Small articles)
		1780–1789 (Large articles)
		1780–1789 (Small articles)

The guild mark (punch of guaranty) for Amiens 1784–1789 was a crossbow ready for discharge. After May 1, 1838, a six-pointed star was used for Amiens silver.

ALENÇON AND CAEN

Punch of Charge	Punch of Discharge	Period
		1774–1780 (Large articles)
		1774–1780 (Small articles)
		1780–1789 (Large articles)
		1780–1789 (Small articles)

The guild mark during the above periods was a potato bug viewed from above.

ARRAS

Guild Mark	Period
	1451
	15th Century
	16th Century

A chair was the guild mark for 1784–1789.

BAYONNE

Guild Mark	Period
	1690

Punch of Charge

 1774–1780 (Large articles)

 1774–1780 (Small articles)

A bird cage was the guild mark for 1774–1780. A footprint was the discharge mark for small articles.

BORDEAUX

Punch of Charge	Punch of Discharge	Period
		1774–1780 (Large articles)
	?	1774–1780 (Small articles)
		1780–1789 (Large articles)
		1780–1789 (Small articles)

BESANÇON

Guild Mark	Period
	1430
	15th Century
	Early 16th Century
	17th Century

BOURGES

Punch of Charge	Punch of Discharge	Period
		1774–1780 (Large articles)
		1774–1780 (Small articles)
		1780–1789 (Large articles)
		1780–1789 (Small articles)

The guild mark for 1774–1780 for small articles (.843) was the head of an ape. For large articles, 1774–1791, a bell denoted the higher standard (.958).

CHÂLONS–SUR–MARNE

Punch of Charge	Punch of Discharge	Period
		1774–1780 (Large articles)
		1774–1780 (Small articles of lower standard. A hand for the higher standard.)
		1780–1789 (Large articles)
		1780–1789 (Small articles)

GRENOBLE

Punch of Charge	Punch of Discharge	Period
		1774–1780 (Large articles)
		1774–1780 (Small articles)
		1780–1789 (Large articles)
		1780–1789 (Small articles)

DIJON

Punch of Charge	Punch of Discharge	Period
		1774–1780 (Large articles)
		1774–1780 (Small articles)
		1780–1789 (Large articles)
		1780–1789 (Small articles)

LA ROCHELLE

Punch of Charge	Punch of Discharge	Period
		1774–1780
		1774–1780
		1780–1789
		1780–1789

LIMOGES

Punch of Charge	Punch of Discharge	Period
		1774–1780
		1774–1780
		1780–1789
		1780–1789

MARSEILLES

Guild Mark	Period
	1760
	1780

MONTPELLIER

Guild Mark	Period
	14th Century
	15th Century
	18th Century

Cripps

Punch of Charge	Punch of Discharge	Period
		1774–1780
		1774–1780
		1780–1789

LYON

Punch of Charge	Punch of Discharge	Period
		1774–1780
		1774–1780
		1780–1789
		1780–1789

MOULINS AND ORLEANS		
Punch of Charge	*Punch of Discharge*	*Period*
		1774–1780
		1774–1780
		1780–1789
		1780–1789

RENNES		
Punch of Charge	*Punch of Discharge*	*Period*
		1774–1780
		1774–1780
		1780–1789
		1780–1789

POITIERS		
Punch of Charge	*Punch of Discharge*	*Period*
		1774–1780
		1774–1780
		1780–1789
		1780–1789

RIOM		
Punch of Charge	*Punch of Discharge*	*Period*
		1774–1780
		1774–1780
		1780–1789
		1780–1789

ROUEN			ST. GERMAIN		
Punch of Charge	*Period*		*Punch of Charge*	*Punch of Discharge*	*Period*
					1780–1789 (Large articles)
	1408				1780–1789 (Small articles)

SOISSONS

	Period
	*circa* 1715

|  | 16th Century |

TOULOUSE

	Period
	18th (?) Century

Punch of Discharge

		1774–1780

TOULOUSE AND MONTAUBAN

Punch of Charge	*Punch of Discharge*	*Period*
		1774–1780
		1774–1780

| | | 1774–1780 |
| | | 1774–1780 |

|  |  | 1780–1789 |
|  | | 1780–1789 |

| | | 1780–1789 |
| | | 1780–1789 |

TOURS			VERSAILLES	
Punch of Charge	*Punch of Discharge*	*Period*	*Punches*	*Period*
		1774–1780	Two large Roman "L"s one reversed; oak leaves intertwined, surmounted by a crown, all in a shaped cartouche	1780–1789 (Large articles)
		1774–1780	P. L. in ornamented script capitals in monogram, all in a shaped cartouche	1780–1789 (Small articles)
		1780–1789		
		1780–1789		

CHAPTER XXVII

Marks on German Plate

AIX-LA-CHAPELLE		ALTENBURG	
Inspection Mark	*Period*	*Inspection Mark*	*Period*
	15th and 16th Century		1639
	15th and 16th Century		1684
	16th Century		
	16th Century		17th–18th Century
	1573–1624 and later		

Aachenes 1705
1705
M
ACH   1723

 1808
(The G may be a warden's mark.)

 Second Half of the 19th Century

The numerals 12, 13, 14, appearing with German marks on silver indicate the number of sixteenths of pure silver contained in the article, 12 being equivalent to .750 fine; 13, .8125, etc.

In modern times the standard of the German Empire has been .800. Goods destined for abroad are made of higher standards and are appropriately marked: .925 "Sterling," .950, etc.

ALTONA		AUGSBURG			
Inspection Mark	Period	Inspection Mark	Period	Inspection Mark	Period
	1703				
	1748		Middle of the 16th Century		
	1761				Middle of 17th Century
	1782				
	1797		16th–17th Century		
	Middle of the 19th Century				
ANSBACH					Early 18th Century
Inspection Mark	Period				
	16th–17th Century				
	17th Century		16th–17th Century		
	17th–18th Century				
	17th–18th Century				
	18th Century				1735–1736
	18th Century				

AUGSBURG—*Continued.*

Inspection Mark	Period	Inspection Mark	Period	Inspection Mark	Period
			1751–1753		1765–1767
	1736–1737				
			1753–1755		1767–1769
	1737–1739				
	1739–1741		1755–1757		1769–1771
			1757–1759		
	1741–1743				1771–1773
	1743–1745		1759–1761		1773–1775
	1745–1747		1761–1763		1775–1777
	1747–1749				1777–1779
	1749–1751		1763–1765		1779–1780

AURICH

Inspection Mark	Period
	16th Century
	19th Century

BADEN–BADEN

Inspection Mark	Period
	16th Century
	16th–17th Century
	17th Century

BAMBERG

Inspection Mark	Period
	15th and early 16th Century
	1618
	1626
	1639
	17th and early 18th Century

BAMBERG—*Continued.*

Inspection Mark	Period
	17th and early 18th Century
	18th Century
	First half of 18th Century
	Middle of 18th Century
	End of 18th Century
	18th and first half of 19th Century

BERLIN	
Inspection Mark	*Period*
	Second half of 17th Century
	First half of 18th Century
	1735 or earlier
	Second half of 18th Century
	18th Century to its close
	19th Century

BIBERACH	
Inspection Mark	*Period*
	18th and 19th Century

BREMEN	
Inspection Mark	*Period*
	19th Century
	17th and 18th Century
	17th Century

BRESLAU	
Inspection Mark	*Period*
	From 1539 to 1553
	16th and early 17th Century
	Early 17th Century
	Middle 17th Century
	Second half 17th Century and to 1721
	1730–1740

BRESLAU—*Continued.*		BRUCHSAL	
		(A town of Baden)	
Inspection Mark	*Period*	*Inspection Mark*	*Period*
	Late 18th Century and to 1842		17th and 18th Century
	Punch used for .8125 silver 1710–1795	**BRUNSWICK**	
		Inspection Mark	*Period*
	Since 1843		End of 16th Century
A	1710–1712		
B	1712–1721		16th–17th Century
B	1721–1727		
C	1727–1737		17th Century
D	1737–1745		
F	1746–1758		
G	1758–1760		Second half of 17th Century
G	1761–1776		
H	1776–1791		
S	1839–1849		Early 18th Century
T	1849–1861		

CASSEL

Inspection Mark	Period
	1658
	17th Century
	17th and 18th Century
	18th Century
E	
F	18th and 19th Century
G	
K	
L	

COBLENZ

Inspection Mark	Period
	18th Century

COLMAR

Inspection Mark	Period
	16th and 17th Century

COLOGNE

Inspection Mark	Period
	16th Century
	16th and 17th Century

The last of these marks combined throughout the second half of the 17th Century but surmounted by date letters A, B, etc.

Inspection Mark	Period
A	
B	
C	Latter half of 17th Century
D	

COLOGNE—*Continued.*

Inspection Mark	Period
	First half of 18th Century
	Middle of 18th Century
	Close of 18th Century

The numerals indicate the number of sixteenths of pure silver, i.e., .8125 or .75.

DAGEBÜLL

Inspection Mark	Period
	17th Century
	17th and 18th Century

DANZIG

Inspection Mark	Period
	16th and 17th Century
	17th Century
	Second half of 17th Century
	17th and early 18th Century

DARMSTADT

Inspection Mark	Period
	16th and 17th Century
	17th and 18th Century
	18th and 19th Century
	19th Century

DAVENSTADT

Inspection Mark	Period
*	Uncertain

DESSAU

Inspection Mark	Period
D	17th Century
D	
D	18th–19th Century
D	
D	19th Century

DILLINGEN

Inspection Mark	Period
	First half 18th Century
	Second half 18th Century

DRESDEN

Inspection Mark	Period
D	16th–17th Century
D	17th Century
*	First quarter of 18th Century
	1730
	1737
	1739
	Middle of 18th Century

*The significance of the numerals 12, 13, 14 is explained in note on p. 315.

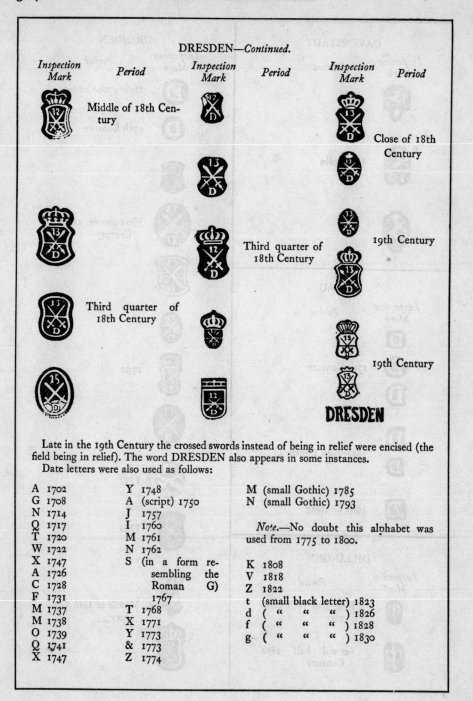

DRESDEN—*Continued.*

Inspection Mark	Period	Inspection Mark	Period	Inspection Mark	Period
	Middle of 18th Century				Close of 18th Century
			Third quarter of 18th Century		19th Century
	Third quarter of 18th Century				19th Century

Late in the 19th Century the crossed swords instead of being in relief were encised (the field being in relief). The word DRESDEN also appears in some instances.

Date letters were also used as follows:

A	1702	Y	1748	M (small Gothic) 1785
G	1708	A (script)	1750	N (small Gothic) 1793
N	1714	J	1757	
Q	1717	I	1760	*Note.*—No doubt this alphabet was
T	1720	M	1761	used from 1775 to 1800.
W	1722	N	1762	
X	1747	S (in a form re-		
A	1726		sembling the	K 1808
C	1728		Roman G)	V 1818
F	1731		1767	Z 1822
M	1737	T	1768	t (small black letter) 1823
M	1738	X	1771	d (" " ") 1826
O	1739	Y	1773	f (" " ") 1828
Q	1741	&	1773	g (" " ") 1830
X	1747	Z	1774	

DÜSSELDORF	
Inspection Mark	**Period**
	17th Century
	17th and 18th Century
	17th and 18th Century
	18th Century
*	

DÜSSELDORF—*Continued.*	
Inspection Mark	**Period**
*	
	18th Century

ELBERFELD	
Inspection Mark	**Period**
	17th Century

ELBING	
Inspection Mark	**Period**
	1657
	1693–1753
	1705
	1742

*The significance of the numerals 12, 13 is explained in the note on p. 315

EMDEN

Inspection Mark	Period
	1474 (?)
	16th Century
	1601
	1603
	1612
	1632
	1634
	1645
	1820

ENGEN

Inspection Mark	Period
	17th Century

ERFURT

Inspection Mark	Period
	16th Century
	16th–17th Century

ERFURT—*Continued.*

Inspection Mark	Period
	First half of 17th Century
	Second half 17th Century
	17th and 18th Century
	First half of 18th Century
	Second half 18th Century

ESSEN

Inspection Mark	Period
	Early 17th Century
	17th and 18th Century

EUTIN

Inspection Mark	Period
	1623

FRANKENSTEIN

Inspection Mark	Period
	Commencement of 18th Century

FRANKFORT-ON-MAIN

Inspection Mark	Period	Inspection Mark	Period
	Up to 1614		
			Middle of 18th Century
	17th Century		
			Middle of 18th Century
	17th–18th Century		
	Early 18th Century		
	Middle of 18th Century		End of 18th Century

FRANKFORT-ON-ODER

Inspection Mark	Period
	17th–18th Century
	1772

FRAUSTADT

Inspection Mark	Period
	17th and 18th Century

FREIBURG
(Baden)

Inspection Mark	Period
	1466
	1528
	16th Century
	1607
	1609

FREIBURG—*Continued.*
(Baden)

Inspection Mark	Period
	17th Century
	18th Century
	18th Century

FREIBURG
(Saxony)

Inspection Mark	Period
	1562
	End of 16th and beginning of 17th Century
	1654
	1658
	1660–1667
	1668
	18th Century
	18th–19th Century

FREISING

Inspection Mark	Period
	End of 17th Century
	18th Century

FRIEDBERG

Inspection Mark	Period
	17th Century

FULDA

Inspection Mark	Period
	circa 1715

FÜRTH

Inspection Mark	Period
	1769

GEBWEILER

Inspection Mark	Period
	End of 17th Century

GEISLINGEN

Inspection Mark	Period
	17th–18th Century

GLATZ

Inspection Mark	Period
	16th Century

GLOGAU

Inspection Mark	Period
	17th Century

GMUND

Inspection Mark	Period
	16th and 17th Century
	17th Century
	17th and 18th Century
	Middle of 18th Century
	18th and 19th Century

GNOIEN

Inspection Mark	Period
	18th Century

GÖRLITZ			GÜSTROW	
Inspection Mark	*Period*		*Inspection Mark*	*Period*
	16th Century		G	End of 17th to middle of 18th Century
	17th Century			Second half of 18th Century
	18th Century		**HALBERSTADT**	
			Inspection Mark	*Period*
GOTHA				Middle of 17th Century
Inspection Mark	*Period*			1697
	17th Century			
	1688			Early 18th Century
	1699			Early 18th Century
GRABOW				
Inspection Mark	*Period*			Middle 18th Century
Three stars above a crescent in a shield.	Uncertain			

HALL
(Swabia)

Inspection Mark	Period
	Second half of 16th Century
	17th Century
	17th Century
	18th Century

HALLE
(Saxony)

Inspection Mark	Period
	16th Century
	17th Century
	17th Century
	17th–18th Century
	18th Century

HAMBURG

Inspection Mark	Period
	End of 16th Century
	16th–17th Century
	17th Century

HAMBURG—*Continued.*

Inspection Mark	Period	Inspection Mark	Period
			Second Half of Century
	17th Century		17th and 18th Century
	1700		
			1711
			1743

The years continued to be represented by date letters.

Inspection Mark	Period
	1762
	(?)
	1785
	1800
	1820
	1821

Inspection Mark	Period
	17th and 18th Century

HANAU	
Inspection Mark	**Period**
	17th Century
	17th and early 18th Century
	Middle 18th Century
	18th Century

HANOVER—*Continued.*	
Inspection Mark	**Period**
	Early 18th Century
	Middle of 18th Century

HANOVER	
Inspection Mark	**Period**
	1640
	1644
	1663
	1665
	1670
	1686

HANOVER–NEUSTADT	
Inspection Mark	**Period**
	17th and 18th Century
	1726

HEIDELBERG	
Inspection Mark	**Period**
	17th and 18th Century
	18th Century

HEILBRONN		JAUER	
Identification Mark	*Period*	*Identification Mark*	*Period*
	1846		18th Century
	19th Century		

HILDESHEIM		KARLSRUHE	
Identification Mark	*Period*	*Identification Mark*	*Period*
	16th Century		Until 1806
	17th Century		
	18th Century		

ILMENAU		KAUFBEUREN	
Identification Mark	*Period*	*Identification Mark*	*Period*
	1700		16th Century

INGOLSTADT		KIEL	
Identification Mark	*Period*	*Identification Mark*	*Period*
	15th and 16th Century		16th–17th Century
	17th Century		17th Century
	18th Century		

KIEL—*Continued.*

Identification Mark	Period
	17th Century
	18th Century
	19th Century

KITZINGEN

Identification Mark	Period
	1595
	18th–19th Century

KÖNIGSBERG

Identification Mark	Period
	1684–1703
	1704–1716
	1714 and later

KÖNIGSBERG—*Continued.*

Identification Mark	Period
	1754–1761
	1766–1772
	1760–1770
	1780–1790
	1784–1786
	1788–1800
	1815
*	1830–1860
	19th Century

*See note on p. 315.

KÖNIGSBERG—*Continued.*		KONSTANZ	
Date Letters		*Identification Mark*	*Period*
a	1713	🛡	1557
C	1714	🛡	
c	1715	🛡	16th Century
D	1740	🛡	
F	1742	🛡	
L	1747	🛡	16th and 17th Century
S	1754	🛡	17th Century
Z	1761		
C	1766	🛡	Early 17th Century
M	1773		
3	1784	🛡	Middle 17th Century
B	1788		
A.	1818	🛡	End of 17th Century
A	1843	🛡	

KONSTANZ—*Continued.*

Identification Mark	Period
	18th Century
	19th Century

LANDSBERG

Inspection Mark	Period
	17th and 18th Century

LANDSHUT

Identification Mark	Period
	16th Century
	1723
	1751

LANDSHUT—*Continued.*

Identification Mark	Period
	Middle of 18th Century
*	End of 18th Century

LEER

Identification Mark	Period
	End of 18th Century

LEIPZIG

Identification Mark	Period
	16th Century
	End of 16th Century
	17th Century and early 18th Century
*	

*See note on p. 315.

LEIPZIG—*Continued.*		LIEGNITZ	
Identification Mark	*Period*	*Identification Mark*	*Period*
	17th and 18th Century		16th and 17th Century
	Early 18th Century		End of 17th Century
		LISSA	
		Identification Mark	*Period*
	18th Century		1741
		LÜBECK	
		Identification Mark	*Period*
			15th Century
			1495
	18th Century		1501
			1507
			Early 16th Century
	1775		

LÜBECK—*Continued.*

Identification Mark	Period
	1540
	Middle 16th Century
	Second half 16th Century
	16th and 17th Century
	1622
	163a
	Middle 17th Century
	18th Century

LUDWIGSBURG

Identification Mark	Period
	19th Century

LÜNEBURG

Inspection Mark	Period
	15th–16th Century
	First half of 16th Century

LÜNEBURG—*Continued.*	
Inspection Mark	Period
	Second half of 16th Century
	16th–17th Century
	1650

LÜNEBURG—*Continued.*	
Inspection Mark	Period
	Early 17th Century
	Beginning of 19th Century

MAGDEBURG	
Inspection Mark	Period
	1622
	1666
	1667
	End of 17th Century
	Early 18th Century
	17th–18th Century

MAINZ

Inspection Mark	Period
	16th Century
	17th Century
	17th Century
	1719
	1761
	19th Century

MANNHEIM

Inspection Mark	Period
	17th and 18th Century
	1717
	1727
*13	1737
	1775

MARIENBURG

Inspection Mark	Period
	17th Century
	17th–18th Century

MARIENWERDER

Inspection Mark	Period
	18th Century

MARKDORF

Inspection Mark	Period
	17th Century

MEMEL

Inspection Mark	Period
	18th Century

MEMMINGEN

Inspection Mark	Period
	16th Century
Same device but in circle	17th Century

MERGENTHEIM

Inspection Mark	Period
	18th Century

*See note on p. 315.

METZ	
Inspection Mark	*Period*
M	1714

MÜLHAUSEN (Alsace)	
Inspection Mark	*Period*
	17th Century
	17th–18th Century
	18th Century

MÜLHAUSEN (Saxony)	
Inspection Mark	*Period*
	1618

MUNICH	
Inspection Mark	*Period*
	16th and 17th Century
	Second half of 17th Century

MUNICH—*Continued.*	
Inspection Mark	*Period*
	1700
	18th Century
	1742
	1752
	1754

MUNICH—*Continued.*

Inspection Mark	Period
	1760
	1762
	1769
	1773
	1784
	1795

MÜNSTER

Inspection Mark	Period
	16th Century
	17th Century

NAUMBURG

Inspection Mark	Period
	16th and 17th Century
	17th Century
	17th Century
	1684

NAUMBURG—*Continued.*

Inspection Mark	Period
	18th Century
	18th Century

NEISSE

Inspection Mark	Period
	1604
	17th and beginning of 18th Century
	1742

NORDEN

Inspection Mark	Period
	18th and 19th Century
	19th Century
	19th Century

NÖRDLINGEN

Inspection Mark	Period
(eagle mark)	17th Century

NUREMBERG

Inspection Mark	Period
(mark)	Early 16th Century
(mark)	
N	Second half of 16th Century
(N mark)	
(N mark)	16th and 18th Century
(N mark)	
(N mark)	
(N mark)	
(N mark)	16th and 18th Century
(N mark)	
(N mark)	
(N mark)	19th Century
(N mark)	

NUREMBERG—Continued.

Date Letters

Mark	Period
A	1766–69
B	1769–73
C	1773–76
D	1776–80
E	1780–83
F	1783–87
G	1787–90
H	1790–94
I	1794–97
K	1797–1800
b	
g	19th Century
f	
g	

OBERGLOGAU

Identification Mark	Period
(heart-shaped mark)	18th Century

OCHSENFURT

Identification Mark	Period
OF	1625

OFFENBURG

Identification Mark	Period
	1515

OSNABRÜCK

Identification Mark	Period
	1692
	1700
	1716

OSTERODE

Identification Mark	Period
O	17th Century
O	1649
O	17th and 18th Century
O	19th Century

ÖOTTINGEN

Identification Mark	Period
	18th Century

PADENBORN

Identification Mark	Period
	17th and 18th Century
	19th Century

PASSAU

Identification Mark	Period
	17th and 18th Century
	18th Century
*	19th Century

PFORZHEIM

Identification Mark	Period
	18th–19th Century
	Gold standard 19th Century
	19th Century
	Gold standard late 19th Century

POSEN

Identification Mark	Period
	17th–18th Century

*See note on p. 315.

POTSDAM

Identification Mark	Period
	18th Century

PRUSSIA

Duty Stamp	Period
	Law of February 12, 1809
	Law of April 25, 1809
	From September 10, 1809, this stamp was used on tax-free church silver

RAPPOLTSWEILER

Inspection Stamp	Period
	1615

RATIBOR

Inspection Mark	Period
	1653

REGENSBURG

Inspection Stamp	Period
	16th–17th Century
	17th Century
	18th Century

RITZEBÜTTEL

Inspection Mark	Period
	18th Century

ROSENHEIM

Inspection Mark	Period
❀	17th Century

ROSTOCK

Inspection Mark	Period
ℝ	1593
ℝ	1600
ℝ	First half of 17th Century
ℝ	

SCHORNDORF

Identification Mark	Period
(shield)	16th Century

SCHWEIDNITZ

Identification Mark	Period
(animal)	17th Century
(animal)	18th Century

SCHWEINFURT

Identification Mark	Period
(eagle)	End of 16th Century
(eagle)	Middle of 17th Century
(eagle)	1681
* $\frac{S}{12}$	1730–1740
$\frac{S}{12}$	1756
S	1807

SCHWERIN

Identification Mark	Period
S in circle	
S in shield	17th and 18th Century

SPEIER

Identification Mark	Period
(towers)	15th Century
(towers)	15th–16th Century
(towers)	16th Century

*See note on p. 315.

STADTAMHOF	
Identification Mark	*Period*
	1767

STETTIN	
Identification Mark	*Period*
	16th–17th Century

STOLBERG–WERNIGERODE	
Identification Mark	*Period*
	18th Century

STRALSUND	
Identification Mark	*Period*
	17th Century

STRASBURG	
Identification Mark	*Period*
	1534–1567
	1567–1616

STRASBURG—*Continued.*	
Identification Mark	*Period*
	1567–1616
	1616–1639
*	1639–1643
	1643–1644
	1654

STRASBURG—*Continued.*

Identification Mark	Period	Identification Mark	Period	Identification Mark	Period	Date Letters
* 13	1655	13	1682	13	1731	1733
13	1656	13	1690	13	1736	
	1659					
	1659	13				1755
13	1662	13	1690–1725	13	1739	D
				13	1749–1751	1761 K
13	1665	13	1725	23		
				13		1769 S
13	1672–1674	13	1725	13	1750–1796	1780
13	1674–1690	13	1728	13		E
		13		13		E

STRAUBING

Identification Mark	Period
	Second half 16th Century

STUTTGART

Identification Mark	Period
	End of 16th Century
	1600
	17th Century
	17th Century
	1700
	1700–1760
	18th–19th Century

STUTTGART—*Continued.*

Identification Mark	Period
	18th–19th Century
	19th Century

SUHL

Identification Mark	Period
	17th Century to 1750 *circa*

THORN

Identification Mark	Period
	17th Century
	18th Century
	1760–1780

TILSIT

Identification Mark	Period
	18th Century
	Early 19th Century

TITTMONING

Identification Mark	Period
	17th Century

TORGAU

Identification Mark	Period
	16th–17th Century
	17th Century

TREBNITZ

Identification Mark	Period
	17th Century

TÜBINGEN

Identification Mark	Period
	1600

TUTTLINGEN

Identification Mark	Period
	1660

ÜBERLINGEN

Identification Mark	Period
	End of 16th Century
	End of 16th Century
	16th–17th Century
	17th Century
	18th Century

ULM		ULM—*Continued.*	
Identification Mark	*Period*	*Identification Mark*	*Period*
	16th Century		17th and 18th Century
	16th–17th Century		
	17th Century		18th Century
		VELBURG	
		Inspection Mark	*Period*
	17th and 18th Century		18th–19th Century
		VERDEN	
		Inspection Mark	*Period*
			17th Century

VILLINGEN	**WERTHEIM**

VILLINGEN

Inspection Mark	Period
	15th and 16th Century
	18th Century

WAREN

Inspection Mark	Period
W in shield	18th Century

WARTHA

Inspection Mark	Period
	18th (?) Century

WEILHEIM

Inspection Mark	Period
	17th–18th Century
	18th Century

WEIMAR

Inspection Mark	Period
	Beginning of 17th Century
	End of 17th Century

WERTHEIM

Inspection Mark	Period
	1660

WESEL

Inspection Mark	Period
	16th Century

WISMAR

Inspection Mark	Period
	16th Century
	17th Century

WOLFENBÜTTEL

Inspection Mark	Period
	1668
	17th Century
	17th and 18th Century

WORMS	
Inspection Mark	Period
	16th and 17th Century
	17th Century
	1730.

WÜRZBURG	
Inspection Mark	Period
	18th Century
	Early 19th Century

WURZEN	
Inspection Mark	Period
	18th Century

ZERBST	
Inspection Mark	Period
	1696
	1700

ZERBST—*Continued.*	
Inspection Mark	Period
	1773
	1752

ZITTAU	
Inspection Mark	Period
	1710
	1731
	1750

ZWEIBRÜCKEN	
Inspection Mark	Period
	18th Century

ZWICKAU	
Inspection Mark	Period
	16th and 17th Century
	17th Century

CHAPTER XXVIII
Marks on Other Continental Plate

AUSTRIA

BOZEN

Inspection Mark	Period
	1708
	Middle of 18th Century
E 1	1824–1866
H 2	1866–1872 Gold
H 2	1872

BRÜNN

Inspection Mark	Period
	1646
	1683
	1769
	1806

CRACOW

Inspection Mark	Period
	1807–1809
	1809–1835
*	1835–1866
	1859

* 1835–1866 etc., indicate the period. Each mark is dated. One shown is 1845; the other is 1859. For numerals 12 and 13 shown in Brünn and Cracow marks see p. 315.

EGER

Inspection Mark	Period
	17th–18th Century
	Beginning of 18th Century
C 7	1868–1872

GRAZ		INNSBRUCK	
Inspection Mark	*Period*	*Inspection Mark*	*Period*
	Late 16th Century		Late 17th Century
	1732		17th and 18th Century
	1743		

KLAGENFURT	
Inspection Mark	*Period*

GRAZ	KLAGENFURT	
1778		1801
1800	**I**	1806–1866

HALL		KLAGENFURT	
Inspection Mark	*Period*	**K**	1866–1867
	Form used from 1824 to 1866. Each year is given. See footnote under Cracow, p. 355.	**G 2**	1868–1872
H	1866–1868	**G 2**	1872

HOTZENPLOTZ		KREMSIER	
Inspection Mark	*Period*	*Inspection Mark*	*Period*
	1769		1769

IGLAU		KREMSIER	
Inspection Mark	*Period*		1769
	1769 (–1776)		1769

LAIBACH

Inspection Mark	Period
	18th Century
	1802
	1806

LEMBERG

Inspection Mark	Period
	1694
	1787–1806

MÄHRISCH–TRÜBAU

Inspection Mark	Period
	16th Century
	1736

NICOLSBURG

Inspection Mark	Period
	1769

OLMÜTZ

Inspection Mark	Period
	1593–1599
	17th Century
	1755
	1769–1776

PRAGUE

Inspection Mark	Period
	16th Century
	Middle of 17th Century
	1673
	1731
	1795
	1800
	1807–1813
	1814–1866

RAGUSA		TRIESTE—*Continued.*	
Inspection Mark	Period	Inspection Mark	Period
	17th or 18th Century	*	1803
			1805

SALZBURG		TROPPAU	
Inspection Mark		Inspection Mark	Period
S			16th–17th Century
	16th Cent		1674
	Close of 16th Century	12	1759
S			1789–1806
S	17th–18th Century		1807–1866

SCHÄRDING		VIENNA	
Inspection Mark	Period	Inspection Mark	Period
	17th Century	W	1524

TRIESTE			Middle of 16th Century
Inspection Mark	Period		From the end of 16th Century to 1674 for silver of .875 standard
*			
	18th Century		
13			1675

VIENNA—*Continued.*

Inspection Mark	Period
	1687
	1692 for silver of .8125 standard
	1737 for silver of .8125 standard
	1737 for silver of .9375 standard
	1764 for silver of .9375 standard
	1807–1812

VIENNA—*Continued.*

Inspection Mark	Period
	1812–1813
	1814 for silver of .8125 standard
	1819–1866 for silver of .9375 standard

ZNAIM

Inspection Mark	Period
	1769

HUNGARY

BUDAPEST

Inspection Mark	Period
*	17th–18th Century
	18th Century
	18th–19th Century

BUDAPEST—*Continued.*

Inspection Mark	Period
	1818
	1854
PESTH	

GRAN

Inspection Mark	Period
	18th–19th Century

*See note on p. 315.

KASCHAU

Inspection Mark	Period
	16th Century
	17th and 18th Centuries
	1800–1866

KECSKEMÉT

Inspection Mark	Period
	16th Century
	1657

KLAUSENBURG

Inspection Mark	Period
	16th and 17th Centuries
	1833

LEUTSCHAU

Inspection Mark	Period
	1664
	17th Century

NEUSATZ

Inspection Mark	Period
	Unknown

NEUSOHL

Inspection Mark	Period
	17th Century
	1813

PRESSBURG

Inspection Mark	Period
	16th Century
	1841
	1864

SCHEMNITZ		TEMESVAR	
Inspection Mark	*Period*	*Inspection Mark*	*Period*
	1576		1838
	17th Century		
	17th–18th Century		
	18th Century		

BELGIUM

Following are the State Assay Office punches, denoting quality for modern silver and gold in Belgium under the law of 1868.

	.900 fine for large pieces of silver		For large pieces of gold .800 fine (19. 2K)
	.800 fine for large pieces of silver		For large pieces of gold .750 fine (18K)
			For small pieces of gold .800 fine
	.900 fine for small pieces of silver		For small pieces of gold .750 fine
	.800 fine for small pieces of silver		Foreign silver

ANTWERP

Hall Mark	Period	Hall Mark	Period	Hall Mark	Period
	Early 16th Century		17th Century		1663
			17th Century		17th Century
					1664
	16th Century		1619		*Circa* 1670
			17th Century		17th Century
					1738
					18th Century
	1609		17th Century		1757
					1772
	16th–17th Century		1662		1783

ANTWERP—*Continued.*

Date Letters

Early 16th Century	**W** 17th Century		**K**	1664
Z 1558–1559	**I** (crowned)		**N** (crowned)	1669
	N (crowned) 1619		(crowned T)	17th Century
16th Century	**D** (crowned) 17th Century		**D**	1680
	F (crowned)		**H**	17th Century
	P (crowned) 17th Century			
I 1565–1568	**Q** (crowned)		**M** (crowned)	1738
X 1581	**F** (crowned) 1662–1663		**63**	1765
A 1609	**G** (crowned)		**72**	1772
R 16th–17th Century	**G** (crowned) 17th Century		**84**	1784

BRUGES

Hall Mark	Period
	17th Century

BRUSSELS

Hall Mark	Period
B	1618
	18th Century

State-Control Mark	
	1618
	18th Century

Date Letter	
O	1618

BRUSSELS—Continued.

Year Date	Period
	1751

GHENT

Hall Mark	Period
G	18th Century

The helmet, crowned, was used as guild mark in the early 16th Century. In the latter half of that period it was uncrowned. These marks were all in profile and looked to the left. In the first half of the 18th Century the helmet (or casque) was uncrowned and full face and continued so throughout the century.

JOURNAY

Hall Mark	Period
	16th Century
	1627

LIÈGE

Hall Mark	Period
	1650–1689
	1724–1763
	1744–1763
	1764–1771

LIÈGE—*Continued.*

Hall Mark	Period
	1772–1784
	1784–1792

LOUVAIN

Hall Mark	Period
	18th Century

MECHELEN

Hall Mark	Period
	1691

MONS		YPRES	
Hall Mark	*Period*	*Hall Mark*	*Period*
	17th Century		
	1766		Second half of 17th Century
			Second half of 18th Century

DENMARK

AALBORG		COPENHAGEN—*Continued.*	
Hall Mark	*Period*	*Hall Mark*	*Period*
	1686		1645
			1663
COPENHAGEN			1707
Hall Mark	*Period*		
	1608		1721
	1610		1725
	1639		

COPENHAGEN—*Continued.*

Hall Mark	Period
	1733
	1736
	1743
	1747

COPENHAGEN—*Continued.*

Hall Mark	Period
	1769
	1783
	1841
	1851

ODENSE

Hall Mark	Period
	1763

HOLLAND

State Stamp	Period	State Stamp	Period
	Law of 1852, silver		For silver less than .833 standard
	Gold		For large pieces of gold .916 standard
	Large silver pieces .934 standard		Mark for imported silverware
	Large silver pieces .833 standard		Mark for imported goldware
	Small pieces of silver both standards		For small foreign pieces (gold and silver)
			Export stamp for silver and gold

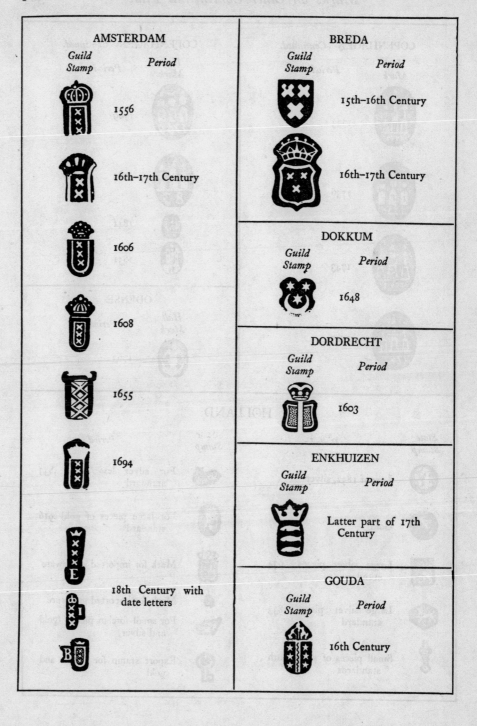

AMSTERDAM		BREDA	
Guild Stamp	*Period*	*Guild Stamp*	*Period*
	1556		15th–16th Century
	16th–17th Century		16th–17th Century
	1606	**DOKKUM**	
		Guild Stamp	*Period*
	1608		1648
	1655	**DORDRECHT**	
		Guild Stamp	*Period*
	1694		1603
		ENKHUIZEN	
		Guild Stamp	*Period*
	18th Century with date letters		Latter part of 17th Century
		GOUDA	
		Guild Stamp	*Period*
			16th Century

THE HAGUE		LEEUWARDEN	
Guild Mark	*Period*	*Guild Mark*	*Period*
	17th Century		17th–18th Century

MAESTRICHT

THE HAGUE		MAESTRICHT	
	17th Century with date letter	*Guild Mark*	*Period*
	17th Century state assay mark		Latter part of 18th Century
	1700		

ROTTERDAM

		ROTTERDAM	
		Guild Mark	*Period*
	18th Century		
			18th Century

HERZOGENBUSCH'S

HERZOGENBUSCH'S		UTRECHT	
Guild Mark	*Period*	*Guild Mark*	*Period*
	17th Century		1614

HOORN

HOORN		UTRECHT	
Guild Mark	*Period*		17th Century
	1640		1710

UTRECHT—*Continued.*

Guild Mark	Period
	18th Century

VLISSENGEN

Guild Mark	Period
	16th–17th Century

ZWOLLE

Guild Mark	Period
	17th Century
	1721
	1726 and later

ITALY

AQUILA

Inspection Mark	Period
	Early 15th Century
	Early 16th Century

BOLOGNA

Inspection Mark	Period
	18th Century

FERRARA

Inspection Mark	Period
	18th Century

FLORENCE

Inspection Mark	Period
	17th–18th Century
	18th Century
	18th Century

GENOA		MODENA	
Inspection Mark	Period	Inspection Mark	Period
	16th Century		18th Century
	18th Century	NAPLES	
		State Stamp	Period
	End of 18th Century		1400
			17th Century
LUCCA			17 (?)
Inspection Mark	Period		
	18th Century		1702
MAILAND			1716
Inspection Mark	Period		
	1810		
	Control-stamp of 1810		1720
MANTUA			
Inspection Mark	Period		1736
	18th Century		

NAPLES—*Continued.*		PARMA	
State Stamp	*Period*	*State Stamp*	*Period*
	Middle of 18th Century		18th Century

NAPLES		ROME	
AP 82	1782	*State Stamp*	*Period*
Guild Mark			17th Century
G C	1700 (?)		Late 17th Century
G B A C	1702		18th Century
N A C	1716		1790 (?)
G D B C	1720		18th and 19th Centuries
D.G.	1736	SOLMONA	
NSC	1742	*State Stamp*	*Period*

PALERMO		SOLMONA	
State Stamp	*Period*	SUL	13 and 14th Centuries
	18th Century	SUL	14th Century and to 1406

SOLMONA—*Continued.*		VENICE	
State Stamp	Period	State Stamp	Period
	1406 to middle of 15th Century		17th–18th Century
	Middle of 15th Century		16th–18th Century
	15th or 16th Century		1805. Stamp for .8125 standard of silver

TURIN			
State Stamp	Period		1805. Stamp for .9375 standard of silver
	18th Century		
	18th Century		1810

PORTUGAL

EVORA		LISBON	
Inspection Mark	Period	Inspection Mark	Period
	1740		17th–18th Century
			18th Century

GUIMARÃES		OPORTO	
Inspection Mark	Period	Inspection Mark	Period
	1790		17th Century

NORWAY

BERGEN		BERGEN—Continued.	
Inspection Mark	*Period*	*Inspection Mark*	*Period*
	1787	DK	circa 1800
	1799	MP	1799
	1812	P	1799
	1820	B	circa 1815
	1799		

CHRISTIANIA

Inspection Mark	*Period*
	18th Century

BERGEN	
	1812
	1820

RUSSIA

The marks on the following pages might lead the reader to believe that 84 in an oblong cartouche was a mark peculiar to the city of Tula. The distinctive town mark is often placed with 84 which designates the Russian standard of silver .903 fine, the unit being divided into ninety parts.

For approximately two centuries Russian silver has been dated, the year being represented by numerals in a straight line, e.g., 1746.

ASTRAKHAN

Inspection Mark	Period
	1771

IRKUTSK or TOBOLSK

Inspection Mark	Period
	1774

BAUSK

Inspection Mark	Period
	18th Century

YAROSLAF

Inspection Mark	Period
	1767

DORPAT

Inspection Mark	Period
	17th Century

KALUGA

Inspection Mark	Period
	Close of 18th Century

GOLDINGEN

Inspection Mark	Period
	18th Century

KAMENETZ-PODOLSKI

Inspection Mark	Period
	1858

KAZAN

Inspection Mark	Period
	1797

KIEV

Inspection Mark	Period
	1794
	19th Century

KOSTROMA

Inspection Mark	Period
	Found on 18th Century silver

LOMZA

Inspection Mark	Period
	1781

MITAU

Inspection Mark	Period
	17th Century

MOSCOW

Inspection Mark	Period
	1734–1741
	1747
	1778
	1780

PERM

Inspection Mark	Period
	18th Century

PSKOF

Inspection Mark	Period
	Unknown

REVAL

Inspection Mark	Period
	16th Century
	17th Century
	18th Century
	18th Century

RIGA

Inspection Mark	Period
	16th Century
	1600
	17th–18th Century
	18th Century

ST. PETERSBURG

Inspection Mark	Period
	1736
СПБ	
1746	1746
1760	1760
1796	1796
1801	1801
1813	18-
	1829–1880

TULA

Inspection Mark	Period
84✳	19th Century

TVER		VOLOGDA	
Inspection Mark	*Period*	*Inspection Mark*	*Period*
	18th Century		18th Century

VILNA		WALK	
Inspection Mark	*Period*	*Inspection Mark*	*Period*
	16th–17th Century		Close of 18th Century

VLADIMIR		WIBORG	
Inspection Mark	*Period*	*Inspection Mark*	*Period*
	18th Century		18th Century
			18th–19th Century

SWEDEN

ARBOGA or ÖREBRO		BORÅS	
Inspection Mark	*Period*	*Inspection Mark*	*Period*
			18th Century
	17th and 18th Centuries		After 1860
	1771		

CHRISTIANSTAD

Inspection Mark	Period
	1647
	17th and 18th Centuries
	1727
	18th and 19th Centuries

EKSJÖ, HEDEMORA, and LINDESBERG

Inspection Mark	Period
	17th Century
	18th Century
	18th Century

Guild Masters' Marks

 	18th Century

GEFLE

Inspection Mark	Period
	18th Century
G	1810

GOTHENBURG

Inspection Mark	Period
	Last half of 18th Century

LINDESBERG

Inspection Mark	Period
 	Close of the 18th Century

LULEÅ

Inspection Mark	Period
	Middle of 18th Century
	Beginning of 19th Century

NORRTELJE

Inspection Mark	Period
	Early 19th Century

ÖREBRO

Inspection Mark	Period
	18th Century

SÖDERHAMN

Inspection Mark	Period
	18th Century

STOCKHOLM

Inspection Mark	Period
	1600
	1647
	1650
	1650
	1674
	1692
	Close of 17th Century and first half of 18th Century

STOCKHOLM—*Continued.*

Inspection Mark	Period
	1700
	1707
	1713
	1716
	1720
	1723
	1724
	1745
	1752
	1756
	1797
STOCK HOLM	1850

TABLE OF DATE LETTERS FOR STOCKHOLM, 1689 TO 1759,
AND FROM THAT YEAR FOR ALL OF SWEDEN.

A = 1689	*A* = 1713	a = 1737	A = 1759	A 2 = 1783
B = 1690	*B* = 1714	b = 1738	B = 1760	B 2 = 1784
C = 1691	*C* = 1715	c = 1739	C = 1761	C 2 = 1785
D = 1692	*D* = 1716	d = 1740	D = 1762	D 2 = 1786
E = 1693	*E* = 1717	e = 1741	E = 1763	E 2 = 1787
F = 1694	*F* = 1718	f = 1742	F = 1764	F 2 = 1788
G = 1695	*G* = 1719	g = 1743	G = 1765	G 2 = 1789
H = 1696	*H* = 1720	h = 1744	H = 1766	H 2 = 1790
I = 1697	*I* = 1721	i = 1745	I = 1767	I 2 = 1791
K = 1698	*K* = 1722	k = 1746	K = 1768	K 2 = 1792
L = 1699	*L* = 1723	l = 1747	L = 1769	L 2 = 1793
M = 1700	*M* = 1724	m = 1748	M = 1770	M 2 = 1794
N = 1701	*N* = 1725	n = 1749	N = 1771	N 2 = 1795
O = 1702	*O* = 1726	o = 1750	O = 1772	O 2 = 1796
P = 1703	*P* = 1727	p = 1751	P = 1773	P 2 = 1797
Q = 1704	*Q* = 1728	q = 1752	Q = 1774	Q 2 = 1798
R = 1705	*R* = 1729	r = 1753	R = 1775	R 2 = 1799
S = 1706	*S* = 1730	s = 1754	S = 1776	S 2 = 1800
T = 1707	*T* = 1731	t = 1755	T = 1777	T 2 = 1801
U = 1708	*U* = 1732	u = 1756	U = 1778	U 2 = 1802
W = 1709	*W* = 1733	w = 1757	W = 1779	W 2 = 1803
X = 1710	*X* = 1734	x = 1758	X = 1780	X 2 = 1804
Y = 1711	*Y* = 1735		Y = 1781	Y 2 = 1805
Z = 1712	*Z* = 1736		Z = 1782	Z 2 = 1806

A 3 = 1807.   A 4 = 1831.   A 5 = 1855.   A 6 = 1879.   A 7 = 1903.

TORSHÄLLA		YSTAD—*Continued.*	
Inspection Mark	*Period*	*Inspection Mark*	*Period*
	18th Century		
			18th Century

ULRICEHAMN

Inspection Mark	*Period*
	Early 19th Century

VASTERÅS

Inspection Mark	*Period*
	18th Century

YSTAD	
Inspection Mark	*Period*
	18th–19th Century
	19th Century
	16th and 17th Centuries

18th Century

18th Century

Close of 18th Century

SWITZERLAND

BADEN		**BADEN**—*Continued.*	
Inspection Mark	*Period*	*Inspection Mark*	*Period*
[mark]	Early 17th Century	[mark]	
[mark]		[mark]	18th Century
[mark]	17th–18th Century	[mark]	
[mark]	16th Century and later		
[mark]	Middle of 17th Century	**BERN**	
[mark]		*Inspection Mark*	*Period*
[mark]	17th Century	[mark]	
[mark]		[mark]	
[mark]	1678	[mark]	16th Century
[mark]	17th Century	[mark]	
[mark]		[mark]	
[mark]	17th–18th Century	[mark]	1690
[mark]		[mark]	1800
[mark]	18th Century		
[mark]		**BIENNE**	
		Inspection Mark	*Period*
		[mark]	18th Century

COIRE

Inspection Mark	Period
	16th–17th Century

EINSIEDELN

Inspection Mark	Period
	17th–18th Century
	18th Century

GENEVA

Inspection Mark	Period
	18th Century

LAUSANNE

Inspection Mark	Period
	18th Century

LUZERN

Inspection Mark	Period
	16th Century
	18th Century

NEUCHÂTEL

Inspection Mark	Period
	17th–18th Century

NEUVEVILLE

Inspection Mark	Period
	17th Century

PAYERNE

Inspection Mark	Period
	16th and 17th Centuries

RAPPERSWIL

Inspection Mark	Period
	16th and 17th Centuries
	18th Century

SURSEE

Inspection Mark	Period
	16th and 17th Centuries
	17th and 18th Centuries

SCHAFFHAUSEN

Inspection Mark	Period
	16th Century
	17th–18th Century
	18th Century

THUN

Inspection Mark	Period
	17th Century

VEVEY

Inspection Mark	Period
	16th and 17th Centuries
	18th Century

SION

Inspection Mark	Period
	16th Century
	17th Century
	18th Century

WINTERTHUR

Inspection Mark	Period
	18th Century

ZUG

Inspection Mark	Period
	1584
	1680
	17th Century
	18th Century

ZÜRICH

Inspection Mark	Period
	1545
	1563
	1563, 1564, 1565
	1608
	1621

ZÜRICH—Continued.

Inspection Mark	Period
	Early 17th Century
	1629
	1631
	17th and 18th Centuries
	1667
	1674
	1779

SPAIN

BARCELONA

Inspection Mark	Period
BARK NONA	15th Century
✠BAROK BA	16th and 17th Century
✠BAR BAR BA BA	16th Century

BURGOS

Inspection Mark	Period
BVRO	Unknown

CALATAYUD

Inspection Mark	Period
CAL	15th–16th Century

CORDOVA

Inspection Mark	Period
COR	15th and 16th Centuries

LA CORUÑA

Inspection Mark	Period
CA RONA	16th Century

LEON

Inspection Mark	Period
1732 / 7N / 13 LEONI	1732

MADRID

Inspection Mark	Period
	18th Century

MUNOZ

Inspection Mark	Period
1712 MVNOZ	Unknown

SARAGOSSA		TOLEDO	
Inspection Mark	*Period*	*Inspection Mark*	*Period*
	15th Century	**TOL**	16th Century
			1600
	16th Century		17th Century

CHAPTER XXIX

Old Sheffield Plate

❖ ❖ ❖N 1743, Thomas Boulsover, of Sheffield, discovered a
❖ I ❖ process of plating silver on copper. This was ninety
❖ ❖ ❖ years before electroplating was invented.

It is important that Boulsover's method—and his method was
followed for nearly a century—of making silver plate should be
understood in order to be able to distinguish real "Old Sheffield
Plate" from the imitation.

An ingot of silver and an ingot of copper were filed and scraped
until two smooth surfaces were obtained. The size of the ingots
would depend upon the size of the plate required, which would
constitute the raw material for the subsequent processes. The
two prepared surfaces, after having been made chemically clean
by washing them in a weak solution of nitric acid, were firmly
pressed together so that they fitted quite evenly. In order thor-
oughly to unite the two faces, they were put under a powerful
hydraulic press. An additional copper plate was then placed on
the silver side of the ingot, but before doing so, either the silver or
copper face was painted with a preparation of chalk to keep the
third piece of metal from fusing to the silver piece—the protection
of the latter from the fire being the object of the introduction of
the cover piece of copper, which, of course, would be used over
and over again.

If it was intended to produce a piece of plated metal with
silver upon both sides, the ingot of copper would be placed be-

tween two pieces of silver, in which case the middle piece would have to be cleaned upon both faces, while the two pieces of silver would only have to be prepared on their opposing faces. In that case, two protecting pieces of copper would have to be employed, each separated from the silver plates it was designed to protect by a coating of chalk. This precaution was necessary in order to prevent all five plates, or in the case of "single plate," all three plates, from fusing together. Where two plates of silver and one plate of copper in between were employed, the resulting product would be "double plate." Where a single ingot of copper and a single ingot of silver were fused together, the product was "single plate." The metal plates were then bound together with iron wire, and the edges where the silver and copper came in contact were treated with a fluxing solution, usually borax. The composite ingot was now ready for the fusing process and was placed in a coke furnace and subjected to great heat until the sheet of silver showed its molten condition by commencing to trickle down the sides of the ingot. It was then removed from the furnace, cooled and cleansed. It was then placed between rollers and rolled out into a sheet of the thickness of the walls of the vessel for the manufacture of which it was to be used. If the finished article was intended to be a coffee pot, a portion of which would have to be thinned by being subjected to a belling-out process, that circumstance would have to be considered in determining the thickness of the silver and copper plate.

This plated sheet of metal would now be used in precisely the same way that a sheet of solid silver, or solid copper, would be employed in the production of the finished article. It is important to note that, when it became necessary to shear off the edges of the metal, a uniform appearance of surface would not be exposed along the cut edge. In the case of double plate, a red line of copper would show between two white lines of silver. It would be

AN OLD SHEFFIELD TRAY SHOWING THE SILVER INSET PLATE

necessary to mask this cut edge, and this necessity affords us the first and most important test for distinguishing genuine "Old Sheffield Plate" from a piece of electroplate. At the present time, this situation could be met by either placing the entire article in a silver-plating solution and by electrical action put in a slight covering of silver over the entire piece, including the exposed edge, or by the process of "sponging" silver on the exposed edge by the use of a silver anode covered with a cloth saturated with a silver solution and the use of the electric current. In the days of Old Sheffield, however, electroplating being unknown, the maker of rolled plate had to employ another method. He met the situation in the very old days by making his silver ingot a trifle larger than the copper one. This would give him a projecting silver flap, which could be folded over the copper edge. This method, however, would only be practicable where the size of the ingot corresponded with the size of the finished article, for instance, a flat dish, and was soon abandoned. Where the plate had to be cut in irregular forms, the exposed edges were covered by a piece of silver wire, which was soldered in place. In many cases, this silver edge, called the "edge of poverty," is plainly perceptible to the eye and can be felt with the fingers.

Unfortunately, this "edge of poverty," which we now look for as desirable evidence of the genuine character of the article under examination, was, before the days of silver plating, regarded as an objectionable feature. Remember that "Old Sheffield Plate" was supposed to take the place of solid silver, and any feature that served to distinguish the substitute from the original was deemed objectionable. The result was that, in the first quarter of the Nineteenth Century, a process was invented which rendered the "edge of poverty" almost invisible, so that the test suggested by the foregoing is rather difficult of application to pieces of genuine plate when produced at that late period. The use of a reading glass or microscope will, however, enable one to discover the point of union between the edge covering and the body of the article.

When it is attempted to take a sheet made of two separate pieces of metal and work it into a very ornate and convoluted surface, or a surface with sharp edges, it will be found that the outer covering, which in this case would be the silver, would be apt to crack and pull away from the metal below because the superficies of the outer pieces of metal, where covering the curve, or the angle, would be greater than the piece below. The makers of Sheffield Plate, therefore, found it more economical to take thin sheets of silver and either hammer or stamp them into the shapes desired. In the case of ornamentation, these pieces could be soldered immediately upon the sides of the vessel to be decorated. When decorated handles had to be applied, a piece of Sheffield Plate could be used for the lower, plain surface section of the handle, while the ornamented upper portion would be made of silver. When put together, the hollow between the silver and Sheffield Plate would be filled with a composition resembling solder. In the case of an electroplated article, the ornamental handles would be cast of a solid piece of brass and then electroplated after having been attached to the body.

This provides us with a second method of distinguishing "Old Sheffield Plate" from a modern plated article. The ornamentation upon the electroplated article, when scratched with a file, will show a hard base metal underneath. In the case of Old Sheffield, the ornamentation, being of silver, will be cut through with much more difficulty and a *soft* metal backing will be disclosed instead of hard brass or copper. The handle of genuine Sheffield will disclose a line of union running along the middle from one terminal of the handle to the other, and the upper or ornamented portion will respond to the same tests as the decoration on the body of the article. This line of union, of course, will be absent in the case of a piece of electroplate, and a test with the file will show the same inner body on the top and bottom of the handle. Everything I have said about the handle will apply to other projecting parts of the article, for example, the feet and the finial (knob) of a coffee-pot lid.

Boulsover's invention was first applied to such articles as harness buckles, and it was not until about the commencement of the reign of George III (1760) that domestic articles were manufactured in any quantity.

It was just at this period that the beauty of English solid silver had reached its zenith, and for a number of years Old Sheffield tea and coffee sets, candelabra, candlesticks, and trays, showed the same beautiful simplicity and grace of outline. The Adam Brothers influenced the designs in Sheffield as they did in silver, and when the "Empire" fashions came into vogue (1800), both solid silver and Sheffield Plate followed the ornate fashions set in furniture. The worst examples of this period were produced in the reign of George IV (1820–1830). As soon as Sheffield plating showed that it could be adapted to the production of articles for the table and for decoration, Sheffield Plate became fashionable and popular. Enormous quantities were produced in the last forty years of the Eighteenth Century. This means that a great number of people were engaged in the industry. The manufacture soon spread beyond Sheffield; in fact, the largest single factory, the Soho Works, was located in Birmingham, under the management of Matthew Boulton, whose work is now valued as of the highest quality.

As might be expected, there were a number of black sheep among the makers of Old Sheffield Plate. The obvious way for them to gouge the public was to reduce the thickness of the silver ingot. This was done to such an extent that some of the rolled plate was no thicker in silver than is now obtained by electrical deposition. This accounts for the number of articles on the market in an almost naked condition, which undoubtedly were at one time Sheffield Plate. The idea that these pieces, now denuded of their silver, have any value is a mistaken one. If the basic work and the design were good, they might be silver plated and be made of some value as electroplated silver.

Even the best pieces of Old Sheffield may show copper where they have been subjected to extraordinary wear, or the piece has been battered, in which case the silver will peel off as it would have done had the manufacturer attempted to turn the plain surface into a highly ornate one. The exposure of the copper is called "bleeding," and if very slight, is not detrimental to the article. If it is so great as to militate against the appearance of the piece, it should be taken to an expert and silver sponged on the bare places. The reason I say it should be taken to an expert is that the ordinary silver-plating plants employ a solution of *pure* silver and use a *pure* silver anode. Old Sheffield, to be sponged properly, should be treated with a solution made of *sterling* silver (i.e., a solution containing about 8 per cent. of copper to 92 per cent. of silver) and a sterling silver anode.

The reason for employing this method is that pure silver would make a glaring white patch on the gray surface of the Sheffield. The ingot of silver employed in the making of the sheet metal contained only about 92 per cent. of silver, and this, with the repeated annealing to which it is subjected while being hammered into shape, accounts for the soft gray colour of the finished product. This colour is approximated when a sterling silver bath and anode are used. The Sheffield process, or rolled-plate process, as it was then called, speedily became known in France, and in a very short time the industry was established there, entirely superseding the method known as "French plating," which had been in use since 1700.

OLD SHEFFIELD ROLLED PLATE OF THE LATER (FLORID) PERIOD

In England, many of the rolled-plate makers had been cutlers; in France, the manufacture of rolled plate was taken up, not by the ordinary manufacturer, but by silversmiths, and their products were taken cognizance of by the authorities of the Goldsmiths' Guild (St. Eloi), who threw about the product the same protection that they did about solid silver. The rules of the guild provided that each piece must be stamped with the mark denoting its quality; for instance, if the basic sheet were composed of nine kilos of copper and one kilo of silver, it would be marked *dixième*, but this term was abbreviated and represented by 10e, 10me, or 10m. Lower grades, or inferior grades, were marked 20me, 30me, and 40 me. It is very doubtful if any manufacturer took advantage of the provisions that enabled him to make the two lower grades of rolled plate. Personally, the author has never seen anything but *dixième* and *vigntième*. The consequence of this genesis of French rolled plate was that the product was much more uniformly beautiful in design than that produced in England by manufacturers without the æsthetic training of the French silversmiths, and was of more uniform good quality. It is very rare, indeed, to see a piece even of *vingtième* showing the copper, unless it be a piece that has been badly dented. Unfortunately, French Sheffield is very rare. The pieces that have most often come under my observation were made by the firm of Balain, whose mark is a grasshopper or locust impaled upon a pin.

There are widespread misapprehensions concerning Old Sheffield. These are due in a large measure to perusal of a number of books that have been written by amateurs without any proper or adequate basis of knowledge. They are also held by people who think that knowledge upon a subject of this sort may be a matter of intuition, and it is indeed difficult to eradicate views that, no matter how erroneous, are regarded as a birthright.

A flagrant error in belief is that Old Sheffield Plate is "hall-marked." Of course, a "hallmark" can only be affixed to solid silver. A more excusable error is that all Sheffield markers put their mark upon their products. As a matter of fact, a very large proportion of the very finest pieces of Old Sheffield Plate are absolutely devoid of marks. On the other hand, "fakes" are abundantly marked, frequently with copies of two or more old marks. One woman collector told the author that in her collection of Old Sheffield she had a number of pieces manufactured by E. P. N. S. This is as if one had said her favourite author was "Mr. Anonymous." E. P. N. S. means electroplate on nickel silver. It was and is employed by a great number of manufacturers in order to give the public an honest and an accurate description of their wares.

Another misconception concerns the presence or absence of the silver inset plate or shield so often found on the sides of wine coolers, dish covers, in the centre of trays, and on the margins of platters. The popular belief is that these *pure* silver shields (the fact that these are pure silver makes them conspicuous against the darker background of Sheffield Plate) denote an extra fine quality of Old Sheffield; in fact, some collectors refuse to purchase pieces that are not so distinguished. A brief consideration of the reason for this innovation (the first inset shield was about 1810) will lead one to a different conclusion. The earlier Sheffield Plate was purposely made with a silver skin so thick that a careful engraver could put on a crest, coat of arms, monogram, or inscription without cutting through to the copper. It occurred to some genius that the old process was an extravagant one, as the piece would be engraved only in one or two places, and in order to provide for that, the silver plate was devised. The only reason for its employment is that the article, except where the plate appears, is too thinly covered with silver to stand engraving. Fortunately, the situation is saved in some measure by the fact that manufacturers of very fine Sheffield found that some of their customers considered the inset plate decorative and followed the fashion without any noticeable depreciation in the quality of their output. As a rule, however, the silver inset plate must be regarded as evidence of inferior quality of plating but not of workmanship. People without the knowledge requisite to identify Old Sheffield Plate find the inset plate a convenient signpost. Those who restrict their collections to articles thus made will voluntarily shut themselves out of the best market.

Very early in the history of the manufacture of rolled plate, a number of manufacturers applied the process, with suitable changes, to the coating of articles of steel, such as knives and forks. In some cases, large spoons and skewers made of pot metal or britannia ware were "close-plated."

Britannia metal was an alloy, used, notably, by the great Sheffield firm of Thomas Dixon & Sons. Dixon & Sons came late on the scene. They were established in 1810 and thirty years later were among the first to adopt the new process of electroplating. They used as a base an alloy which they stamped "Britannia." Unfortunately, this was not a stable or static compound. For some reason, probably galvanic action set up by the proximity of different metallic elements, or perhaps merely oxidation, this metal has with the effluxion of time become porous and rotten. When the mutable character of the alloy became apparent, it was abandoned, and bell-metal, called "nickel silver," was employed —an alloy of nickel, copper, and tin and a very small proportion of zinc or antimony; the formula is variable but always adapted to produce a hard yellow metal. This makes such an admirable base that in England it has almost entirely superseded copper, and it is this metal, when plated, that is properly stamped E. P. N. S.

Old Sheffield is nearly always upon copper. Brass, however, has sometimes been employed. Many of the pieces of so-called

"Sheffield" on the market consist of a cast base electroplated. The old Sheffield pieces, of course, were hammered out by hand, except as to the mounts and handles, which were stamped and backed as I have described. Where a casting is employed, the use of a microscope will disclose a rather porous-looking surface—a feature, of course, that is entirely absent from a piece of metal that has been subjected to much hammering in the course of manufacture.

The reader who wishes to learn every detail of the manufacture of Old English Sheffield should peruse Mr. Frederick Bradbury's masterly work, *History of Old Sheffield Plate*. It is the only authoritative book upon that subject. Mr. Bradbury's ancestors were prominent makers of rolled plate in the Eighteenth Century, and the firm has had a continued existence from then until the present day, when it still occupies the foremost position among Sheffield silversmiths.

I have said that many of the handsomest and most valuable pieces of Old Sheffield are unmarked. That is not the result of chance alone. Prior to 1773, some eighteen makers of rolled plate in Sheffield and Birmingham—by no means all of the manufacturers in those cities—used marks. In that year, the law establishing an assay office in Sheffield struck at certain manufacturers of plated ware whose marks resembled hall marks, by prohibiting the striking of a letter or letters on articles made of metal, plated or covered with silver. Ten years later, in 1784, a law was passed which enabled the platers who were engaged in trade in Sheffield, or within a hundred miles thereof, to impress their goods with their names "together with any mark, figure, or device at the end of the name, such figure not being an assay office device for sterling silver or in imitation thereof." Such mark or marks must be approved and registered by the assay authorities.

During the intervening decade, no marks had been affixed to

EXAMPLES OF FRENCH SHEFFIELD OF THE EMPIRE PERIOD

Dish warmers with lamps and stands

Old Sheffield Plate, and that happens to have been the most prolific decade in the history of the industry. It was also the best period from an artistic standpoint.

It should be noted that, under the law of 1784, it was not obligatory for the maker to mark his wares, and he must not do so without registration. There was a penalty of £100 for any violation of the statute.

Sixteen makers registered their marks in 1784, and many did not; so that we cannot say with certainty that any unmarked piece was made before 1784. However, that fact, coupled with the design of the piece—fashions were closely followed by silversmiths and Sheffield Plate makers—does enable one very often to fix the period of manufacture with reasonable certainty.

In 1785, seven Sheffield makers registered. One or two each year added their marks and names to the official list until 1807, when, for some reason, eighteen Birmingham manufacturers of rolled plate recorded their marks at the Sheffield assay office. Between 1808 and 1836 (both years inclusive), fifty-five Birmingham and nineteen Sheffield firms or individuals recorded their marks. No marks have been entered since.

It should be carefully noted that some of the marks put on old Sheffield have been used upon electroplate after the rolled-plate maker had changed his product as the result of the invention of electroplating. The crossed arrows (T. & J. Creswick) is an example. It is now used by Hutton & Company, successors to the old firm, on electroplate.

Frequently, on a piece of Old Sheffield, one will find marks other than a maker's mark. It may be of one or more letters, figures, or a symbol, such as a sun or two concentric circles. These are workmen's marks. Sometimes workmen would leave one factory and go to another, so that we find the identical workmen's mark upon pieces of different makers.

CHAPTER XXX

Sheffield Platers and Their Marks

APPROXIMATE DATES OF THE MANUFACTURERS' EARLIEST CONNECTION WITH THE FUSED PLATE INDUSTRY PREVIOUS TO 1773

Name of Firm.	Maker's Marks.	Date.	Location.	Trade Description.
Boulsover Thomas...	No Mark Traced.	1743	Sheffield, Norfolk Street	Cutler, Button and Box maker.
Hancock Joseph ...	IOSᴴ HANCOCK SHEFFIELD. IH	1755	Sheffield, Union Street—High Street	Cutler, and maker of Plated Hollow-ware.
Smith Nathaniel ...	NS *	1756	Sheffield, Waingate ...	Cutler.
Law Thomas	TH° LAW LAW	1758	Sheffield, Baker's Hill ...	Silver Cutler & makers of Plated Hollow-ware and Candlesticks
Tudor & Leader ...	T&C°	1760	Sheffield, Sycamore Works	Silver and Plate manufacturers.
Fenton Matthew&Co	†	1760	Sheffield, Mulberry St....	Do.
Unidentified ...		1760	Sheffield	Plate manufacturers
Unidentified ...		1760	Sheffield	Do.
Unidentified ...		1760	Sheffield	Do.
Hoyland John & Co.		1764	Sheffield, Union Street...	Silver and Plate manufacturers.
Boulton & Fothergill	B•F	1764	Birmingham	Do.
Roberts Jacob & Samuel	JSR *	1765	Sheffield, Pond Hill ...	Silver and Plated Cutlery manufacturers
Winter John & Co.	IW †	1765	Sheffield	Silver and Plate manufacturers.
Morton Richard ...		1765	Sheffield, Brinsworth Orchard	Do.
Rowbotham J. & Co.	IR *	1768	Sheffield, Norfolk Street	Do.
Ashforth, Ellis & Co		1770	Sheffield, Holy Croft ...	Cutlers and Plate manufacturers.
Ryland William ...	No Mark Traced.	1770	Birmingham	Plater.
Littlewood J. ...	PLATED	1772	Sheffield, Westbar Green	Plater and Silversmith.

* Marks used on plated and silver cutlery.
† It is only presumed that these marks were used by this firm.

EXTRACTS FROM LISTS OF MANUFACTURERS FROM "SKETCHLEY'S SHEFFIELD DIRECTORY," 1774
NO MARKS LEGALISED ON PLATED ARTICLES, ACCORDING TO THE ACT 1773

Name of Firm.	No Maker's Marks Used.				Location.		Trade Description.
Bunbury Thomas ...	...	...	...	...	Sheffield, Norfolk Lane ...		Silversmith.
Elliott Thomas ...	...	...	...	...	Do.	John Lane	Silversmith.
Ellis Thomas ...	...	...	...	...	Do.	Norfolk Street ...	Silver Plater.
Fenton, Creswick & Co.	...	...	...	...	Do.	Mulberry Street ...	Silver & Plated manufacturers.
Greaves Johanadab	...	...	...	...	Do.	Church Lane ...	Plated Snuff Box maker.
Hoyland John & Co.	...	...	...	...	Do.	Union Street ...	Platers, Refiners, Button and Box makers.
Kirk Joseph	...	...	...	...	Do.	at the Wheat Sheaf, Waingate	Silversmith.
Margreave, Marsden & Brocklesby	...	...	...	...	Do.	above the Town Head Crofts	Silver and Bristol Stone Sleeve Button makers.
Marsden William ...	...	...	...	...	Do.	White Croft... ...	Plater.
Morton Thomas ...	...	...	...	...	Do.	New Church Street	Plater.
Morton Richard & Co.	...	...	...	...	Do.	Fargate	Platers & Silver Manufacturers.
Rowbotham John & Co.	...	...	...	...	Do.	Norfolk Street ...	Silversmiths and Platers,
Tonks William ...	...	...	...	...	Do.	West Bar Green ...	Plated Buckle and Spur maker.
Tudor & Leader ...	...	...	...	...	Do.	Sycamore Hill ...	Silver & Plated manufacturers of Pitchers; Coffee Pots, Candlesticks, Tureens, Waiters, &c.
Wilson Joseph ...	...	...	...	...	Do.	Highfield	Silversmith, Plater, Saw maker, Tobacco and Snuff manufacturer.
Winter, Parsons & Hall	...	...	...	...	Do.	High Street	Silversmiths and Platers,
Boulton Matthew ...	...	...	...	...	Birmingham, Soho Works ...		Silversmith and Plater.
Ryland Wm. ...	...	...	...	...	Birmingham		Plater.

(FROM BIRMINGHAM DIRECTORY FOR THE YEAR 1777.)

Name of Firm.	No Maker's Marks Used.				Location.		Trade Description.
Boulton Matthew ...	...	...	...	...	Birmingham, Soho Works ...		Silver and Plate manufacturer.
Ryland William ...	...	...	...	...	Birmingham		Plater.

EXTRACTS FROM LISTS OF MANUFACTURERS FROM "BAILEY'S NORTHERN DIRECTORY," AND OTHER SOURCES. 1781

Name of Firm.	No Maker's Marks Used.				Location.	Trade Description.
Allen Thomas ...	...	...	...	...	Sheffield, Bailey Street ...	Snuffer maker.
Ashforth, Ellis & Co.	...	...	...	...		Platers.
Burdett John ...	...	...	...	...	Do Pea Croft	Brass Dog Collar Silver Sleeve Button, Silver-plated & Metal Seal Maker.
Henfrey John ...	...	...	...	...		Fine Scissor & Snuffer maker.
Henfrey Samuel ...	...	...	...	...	Do. Spring Street ...	Steel Spring Snuffer, Scissor and Steel Cat maker.
Holy Daniel & Co. ...	...	...	...	...	Do. Norfolk Street ...	Platers.
Kippax & Nowill ...	...	...	...	...	Sheffield, (Nowill & Kippax, High Street in 1787)	Wholesale Cutlers and Silversmiths.
Law Thomas & Co. ...	...	...	...	...	Sheffield, Norfolk Street ...	Platers and Silver Cutlers.
Littlewood John ...	...	...	...	...	Do. Westbar Green ...	Manufacturer of Silver-handled Knives and Forks.
Madin & Trickett ...	...	...	...	...	Do. Farfield, near ...	Cutlers and Platers.
Mappin Jonathan ...	...	...	...	...	Do. Fargate	Plater and Cup Maker.
Roberts, Eyre & Co.	...	...	...	...	Do. Union Street... ...	Silversmiths and Platers.
Rowbotham John ...	...	...	...	...	Do. Norfolk Street ...	Silversmith and Cutler.
Sykes John & Dennis	...	...	...	...	Do. (Pinstone Lane in 1787)	Manufacturers of Wood, Ivory, Silver & Plated Table Knives and Forks.
Tudor & Leader ...	...	...	...	...	Do. Sycamore Hill ...	Silversmiths and Platers.
Winter, Parsons & Hall	...	...	...	...	Do. Market Place ...	Platers.
Withers Benjamin & Co.	...	...	...	...	Do. Pinstone Cross Lane	Manufacturers of Silver, Ivory, Plated and Wood Handled Knives & Forks, and Stamped Pen Knives.
Younge, Greaves & Hoyland	...	...	...	...	Do. Union Street... ...	Silversmiths and manufacturers of Plated Wares and Buttons.
Fenton, Creswick & Co.	...	...	...	...	Do. Mulberry Street ...	Silversmiths and Platers.
Boulton & Fothergill	...	...	...	...	Birmingham, Soho Works and Green Lettice Lane, Cannon Street. London	Manufacturers of Hardware.
Ryland William ...	...	...	...	...	Birmingham	Plater.

LIST OF MAKERS AND MARKS USED BY MANUFACTURERS OF FUSED PLATED AND CLOSE PLATED ARTICLES AFTER THE PASSING OF THE ACT OF 1784.

The words "close plater," given in this list, signify that the makers so described made articles plated on iron or steel. Marks struck on close plated articles can usually be identified by the splitting up or duplicating in various ways of the makers' names, initials, and devices, forming separate shields as ▪▪▪▪ and ▪▪▪▪. Different forms of the letters s and p. s. were used to denote steel, or plated steel. The dates recorded are the earliest that can be traced of firms using their marks. The trade descriptions are taken from old manuscripts, ledgers and directories. Where a § is fixed against a device it signifies that this mark was not registered at the Sheffield Assay Office. The abbreviation "B. M." (in trade description) signifies Britannia Metal.

Name of Firm.	Maker's Marks.	Date.	Location.	Trade Description.
Ashforth G. & Co. ...		1784	Sheffield, Angel Street ...	Platers and Silversmiths
Fox T. & Co.		1784	Do. ...	Do. do.
Green W. & Co. ...		1784	Do. Eyre Street	Do. do.
Holy D., Wilkinson & Co.		1784	Do. Mulberry Street	Do. do.
Law T. & Co. ...		1784	Do. Norfolk Street ...	Do. do.
Parsons J. & Co.		1784	Do. Market Place ...	Do. do.
Smith N. & Co. ...		1784	Do. Waingate ...	Do. do.
Staniforth, Parkin & Co.		1784	Do.	Platers and Cutlers
Sykes & Co.		1784	Do. Pinstone Lane ...	Platers and Silver Cutlers
Tudor, Leader & Nicholson		1784	Do. Sycamore Hill ...	Platers and Silversmiths
Boulton M. & Co.		1784	Birmingham, Soho Works	Do. do.
Dixon T. & Co. ...		1784	Birmingham	Platers
Holland H. & Co. ...		1784	Do.	Platers and Silversmiths
Moore J.	§	1784	Do.	Plater and Silversmith
Smith & Co.		1784	Do.	Platers

§ Unregistered marks.

Name of Firm.	Maker's Marks.	Date.	Location.	Trade Description.
Beldon, Hoyland & Co...		1785	Sheffield	Platers and Silversmiths
Brittain, Wilkinson & Brownill		1785	Do.	Do. do.
Deakin, Smith & Co. ...		1785	Do. Hawley Croft ...	Do. do.
Love J. & Co. ... ... (Love, Silverside, Darby & Co.)		1785	Do. Pea Croft ...	Do. do.
Morton R. & Co. ...		1785	Do. Brinsworth Orchard	Do. do.
Roberts, Cadman & Co.		1785	Do. Eyre Street ...	Do. do.
Roberts J. & S.		1786	Do. Union Street	Do. do.
Sutcliffe R. & Co. ...		1786	Do. King Street	Do. do.
Bingley W.		1787	Birmingham	Plater
Madin F. & Co. ...		1788	Sheffield, Far Field ...	Platers and Silversmiths
Jervis W.		1789	Do. White Croft ...	Plater and Silversmith
Colmore S.	§	1790	Birmingham	Plater
Goodwin E.		1794	Sheffield, The Park ...	Plater and Silversmith
Watson, Fenton & Bradbury		1795	Do. Mulberry Street	Platers and Silversmiths
Froggatt, Coldwell & Lean		1797	Do. Eyre Street, ...	Platers, Silversmiths, & B.M. manufacturers
Green J. & Co. ...	*	1799	Do. Market Place ...	Platers and Silversmiths
Goodman, Gainsford & Fairbairn		1800	Do. 18, Hawley Croft	Platers, Silversmiths and Factors
Ellerby W.	§	1803	London	Close Plater
Garnett W.		1803	Sheffield, Bridge Houses...	Plater
Holy D., Parker & Co. ...		1804	Do. Mulberry Street	Platers and Silversmiths

* Green, Roberts, Moseley & Co.   This firm commenced from this date to use the mark formerly struck by their predecessors J. Parsons & Co.

§ Unregistered marks.

Name of Firm.	Maker's Marks.	Date	Location.	Trade Description.
Newbould W. & Son ...		1804	Sheffield, The Moor ...	Platers
Drabble I. & Co. ...	*	1805	Do. Eyre Street ...	Platers and Silversmiths
Coldwell W.		1806	Do. do. ...	Plater, &c.
Hill D. & Co.	§ ||	1806	Birmingham	Close Platers
Law J. & Son	†	1807	Sheffield	Platers
Butts T.		1807	Birmingham	Close Plater
Green J.		1807	Do.	Do.
Hutton W.	‡	1807	Do.	Do.
Law R.		1807	Do.	Do.
Linwood J.		1807	Do.	Do.
Linwood W.		1807	Do.	Do.
Meredith H.		1807	Do.	Do.
Peake		1807	Do.	Do.
Ryland W. & Son ...	§ ||	1807	Do.	Platers, Close Platers and Silversmiths
Scot W.		1807	Do.	Close Plater
Silkirk W.	§	1807	Do.	Do.
Thomason E. & Dowler...	§	1807	Do.	Close Platers, &c.
Tonks Samuel		1807	Do. Bromsgrove Rd.	Plater

* Previous to this date this mark was used by D. Holy, Wilkinson & Co.

† Tudor & Co. having retired from business in 1804, this would appear to be a re-registration of their mark by J. Law & Son at the Sheffield Assay Office in 1807.

‡ See also 1831, 1837, 1839, 1849.

\|\| These marks were probably used at a later date.

§ Unregistered marks.

Name of Firm.	Maker's Marks.	Date.	Location.	Trade Description.
Waterhouse & Co.		1807	Birmingham	Platers and Silversmiths
Wilmore Joseph ...	§	1807	Do.	Plater, Worker and Silversmith
Gainsford R.		1808	Sheffield	Plater, Close Plater and Silversmith
Hatfield A.		1808	Do. Pepper Alley ...	Close Plater and Silversmith
Banister W.		1808	Birmingham	Close Plater
Gibbs G.		1808	Do.	Do.
Hipkiss J.		1808	Do.	Close Plater and Silversmith
Horton D.		1808	Do.	Close Plater
Lea A. C.		1808	Do.	Close Plater and Silversmith
Linwood M. & Sons ...		1808	Do.	Do. do.
Nicholds J.		1808	Do. 13, Foredrough Street	Maker of Plated Liquor and Cruet Stands, Teapots, Curbs, Spoons, etc.
Beldon G.		1809	Sheffield	Plater
Wright J. & Fairbairn G.		1809	Do.	Platers and Silversmiths
Cheston T.		1809	Birmingham	Plater and Silversmith
Harrison J.		1809	Do.	Plater
Hipwood W.		1809	Do.	Close Plater
Horton J.		1809	Do.	Plater and Silversmith
Silk R.		1809	Do.	Close Plater
Howard S. & T. ...	§	1809	London	Do.
Smith, Tate, Nicholson & Hoult		1810	Sheffield, Arundel Street ...	Platers and Silversmiths
Dunn G. B.		1810	Birmingham	Close Plater of Dessert Knives and Forks, Spoons, Ladles, Fish Knives, Snuffers, etc.

§ Unregistered marks.

Name of Firm.	Maker's Marks.	Date.	Location.	Trade Description.
Hanson M.		1810	Birmingham	Close Plater
Pimley S.		1810	Do.	Close Plater
Creswick T. & J. ...	§*	1811	Sheffield, Porter Street ...	Platers and Silversmiths
Stot B.		1811	Do. Duke St., Park	Close Plater
Watson, Pass & Co. (late J. Watson)		1811	Do. Hartshead ...	Platers and Silversmiths
Lees G.	†	1811	Birmingham	Fancy Plater
Pearson R.		1811	Do. Princes Street ...	Plater in general
White J. (White & All-good)		1811	Do.	Platers and Military Ornament makers
Kirkby S.		1812	Sheffield, Carver Lane ...	Plater and Silversmith
Allgood J.		1812	Birmingham, Essex Street	Close Plater
Allport E.	§	1812	Do. Cannon Street ...	Do.
Gilbert J.		1812	Do. Legge Street ...	Do.
Hinks J.		1812	Do.	Plater and maker of Plated articles
Johnson J.		1812	Do. New Inkleys ...	Sword Hilt maker and Steel worker
Small T.		1812	Do.	Plater in general and Japanner
Smith W.		1812	Do.	Jeweller and Button maker
Younge S. & C. & Co. ...		1813	Sheffield, Union Street ...	Platers and Silversmiths
Thomas S.		1813	Birmingham, 45, Thorp-st.	Close Plater
Tyndall J.		1813	Do. Moseley St.	Do.
Best H.		1814	Do. Great Charles-st.	Do.
Cracknall J.		1814	Do.	Plate maker, Table and Tea Spoons, Sugar Tongs, Caddie Shells, &c.
Jordan T.		1814	Do.	Close Plater

* Found on close plated goods, the initials are also found on silver goods.
† Found on close plated goods.   § Unregistered marks.

Name of Firm.	Maker's Marks.	Date.	Location.	Trade Description.
Woodward W.		1814	Birmingham, Bishopgate Street	Close Plater
Lilly John		1815	Birmingham, St. Paul's Square	Close Plater and Military Ornament maker
Best & Wastidge ...		1816	Sheffield	Platers
Ashley		1816	Birmingham	Do.
Davis J.		1816	Do.	Japanner
Evans S.		1816	Do.	Maker of Plated articles
Freeth H.		1816	Do. Upper Priory ...	Plater
Harwood T.		1816	Do.	Close Plater
Lilly Joseph		1816	Do.	Plater and maker of Curbs, Spoons, &c.
Turley S.		1816	Do.	Plater and maker of plated articles
Cope C. G.		1817	Do. Edmond Street	Do. do.
Pemberton & Mitchell ...		1817	Do.	Jewellers, Silversmiths, Watch and Clock makers
Shephard J.		1817	Do.	Maker of Plated Coach Harness, Furniture, Bits, Stirrups, Knives and Snuffers
Markland W.		1818	Do.	Maker of Plated Spoons, Tongs, Caddie Shells, Tea Canisters, Soup, Toddy, and Punch Ladles, Teapots, Sugar Basins, Cake, Fruit and Bread Baskets, Plated Saddle Nails, &c.
Corn J. & J. Sheppard ...		1819	Do. Exeter Row ...	Close Platers
Rogers J.		1819	Do. New Street ...	Harness Plater
Hall W.		1820	Do.	Close Plater
Moore F.		1820	Do. William Street ...	Fancy Plater
Turton J.		1820	Do. 8, Church Street	Close Plater and maker of fused Plated Tea Spoons and Tongs

* These marks were probably used at a later date.   § Unregistered marks.

Name of Firm.	Maker's Marks.	Date.	Location.	Trade Description.
Blagden, Hodgson & Co.		1821	Sheffield, Nursery Street...	Platers and Silversmiths
Holy D. & G.	HOLY SN C SHEFFIELD *	1821	Do. Mulberry Street	Do. do
Needham C.	C NEEDHAM MAKER SHEFFIELD §	1821	Sheffield, Willey Street ...	Maker of Plated Tankards and Measures
Sansom T. & Sons ...	SAN SOM	1821	Do.	Maker of Plated goods
Child T.	CHILD	1821	Birmingham	Plater and Pawnbroker
Smith I.	SMITH	1821	Do.	Close Plater and Harness Buckle maker
Worton S.	S WORTON	1821	Do. Near the Five Ways	Close Plater
Rodgers J. & Sons ...	J R G R / ROD GERS	1822	Sheffield, Norfolk Street...	Cutlers, Silver Cutlers and Factors
Bradshaw J.		1822	Birmingham, 3, Goff St....	Close Plater
Briggs W.	§	1823	Sheffield, Carver Street ...	Silversmith and Plater
Harrison G.	GH § / GH §	1823	Birmingham	Close Plater
Smallwood J.	§	1823	Do. ...	Do.
Causer J. F.	CAUSER	1824	Do. 4, Nicholson St.	Merchant and Factor
Jones	JONES	1824	Do. Show room, New Street	Gold and Silversmith, Medallist, &c.
Tonks & Co.	TONKS	1824	Birmingham	Close Platers
Roberts, Smith & Co. ...	§	1828	Sheffield, 5, Eyre Street ...	Platers and Silversmiths
Smith J. & Son	§	1828	Do. Arundel Street...	Cutlers and Silversmiths
Askew	A SKEW MAKER NOTTINGHAM §	1828	Nottingham	Maker of Plated Tankards and Measures
Hall Henry	§	1829	Birmingham, 51, Shadwell Street	Close Plater
Hobday J.	§	1829	Birmingham	Do.
Watson J. & Son ...		1830	Sheffield	Platers and Silversmiths

* Mark used on plated handled cutlery on steel blade is stamped "D. & G. HOLY, SHEFFIELD."

§ Unregistered marks.

Name of Firm.	Maker's Marks.		Datd.	Location.	Trade Description.
Bishop Thomas... ...	[marks]	§	1830	Birmingham, 24, St. Paul's Square	Goldsmith and Jeweller
Hutton W.	[marks]	*	1831	Sheffield	Close Plater
Atkin Henry	[marks]	§	1833	Do. 32, Howard St....	Gold, Silver and Plated Cutlery manufacturer
Waterhouse I. & I. & Co.	[marks]		1833	Sheffield	Platers and Silversmiths
Watson W.	W. WATSON MAKER SHEFFIELD	§	1833	Do. 15, Arundel Street (until 1812 partner in firm of Watson & Bradbury)	Plater and Silversmith
Dixon J. & Sons ...	D ✳ S / D ✳ S / [mark] J / G⚜R DIXON'S IMPERIAL / [octagonal mark] DIXON'S	§ § § §	1835	Do. Cornish Place ...	Makers of Plated Silver and B.M. goods
Smith J.	JOSEPHUS SMITH	§	1836	Do. 48, South Street	Maker of Plated Tankards and Measures
Waterhouse, Hatfield & Co.	[mark]		1836	Do. Portobello Place	Platers and Silversmiths
Wilkinson H. & Co. ...	[mark]	†	1836	Do. Norfolk Street ...	Do. do
Hutton W.	[marks]	‡	1837	Do.	Close Plater
Hutton W.	H & S T	‖	1839	Do.	Do.
Prime J.	[marks] PS / [marks] / [marks]	§ § § §	1839	Birmingham	Close Plater
Walker, Knowles & Co.	[mark]	§	1840	Sheffield, 47, Burgess St.	Platers and Silversmiths
Waterhouse George & Co.	W & C S	§	1842		
Smith, Sissons & Co. ...	[mark]		1848	Do. 5, Eyre Street ...	Do. do.
Padley, Parkin & Co. ...	[mark]		1849	Do. Watson Walk	Do. do.

* See also 1807, 1837, 1839, 1849.
† The cross keys mark is registered this year at the Sheffield Assay Office for the third time.
‡ This mark was originally registered by Scot in 1807; for previous marks used by Hutton see 1807, 1831.
‖ The same firm as above, and in 1831 but with the 1807 mark reversed.
§ Unregistered marks.

Name of Firm.	Maker's Marks.	Date.	Location.	Trade Description.
Hutton W.	⬛⬛⬛⬛⬛ *	1849	Sheffield	Close Plater
Mappin Bros.	⬛⬛⬛ †	1850	Do. Baker's Hill ...	Silver and Plated Cutlery Manufacturers
Oldham T.	⬛ §	1860	Nottingham	Maker of Plated Tankards and Measures
Roberts & Briggs ...	R & B X ‡§	1860	Sheffield, 38, Furnival Street	Silver and Plated Ware Manufacturers

* See note (‖) on previous page.
† Possibly this mark was purchased from M. Boulton & Co., of Birmingham, at their dissolution in 1848.
‡ Since 1863 Roberts & Belk.
§ Unregistered marks.

MISCELLANEOUS MARKS WHICH HAVE NOT BEEN TRACED.

Maker's Marks.	Description of article from which marks are taken.	Approximate date of manufacture.
⬛⬛⬛	Fused Plated 1-pint Tankard	1780-1790
⬛ BEST PLATE	Do. Sugar Tongs	1790
SILVER	Do. Sauce Boat	1790
⬛⬛⬛⬛	Do. Pierced Fish Slice, with Plated Handle... ...	1790-1800
Do.	Do. Wine Coolers, with Lion Mask Handles ...	1790-1800
R·JEWESSON MIDDLETON&CO	Do. Tankard	1800-1810
W.B.PINE 352 STRAND	Do. Folding Ear Trumpet, with Silver Filled Floral Mounts (see page 390.)	1815-1825
⬛⬛⬛⬛	Do. Salt Cellar, with Wire Supports for Glass ...	1815-1825
WILSON	Fused Plated 5-light Candelabra, 29 in. high.	1815-1825
GILBERT LONDON	Fused Plated small Telescope (see page 390)	1840
⬛	Fused Plated pointed end Snuffer Tray (see page 328.) ...	1840
RWAW ⬛⬛	Close Plated Dessert Knife...	1840
PAT ENT ⬛ PAT ENT	Close Plated Article	1840
⬛⬛⬛⬛	Snuffers, made of Argentine Metal, with Filled Silver Mounts...	1850
SALT ⬛⬛	Close Plated Dessert Knife	1850
⬛⬛⬛⬛	Do. Marrow Scoop	1850
⬛⬛⬛⬛	Ivory Handled Dessert Knife, Close Plated Blade	1850

* T. Middleton, Rd. Jewesson, G. Ashford and G. Frost are registered, as a firm of silver plate workers, at the Sheffield Assay Office, 2/4/1798.

Name of Firm.	Maker's Marks.	Date	Location.	Trade Description.
Hutton, W. ...		1840 *	Sheffield	Close Plater
Mappin Bros. ...		1870 †	Do. Baker's Hill ...	Silver and Plated Cut-lery Manufacturers
Oldham, T. ...		1860 §	Nottingham ...	Maker of Plated Tan-kards and Measures
Roberts & Briggs ...		1850 ‡	Sheffield, 78, Furnival Street	Silver and Plated Ware Manufacturers

* See note (B) on previous page.
† Possibly this mark was purchased from M. Boulton & Co., of Birmingham, at their dissolution in 1848.
‡ Since 1905 Roberts & Belk.
§ Unregistered marks.

MISCELLANEOUS MARKS WHICH HAVE NOT BEEN TRACED.

Maker's Marks.	Description of article from which marks are taken.	Approximate date of manufacture.
	Fused Plated 2-pint Tankard	1760-1770
	Do. Sugar Tongs	1790
	Do. Sauce Boat	1790
	To. Pierced Fish Slice, with Plated Handle ...	1790-1800
Do.	Do. Wine Coolers, with Lion Mask Handles ...	1790-1800
*	Do. Tankard	1800-1810
	Do. Folding Bar Trumpet, with Silver Filled Floral Mounts (see page 390)	1815-1825
	Do. Salt Cellar, with Wire Supports for Glass ...	1815-1825
	Fused Plated 3-light Candelabra, 23 in. high. ...	1815-1825
GILBERT LONDON	Fused Plated small Telescope (see page 390) ...	1840
	Fused Plated pierced and Scallop Tray (see page 296)	1860
	Close Plated Dessert Blades	1860
	Close Plated Article	1860
	Sauiltra, made of Argentine Metal, with Filled Silver Mounts	1850
	Close Plated Dessert Knife	1850
	Do. Marrow Scoop	1850
	Ivory Handled Dessert Knife, Close Plated Blade ...	1850

* T. Middleton, Rd. Jessamine, G. Ashford and G. Frost are registered, as a firm of silver plate workers, at the Sheffield Assay Office, 1/4/1796.

GENERAL INDEX

General Index

Makers' marks and date letters are not indexed in the following pages. A comprehensive index to the marks of English, Scotch, Irish, and British colonial silversmiths will be found at p. 211. See also the alphabetical list of American silversmiths and their marks, pp. 239–292.

Gebweiler, mark used at, 329.
Gefle, marks used at, 379.
Geislingen, mark used at, 329.
Geneva, marks used at, 384.
Genoa, marks used at, 371.
Germany, silver of, 315–354.
Ghent, marks used at, 364.
Glasgow, marks used at, 178–181.
Glatz, mark used at, 329.
Glogau, mark used at, 329.
Gmund, marks used at, 329.
Gnoien, mark used at, 329.
Gold, hallmarking of in England, 31 (footnote).
Goldsmiths in England recognized as a corporate body, 3.
Görlitz, marks used at, 330.
Gotha, marks used at, 330.
Gothenburg, marks used at, 379
Gouda, marks used at, 368.
Grabow, mark used at, 330.
Gran, mark used at, 359.
Graz, marks used at, 356.
Greenock, marks used at, 184.
Grenoble, marks used at, 310.
Guimraes, Marks used at, 373.
Güstrow, marks used at, 330.

Hague, The, marks used at, 369.
Halberstadt, marks used at, 330.
Hall (Austria), marks used at, 356.
Hall (Germany), marks used at, 331.
Halle (Saxony), marks used at, 331.
Hallmarks, absence from English silver no proof of fraud, 16; popular misconception regarding Sheffield plate, 395.
Hamburg, marks used at, 331, 332.
Hanau, marks used at, 333.
Hanover, marks used at, 333.
Hanover-Neustadt, marks used at, 333.
Harrison, the Reverend William, his *Description of England*, 5.
Harp, crowned, sterling mark of Dublin, 191.
Hedemora, Eksjö, and Lindesberg, marks used at, 379.
Heidelberg, marks used at, 333.
Heilbronn, marks used at, 334.
Henry VII, 3, 4.
Henry VIII, 4, 5.
Herzogenbusch's, marks used at, 369.
Hibernia, figure of, duty and their town mark of Dublin, 193.
Hildesheim, marks used at, 334.
Hogarth, William, his influence on the designing of English silver, 8.
Holland, silver of, 367–370.
Hoorn, mark used at, 369.
Hotzenplotz, mark used at, 356.

Huguenot silversmiths in England, 9.
Hull, marks used at, 154.
Hull, John, "American" silversmith, 235.
Hungary, silver of, 359–361.

Iglau, mark used at, 356.
Ilmenau, mark used at, 334.
Index to the marks of English, Scotch, and Irish silversmiths, 211.
Ingolstadt, marks used at, 334.
Innsbruck, marks used at, 356.
Inset plate on Old Sheffield ware, its purpose and the popular exaggeration of its value, 396.
Inverness, marks used at, 187.
Ireland, silver of, 191–210.
Irkutsk or Tobolsk, mark used at, 375.
Italy, silver of, 370–373.

Jamaica, mark used on the island of, 163.
Jauer, marks used at, 334.
Jesse, David, American silversmith, 235.
Journay, marks used at, 364.

Kaluga, mark used at, 375.
Kamenetz-Podolski, mark used at, 375.
Karlsruhe, marks used at, 334.
Kaschau, marks used at, 360.
Kaufbeuren, mark used at, 334.
Kazan, mark used at, 376.
Kecskemét, marks used at, 360.
Kiel, marks used at, 334, 335.
Kiev, marks used at, 376.
King's Lynn, marks used at, 156.
Kitzingen, marks used at, 335.
Klagenfurt, marks used at, 356.
Klausenburg, marks used at, 360.
Königsberg, marks used at, 335, 336.
Konstanz, marks used at, 336, 337.
Kostroma, mark used at, 376.
Kremsier, marks used at, 356.

La Coruña, mark used at, 387.
Laibach, marks used at, 357.
Lamerie, Paul, English silversmith, 12.
Landsberg, mark used at, 337.
Landshut, marks used at, 337.
Lausanne, mark used at, 384.
La Rochelle, mark used at, 310.
Leeds, marks used at, 162.
Leer, mark used at, 337.
Leeuwarden, mark used at, 369.
Leicester, marks used at, 155.
Leipzig, marks used at, 337, 338.
Lemberg, marks used at, 357.
Leon, marks used at, 387.
Leopard's head crowned, in a measure restricted to articles made in London, 1, 22, 30; used in conjunction with town mark in Exeter, 1721–

396th info on Old Sheff Plate